KulturConfusão – On German-Brazilian Interculturalities

Interdisciplinary German Cultural Studies

Edited by
Irene Kacandes

Volume 19

KulturConfusão – On German-Brazilian Interculturalities

Edited by
Anke Finger, Gabi Kathöfer and Christopher Larkosh

DE GRUYTER

Acknowledgment
We would like to express our gratitude to the Humanities Institute
and the Scholarship Facilitation Fund at the University of Connecticut
for their generous support of this book project.

ISBN 978-3-11-068279-3
e-ISBN [PDF] 978-3-11-040822-5
e-ISBN [EPUB] 978-3-11-040844-7
ISSN 1861-8030

Library of Congress Cataloging-in-Publication Data
A CIP catalog record for this book has been applied for at the Library of Congress.

Bibliographic information published by the Deutsche Nationalbibliothek
DThe Deutsche Nationalbibliothek lists this publication in the Deutsche Nationalbibliografie;
detailed bibliographic data are available on the Internet at http://dnb.dnb.de.

© 2019 Walter de Gruyter GmbH, Berlin/Boston
Dieser Band ist text- und seitenidentisch mit der 2015 erschienenen gebundenen Ausgabe.
Cover image: © Tourist-Service Ostseebad Schönberg
Druck und Bindung: CPI books GmbH, Leck
♾ Printed on acid-free paper
Printed in Germany

www.degruyter.com

Table of Contents

Anke Finger, Gabi Kathöfer, and Christopher Larkosh
KulturConfusão: On German-Brazilian Hybridities and Intercultural Hermeneutics —— 1

Indigenous Projections

Ute Ritz-Deutch
Germans and Indians in Brazil: The Transatlantic Construction of Ethnic Identity in the Discourse of Indian Protection —— 21

Fernando Clara
"Paradise with Black Angels": Brazil in Eighteenth-Century Germany —— 43

Gabi Kathöfer
Devouring Culture: Cannibalism, National Identity, and Nineteenth-Century German Emigration to Brazil —— 71

Thomas O. Beebee
Cultural Entanglements and Ethnographic Refractions: Theodor Koch-Grünberg in Brazil —— 95

Everyday Cultures and Media

Ricarda Musser
German-Brazilian Cultural Exchange in the Times of the Dictatorship: The Cultural Magazine *Intercâmbio* —— 119

Andrew W. Hurley
From Documentation to Dialogue: On Bringing Brazilian Popular Music and Jazz to West Germany —— 137

Ulrike Schröder
Conceptual Metaphors: A Culture-Specific Construction of Meaning Using the "Life Is War" Metaphor in Brazilian and German Rap Lyrics —— 159

Wolfgang Fuhrmann
Transnational Film History? Um Cinema Teuto-Brasileiro —— 179

Literary Fusions and Interstitial Spaces

Horst Nitschack
**Tropical Subjectivity and the European Tradition of *Bildung*:
Macunaíma, a Hero Without a Character, by Mário de Andrade —— 201**

Marlen Eckl
"Everywhere Paradise Is Lost": The Brazilian National Myth in the Works of Refugees of Nazism —— 219

Christopher Larkosh
Submarine: Germany Resurfacing in the Contemporary Brazilian Novel —— 247

Edith Wolfe
"Exiled from the World": German Expressionism, Brazilian Modernism, and the Interstitial Primitivism of Lasar Segall —— 267

Rainer Guldin
Between São Paulo and Stuttgart: Multilingualism, Translation, and Interculturality in Haroldo de Campos's and Vilém Flusser's Work —— 301

Contributors —— 319

Index —— 323

Anke Finger, Gabi Kathöfer, and Christopher Larkosh
KulturConfusão: On German-Brazilian Hybridities and Intercultural Hermeneutics

> If you have an incredible idea
> It's better to write a song.
> It's been proven it's only possible
> To philosophize in German.
> – Caetano Veloso, "Língua" (Vêlo, 1984)

Is it really possible to philosophize only in German or truly preferable to write a song in Brazilian Portuguese? Improbable. A listener of Caetano Veloso's song "Língua" would do well to take this statement with a grain of salt and an even greater measure of irony. After all, these words, which have come to rest at the intersection between these two cultures, seem to connote the exact opposite. Caetano himself sings songs in a wide range of languages; ultimately, how we articulate our ideas, feelings, and histories between languages and cultures is often dependent on the place, language, and culture in which they emerge.

Long before and long after Herder and Hegel, ample attention has been given to the ways in which a national language and accompanying nation-state identities and ideologies shape cultural politics and secure a country's or group's perceived place in relation to others in the world. And yet this discussion is no longer limited to such philosophy in its strictest sense; today, popular music and philosophy are as permeable to one another as are national or regional cultures, even those apparently opposed to one another, as Brazil and Germany are represented in Caetano's music. One need only listen to him and other representatives of the música popular brasileira (MPB) movement, or Brazilian classical pieces such as Heitor Villa-Lobos's *Bachianas brasileiras*, or more recent transatlantic electronic music, to recognize that one can indeed philosophize through music, just as one can create music and poetry through philosophy. The borders, however separate they might appear at first glance, are already confused; this is one of the main purposes of this collection: to recognize and explore the poetry, originality, and creativity of these culturally confused spaces.

The analyses of German-Brazilian confused spaces and interculturalities contained in this collection offer a timely introduction to and retheorization of the intercultural paradigm for the humanities and literary and cultural studies. This collection attempts to revisit movements of interculturality between Germany and Brazil over a broad historical period from the early Modern period to the present day, examining the ways authors, translators, artists, and other intellectuals attempt to address the growth and development of society, intervene in the construction and transformation of their cultural identities, and observe the introduction of differing cultural elements in and beyond the limits of the nation. The contributors include international scholars from a variety of disciplines, including German studies, Brazilian and Lusophone studies, art history, and literature. The chapters cover a range of works and media, from the eighteenth century onward to the contemporary moment, and the issues they address have relevance not only in the scholarly disciplines involved but also for questions of current cultural practices and the connection of these practices to all forms of media. The collection therefore aims to inform and inspire scholars in numerous fields, most prominently literary and cultural studies, history, art history, anthropology, and international studies.

Specifically, *KulturConfusão* provides a critical investigation of two historically entwined but, in juxtaposition, underinvestigated, cultures, Germany and Brazil, by examining emerging cultural hybridities, as Peter Burke has described them,[1] via the concept of interculturality. Humanities and social science scholarship on Germany and Brazil has focused on Germans' history of immigration to Brazil or on Brazilians' presence in Germany, but inquiries into personal, public, or generally creative encounters as presented in literature, film, and other media that engage both viewpoints remain largely absent. Beginning with Hans Staden's sixteenth-century account of Brazil, hotly debated among anthropologists, questions of authenticity, colonization and coloniality, emigration, exile, dialogue, cultural value systems, cultural production, cultural practice, and cultural identity, though not without answers, linger in various areas of research, and scholars rarely meet to investigate them together. *KulturConfusão* seeks to address these questions from interdisciplinary perspectives with the purpose of putting into dialogue the cultures under investigation, Brazilian and German, and between disciplines such as literature, history, linguistics, film studies, philosophy, art, and art history. Thus, the volume builds on Walter Mignolo's concept of "border thinking,"[2] on liminality, and on enculturation and acculturation to help develop theories and models with which to engage and examine the interculturality of global encounters in history and in the present.[3]

---

1 Peter Burke, *Cultural Hybridity* (Cambridge: Polity, 2009).
2 Walter Mignolo, *Local Histories/Global Designs. Coloniality, Subaltern Knowledges, and Border Thinking* (Princeton, NJ: Princeton University Press, 2000).
3 There is little research or theory to guide a comprehensive understanding of German-Brazilian relations at this point. For example, German studies scholars have focused mainly on the depiction of "the Other" in German travelogues and literary texts (Maria Cortez, "Zwischen gut und Böse," 2006; Cerue Diggs, "Brazil After Humboldt," 2008; Gerson Roberto Neumann, *Brasilien*

The collection serves, then, as a case study for intercultural investigations because it calls into question the boundaries by which we understand cultures, their products, practices, and perspectives. Although cultural production as a national construction has been under investigation for some time now, this collection seeks to move the debate further by calling into question some of the cultural production models with which much of cultural studies has been engaged over the past decades and rebooting the conversation about and usage of interculturality by suggesting lineages, theories, and expressions in the humanities, shifting outside of or away from a more pragmatic use of the concept that includes, invariably, business, sports, education, and the paradigm of the "global." We are acknowledging hereby a number of disciplinary traditions that intersect in the concept of the intercultural that has informed the study of cultures, groups, and civilizations for centuries. As Jeremy Smith put it,

> Europe's civilisational consciousness was nourished by received ideas on the Americas and its supposed primitivity. The latter circulated widely in Europe establishing a shared fund of understanding. From that fund, metaphors of savagery could be drawn that set standards of progress with which Europeans could persuade themselves of their essential civility. Overall, this degree of cultural transmission highlights a substantial intercultural dimension of the Colombian collision, which cannot be ignored, even though it equally cannot be characterised as an intercivilisational encounter.[4]

With its focus on Brazil and Germany, the collection also connects a new set of countries to locate, identify, and define angles that have the potential to ques-

---

ist nicht weit von hier!, 2005) or concentrated on politics of identity in texts by German immigrants (Ana-Isabel Aliaga-Buchenau, "German Immigrants in Blumenau, Brazil," 2007). Similar research foci become apparent in the few historical and anthropological studies on the topic: Scholars deliberate the sociohistorical causes and implications of German emigration to Brazil (Mack Walker, *Germany and the Emigration 1816–1885*, 1964; Peter Marschalck, *Deutsche Überseewanderung im 19. Jahrhundert*, 1973; Fritz Sudhaus, *Deutschland und die Auswanderung nach Brasilien im 19. Jahrhundert*, 1940) or discuss the authenticity of German descriptions of Brazil and its indigenous tribes (Hubertus Rescher, *Die deutschsprachige Literatur zu Brasilien von 1789–1850*, 1979; Neil L. Whitehead, "Hans Staden and the Cultural Politics of Cannibalism," 2000; Michaela Schmölz-Häberlein and Mark Häberlein, "Hans Staden, Neil L. Whitehead, and the Cultural Politics of Scholarly Publishing," 2001; Debora Bendocchi Alves, *Das Brasilienbild der deutschen Auswanderungswerbung im 19. Jahrhundert*, 2000), whereas several other scholars have accentuated the preservation of German cultural traditions in Brazil. Only a few of these studies address questions of hybridization, and none of them highlight processes of intercultural collision and negotiation.

4 See the entire article by Jeremy Smith on the sociological differentiation between intercivilisational and intercultural encounters. "Civilisational Analysis and Intercultural Models of American Societies," *Journal of Intercultural Studies* 30.3 (2009): 233–248.

tion established associations, such as Germany and France, or the United States and Great Britain. It thereby cross-cuts and short-circuits a familiar geography or comfortable vantage points by putting together cultures that are not obvious partners: They have a history and present of engagement that has the potential to challenge or question other, more fixed engagements, by providing a different constellation (south/north, developing/industrial, colonized/colonizer) of how to generate, process, and interpret cultural products, practices, and perspectives.

At stake in ongoing investigations and reinterpretations of geocultural interaction over time and within different sectors is an embrace of *confusão*, of a process-oriented, fluid, evolving, possibly elusive model for distinguishing, reading, and interpreting cultural interaction in certain moments of time and space. These interactions cannot be marked by the static concepts or imagery of clichés and stereotypes. They are of a distinctly hybrid nature that represents fleetingness, haphazardness, and chance. What fits best, in our minds, for this kind of waxing and waning, this type of fluid sense-making, is a model of intercultural hermeneutics, what Dallmayr calls an "experimental approach, the approach of hermeneutical inquiry."[5] If we understand hermeneutics to signify the active engagement with interpretation, then – with the assumption that interpretation is a dialogic practice, also emphasized by Dallmayr – the fluidity and hybridity of interactions between cultures, groups, and civilizations depends and feeds on how each group communicates its world view in conjunction with its sense of self. Or, from the perspective of stereotype research, autostereotypes matter as much as heterostereotypes, given the hermeneutic practice of dialoging intraculturally and interculturally. Accordingly, although the editors and contributors question area studies models still linked to epistemologies of national boundaries and the scholarship that has focused on the prefixes "cross-" and "trans-," among other critiques, the central argument of this collection, decisively, lies in bringing the paradigm of the "intercultural" into critical humanities, and especially to literary and cultural studies. This paradigm connotes cognitive, affective, and communicative abilities that enable a certain translational and interpretive process by which distinct or interlaced concepts from different cultural areas or epistemologies reveal their cultural programming and branding; they interact, in contrast to merely being adjacent to each other or mutually acknowledging, and they creatively and productively engage with the fluctuating cultural frameworks. If a method with which most of the authors in this collection work is to be identified, it would be comparative. However, anthropology, media studies,

---

[5] Fred Dallmayr, "Hermeneutics and Inter-cultural Dialog: Linking Theory and Practice," *Ethics & Global Politics* 2.1 (2009): 23–39.

history, and other fields play into each contribution, making any methodological engagement simultaneously interdisciplinary, comparative, and relational. One could even argue, with Merleau-Ponty, that the "body" of each discipline, each subfield, and each group is "touched" such that the paradigm of the intercultural also applies to meta-levels such as research in and of itself: "the trespass of oneself upon the other and of the other upon me."[6] Each author works from her or his (inter)disciplinary field, applying certain methods (e.g. from linguistics) to collect and present data, to analyze and interpret. The flow of intercultural hermeneutics, as practice and as content focus, emerges from the entirety of the contributions itself and supplies a much-needed reengagement of the intercultural paradigm in today's practice of the humanities.

The paradigm of the "intercultural" and of its interdisciplinary "home" field, intercultural communication, has so far been relegated to serve more as a utilitarian concept, at least from a general humanist's perspective: In the United States, it is relevant for doing business interaction across the world, that is, to engage knowledgeably and meaningfully with people from other cultures or nations for – sometimes – joint success in the global marketplace, often backed up by study abroad programs that replace intercultural with global studies (geopolitical and economic) foci. Within European humanities, however, intercultural literary studies and intercultural philosophy, for example, are contributing significantly to an understanding of mobility and immigration, beyond the confines of political and social studies. What has emerged, then, is a development of H. G. Gadamer's method, that is, the notion of an intercultural hermeneutics framed by a certain fixity of horizons, based on a cross-cultural subject that facilitates an analysis and understanding of motion, nonfixedness, as it expands beyond mere comparison:

> A cross-cultural subject [...] understands that one cannot fully capture and comprehend the other in a dialogical encounter because another culture is never an enclosed horizon. Cultures like individuals are always involved with others, are always in motion. [...] Actors in cross-cultural encounters would seek to enlarge their horizons – or in Gadamer's account – achieve a fusion of horizons but this fusion is not premised on a transcendental position because self and other are always situated.[7]

The intriguing use of concepts here is that of the "actor" in an intercultural or cross-cultural endeavor. As R. Radhakrishnan has pointed out, when it comes

---

[6] Quoted in Fred Dallmayr, "Hermeneutics and Inter-cultural Dialog: Linking Theory and Practice," *Ethics & Global Politics* 2.1 (2009): 35.

[7] Vince Marotta, "Intercultural Hermeneutics and the Cross-cultural Subject," *Journal of Intercultural Studies* 30.3 (2009): 270.

to comparisons, the challenge to overcome is an implied line of demarcation between perceived "life worlds," between the horizon of one subject alongside that of another: "What starts out as a neutral and disinterested comparison of modes inevitably turns into a comparison between life worlds and ways of being. Where and how does one draw a critical line between ways of being and ways of knowing?" Invariably, according to Radhakrishnan, "comparisons are never disinterested."[8] However, cross-culturally interacting subjects act (take action) and act (take on roles), opened up to different ways of being and knowing. The engagement, dialogue, supplies versatility, hybridization of the subject itself, reflecting the impossibility of a closed horizon back on herself or himself; the subject as such becomes open, nonfixed, and in motion.

Bernhard Waldenfels has taken the concept of openness and the impending encounter of the unfamiliar further and argues for an alien science when it comes to the gaps or pitfalls of communication and interaction that we cannot bridge or generate on our own: "The alien, which takes us outside ourselves and lets us transcend the boundaries of the specific order, cannot be anything that we bring about by our own volition." His notion of the alien supports an intercultural engagement that will always be fraught with the extraordinary, the unfamiliar, the suspicious – and as such represents a necessary, productive flipside or underbelly of intercultural engagement to begin with:

> The ambiguity expressed in this word [alien], which includes a suffering, saves us from a harmless interpretation of the alien. Only if we start elsewhere, in a place where we have never been and will never be, can we testify to such a happening, which is certainly not limited to intercultural experiences, yet develops a special virulence for them. I wish to designate speech that comes from an alien place as response. Responding to the alien means more than sense understanding and more than norm-guided communication, no matter how important all of these are. Intercultural experience cannot help but become weak interculturalism unless it – to speak with Celan – always again "goes through a pause."[9]

Consequently, the contribution this collection can make is also soliciting a response from the alien by (a) helping conceptualize and theorize the paradigm of the "intercultural" and of intercultural hermeneutics for the humanities as it presents a new development, a new vantage point, for cultural studies scholarship and for transnational studies; (b) addressing not the border, the liminal-

---

[8] R. Radhakrishnan, "Why Compare?," in Rita Felski and Susan Stanford Friedman, eds., *Comparison. Theories, Approaches, Uses* (Baltimore, MD: Johns Hopkins University Press, 2013), 15–16.
[9] Bernhard Waldenfels, *Phenomenology of the Alien* (Chicago: Northwestern University Press, 2011), 84.

ity, the challenge to reading and interpreting in another cultural frame but the perforation, the gaps and holes, that which is permeable, to uncover the processes of cultural programming and branding (including stereotypes) and reflect on one's own; and (c) presenting modes and modalities of dialogue that speak to cultural hybridization via *confusão* and interculturality. It presents as a mode of being in flux, in change, gauging the various moments of interaction and engagement rather than determining fixed frameworks within which to operate now and in the future. In that sense, "Brazilian" and "German," whether in music or in philosophy, are already confusing because these national labels, as adjectives, reduce a history of muddled identities, viewpoints, and experiences to supposedly neat horizons. The perceived acting out or acting as a Brazilian or a German, to remind ourselves of Radhakrishnan's concept, already presents a dialogic engagement that is fraught with hermeneutic pitfalls. It is here that the analyses of gaps, fissures, and perforations accompanying encounters and dialogues prove the most fruitful and give rise to new questions about the history of intercultural encounters and their confusions.

What type of narrative, and what kind of "hermeneutical inquiry," to hark back to Dallmayr, marks the beginning of these encounters? The most important German travel account in the sixteenth century and, as it has been argued, in premodern times, is Hans Staden's *Warhaftige Historia und Beschreibung eyner Landtschafft der wilden nacketen, grimmigen Menschfresser-Leuthen in der Newenwelt America gelegen* [*The True History and Description of a Country Populated by a Wild, Naked, and Savage Man-munching People, Situated in the New World, America*] (1557). The German soldier Staden (1525–1579) traveled to Brazil twice (in 1547–1549 and 1549–1555). At the end of his second journey, he was held captive by the Tupinambá people for nine months. In his famous report, he reflected on his experience and observations of Brazilian nature and, more importantly, the tribe's rituals and cannibalistic practices. The *Warhaftige Historia* originally comprised 178 folios (in quarto format) and 44 woodcut illustrations and was published in numerous editions and several languages.

Hans Staden's "Bestseller der Reiseliteratur"[10] has been classified as "a fundamental text in the history and discovery of Brazil."[11] More importantly, his descriptions of Brazil's cannibalistic culture and natural wilderness count as a central point of reference in the history of German-Brazilian interculturalities. On one hand, the text facilitated the emergence of Brazil in the German mind and

---

10 See Annerose Menninger, "Hans Stadens Warhaftige Historia. Zur Geschichte eines Bestsellers der Reiseliteratur," *Geschichte in Wissenschaft und Unterricht* 9 (1984): 509–523.
11 Neil L. Whitehead, "Hans Staden and the Cultural Politics of Cannibalism," *Hispanic American Historical Review* 80 (2000): 721.

provided a template for explorations in subsequent centuries, such as the observations by Prince Maximilian Alexander Philipp von Wied-Neuwied (1782–1867), naturalists Carl Friedrich Philipp von Martius (1794–1868) and Johann Baptist von Spix (1781–1826), explorer Ida Pfeiffer (1797–1858), Prince Adalbert of Prussia (1811–1873), physician Robert Avé-Lallemant (1812–1884), traveler Friedrich Gerstäcker (1816–1872), Princess Theresa of Bavaria (1850–1925), or ethnologist Theodor Koch-Grünberg (1872–1924), to name but a few.

Through the plethora of reports, the Brazilian jungle, literally and metaphorically, became an important imaginary space for the German nation. What Susanne Zantop convincingly pointed out in her groundbreaking study *Colonial Fantasies* with regard to Spanish-speaking South America holds true for Brazil, too: Although Germans never held colonial power over Brazil, the country became "an imaginary testing ground for colonial action" in the eighteenth and nineteenth centuries and "provided an arena for creating an imaginary community and constructing a national identity in opposition to the perceived racial, sexual, ethnic, or national characteristics of others, Europeans and non-Europeans alike."[12] Thus, the imagination and definition of Brazilian nature was of central importance for the construction of the Romantic idea(l) of a German *Kulturnation*.

The German immigrant presence in Brazil constitutes another critical aspect in the history of German-Brazilian encounters. In the nineteenth century, Brazil became the third most popular emigration destination for Germans. At the turn of the twentieth century, about 100,000 Germans had emigrated to Brazil, and more than 100 colonies had been established, most of them in the southern part of the country. However, these settlements in Brazil were not just a German affair; emigration left its marks on both countries. In fact, it was the Brazilian leadership that organized German immigration, as it was connected both to the persistent labor shortage in Brazil and the increasing international pressure on the imperial regime to abolish slavery. Although early nineteenth-century German immigrants may not have directly replaced slaves of African ethnic origin in southern Brazil, European immigrants did come to occupy a privileged place in Brazilian society that indigenous, African, and mixed-race people did not have the same economic opportunities to fill, given the preexisting racial hierarchies. Moreover, increased German immigration was often promoted as the ideal way to ensure white racial supremacy in Brazil, although it was numerically insignifi-

---

12 Susanne Zantop, *Colonial Fantasies. Conquest, Family, and Nation in Precolonial Germany, 1770–1870* (Durham, NC: Duke University Press, 1997), 6, 7. Although *Colonial Fantasies* failed to address the German fixation on Brazil, it offers a useful theoretical framework for this essay collection.

cant in comparison to that of other immigrant groups (Italian, Spanish, and Portuguese). In this way, it can be argued that German settlement still contributed to the continuing displacement and socioeconomic marginalization of nonwhite populations in Brazil.[13]

Predictably, the German presence in Brazil caused fierce discussion about cultural identity in Germany as well as in Brazil in the subsequent century. Most German colonies in southern Brazil were established in remote rural areas, and they remained in isolation and tended to exclude other ethnic groups for centuries. Furthermore, by the end of the nineteenth century, the Teuto-Brazilians had became the most dominant minority in the southern provinces; they had created their own society within a society with numerous institutions and associations, their own schools, churches, and towns – a "large, diverse, and structured community with its own values, attitudes, language, and folkways"[14] that celebrated its presumed essential Germanness.

In Brazilian society, a more sociopolitically engaged intercultural encounter gained significant momentum after the Week of Modern Art in 1922 and continued throughout the Modernist period, propelled by a strong creative engagement with the urban space of São Paulo and by two of the essential texts of Brazilian Modernism: Mário de Andrade's *Paulicéia desvairada* (1922) and Oswald de Andrade's *Manifesto antropófago* (1928).

Andrade's manifesto proclaimed that "Brazil must neither ape nor reject European civilization, but 'devour' it, adapting its strengths and incorporating them into the native self."[15] It was based on Staden's description of the Tupi peoples and states unequivocally:

> Cannibalism alone unites us. Socially. Economically. Philosophically. The world's single law. Disguised expression of all individualism, of all collectivism. Of all religions. Of all peace treaties. Tupi or not Tupi, that is the question.[16]

---

[13] The abolishment of slavery was mainly the result of international pressure (especially from England) and racist theory apparent in the writings of prominent figures of the abolition movement, such as Jaoquim Nabuco. In his speeches, Nabuco distinguished between the superior, white race and the inferior, black and yellow. He called for a flow of European immigration bearing human and universal values. Like Nabuco, many so-called social reformers of the nineteenth century expressed the desire for whites' omnipresence and omnipotence in Brazil.
[14] Frederick Luebke, "A Prelude to Conflict: The German Ethnic Group in Brazilian Society, 1890–1917," *Ethnic and Racial Studies* 6.1 (1983): 2.
[15] Leslie Bary, "Oswald de Andrade's 'Cannibalist Manifesto,'" *Latin American Literary Review* 19.38 (1991): 13.
[16] Bary, 38.

By appropriating Staden's descriptions of Brazil's cannibalistic nature, the Modernist movement reinterpreted their country's colonial history and asserted Brazil's unique cultural identity against the colonial powers. The cannibalistic incorporation of a series of foreign texts and bodies manifested itself in twentieth-century Brazil through translation, transculturation, and migration.

Academics, artists, and cultural practitioners in both Europe and Latin America have continually reached out to other cultures for inspiration over the course of the century and contributed substantially to these global intellectual trends, whether to Marxism and psychoanalysis from the early twentieth century, to Latin American discourses of transculturation and liberation in the mid-twentieth century, to poststructuralist and other critical and theoretical tools concurrently circulating in Western Europe and North America in more recent years. Without a doubt, professional associations for comparative literature, translation studies, and intercultural studies in Brazil, Germany, and beyond have also done much to intensify these cross-cultural communications and an analysis of any historical infusions and confusions.

The contributions herein, taking seriously these kinds of identity formations, confusions, and imaginations, observe a varied and complex set of multidirectional movements between Germany and Brazil over a broad historical period, from the Early Modern era to the present day. They examine the ways authors, translators, artists, and other intellectuals attempt to address the growth and development of society, intervene in the construction and transformation of their cultural identities, and witness the introduction of differing cultural elements in and beyond the limits of the nation, as well as other constructs of cultural and ethnic identity. The chapters cover a wide range of literary works and media, and the issues they address, to say nothing of the diversity in their methodological and theoretical approaches, have relevance not only for the scholarly disciplines involved but also for questions of current cultural practices and the connection of these practices to all forms of media. And although German-Brazilian *confusão* cannot be marked by the static concepts or imagery of clichés and stereotypes, there are numerous recurring themes that serve as common denominators in the history of German-Brazilian interrelations. Accordingly, the collection is divided into three sections, each of which aims to present key vantage points, positions, and perspectives that will be necessary as we continue to observe, encounter, engage with, change viewpoints, and thus renew the ongoing discussion of German-Brazilian intercultural encounters and relations.

The first section, "Indigenous Projections," is concerned with the representations of ethnic (mis)encounter and racialization over the last four centuries of cultural contact between Europe and South America. On one hand, it centers around images of Brazil's indigenous people who were defined, first and foremost, by numerous European travelogues and scientific reports on Brazil. To point out that ethnography played a significant role in the establishment of racial and ethnic hierarchies would be an understatement, once again revealing the hermeneutics of racialization at play in this emergent discipline that cast itself in the service of science. On the other hand, in any discussion in which Germany and Brazil find themselves culturally or historically juxtaposed, many familiar with racial realities of Brazil will also think of the German-Brazilian community as an ethnic one: the second-largest German diaspora in the world after the United States, which chose to reside in villages made up of typically German Stockwerk-Häuser, drinking beer and eating sausages at racially exclusive ethnic festivals.

By highlighting interdependencies between the ethnic and racial identity construction of both groups, this first section of *KulturConfusão* seeks to expand conventional binary models such as Zantop's theory of German colonial fantasies; it invites its readers to ponder the historical evolution of existing racial and ethnic hierarchies and, more importantly, to search for alternatives to unitary forms of national and ethnic identity.

The chapters in the first section, "Indigenous Projections," build their analyses of ethnic encounters on models of triangulation and mediation to deconstruct and critique static concepts of identity or imagery of clichés and stereotypes. Fernando Clara investigates the blind spots inherent to an incomplete timeline of German-Brazilian interrelations, pointing to a wide gap especially in the seventeenth and eighteenth centuries. With his contribution, he seeks to lay bare the intertextuality of many of the German texts on Brazil. Thus, the Brazil in the late eighteenth-century German mind was very much a "land determined in Europe and by Europe," and its definition was influenced by the complex interweaving of nature and nation at this time: With the accentuation that "the Nation was the Nature," Clara argues, the "process of colonization was completed."

Ute Ritz-Deutch takes a close look at the metadebates involving the fate of indigenous populations in Brazil, a political conundrum including more than just the South American states and moving into a global arena around 1900. More precisely, Ritz-Deutch draws attention to a topic that most studies on German settlements in Brazil ignore: violent conflicts between German-Brazilians and indigenous peoples of southern Brazil. Moreover, she examines how debates on the atrocities by the German-Brazilian communities were embedded in the ethnic and national identity formation on both sides of the Atlantic.

Similarly, Gabi Kathöfer's contribution to this section resituates the history of German emigration to Brazil in the nineteenth century by taking into account both the colonial chronicles of Hans Staden and the identity-constructing Brazilian narrative of *antropofagía* as developed by Modernist poet Oswald de Andrade in the 1920s. Reading cannibalism as a "cipher for intercultural influence and conflict," Kathöfer positions German emigration to Brazil in the intersection of German colonial desire and its subversion by Brazilian Modernists and reveals the translational dynamics between the two cultures in the nineteenth and early twentieth century.

Finally, Thomas Beebee's article on ethnographer Theodor Koch-Grünberg examines the role played by Germans as cultural mediators and translators in the Brazilian cultural project of appropriating "the Indian." Koch-Grünberg's interactions and observations as seen in his writings provide a perspective of a Brazilian indigenous population very much in flux and in direct relation to his study of various levels of Brazilian society and his idea of Brazilian pseudocivilization; Koch-Grünberg's writing "shows the inescapable triangulation and mediation of the ethnographic gaze through the presence of the third party, who is neither Indian nor European but Brazilian."

In "Everyday Cultures and Media," authors from different disciplines examine a variety of media formats and cultural products to convey a changing landscape of political and cultural communication practices. The pairing of Germany and Brazil, however random or arbitrary it may appear, calls forth different associations to different people. Some might say that the combination of Germany and Brazil sounds more like a soccer match, however friendly, than a scholarly volume, and many geopolitical theorists have endeavored to remind us that cultural politics is a game of shifting fortunes. In August 2011 the German national team broke an 18-year losing streak against Brazil. But the sides were not always so clear in such a matchup. Dunga, the well-known Brazilian soccer player of German-Italian descent, was instrumental in Brazil's 1994 World Cup victory, at the same time that he was under contract for Stuttgart FC (1993–1995). Even so, the story of German-Brazilian soccer stars begins much earlier, with Arthur Friedenreich (1892–1969), son of a German father and Afro-Brazilian mother, who was one of the first players to break the color barrier in Brazilian soccer, paving the way for other players of color in the country.

While addressing commonplaces, we might also turn our attention to the image of German-Brazilian women. Many throughout the world who pay attention to pop culture may think first of blonde, blue-eyed entertainers such as Xuxa or supermodel Gisele Bündchen. Those whose memory goes back further in time might also recall Vera Fischer, Miss Brazil 1969, from the largely German-Brazilian city of Blumenau, Santa Catarina. Speaking about her German background in an interview to promote her autobiography, she had this to say: "My father was German, a Nazi. He ordered me to read Hitler and hit me a lot. [...] I fought a lot with my father; I confronted him. But I also admired him."[17] Known for her acting career in telenovelas and the quintessentially São Paulo film genre known as the *pornochanchada*, Vera Fischer is revealed in her own words not simply as a two-dimensional centerfold but as a woman who proved capable of overcoming her status as a sex symbol, one all too aware from early on of the challenges of negotiating one's own femininity at the historical crossroads of two authoritarian regimes and at the forefront of a strongly established entertainment and popular culture.

Similarly, the chapters in the second section of this collection draw our attention to cultural crossroads, examples of intercultural negotiation, hybridization, and appropriation in journalism, music, and film to account for the nuances that arise between or even beyond spaces marked primarily by a single cultural and national identity. Ricarda Musser reintroduces us to *Intercâmbio*, the German-produced journal for cultural relations with Brazil from the 1930s, and points to its cultural marketing strategies heavily influenced by Nazi propaganda, discourses that were, perhaps not surprisingly, enthusiastically welcomed in Brazil during the period of the Estado Novo military dictatorship. Although the journal's official purpose was to mediate between German and Brazilian culture, it negotiated cultural and racial hierarchies between and within the two countries and, moreover, contributed to the ethnic definition of the German-Brazilian community.

In contrast, Andrew Hurley remarks on the liberating mediation of Brazilian jazz and bossa nova music to post-1945 West German audiences, particularly in the 1960s and 1970s. With Brazilian music popularized on German radio and television and resulting in a boom in sales of Brazilian recordings, Hurley shows how this was a multifaceted enterprise that positioned musicians and the music industry at the intersection of increasing hybridization and intercultural encounter between the two countries and their cultural institutions.

Hip-hop and rap lyrics are the subject of Ulrike Schröder's contribution to the volume. A linguistic project that analyzes the use of common operative metaphors in German and Brazilian lyrics, Schröder's investigation into the rise of hip-hop in the two countries traces three stages or mechanisms of reterritorialization in speech communities: transculturation, hybridization, and finally indigenization, the absorption of local singularities, which are then integrated into a new cultural style. Schröder's study also reveals that the fusion of globally circulating hip-hop cultures and regional cultures "does not result simply in unidirectional adoption and assimilation but rather in different forms of recontextual-

---

[17] Vera Fischer, *Vera, a Pequena Moisi* (Porto Alegre, Brazil: Editora Globo, 2007). No page number.

ization" according to the particular communicative structures and different cultural contexts and frames in both countries.

Concluding this section is a chapter on German films in Brazil in the 1920s and 1930s by Wolfgang Fuhrmann, who intertwines political, cultural, aesthetic, and technical elements when analyzing the medium of film and its intercultural potential in a transnational context. Similar to Musser's analysis of the journal *Intercâmbio*, Fuhrmann's chapter interprets the distribution and reception of German films in Brazil not only with regard to German fascistic propaganda abroad but also, and more importantly, in the context of "the dynamics of an active and sometimes very peculiar Teuto-Brazilian culture."

The last section, "Literary Fusions and Interstitial Spaces," is dedicated to cultural production in literature and art. The German-Brazilian *confusão* might easily be recognized in literary figures such as poet Hilda Hilst (1930–2004), whose family originated in Alsace, or novelist Lya Luft (b. 1938), who maintained in a recent interview that, although critics from other parts of Brazil do not consider her truly Brazilian because of her background, she does not desire to be European: "Alemão fica bom depois de algumas gerações amaciando no Brasil" ("German becomes all right after a few generations mellowing in Brazil").[18] Luft is also an accomplished translator of more than 100 books from both German and English, responsible for the Portuguese versions of works by Günter Grass, Hermann Hesse, Rainer Maria Rilke, and Thomas Mann. These women are dedicated to not only creating their own visions of Brazilian culture but also transforming it, thereby challenging the predominance of the beauty queens or supermodels in the popular imagination, who have all too often captured attention with their European complexion and features, thereby calling into question the persistent myths of racial democracy and equality.

Another famous example for interstitial spaces is the architecture of Oscar Niemeyer (1907–2012), one of the most important international modern architects, who designed the main buildings of the Brazilian capital, Brasília, the United Nations headquarters in New York, and numerous buildings in Brazilian cities, as well as one in the Hansaviertel in West Berlin. His views of modernity are informed by his own longstanding political allegiances to communism, which earned him the status of persona non grata during the military dictatorship in Brazil from 1964 to 1985. One of Niemeyer's collaborators, landscape architect Roberto Burle Marx (1909–1994), was the son of a German immigrant born in Stuttgart and raised in Trier (in fact, Karl Marx was his grandfather's cousin);

---

[18] Lya Luft, "A cultura alemã me influenciou muito," http://www.dw-world.de/dw/article/0,,1437528,00.html. *Deutsche Welle* 25.12 (2004).

after studying painting in Germany in the late 1920s, he returned to Brazil and is credited with introducing modernist landscape architecture to Brazil.

The chapters in this last section of *KulturConfusão* provide additional examples for German-Brazilian interculturalities in art and, more importantly, approaches to the analysis of literature and art as culturally confused spaces beyond the limits of nation-oriented fixed frameworks. Horst Nitschack concentrates on a comparative discussion of one of the most iconic texts in Brazilian literature, Mário de Andrade's *Macunaíma,* alongside the emblematic example of the German bildungsroman, Goethe's *Wilhelm Meister.* Rather than consider *Macunaíma* a failed attempt at replicating this genre in the context of Brazilian modernism, Nitschack claims an "elective affinity between the two" to point to a "common desire for a future national culture in which the subjectivity of its citizens may develop."

Christopher Larkosh focuses on nonnormative representations of gender and sexuality in the context of the virtual transnational imaginary of Nazi Germany as it resurfaces in the contemporary Brazilian novel, above all in the work of novelist João Gilberto Noll. By analyzing his 2008 novel *Acenos e afagos* and uncovering traces of the discussions of the author's ethnic origins in his work against the broader backdrop of German, Brazilian, and global cultural production, he proposes a renewed critical discussion on the rise and reemergence of totalitarianism.

German writers as refugees escaping the horrors of Nazi Germany contributed significantly to the Brazilian literary landscape after the 1930s, and many of them were susceptible to imagining the Brazilian society and landscape both as an Edenic paradise and as a space with unlimited future potential. In their writings, they also often stumbled on a set of cultural and political barriers, as Marlen Eckl conveys in her article. Thus, the Brazil the authors portray in their texts is the result of a *KulturConfusão* all their own, a process of intercultural comparison and negotiation of the meaning of home and belonging.

Edith Wolfe concentrates on Lithuanian-born and German-educated Brazilian immigrant painter Lasar Segall and his role of the "outsider within." Wolfe's analysis of his body of work centers on the critical distance to both German expressionism and Brazilian modernism, but it also reveals "unexpected similarities in purpose and practice between German colonialist and Brazilian postcolonial aesthetics." Examining the artist's interstitial gaze, Wolfe makes the case for the potential of a German-Brazilian postcolonial aesthetics and alternative understanding of modernity via the incorporation of migrant, ethnic, and other identities.

Concluding this section, as well as the collection as a whole, is Rainer Guldin's analysis of the intercultural relations between concrete poetry movements in Stuttgart and São Paulo. Through an examination of the complexities of literary translation of Vilém Flusser's 1966 German version of Haroldo de Campos's prose poem *Galáxias,* Guldin discusses the status of the multilingual text and the question of its (un)translatability. Moreover, he concludes that we should reinterpret all intercultural dialogues "as creative translational acts during which the foreign and the familiar are playfully reinvented."

As all chapters in this book demonstrate, Germany and Brazil remain two major global players that continue to attract one another, create stories about each other, if only from afar, a distance between them continually undercut by new technologies and differing forms of dialogue and hermeneutics. In the same way that each has been paired with a number of economic, cultural, and strategic partners (the United States, France, the United Kingdom, or regional counterparts in the rest of Latin America, the former Soviet Bloc, or elsewhere in the world, especially in Asia and Africa), Germany and Brazil are in a unique moment to explore the ways that their role as emerging regional and transnational superpowers will play out over the next century, whether as part of continental groups such as Mercosul and the European Union or in more extensive global configurations of both conventional and soft power, or in the various forms of cultural and media productions and cross-cultural enactment that inspire, cross-fertilize, and generate room and matter for intercultural debate, based on hermeneutic inquiry.

References

Aliaga-Buchenau, Ana-Isabel. "German Immigrants in Blumenau, Brazil: National Identity in Gertrud Gross-Hering's Novels." *The Latin Americanist* (2007): 5–21.

Alves, Débora Bendocchi. *Das Brasilienbild der deutschen Auswanderungswerbung im 19. Jahrhundert* (Berlin: Wissenschaftlicher Verlag Berlin, 2000).

Bary, Leslie. "Oswald de Andrade's 'Cannibalist Manifesto.'" *Latin American Literary Review* 19.38 (1991): 35–37.

Burke, Peter. *Cultural Hybridity* (Cambridge: Polity, 2009).

Cortez, Maria Teresa. "Zwischen Gut und Böse: die Darstellung Brasiliens in der Erzählung *Die Auswanderer nach Brasilien oder die Hütte am Gigitonhonha* von Amalie Schoppe." *Hebbel Jahrbuch* 61 (2006): 53–71.

Dallmayr, Fred. "Hermeneutics and Inter-cultural Dialog: Linking Theory and Practice." *Ethics & Global Politics* 2.1 (2009): 23–39.

Diggs, Cerue. "Brazil After Humboldt: Triangular Perceptions and the Colonial Gaze in Nineteenth-Century German Travel Narratives" (Diss., University of Maryland, 2008).

Fischer, Vera. *Vera, a Pequena Moisi* (Porto Alegre, Brazil: Editora Globo, 2007).

Luebke, Frederick. "A Prelude to Conflict: The German Ethnic Group in Brazilian Society, 1890–1917." *Ethnic and Racial Studies* 6.1 (1983): 1–17.

Luft, Lya. "A cultura alemã me influenciou muito." http://www.dw-world.de/dw/article/ 0,,1437528,00.html. *Deutsche Welle* 25.12 (2004). 29 July 2013.

Marotta, Vince. "Intercultural Hermeneutics and the Cross-cultural Subject." *Journal of Intercultural Studies* 30.3 (2009): 270.

Marschalck, Peter. *Deutsche Überseewanderung im 19. Jahrhundert* (Stuttgart: Klett, 1973).

Menninger, Annerose. "Hans Stadens Warhaftige Historia. Zur Geschichte eines Bestsellers der Reiseliteratur." *Geschichte in Wissenschaft und Unterricht* 9 (1984): 509–523.

Mignolo, Walter. *Local Histories/Global Designs. Coloniality, Subaltern Knowledges, and Border Thinking* (Princeton, NJ: Princeton University Press, 2000).

Neumann, Gerson Roberto. *Brasilien ist nicht weit von hier! Die Thematik der deutschen Auswanderung nach Brasilien in der deutschen Literatur im neunzehnten Jahrhundert (1800–1871)* (Frankfurt am Main: Lang, 2005).

Radhakrishnan, R. "Why Compare?," in Rita Felski and Susan Stanford Friedman, eds., *Comparison. Theories, Approaches, Uses* (Baltimore, MD: Johns Hopkins University Press, 2013), 15–16.

Rescher, Hubertus. *Die deutschsprachige Literatur zu Brasilien von 1789–1850. Widerspiegelung brasilianischer Sozial- und Wirtschaftsstrukturen von 1789–1850 in der deutschsprachigen Literatur desselben Zeitraums* (Frankfurt am Main: Lang, 1979).

Schmölz-Häberlein, Michaela, and Mark Häberlein. "Hans Staden, Neil L. Whitehead, and the Cultural Politics of Scholarly Publishing." *Hispanic American Historical Review* 81 (2001): 745–751.

Smith, Jeremy, "Civilisational Analysis and Intercultural Models of American Societies." *Journal of Intercultural Studies* 30.3 (2009): 233–248.

Sudhaus, Fritz. *Deutschland und die Auswanderung nach Brasilien im 19. Jahrhundert.* (Hamburg: Hans Christians Verlag, 1940).

Waldenfels, Bernhard. *Phenomenology of the Alien* (Chicago: Northwestern University Press, 2011).

Walker, Mack. *Germany and the Emigration 1816–1885* (Cambridge, MA: Harvard University Press, 1964).

Whitehead, Neil L. "Hans Staden and the Cultural Politics of Cannibalism." *Hispanic American Historical Review* 80 (2000): 721–751.

Zantop, Susanne. *Colonial Fantasies. Conquest, Family, and Nation in Precolonial Germany, 1770–1870* (Durham, NC: Duke University Press, 1997).

Indigenous Projections

Ute Ritz-Deutch
Germans and Indians in Brazil: The Transatlantic Construction of Ethnic Identity in the Discourse of Indian Protection

The construction of ethnic identity takes place in a complex social field, in which the Other and the maintenance of conceptual and physical boundaries with the Other are vitally important. This process is never homogeneous but case specific, taking on different manifestations across time and space and depending greatly on the particular actors involved. In this chapter I examine the conflicts between German-Brazilians and indigenous peoples of southern Brazil at the turn of the twentieth century and how the ensuing debates were embedded in the ethnic and national identity formation on both sides of the Atlantic. In particular, I look at the transatlantic discourse on Indian protection in Brazil, which entered an intensive phase in 1908 after the Sixteenth International Congress of Americanists in Vienna, during which Czech ethnologist Alberto Frič publicly accused Europeans in Brazil of participating in the "modern conquista" of South America by committing atrocities against Indians.[1]

After the Vienna Congress, advocates in São Paulo and Rio de Janeiro who had been arguing for government intervention on behalf of Indians became even more determined to find a political solution. They embarked on a campaign that within two years led to the creation of Brazil's first federal Indian Protection Service, the *Serviço de Proteção aos Índios* (SPI). During the service's inaugura-

---

[1] Alberto Frič, "Völkerwanderungen, Ethnographie und Geschichte der Konquista in Südbrasilien," in *Verhandlungen des XVI. Internationalen Amerikanisten Kongress: Wien 9. bis 14. September 1908* (Nendeln, Liechtenstein: Kraus Reprint, 1968) [hereinafter Verhandlungen], 63–67. See also Ute Ritz-Deutch, "Alberto Vojtěch Frič, the German Diaspora, and Indian Protection in Southern Brazil, 1900–1920: A Transatlantic, Ethno-Historical Case Study" (PhD diss., Binghamton University, 2008). See also Josef Kandert, "Alberto Vojtěch Frič – on the Centenary of his Birth," *Annals of the Náprstek Museum* 11 (1983): 111–160; H. Glenn Penny, "The Politics of Anthropology in the Age of Empire: German Colonists, Brazilian Indians, and the Case of Alberto Vojtěch Frič," *Comparative Study of Society and History* (2003): 249–280. I realize that the terms *Indians* and *índios* are problematic, but these are the terms prevalent in the primary sources. Instead of the derogatory term *Bugre*, I use *Xokleng* or *Kaingang* because these were the groups generally referred to during this discourse.

tion address, Brazil's minister of agriculture recognized the Vienna Congress as being a catalyst in this process.²

The Xokleng of Santa Catarina and the Kaingang of São Paulo, who are at the center of this discourse on Indian protection, are of strategic importance in the history of Indian-Brazilian relations.³ By the turn of the twentieth century, most indigenous groups in southern Brazil had already been subjugated, decimated, or pushed out of the area; however, the Xokleng and Kaingang were among the last groups to offer major resistance in the South, which led to brutal responses by Brazilians.⁴ These clashes were more than minor regional struggles; here on the remaining frontiers of the South, Indian–white conflicts were among the most intense in all of Brazil at that time.⁵ The so-called pacification of these groups was also the first task of the Indian Protection Service, and indeed the beginning of federal Indian protection for the entire nation.⁶ Considering that Brazil from its beginnings as a Portuguese colony has had a very troubling and often brutal history with its indigenous population, it is noteworthy that the need for more humane policies was articulated in opposition to foreign (German) influence.

---

2 David Hall Stauffer, "The Origin and Establishment of Brazil's Indian Service: 1889–1910" (PhD diss., University of Texas, 1955), 304. In this chapter I refer to São Paulo generally as being part of southern Brazil. However, officially *the South* refers to the three southernmost states, Rio Grande do Sul, Santa Catarina, and Paraná, whereas São Paulo and Rio de Janeiro are considered to be part of the Southeast.
3 The Xokleng are known by several names, including *Shokleng*. The Kaingang (Caingang) are also known as Coroado. Regionally the Xokleng and Kaingang continue to be called Botocudo or by the infamous generic term *Bugre*, which is the most common term found in the primary sources. See also Sílvio Coelho dos Santos, *Os índios Xokleng: memória visual* (Florianópolis: Ed. da Universidade Federal de Santa Catarina, 1997), 20. The Xokleng and Kaingang belong to the Gê (Jê) linguistic group and are culturally related. Although some of their territory overlaps, the Kaingang have a wider range that extends into São Paulo (which formerly included the present state of Paraná).
4 See Shelton H. Davis, *Victims of the Miracle: Development and the Indians of Brazil* (Cambridge, England: Cambridge University Press, 1977).
5 David Hall Stauffer, "The Origin and Establishment of Brazil's Indian Service: 1889–1910" (PhD diss., University of Texas, 1955), 47. Most secondary sources, which reference Stauffer's dissertation, see the Xokleng massacres and the 1908 Congress in Vienna as leading to the creation of the SPI. Pinheiro stresses that it was the massacres against the São Paulo Kaingang that elicited strong protests in the media and led to the agency's creation. Niminon Suzel Pinheiro, "Terra não é Troféu de Guerra," in *Novas contribuições aos estudos interdisciplinares dos Kaingang*, ed. Kimiye Tommasino et al. (Paraná: Editora da Universidade Estadual de Londrina, 2004), 367.
6 John Hemming, *Die If You Must: Brazilian Indians in the Twentieth Century* (London: Macmillan, 2003), 28, 40.

The discourse about the fate of Brazil's Indians was transatlantic, far exceeding the national boundaries of Brazil. In Germany it involved ethnologists, museum directors, government representatives, and colonial propagandists, whereas in Brazil it engaged German-Brazilian settlers and propagandists, Brazilian nativists, scientists, and political activists. The controversy was deeply embedded in the transatlantic circulation of ideas and mediated through personal and official letters, press releases and political pamphlets, articles in newspapers and scientific journals, and presentations at national and international congresses. The actors in this case often articulated the interests of German immigrants as destructive to the interests of indigenous peoples. In other words, Indian protection was debated in the wider matrix of ethnic identity construction, in which Germans in Brazil were used to argue either for or against the protection of Brazil's indigenous peoples.

The Sixteenth International Congress of Americanists can be seen as a watershed moment in the controversy over the plight of Brazil's Indians, although activists such as Alberto Frič had been engaged on these issues for some time. In the years leading up to the congress, Frič, who had been contracted by the Royal and Imperial Museums of Ethnology in Berlin and Hamburg to collect ethnographic artifacts in South America, had become politically active after witnessing the plight of American Indians first hand. In early 1907 he had already accused the well-known German colony Blumenau in Santa Catarina of hiring Indian hunters or so-called *bugreiros* to hunt, kill, and enslave the Xokleng in the hinterland, a charge that was not without merit, although Germans were not the only settlers involved. All Brazilian farmers, including Italian–Brazilians living in the mountainous regions (*serra*), feared Indian attacks and mobilized revenge raids if these happened.[7] German-Brazilian communities were therefore not unique. Even the government of Santa Catarina hired *bugreiros* and paid them out of state coffers. Martinho Bugreiro, the most infamous of these state-financed hunters, even boasted to government officials during an inquiry that he had killed a thousand Indians, yet he suffered no consequences.[8] However, Frič's

---

7 In the interior of Santa Catarina, Brazilians of German and Italian origin were the largest ethnic groups, whereas coastal areas were more ethnically diverse. Often settlers had been sold dubious titles in the Serra do Mar and Serra Geral and ended up homesteading in Indian territory without initially realizing it. During revenge raids men were generally killed, and children along with one or two women were brought into town.

8 See Dorvalino Eloy Koch, *Tragédias Euro-Xokleng e contexto* (Brusque, Santa Catarina: Author, 2002), 151. See also Daércio Kieser, *Um discurso para justificar a ação Bugreira* (Florianópolis, Santa Catarina: Universidade Federal de Santa Catarina, 1994); Enéas Athanázio, "Martinho Bugreiro: criminoso ou herói?" *Separata de Blumenau em Cadernos* (September 1984): 1–11; Rosi-

opposition was specifically articulated against German colonists in Santa Catarina and the ongoing warfare with the Xokleng, whose population had already been decimated and at most numbered 1,500 people by the turn of the twentieth century.[9]

Attitudes about the Xokleng were not monolithic, and residents of Blumenau differed significantly in their opinions about the local Indians. Many German-Brazilians who lived on farms in remote areas feared the Xokleng and saw them as a personal threat that should be eliminated. When newspapers reported on raids conducted against the Xokleng, they generally listed as a matter of fact the number of people killed or injured, the artifacts the hunters had collected, and the number of children they brought back into town, which were handed over to local churches or placed into families. In these accounts the Xokleng were treated as "wild Indians," and little thought was given to the causes of the conflicts or the psychological devastation the raids had on the surviving children.[10] However, not everyone in Blumenau was callous. Hugo Gensch, a physician and humanitarian who had adopted one of the Xokleng children and by all accounts treated her with kindness and consideration, frequently wrote articles in which he denounced the *bugreiros* and their activities.[11]

Indian–white conflict did not just occur in Santa Catarina, however. Clashes in the state of São Paulo were even more intense and involved the large-scale punitive campaigns directed against the more numerous Kaingang Indians, who had an estimated population of 10,000 people.[12] It is therefore not surprising that after the Vienna Congress the center of action in Brazil shifted northward.

---

lene Alves, "Bugres: as notícias correm!," in *Visões do Vale: perspectivas historiográficas recentes*, ed. Cristina Ferreira and Méri Frotscher (Blumenau: Nova Letra, 2000).

9 According to anthropologist Greg Urban, at this time the Xokleng numbered from 600 to 1,500 people. See Greg Urban, "A Model of Shokleng Social Reality" (PhD diss., University of Chicago, 1978), 47.

10 See for example, "Expedição contra os Bugres," *Novidades* (Itajaí), March 1905. Reprinted in *Notícias de "Vicente Só": Brusques – Ontem e Hoje* VII.27 (1983): 167–168.

11 Gensch wrote a short book on his adopted daughter and her transition into the "civilized world," which was distributed at the Vienna Congress. See Hugo Gensch, "Die Erziehung eines Indianerkindes: praktischer Beitrag zur Lösung der südamerikanischen Indianerfrage," in *Verhandlungen des XVI. Internationalen Amerikanisten Kongresses: Wien 9. bis 14. September 1908* (Nendeln, Liechtenstein: Kraus Reprint, 1968).

12 On Kaingang studies see Wilmar da Rocha D'Angelis, *Toldo Chimbangue: história e luta em Santa Catarina* (Xanxerê, Santa Catarina: Conselho Indigenista Missionário-Regional Sul, 1984); Lúcio Mota et al., eds., *Novas contribuições aos estudos interdisciplinares dos Kaingang* (Londrina, Paraná: Editora Universidade Estadual de Londrina, 2004); Francisco Silva Noelli, ed., *Bibliografia Kaingang: referências sobre um povo jê do sul do Brasil* (Londrina, Paraná: Editora Universidade Estadual de Londrina, 1998).

During this phase of the discourse Brazilian activists targeted Hermann von Ihering, German-born director of the Paulista Museum, and used his anti-Indian rhetoric to argue that Brazil must free itself from the dominance of German science and follow its own path of national self-realization by protecting its indigenous populations. The need for Indian protection was therefore articulated in direct opposition to German presence in Brazil, including German-Brazilian colonists and the perceived domination of German science.

The conditions and issues in São Paulo differed significantly from those in Santa Catarina, where Euro-Brazilians were mostly small-scale farmers who felt vulnerable to Indian attacks and abandoned by their government. Communities such as Blumenau primarily financed the *bugreiro* raids against the Xokleng, who were often accused of raiding farms, stealing livestock, or injuring colonists. These attacks and the subsequent counterattacks were characteristic of the conflicts that had been going on since Europeans first settled the mountainous interior of the region in the nineteenth century. By then the Xokleng, who were once engaged in agriculture on the highlands (*Planalto*) of Paraná and São Paulo, had been driven from their homes and reduced to roving bands depending on raids as part of their subsistence strategy.[13]

The decline of Xokleng communities was thus inextricably connected to Brazilian expansion into São Paulo and the Indian wars on the Planalto. Here the Kaingang were among the last indigenous peoples to offer fierce resistance to Brazil's westward expansion in the South, in particular to the construction of the Northwest Railroad (*Estrada de Ferro do Noroeste*) into their territory. The railroad was important for coffee producers on the highlands because it connected them with the Paraná River in the West and hence the entire La Plata river system.[14] Not surprisingly, the attacks against the Kaingang were organized by larger militias, and many Brazilians saw elimination of these fierce warriors as necessary to Brazil's westward expansion and economic development.[15]

In São Paulo, where large coffee plantations were the norm rather than small-scale farms, the atrocities committed against the Kaingang could not be blamed on the German colonists there, whose history and settlement patterns were significantly different from those in Santa Catarina or Rio Grande do Sul.

---

13 See Greg Urban, "Interpretations of Inter-Ethnic Contact: The Shokleng and Brazilian National Society, 1914–1916," *Ethnohistory* 32.3 (1985): 224.
14 See Correia das Neves, *Historia da Estrada de Ferro Noroeste do Brasil* (São Paulo: Bauru, 1958).
15 See John Hemming, *Die If You Must: Brazilian Indians in the Twentieth Century* (London: Macmillan, 2003), chapter 1. The atrocities committed against the Kaingang of São Paulo were already well known before Alberto Frič became active.

Furthermore, in São Paulo the state itself financed the penetration into Kaingang territory and even supplied railroad workers with weapons. However, instead of taking on the government and its policies directly, advocates for Indian protection found a convenient scapegoat in Hermann von Ihering because he seemingly defended the eradication of the Kaingang. By focusing their efforts on the German (hence foreign) element in their society, Brazilian activists could launch an effective critique without seeming to be unpatriotic.

Alberto Frič had already conducted ethnographic research in South America in previous years and was therefore familiar with attacks against Indians in southern Brazil. However, his third South American journey from 1906 to 1908 was the beginning of his political activism and his participation in the transatlantic discourse on Indian protection.[16] In September 1906 he circulated a petition at the Freethinker Congress in Buenos Aires demanding that the Indians of South America be protected instead of persecuted.[17] Frič was subsequently invited to southern Brazil by Pedro Trompowsky Taulois, a fellow activist who had been inspired to create the Liga Patriotica para Catechese dos Selvicolas (Patriotic League for the Education of Indians). The two ended up collaborating on a political pamphlet, *As Matanças de Bugres e o Urwaldsbote* (*The Killing of Bugre Indians and the Urwaldsbote*), which was published in early 1907.[18] The 40-page book introduced Frič as "pacificador dos Indios" and targeted the widely circulated Blumenau newspaper *Der Urwaldsbote* for its anti-Indian and anti-Brazilian views.[19]

---

[16] See also Ute Ritz-Deutch, "Alberto Vojtěch Frič, the German Diaspora, and Indian Protection in Southern Brazil, 1900–1920: A Transatlantic, Ethno-Historical Case Study" (PhD diss., Binghamton University, 2008), 6.

[17] On Frič's advocacy at the Freethinker Congress (Congreso do Livre Pensamento), held on 23 September 1906 in Buenos Aires, see Edilberto Trevisan, "Vultos Tchecos no Brasil e no Paraná," *Boletim do Instituto Histórico, Geográfico Paranaense* 37 (1980): 9–55.

[18] Pedro Trompowsky Taulois, *As matanças de Bugres e o "Urwaldsbote"* (Coritiba, Brazil: Impressora Paranaense, 1907). See also Sílvio Coelho dos Santos, "Fric, a 'Liga Patriotica' e os Índios," *Anais do Congresso de História e Geografia de Santa Catarina* (Florianópolis), 4–7 September 1996. Taulois was later invited to work for the SPI.

[19] Brazilian scholars in Santa Catarina continue to analyze the publications of *Der Urwaldsbote* today, because the paper also had a reputation for promoting Germandom and being hostile to assimilation efforts. Several articles have been translated into Portuguese and appear in the journal *Blumenau em Cadernos*, which is published by the Arquivo Histórico José Ferreira da Silva in Blumenau. See "Der 'Paiz' und die Indianerkatechese," *Der Urwaldsbote*, 9 November 1912 and 13 November 1912. Reprinted in *Blumenau em Cadernos* XLI.4 (April 2000): 7–21. Another local paper, the *Blumenauer Zeitung*, tended to promote a more moderate approach to the Indian problem. Like most German papers in Brazil, neither *Der Urwaldsbote* nor the *Blumenauer Zeitung* survived the Vargas regime and World War II.

In March 1907, when Frič traveled to Blumenau, *As Matanças* was already well known, and because he had accused the community of advocating for the destruction of the Bugres (Xokleng), residents did not receive him kindly. They saw his charges as damaging to the reputation of Germans in Brazil and felt strongly compelled to discredit him. Apparently Frič also had a penchant for getting into political discussions and criticizing the German Empire and Germans in Brazil, which seemed especially egregious to residents of Blumenau because he introduced himself as a "representative" of the German imperial museums who had contracted him to collect ethnographic artifacts.[20] When Gustav Salinger, the German consul stationed in Blumenau, felt compelled to inquire about Frič, the Blumenau men who responded to his request all noted that the Czech ethnologist exhibited "inappropriate behaviors" and damaged Germany's reputation abroad.[21] They also described Frič as a rabid Czech nationalist and hater of Germans.

These letters and a copy of *As Matanças de Bugres e o Urwaldsbote* were promptly forwarded to the German Foreign Office (Auswärtige Amt) in Berlin, which thereafter kept an extensive file on his activities. As a result of these petitions from Blumenau, Frič's museum contract with Berlin was revoked by June of that year, reportedly by orders of the minister in the Foreign Office.[22] The rebuke of Frič's activism thus led to concrete government action at an impressive speed, indicating Germany's continued concern with the German diaspora in Brazil and the severity of the threat he was thought to pose.

When Frič returned to Europe in 1908 to bring his charges to the International Congress of Americanists, numerous people in attendance, among them the museum directors who had originally contracted with him, knew of his political activities in Blumenau and his reputation as a troublemaker. Even though Frič at this particular venue did not specifically accuse German-Brazilians in Santa Catarina, his colleagues and the journalists covering the congress felt nonetheless compelled to dismiss his charges, discredit his character, and defend the reputa-

---

20 Although Frič was contracted to collect ethnographic artifacts, he was not officially employed by these institutions.
21 Gustav Salinger sent the letters he received from Blumenau residents to the Foreign Office in Berlin, 22 July 1907. See Bundesarchiv Berlin, Auswärtiges Amt [hereinafter AA], R901, 37874: 16.
22 It took a mere three months from the time Frič traveled to Blumenau to the time the Berlin museum revoked his contract via telegram. Bode, in the administration of the Berlin museum, informed Frič that the action was taken because of complaints against him. Bode to Frič, 16 July 1907. AA, R901, 37874: 28–31.

tion of German colonists in southern Brazil.[23] The discussions in the German-speaking press lasted nearly six weeks, and as Karl von den Steinen from Berlin's Museum of Ethnology lamented, this "political incident" received more public attention than the entire congress.[24] Many of the opinions expressed in newspaper articles during these weeks reiterated what Germans on both sides of the Atlantic had been writing in letters and articles for years, namely that German-Brazilians in Blumenau were exemplary and hardworking people – the pride of Germandom abroad.[25]

Alberto Frič had made a strategic decision to challenge Blumenau, because it was one of the most well-known German colonies in Brazil and one of the most successful communities in Santa Catarina, a state in which German-Brazilians made up a remarkable 20 percent of the entire population. Southern Brazil in general and Blumenau in particular also continued to receive attention in the German Empire, where newspapers and colonial publications highly praised the German community as a shining example of German cultural preservation.[26] Blumenau, which had been founded in 1850 as a private colony by Dr. Blumenau, was clearly an important node in the transatlantic discursive network. The *município*, which by the early twentieth century was one of the three greatest industrial centers of the state, also gained a lot of attention in the Brazilian

---

[23] For a discussion of the congress and the coverage in the German-speaking press, see Ute Ritz-Deutch, "Alberto Vojtěch Frič, the German Diaspora, and Indian Protection in Southern Brazil, 1900–1920: A Transatlantic, Ethno-Historical Case Study" (PhD diss., Binghamton University, 2008), 35–81. Frič's assertions prompted a response from museum directors and government officials. See "Völkerkunde in Brasilien: Anklagen gegen das Berliner Ethnographische Museum," *Berliner Tageblatt*, 15 September 1908. AA, R901, 37875: 13. Professor Seler wrote an editorial defending the Brazilian government. See *Berliner Tageblatt* 479, 19 September 1908.

[24] Karl von den Steinen, "Fric und kein Ende," *Berliner Tageblatt*, 13 October 1908. AA, R901, 37875: 41.

[25] For example, the *Vossische Zeitung* already published an article about Germans in Brazil right after Frič had run afoul in Blumenau the previous year. The newspaper was published in Berlin, although some of the readership was in Brazil. See "Amerika: die Deutschen in Brasilien," *Vossische Zeitung* 228.2 (Suppl., 17 May 1907).

[26] The highest total number of Germans was in Rio Grande do Sul; however, Santa Catarina had the highest percentage of Germans. Today 35 percent of the people in Santa Catarina claim German ancestry, followed by 33 percent claiming Italian descent. For various statistics about the number of Germans in Brazil, see Leslie Bethell, ed., *The Cambridge History of Latin America*, Vol. V (Cambridge, England: Cambridge University Press, 1986), 779 and 782–783. Although statistics are difficult to establish, it has generally been estimated that at the eve of World War I, between 350,000 and 400,000 Germans resided in Brazil. It is not clear how many of them were German citizens.

media.²⁷ Here, however, pride in German culture was not universally appreciated, and some Luso-Brazilians were even suspicious of Germans in southern Brazil and questioned their loyalty to the young Brazilian Republic, especially during moments of crisis.²⁸

Although many Germans in Brazil stayed connected to Germany by subscribing to German newspapers, maintaining written communications with family members, or even visiting Germany if they had the means, this desire to maintain a bond was not one-directional. The German government, academic institutions, private businesses, and various associations also facilitated an ongoing relationship with the German diaspora in Brazil. This transatlantic exchange therefore took place in the private as well as the public sphere. The ongoing interest in German communities in Brazil was also vividly expressed through a variety of colonial publications, which frequently discussed the official German colonies in Africa and elsewhere but also periodically covered German communities in Brazil, lauding them for their heroic physical and cultural survival.²⁹

In addition, well-known colonial publicists such as Friedrich Fabri, Otto Tannenberg, and Robert Jannasch considered Brazil to have the greatest potential for German influence in South America.³⁰ *The Handbook of Germandom Abroad* (*Handbuch des Deutschtums im Auslande*), which covered German communities all over the world, also considered southern Brazil as an important center of in-

---

27 Todd Diacon, *Millenarian Vision, Capitalist Reality: Brazil's Contestado Rebellion, 1912–1916* (Durham, NC: Duke University Press, 1991), 11–12.
28 The term *Luso-Brazilian* refers to Brazilians of Portuguese origin; however, the term was more generally used in contradistinction to German-Brazilians, especially in German sources. Therefore, the ethnic identity of Luso-Brazilians was more mixed than the term may imply. On the ethnic tensions between Luso-Brazilians and German-Brazilians before and during World War I, see Frederick C. Luebke, *Germans in Brazil: A Comparative History of Cultural Conflict During World War I* (Baton Rouge: Louisiana State University Press, 1987). Also see Luebke, "A Prelude to Conflict: The German Ethnic Group in Brazil, 1890–1917," *Ethnic and Racial Studies* 6.1 (January 1983).
29 For a discussion about German literature on immigration to Brazil, see Gerson Roberto Neumann, *Brasilien ist nicht weit von hier! Die Thematik der deutschen Auswanderung nach Brasilien in der deutschen Literatur im 19. Jahrhundert (1800–1871)* (Frankfurt am Main: Peter Lang, 2004).
30 See Friedrich Fabri, *Bedarf Deutschland der Colonien? Does Germany Need Colonies? Eine politisch-ökonomische Betrachtung von D[r. Theol.] Friedrich Fabri*, 3rd ed. Trans. and ed. E. C. M. Breuning and M. E. Chamberlain, *Studies in German Thought and History*, Vol. 2 (Lewiston, NY: The Edwin Mellen Press, 1998); Otto Richard Tannenberg, *Groß-Deutschland: die Arbeit des 20. Jahrhunderts* (Leipzig: Bruno Volger Verlagsbuchhandlung, 1911); and Robert Jannasch, "Die praktischen Aufgaben der deutschen Auswanderungspolitik," in *Verhandlungen des Deutschen Kolonialkongresses 1902 zu Berlin* (Berlin, 1903).

fluence, where German culture had greater chances of surviving than elsewhere. It also noted that the Germans in Blumenau and Joinville were largely responsible for the positive reputation German-Brazilian communities enjoyed on both sides of the Atlantic.[31]

German culture in southern Brazil found expression in a multitude of associations, including music clubs, sports clubs, rifle clubs, mutual benefit societies, library associations, and professional organizations, such as Handelsvereine.[32] In Blumenau associational life was generally strong, and the community also had branch offices of the General German School Association (Allgemeiner Deutscher Schulverein), the Pan-German League, and the German Navy League.[33] Private German-language schools in the Blumenau *município* outnumbered Portuguese-language state schools by ten to one, and statewide more than three-quarters of private schools taught in German. Many of the schools, and the Protestant parishes, were financially supported by official and private funds from Germany.[34]

Given the strength of German institutions, including German schools, German Protestant churches, and German associations in the region, it is not surprising that advocates of German colonialism focused their attention on Santa Catarina. Propagandists argued that Germans who emigrated should not be lost to the German nation, and therefore they recommended southern Brazil as an ideal destination where Germandom could be most easily preserved.[35] Tannenberg described southern Brazil as a country of German culture, and pastor Faulhaber of Blumenau even suggested that Germandom should expand over all of South America.[36] R. Sernau, one of the directors of the Hansa-Hammonia

---

[31] See W. Dibelius and G. Lenz, eds., *Handbuch des Deutschtums im Auslande*, 2nd ed. (Berlin: Allgemeiner Deutscher Schulverein zur Erhaltung des Deutschtums im Auslande, 1906) [hereinafter Dibelius], 375.
[32] See Frederick C. Luebke, *Germans in Brazil: A Comparative History of Cultural Conflict During World War I* (Baton Rouge: Louisiana State University Press, 1987), 47.
[33] Dibelius, 403.
[34] At the turn of the twentieth century, the county of Blumenau had 10 state schools and 113 private schools enrolling 520 and 5,011 children, respectively. See Frederick C. Luebke, *Germans in Brazil: A Comparative History of Cultural Conflict During World War I* (Baton Rouge: Louisiana State University Press, 1987), 51. There were approximately 3,000 German schools abroad, 1,000 of which were in Brazil. See Dibelius, 401.
[35] R. Sernau, "Zur Frage der Auswanderung," *Deutsche Kolonialzeitung* 3 (1886): 133–134; and Alfred Hettner, "Das Deutschtum in Südbrasilien," *Geographische Zeitschrift* 8.11 (1902): 609.
[36] Otto Richard Tannenberg, *Groß-Deutschland: die Arbeit des 20. Jahrhunderts* (Leipzig: Bruno Volger Verlagsbuchhandlung, 1911), 266; and H. Faulhaber, "Deutschtum in Südbrasilien," *Beiträge zur Kolonialpolitik und Kolonialwirtschaft* 1 (1899–1900): 436.

colony in Santa Catarina, claimed that the German government should support Germandom abroad because it was "good national colonial politics" and a national duty.[37]

Travel literature and memoirs of Germans who had spent some years in Brazil were also widely available to the German-reading public, although until recently few of these works were translated into Portuguese. On one hand, these articles and books introduced readers in Germany to Brazil and intended to educate potential immigrants about the challenges they would face. On the other hand, these works also served the purpose of strengthening German identity on both sides of the Atlantic, by comparing positive attributes of Germans with negative attributes of Luso-Brazilians. Such writings were generally laced with prejudice and generalizations, especially from our present-day vantage point.[38] In the older sources Luso-Brazilians were often depicted as lazy, dirty,

---

37 See R. Sernau, "Zur Frage der Auswanderung," *Deutsche Kolonialzeitung* 3 (1886), 134; also Alfred Hettner, "Das Deutschtum in Südbrasilien," *Geographische Zeitschrift* 8.11 (1902): 626.
38 Among primary sources see José Deeke, *Das Munizip Blumenau und seine Entwicklungsgeschichte in drei Bände* [sic] (São Leopoldo, Brazil: Rotermund, 1910); Gustav Stutzer, *Das Itajahy-Thal und die Kolonie Blumenau in Süd-Brasilien, Provinz Santa Catharina* (Goslar am Harz: L. Koch, 1883); Karl August Wettstein, *Brasilien und die Deutsch-Brasilianische Kolonie Blumenau* (Leipzig: Verlag von Friedrich Engelmann, 1907). As I have previously noted, even the secondary sources authored by Germans or German-Brazilians decades ago tend to be uncritical and focus primarily on the positive contributions Germans in Brazil made. See Carlos Fouquet, *Der deutsche Einwanderer und seine Nachkommen in Brasilien 1808–1824–1974* (São Paulo: Instituto Hans-Staden, 1974); Hartmut Fröschle, ed., *Die Deutschen in Lateinamerika: Schicksal und Leistung* (Tübingen: Horst Erdmann Verlag, 1979); Karl H. Oberacker, *Der deutsche Beitrag zum Aufbau der brasilianischen Nation* (São Paulo: Herder Editora Livraria, 1955). See also Ute Ritz-Deutch, "Alberto Vojtěch Frič, the German Diaspora, and Indian Protection in Southern Brazil, 1900–1920: A Transatlantic, Ethno-Historical Case Study" (PhD diss., Binghamton University, 2008), 10–11. For German immigration to Latin America see Klaus J. Bade, ed., *Deutsche im Ausland – Fremde in Deutschland: Migration in Geschichte und Gegenwart* (Munich: Verlag C. H. Beck, 1992); and Günther J. Bergmann, *Auslandsdeutsche in Paraguay, Brasilien, Argentinien* (Berlin: Westkreuz Verlag, 1994). Scholars in Brazil continue to study the role of German-Brazilian communities in a more nuanced fashion. See Cristina Ferreira and Méri Frotscher, eds., *Visões do Vale: perspectivas historiográficas recentes* (Blumenau: Nova Letra, 2000); Toni Vidal Jochem, *Pouso dos imigrantes* (Florianópolis, Santa Catarina: Papa-Livro, 1992); Cláudia Mauch and Naira Vasconcellos, *Os Alemães no Sul do Brasil: cultura, etnicidade, história* (Canoas, Brazil: Ed. Universidade Luterana do Brasil, 1994); Ivo M. Theis, Marcos Antônio Mattedi, and Fabricio Ricardo de Limas Tomio, eds., *Nosso passado (in)comum: contribuições para o debate sobre a história e a historiografia em Blumenau* (Blumenau: Ed. Universidade Regional de Blumenau, 2000).

unmotivated, and untrustworthy, whereas German-Brazilians were described as hard-working, efficient, clean, and reliable.[39]

The public in Germany was thus able to keep informed about the German diaspora in Brazil through colonial publications, specialist journals, and travelogues. Even newspapers published in Berlin, which targeted an educated readership, such as the *Vossische Zeitung* and the daily *Berliner Tageblatt*, periodically published articles on German-Brazilian communities. They often deplored the difficult conditions in Brazil while lauding the Germans there for their tenacious survival.[40] Southern Brazil was not on the daily agenda of these newspapers but was given particular attention when transnational controversies were unfolding, as they did after the Vienna Congress.

Alberto Frič, whose activism had started the fire, withdrew from the debate after the media coverage in the German-speaking press had died down. The discourse had by then shifted to Brazil, and Hermann von Ihering became the new lightning rod when he argued that German colonists (and not Brazilian Indians) deserved the protection of the Brazilian government. Activists in São Paulo and Rio de Janeiro now focused on Ihering and the German science he represented to argue their case in Brazilian newspapers and scientific journals.

The debate was moved forward by just a handful of dedicated people. As David Hall Stauffer notes, the SPI was not created as a result of parliamentary debates or public lecture campaigns, nor did it come about in the wake of public demonstrations. Rather, it was the result of the tireless efforts of those who exercised their agency, devoted their time, talents, and efforts to the cause, and exerted direct pressure on government officials.[41] The public debate then included not the public at large but scientists, activists, and positivists who were seemingly spurred into action by Frič's denunciations.

Brazilian activists had several reasons for targeting Hermann von Ihering, who had already alienated his colleagues at the museums in São Paulo and Rio de Janeiro by maintaining strong intellectual ties to Europe and treating

---

39 See for example Jorge Luiz da Cunha and Angelika Gärtner, "Darstellung der deutschen und brasilianischen Kultur im Reisebericht von Herrmann [sic] Meyer aus den Jahren 1898 und 1899 über die deutschen Kolonien in Rio Grande do Sul," in *Anais do VI Seminário Nacional de Pesquisadores da História das Comunidades Teuto-Brasileiras*, ed. Isabel Cristina Arendt and Marcos Antonio Witt (Rio Grande do Sul: Editora Oikos, 2004), 100–118.
40 See for example, *Vossische Zeitung*, 17 May 1907.
41 David Hall Stauffer, "The Origin and Establishment of Brazil's Indian Service: 1889–1910" (PhD diss., University of Texas, 1955), 308.

his Brazilian colleagues with contempt.⁴² These professional animosities undoubtedly played a role in the controversy. Because Ihering had already created tensions in his professional capacity as a scientist, his apparent embracing of social Darwinism only made matters worse. Although he intended to bring the plight of immigrants to national attention, his efforts backfired and instead fueled the controversy over the so-called Indian question.⁴³

It is also important to remember that Ihering worked and published in São Paulo, a wealthy state that pursued its own immigration policies and was arguably more formidable than the weak federal government. In São Paulo several powerful forces converged, and the state often colluded with railway companies and large landowners (*fazendeiros*) to disenfranchise poor farmers and indigenous peoples.⁴⁴ When Ihering was arguing in favor of "progress" he seemed to align himself with large-scale development projects, including railroad construction penetrating into Kaingang territory, that were funded by Brazilian and international capital.⁴⁵

Many Brazilian intellectuals believed that displacing the Indians from their land might be regrettable but was nonetheless necessary in order for Brazil to become a modern nation. Consequently, there had been little critique of the government or the large landowners over such issues. After the congress in Vienna, however, Brazilians felt compelled to review this position, and advocates argued more strongly that Indians should be protected or at least left alone. Hermann von Ihering, on the other hand, was asserting that the Brazilian government should offer greater protection to (German) immigrants who made productive

---

42 See Lilia Moritz Schwarcz, *The Spectacle of the Races: Scientists, Institutions, and the Race Question in Brazil, 1870–1930*. Trans. Leland Guyer (New York: Hill and Wang, 1999), 86–92.
43 David Hall Stauffer, "The Origin and Establishment of Brazil's Indian Service: 1889–1910" (PhD diss., University of Texas, 1955), 129–130.
44 Todd A. Diacon, *Stringing Together a Nation: Cândido Mariano da Silva Rondon and the Construction of a Modern Brazil, 1906–1930* (Durham, NC: Duke University Press, 2004), 59.
45 In São Paulo capital for railroad construction often came from wealthy coffee plantation owners, whereas the North and South of Brazil were almost completely dependent on foreign capital. See Maria da Guia Santos, *Aussenhandel und industrielle Entwicklung Brasiliens unter besonderer Berücksichtigung der Beziehung zu Deutschland (1889–1914)* (Munich: Wilhelm Fink Verlag, 1984), 186. By the end of the nineteenth century, Britain, the United States, and Germany were the biggest investors in Brazil and received most of its exports, between three-fifths and three-quarters. Thomas E. Skidmore and Peter H. Smith, *Modern Latin America* (New York: Oxford University Press, 2001), 148.

contributions to the Brazilian economy and state rather than the Kaingang Indians, who stood in the way of progress.[46]

Advocates of Indian protection seized the opportunity to decry Ihering's opinions and argued that Brazil must follow its own path by protecting its indigenous populations. This discourse therefore also played itself out in the broader context of Brazilian nation building and the efforts of intellectuals to establish a true Brazilian identity.[47] By associating the evils of development with a foreign and imported science, Brazilians could evoke a sense of nationalist pride without necessarily holding their own government accountable.[48]

Ihering had already made derogatory comments about Indians in his monograph *The Anthropology of the State of São Paulo*, which had originally been drafted for the 1904 Universal Exhibition in St. Louis, but because the publication was not in Portuguese, few Brazilians had taken notice. However, when the Portuguese translation was published directly after the Vienna Congress, his remarks received attention, partly because anti-German sentiment in Brazil was already high and fears of the so-called German peril had been circulating in the Brazilian, British, and American press.[49]

It should be noted that the second edition of Ihering's article on the scholarship of Indians in the state of São Paulo was a work of more than 50 pages, in which only some paragraphs were offensive.[50] However, when translated from English to Portuguese, his statements became even more extreme. In the original Ihering wrote that the demise of the Indians was inevitable, but the translated version implied that he would support a program of extermination. Brazilian positivists and scientists made sure that this view was widely publicized, and eventually even agricultural minister Rodolfo Miranda and Cândido Mariano da Silva Rondon, who was already considered a hero for his work with Indians on the frontier and who would become the SPI's first director, both joined the

---

[46] In his published articles Ihering made generic reference to backwoodsmen or European immigrants. However, in his speeches he sometimes specifically referred to German immigrants.
[47] Most Brazilian intellectuals were strongly influenced by European philosophies and ideologies. However, as Schwarcz points out, they did not accept these ideologies uncritically but instead transmuted and modified them to fit their own realities. See Lilia Moritz Schwarcz, *The Spectacle of the Races: Scientists, Institutions, and the Race Question in Brazil, 1870–1930*. Trans. Leland Guyer (New York: Hill and Wang, 1999), 88–89.
[48] David Hall Stauffer, "The Origin and Establishment of Brazil's Indian Service: 1889–1910" (PhD diss., University of Texas, 1955), 69.
[49] Regarding the German peril, see Sylvio Roméro, *O allemanismo no Sul do Brasil: seus perigos e meios de os conjurar* (Rio de Janeiro: Heitor Ribeiro & Co., 1906).
[50] See Hermann von Ihering, *The Anthropology of the State of S. Paulo, Brazil*, 2nd ed. (São Paulo: Diario Official, 1906), 12.

controversy and chastised von Ihering. Although some of these advocates had differing visions about the protection of Indians and later argued strenuously among themselves, they were united in their opposition to the German-born director.

Originally, when the Rio daily *Jornal do Comércio* published notices about the Vienna Congress, it called on the Brazilian government to abolish Indian slavery, but it did not repeat Frič's accusations against the German communities in Santa Catarina.[51] At this point, then, Indian protection in Brazil was not yet entirely framed in opposition to Germans. However, several weeks later, when Sílvio Almeida published an article on the front page of the *Estado de São Paulo*, he specifically targeted Hermann von Ihering. From this moment on, the attacks against Indian massacres became focused on just one person and the interpretation of statements he had made four years earlier. In an article published in Rio's *Jornal do Comércio*, Luís Bueno Horta Barbosa urged his readers to condemn "this ruthless and barbaric theory of a scientist alien to our sentiments."[52] The mistreatment of Indians in Brazil could now be denounced as being an example of "German scientific reasoning unworthy of the Brazilian people."[53]

Advocacy on this issue continued throughout 1909, although in different venues, this time involving scientists and scholarly societies. The Centro de Ciências, Letras e Artes in Campinas created a committee to promote the protection of Indians (Commissão Promotora da Defesa dos Indígenas). Even though Ihering had pulled out of the public controversy, committee members continued their attacks against him. Speeches and articles either quoted Ihering or referred to his less than diplomatic statements before appealing for Indian protection.[54] Perhaps the most stinging rebuke against Ihering came with the publication of a telegram Rondon sent to Rio de Janeiro, claiming that despite what the "von Iherings of all times" may advocate, Indians of all tribes are intelligent and just as capable of love and goodness as any "civilized westerner."[55]

In both Santa Catarina and São Paulo, the massacres of Brazilian Indians were portrayed as being connected to Germans, and by logical extension Indian

---

51 *Jornal do Comércio*, 15 September 1908 and 16 September 1908.
52 Luis Bueno Horta Barbosa, "Em defesa dos indigenas brasileiros," *Jornal do Comércio* (Rio de Janeiro), 11 November 1908.
53 David Hall Stauffer, "The Origin and Establishment of Brazil's Indian Service: 1889–1910" (PhD diss., University of Texas, 1955), 88.
54 David Hall Stauffer, "The Origin and Establishment of Brazil's Indian Service: 1889–1910" (PhD diss., University of Texas, 1955), 160.
55 Rondon, "O exterminio dos indios," *Jornal do Comércio*, 11 February 1909.

protection was seen as a means to limit German influence in southern Brazil, which was related to both the presence of German-Brazilian communities in the South and the dominance of German science in Brazil. Although many of the attacks had been directed against Ihering, one of the most prominent German scientists in Brazil at that time, he was not the only cause for discontent. Brazilian intellectuals were also opposed in general to Germany's predominance in a number of scientific fields, including Brazilian ethnology.[56]

At the time of the 1908 Congress, for example, German and Austrian museums had greater holdings of Brazilian artifacts than Brazilian institutions. In Vienna the collection of Johann Natterer, which had an inventory of more than 2,000 items, had been curated to coincide with the congress. Brazilians attending the event probably would have seen the exhibition.[57] Furthermore, much of the anthropological literature was published in German, and Brazilian scientists had to learn German if they wanted to keep up with the scholarship, which caused resentment in Brazil. Not surprisingly, when the Congresso Brasiliero de Geografia met in September 1909 to discuss Indian protection, the plenary session also concluded that "legislation should be passed that would prohibit foreign museums from collecting artifacts."[58] These efforts were clearly directed against German institutions, including the museums that had contracted Frič to collect on their behalf.

The discourse involving the protection of Brazil's Indians in the early twentieth century thus played itself out on several levels and in a complex field of relations that encompassed local conditions, national reputation, and international competition. Advocates of Indian protection such as Frič and Taulois blamed German-Brazilians for the violent conflicts with the Xokleng in Santa Catarina, whereas indigenistas in São Paulo and Rio de Janeiro framed their efforts on behalf of the Kaingang in opposition to German science. Both of those positions not only polarized the debate, they also made it possible, at least in these early stages of Indian protection, to shift attention away from the underlying causes of these violent conflicts, namely the development of Brazil's South,

---

56 On German scientific contributions see Egon Schaden, "Der deutsche Beitrag zur brasilianischen Ethnologie," *Staden Jahrbuch* (São Paulo) 29 (1981): 9–17. Although German scientists studied Brazil throughout the nineteenth century, the great age of German expeditions in South America started with Karl von den Steinen's exploration of the Xingu in 1884 and lasted until 1914. Steinen was one of the directors at the Berlin Museum of Ethnology, and he had originally been supportive of Frič before his political activism became a liability.
57 See E. Becker-Donner et al., *Brasiliens Indianer* (Vienna: Museum für Völkerkunde, 1971), 3.
58 David Hall Stauffer, "The Origin and Establishment of Brazil's Indian Service: 1889–1910" (PhD diss., University of Texas, 1955), 183.

and the contradictory goals of Brazilian positivists, who wanted to bring "order and progress" to Indians without destroying them. In the years after the Indian Protection Service was created, it became increasingly difficult to avoid such internal criticism.

This particular case study, involving the German diaspora in Brazil and the survival of the Xokleng and Kaingang, highlights the complicated juncture of scholarly networks, ethnic identity, and political advocacy in the context of nation building. The rhetoric pervasive in the letters, pamphlets, articles, and other nonfiction sources offers unique insights into the construction of ethnic otherness, although this particular moment of crisis also has its inherent limits and does not necessarily represent the day-to-day coexistence of the various ethnic groups in southern Brazil. During times of increased ethnic tensions the rhetoric various people used was designed to achieve political change; therefore, the discourse tended to polarize positions and exaggerate ethnic identities and conflicts. Adversaries were depicted in the broadest and most general terms, which obscured the diversity of those involved.

Identities are complicated and multifaceted, yet this complexity is at times difficult to extract from the primary sources. For a community the size of Blumenau it would be impossible to have a homogenous population, and by the early twentieth century other ethnic groups had settled in the area, among them Italians, Poles, and Luso-Brazilians. Not surprisingly, diversity also existed within the German community, which was integrated into Brazilian society to different degrees.[59] Many residents in Blumenau were proud of their German heritage, yet at the same time they identified themselves as Brazilian citizens and considered southern Brazil as their homeland. However, people who had recently come to Brazil as teachers, pastors, businesspeople, or German government officials were less attached to Brazil. They not only hoped to return to Germany but often argued that German culture needed to be preserved.[60] Others in Brazil were almost completely beyond the reach of German influence, including the impoverished German peasant farmers known as *caboclos* who had disappeared into the backwoods many generations before. In short, there was diversity

---

59 On the diversity of these German-Brazilian communities see Emílio Willems, "Zur sozialen Anpassung der Deutschen in Brasilien," *Kölner Zeitschrift für Soziologie*. New Series of the *Kölner Vierteljahrshefte für Soziologie* 1 (1948/9): 316–323; and "Some Aspects of Cultural Conflict and Acculturation in Southern Rural Brazil," *Rural Sociology* 7.4 (1942): 375–384.
60 For example, the Blumenau residents who wrote letters of complaint to the German consulate in Blumenau were German citizens. Several people who authored articles and books were Protestant pastors or directors of German colonies in Brazil, among them Gustav Stutzer, H. Faulhaber, and R. Sernau. Others were explorers or businesspeople.

among Germans in Brazil. Furthermore, a person's identity could change over time.

This complexity and fluidity of identity, which sometimes stressed Germanness and other times Brazilianness, is also reflected in an ambiguity about citizenship. Because the sources are generally mute about citizenship, it is difficult to ascertain what role citizenship played in the construction of ethnic identity among German-Brazilians. In this particular discourse those who retained their German citizenship were often more outspoken in Brazil in their defense of German culture. It would be insightful to have this phenomenon studied more broadly.

Given the complexity of individuals, it is therefore a challenge to separate the multiple layers of identity and to make clear distinctions between German citizens and Brazilian citizens in that region. Furthermore, ethnic identity is only one of the components in a complex identity matrix. Citizenship is part of a multilayered identity, which was publicly used under certain circumstances but remained opaque at other times. Citizenship was not necessarily the glue that bound the community, and often a strong sense of German identity was based simply on common language and culture, regardless of citizenship. This construction and adaptation of German ethnic identity in southern Brazil clearly transcended notions of citizenship and the territorial boundaries of both Germany and Brazil, and identity was continuously articulated across the Atlantic.

There is potential for future research projects regarding German-Brazilian identity formation. Although archives such as the Arquivo Estado do São Paulo and the Instituto Martius-Staden have large holdings, some of them have not been systematically studied. Furthermore, local archives such as the Arquivo Histórico in Blumenau have items in their collection that are unique and not available elsewhere.[61] To speak more broadly about the construction and adaptation of German identity, it is important to engage in comprehensive studies of the archival sources in Germany and in Brazil and to reexamine and reinterpret the available secondary sources, which have often been uncritical about the conflicts between German-Brazilians and indigenous peoples. Brazilian scholars have examined these conflicts more widely and also continue to explore

---

61 For example, the Martius Staden Institute has large volumes of confessional literature from Protestant congregations. Although I have not addressed religious affiliation in this chapter, it was nonetheless an important aspect of identity formation, especially for Protestants living in a predominantly Catholic country. In general German Catholics were more likely to intermarry with Catholics from other ethnic groups, whereas middle-class German Protestants clung more tenaciously to their German identity. Not surprisingly, in Brazil Protestant pastors working with German congregations often spoke out against assimilation.

the challenges of integrating German communities into the larger Brazilian nation. It is my hope that this case study will inspire students and researchers to build on this scholarship and to contribute to the emerging field of German-Brazilian relations.

References

Alves, Rosilene. "Bugres: As Notícias correm!," in *Visões do Vale: perspectivas historiográficas recentes*. Ed. Cristina Ferreira and Méri Frotscher (Blumenau: Nova Letra, 2000).
"Amerika: Die Deutschen in Brasilien." *Vossische Zeitung* 228.2, Suppl. (17 May 1907).
D'Angelis, Wilmar da Rocha. *Toldo Chimbangue: história e luta em Santa Catarina* (Xanxerê, Santa Catarina: Conselho Indigenista Missionário-Regional Sul, 1984).
Athanázio, Enéas. "Martinho Bugreiro: criminoso ou herói?" Separata de *Blumenau em Cadernos* (September 1984): 1–11.
Bade, Klaus J., ed. *Deutsche im Ausland – Fremde in Deutschland: Migration in Geschichte und Gegenwart* (Munich: Verlag C. H. Beck, 1992).
Becker-Donner, E., et al. *Brasiliens Indianer* (Vienna: Museum für Völkerkunde, 1971).
Bergmann, Günther J. *Auslandsdeutsche in Paraguay, Brasilien, Argentinien* (Berlin: Westkreuz Verlag, 1994).
Bethell, Leslie, ed. *The Cambridge History of Latin America* (Cambridge, England: Cambridge University Press, 1984–1986).
Cunha, Jorge Luiz da, and Angelika Gärtner. "Darstellung der deutschen und brasilianischen Kultur im Reisebericht von Herrmann [sic] Meyer aus den Jahren 1898 und 1899 über die deutschen Kolonien in Rio Grande do Sul," in *Anais do VI Seminário Nacional de Pesquisadores da História das Comunidades Teuto-Brasileiras*. Ed. Isabel Cristina Arendt and Marcos Antonio Witt (Rio Grande do Sul: Editora Oikos, 2004).
Davis, Shelton H. *Victims of the Miracle: Development and the Indians of Brazil* (Cambridge, England: Cambridge University Press, 1977).
Deeke, José. *Das Munizip Blumenau und seine Entwicklungsgeschichte in drei Bände* [sic] (São Leopoldo, Brazil: Rotermund, 1910).
Diacon, Todd A. *Millenarian Vision, Capitalist Reality: Brazil's Contestado Rebellion, 1912–1916* (Durham, NC: Duke University Press, 1991).
Diacon, Todd A. *Stringing Together a Nation: Cândido Mariano da Silva Rondon and the Construction of a Modern Brazil, 1906–1930* (Durham, NC: Duke University Press, 2004).
Dibelius, W., and G. Lenz, eds. *Handbuch des Deutschtums im Auslande*, 2nd ed. (Berlin: Allgemeiner Deutscher Schulverein zur Erhaltung des Deutschtums im Auslande, 1906).
"Expedição contra os Bugres." *Novidades* (Itajaí), March 1905. Reprinted in *Notícias de "Vicente Só": Brusques – Ontem e Hoje* VII.27 (1983): 167–168.
Fabri, Friedrich. *Bedarf Deutschland der Colonien? Does Germany Need Colonies? Eine politisch-ökonomische Betrachtung von D[r. Theol.] Friedrich Fabri*, 3rd ed. Trans. and ed. E. C. M. Breuning and M. E. Chamberlain. *Studies in German Thought and History*, Vol. 2 (Lewiston, NY: The Edwin Mellen Press, 1998).

Faulhaber, H. "Deutschtum in Südbrasilien." *Beiträge zur Kolonialpolitik und Kolonialwirtschaft* 1 (1899–1900): 435–438.

Ferreira, Cristina, and Méri Frotscher, eds. *Visões do Vale: perspectivas historiográficas recentes* (Blumenau: Nova Letra, 2000).

Fouquet, Carlos. *Der deutsche Einwanderer und seine Nachkommen in Brasilien 1808–1824–1974* (São Paulo: Instituto Hans-Staden, 1974).

Frič, Alberto. "Völkerwanderungen, Ethnographie und Geschichte der Konquista in Südbrasilien," in *Verhandlungen des XVI. Internationalen Amerikanisten Kongresses: Wien 9. bis 14. September 1908* (Nendeln, Liechtenstein: Kraus Reprint, 1968), 63–67.

Fröschle, Hartmut, ed. *Die Deutschen in Lateinamerika: Schicksal und Leistung* (Tübingen: Horst Erdmann Verlag, 1979).

Gensch, Hugo. "Die Erziehung eines Indianerkindes: Praktischer Beitrag zur Lösung der südamerikanischen Indianerfrage," in *Verhandlungen des XVI. Internationalen Amerikanisten Kongresses: Wien 9. bis 14. September 1908* (Nendeln, Liechtenstein: Kraus Reprint, 1968.)

Hemming, John. *Die If You Must: Brazilian Indians in the Twentieth Century* (London: Macmillan, 2003).

Hettner, Alfred. "Das Deutschtum in Südbrasilien." *Geographische Zeitschrift* 8.11 (1902): 609–626.

Ihering, Hermann von. *The Anthropology of the State of S. Paulo, Brazil*, 2nd ed. (São Paulo: Diario Official, 1906).

Jannasch, Robert. "Die praktischen Aufgaben der deutschen Auswanderungspolitik," in *Verhandlungen des Deutschen Kolonialkongresses 1902 zu Berlin* (Berlin, 1903), 587–592.

Jochem, Toni Vidal. *Pouso dos imigrantes* (Florianópolis, Santa Catarina: Papa-Livro, 1992).

Kandert, Josef. "Alberto Vojtěch Frič – on the Centenary of His Birth." *Annals of the Náprstek Museum* 11 (1983): 111–160.

Kieser, Daércio. *Um discurso para justificar a ação bugreira* (Florianópolis, Santa Catarina: Universidade Federal de Santa Catarina, 1994).

Koch, Dorvalino Eloy. *Tragédias Euro-xokleng e contexto* (Brusque, Santa Catarina: Author, 2002).

Luebke, Frederick C. *Germans in Brazil: A Comparative History of Cultural Conflict During World War I* (Baton Rouge: Louisiana State University Press, 1987).

Luebke, Frederick C. "A Prelude to Conflict: The German Ethnic Group in Brazil, 1890–1917." *Ethnic and Racial Studies* 6.1 (January 1983).

Mauch, Cláudia, and Naira Vasconcellos. *Os Alemães no Sul do Brasil: cultura, etnicidade, história* (Canoas, Brazil: Ed. Universidade Luterana do Brasil, 1994).

Mota, Lúcio, et al., eds. *Novas contribuições aos estudos interdisciplinares dos Kaingang* (Londrina, Paraná: Editora Universidade Estadual de Londrina, 2004).

Neumann, Gerson Roberto. *Brasilien ist nicht weit von hier! Die Thematik der deutschen Auswanderung nach Brasilien in der deutschen Literatur im 19. Jahrhundert (1800–1871)* (Frankfurt am Main: Peter Lang, 2004).

Neves, Correia das. *Historia da Estrada de Ferro Noroeste do Brasil* (São Paulo: Bauru, 1958).

Noelli, Francisco Silva, ed. *Bibliografia Kaingang: referências sobre um povo jê do sul do Brasil* (Londrina, Paraná: Editora Universidade Estadual de Londrina, 1998).

Oberacker, Karl H. *Der deutsche Beitrag zum Aufbau der brasilianischen Nation* (São Paulo: Herder Editora Livraria, 1955).
"Der 'Paiz' und die Indianerkatechese." *Der Urwaldsbote,* 9 November 1912 and 13 November 1912. Reprinted in *Blumenau em Cadernos* XLI.4 (April 2000): 7–21.
Penny, H. Glenn. "The Politics of Anthropology in the Age of Empire: German Colonists, Brazilian Indians, and the Case of Alberto Vojtěch Frič." *Comparative Study of Society and History* (2003): 249–280.
Pinheiro, Niminon Suzel. "Terra não é troféu de guerra," in *Novas contribuições aos estudos interdisciplinares dos Kaingang.* Ed. Kimiye Tommasino et al. (Paraná: Editora da Universidade Estadual de Londrina, 2004).
Ritz-Deutch, Ute. "Alberto Vojtěch Frič, the German Diaspora, and Indian Protection in Southern Brazil, 1900–1920: A Transatlantic, Ethno-Historical Case Study" (PhD diss., Binghamton University, 2008).
Roméro, Sylvio. *O Allemanismo no Sul do Brasil: seus perigos e meios de os conjurar* (Rio de Janeiro: Heitor Ribeiro & Co., 1906).
Santos, Maria da Guia. *Aussenhandel und industrielle Entwicklung Brasiliens unter besonderer Berücksichtigung der Beziehung zu Deutschland (1889–1914)* (Munich: Wilhelm Fink Verlag, 1984).
Santos, Sílvio Coelho dos. "Fric, a 'Liga Patriotica' e os Índios." *Anais do Congresso de História e Geografia de Santa Catarina* (Florianópolis), 4–7 September 1996.
Santos, Sílvio Coelho dos. *Os Índios Xokleng: memória visual* (Florianópolis: Ed. da Universidade Federal de Santa Catarina, 1997).
Schaden, Egon. "Der deutsche Beitrag zur brasilianischen Ethnologie." *Staden Jahrbuch* (São Paulo) 29 (1981): 9–17.
Schwarcz, Lilia Moritz. *The Spectacle of the Races: Scientists, Institutions, and the Race Question in Brazil, 1870–1930.* Trans. Leland Guyer (New York: Hill and Wang, 1999).
Sernau, R. "Zur Frage der Auswanderung." *Deutsche Kolonialzeitung* 3 (1886): 133–134.
Skidmore, Thomas E., and Peter H. Smith. *Modern Latin America* (New York: Oxford University Press, 2001).
Stauffer, David Hall. "The Origin and Establishment of Brazil's Indian Service: 1889–1910" (PhD diss., University of Texas, 1955).
Stutzer, Gustav. *Das Itajahy-Thal und die Kolonie Blumenau in Süd-Brasilien, Provinz Santa Catharina* (Goslar am Harz: L. Koch, 1883).
Tannenberg, Otto Richard. *Groß-Deutschland: die Arbeit des 20. Jahrhunderts* (Leipzig: Bruno Volger Verlagsbuchhandlung, 1911).
Taulois, Pedro Trompowsky. *As matanças de Bugres e o "Urwaldsbote"* (Coritiba, Brazil: Impressora Paranaense, 1907).
Theis, Ivo M., Marcos Antônio Mattedi, and Fabricio Ricardo de Limas Tomio, eds. *Nosso passado (in)comum: contribuições para o debate sobre a história e a historiografia em Blumenau* (Blumenau: Ed. Universidade Regional de Blumenau, 2000).
Trevisan, Edilberto. "Vultos Tchecos no Brasil e no Paraná." *Boletim do Instituto Histórico, Geográfico Paranaense* 37 (1980): 9–55.
Urban, Greg. "Interpretations of Inter-Ethnic Contact: The Shokleng and Brazilian National Society, 1914–1916." *Ethnohistory* 32.3 (1985): 224–244.
Urban, Greg. "A Model of Shokleng Social Reality" (PhD diss., University of Chicago, 1978).

Wettstein, Karl August. *Brasilien und die deutsch-brasilianische Kolonie Blumenau* (Leipzig: Verlag von Friedrich Engelmann, 1907).

Willems, Emílio. "Some Aspects of Cultural Conflict and Acculturation in Southern Rural Brazil." *Rural Sociology* 7.4 (1942): 375–384.

Willems, Emílio. "Zur sozialen Anpassung der Deutschen in Brasilien." *Kölner Zeitschrift für Soziologie*. New Series of the *Kölner Vierteljahrshefte für Soziologie* 1 (1948/9): 316–323.

Fernando Clara
"Paradise with Black Angels": Brazil in Eighteenth-Century Germany

Nature and nation

Academic research on the German-Brazilian encounters of the last five centuries generally seems to follow two or three main traditional paths. On one hand, it apparently inherits the powerful historical and somewhat mythical perspective on Brazil that was built after Staden's *Wahrhaftige Historia* and therefore cannot help acknowledging the exoticism of the place and its natives as the main subject of its analysis and interests. On the other hand – in what could be seen as a countereffort to rationalize discourse and dissolve the fears and phantasies brought up by Staden's mythical images of wilderness – it thrives to follow the new scientific perspectives, focusing on the major expeditions that took place in the first half of the nineteenth century (Langsdorff, Spix and Martius, Maximilian of Wied-Neuwied, or Wilhelm von Eschwege, to name only a few of the most well known). More recently, the so-called German-Brazilian studies (*estudos teuto-brasileiros*) bring forth another kind of people and issues to the global picture, because they adopt a sociological point of view and concentrate mainly on themes such as immigration, colonization, and cultural interaction between Brazil and Germany from the late nineteenth century to the present day. Broadly speaking, *nature* and *nation* are thus the two keywords that would probably best characterize the thematic core of this field of research.

However, the fact that both these keywords are often used in a fuzzy, indiscriminate way – in Brazil's representations *nature* and *nation* are often indistinguishable[1] – leads analytical discourse to a certain absolutization of its object of study, hence silencing, disregarding, or sometimes merely overlooking the prob-

---

1 To some extent one could say that in the case of Brazil the emergence of the nation coincides with the discovery of its nature. The fact that most of the scientific travel books by the aforementioned authors mentioned were published in the years immediately before or after the independence of Brazil is far from being a coincidence and undoubtedly contributes to this characteristic indistinction between nature and nation, an indistinction that has marked the European views of Brazil from the nineteenth century on, is still present in some contemporary research in these areas, and, as might be expected, has been crystallized in contemporary pop culture (among many possible examples, see the popular song "País Tropical," recorded in 1969 by Jorge Ben).

lematic interaction of these two concepts as obvious cultural constructs and the complex network of European perspectives, and again also of interests, that are involved in the production of knowledge and discourse on Brazil.[2]

Furthermore, one cannot help noticing that between Staden's book (1557) and the Spix–Martius expedition (1817–1820), for instance, there is a lapse of time that appears to be of minor interest for this more traditional research, as the works dealing with European representations of Brazil during the seventeenth and eighteenth centuries are only a few exceptions.[3] Finally, it should also be noted that magazines, periodicals, or other kinds of shorter occasional texts are seldom taken into account by this otherwise vast and rich scholarly research, which appears to be focused primarily on the analysis of monographs and books. And this means that a central public space of knowledge exchange, information, and production – especially when one considers Germany of the seventeenth and eighteenth centuries[4] – is left aside as a blind spot that could

---

[2] See the relevant issues raised in Georg Wink's dissertation *Brasilien als "vorgestellte Gemeinschaft"? Eine kulturwissenschaftliche Untersuchung der Erzählung Brasiliens vom Reich zur Nation im lateinamerikanischen Kontrast* (PhD diss., Mainz, 2008) and the complex conceptual framework apparently needed to make the European concept of nation usable in a South American context, a conceptual framework which in the specific case of Brazil must also include, according to the same author (107), "the particularities of the Portuguese empire Policy" ("[die] Besonderheiten der portugiesischen Reichspolitik"). Unless otherwise noted, all translations from German and Portuguese are the author's.

[3] Two of these more recent exceptions are provided by the essays of Franz Obermeier, "Brasilien in der englischen Reiseliteratur der Kolonialzeit," *Jahrbuch für Geschichte Lateinamerikas/Anuario de Historia de América Latina* 41 (2004): 373–398 and "Die französischen Aufklärer und Brasilien, Brasilien in Raynals Histoire philosophique des deux Indes," *Literaturwissenschaftliches Jahrbuch* 50 (2009): 81–113, which deal respectively with English and French literature on Brazil of the seventeenth and eighteenth centuries; see also Michel de Certeau's outline of a project dedicated to the analysis of "Travel Narratives of the French to Brazil: Sixteenth to Eighteenth Centuries," *Representations* 33 (1991): 221–226. As far as Germany goes, see Oscar Canstatt, *Kritisches Repertorium der deutsch-brasilianischen Literatur* (Berlin: Reimer, 1902–1906) and Martin Franzbach's modest bibliographical attempt, "Versuch einer chronologischen Bibliographie der Reisebeschreibungen, geographischen, historischen und theologischen Spezialwerke über Brasilien im deutschen Sprachraum 1504–1800," *Jahrbuch für Geschichte Lateinamerikas/Anuario de Historia de América Latina* 7 (1970): 146–156; though limited to Rio de Janeiro, see also Paulo Berger's *Bibliografia do Rio de Janeiro de viajantes e autores estrangeiros 1531–1900*, 2nd ed. (Rio de Janeiro: Secretaria de Estado de Educaça˜o e Cultura, RJ, 1980).

[4] Regarding the crucial role played by periodicals and magazines in building a public sphere of knowledge exchange, information, and production in seventeenth- and eighteenth-century Germany, see the essays included in chapter V ("Periodische Formen des wissenschaftlichen Denkens, Schreibens und Publizierens") of Ulrich Johannes Schneider (ed.), *Kulturen des Wissens im 18. Jahrhundert* (Berlin: De Gruyter, 2008), 229–258, the extensive bibliographical-analytical

jeopardize the completeness (not to mention the credibility) of the global picture of Brazil produced in this area of study.

Rescher's dissertation[5] could be considered an important breakthrough, as far as this period of German-Brazilian interactions is concerned, and no doubt it has the merit of systematically showing (probably for the first time) the richness and abundance of these intercultural relations during the period in question. Yet Rescher's work barely touches a what one could call background informational and occasional texts on Brazil that were published in German periodicals and magazines of the time, background texts where, besides the expected scientific and mythical landscapes, a somehow distinct Brazil seems to emerge, one that is said to bear similarities to Portugal (or even to Germany) despite its otherness. Almost the same could be said about some of the essays gathered in an issue of the *Revista da Universidade de São Paulo* dedicated to "The Brazil of Travelers" ("O Brasil dos Viajantes").[6] Even though the perspective changes (as one would expect from papers published in the mid-1990s and already aware of the cultural and postcolonial studies turn in the humanities), many of the aforementioned insufficiencies that affected Rescher's dissertation still persist.

This chapter focuses on some of these silences and blind spots by concentrating on the Brazil depicted and at the same time produced by several German texts published mainly in periodicals, magazines, and encyclopedias of the late eighteenth century. Considering the extensive (yet not exhaustive) bibliography available and, on the other hand, the fact that this same bibliography is only rarely brought up in this area of research, the analysis will provide a global overview of the dynamics of this eighteenth-century German Brazil (how did it evolve? what changes did it undergo? which perspectives were involved in its making?) rather than specific and more detailed interpretations of the texts.

---

studies of Paul Hocks and Peter Schmidt, *Literarische und politische Zeitschriften 1789–1805. Von der politischen Revolution zur Literaturrevolution* (Stuttgart: Metzler, 1975), and *Index zu deutschen Zeitschriften der Jahre 1773–1830* (Nendeln, Liechtenstein: KTO Press, 1979); Jürgen Wilke's *Literarische Zeitschriften des 18. Jahrhunderts 1688–1789* (Stuttgart: Metzler, 1978); or Alfred Adolph Estermann's *Die deutschen Literatur-Zeitschriften 1815–1850: Bibliographien, Programme, Autoren*, Vol. 1: *Zeitschriften mit Erscheinungsbeginn 1645–1814* (Munich: Saur, 1991) and *Kontextverarbeitung. Buchwissenschaftliche Studien*, ed. Klaus-Dieter Lehmann and Klaus G. Saur (Munich: Saur, 1998), among several others.

5 Hubertus Rescher, *Die deutschsprachige Literatur zu Brasilien von 1789–1850: Widerspiegelung brasilianischer Sozial- und Wirtschaftsstrukturen von 1789–-1850 in der deutschsprachigen Literatur desselben Zeitraums* (Bern, Switzerland: Peter Lang, 1979).

6 *Revista USP* 30 (1996), http://www.usp.br/revistausp/30/SUMARIO-30.htm, 19 June 2014.

What nature? Which nation?

A brief look at some of the titles of articles listed in the References at the end of this chapter hardly comes as a surprise, considering the traditional thematic landscape briefly outlined before: Nature clearly dominates the authors' and public's interests,[7] immediately followed by a variety of themes undoubtedly motivated by the political, national contemporary contexts.[8]

---

[7] See José Bonifácio d'Andrada e Silva, "Ueber die brasilianischen Diamanten," *Magazin für das Neueste aus der Physik und Naturgeschichte* 9.2 (1794): 47–54; the anonymously published essays "Naturgeschichte der brasilischen Spinne," *Berlinische Sammlungen zur Beförderung der Arzneywissenschaft, der Naturgeschichte, der Haushaltungskunst, Kameralwissenschaft und der Dahin einschlagenden Litteratur* 5 (1773): 66–68; "Aus Brasilien," *Gartenkalender* 3 (1784): 136–138; "Der Brasilianische Großkopf," *Neue Bilder-Gallerie für Junge Söhne und Töchter zur Angenehmen und Nützlichen Selbstbeschäftigung aus dem Reiche der Natur, Kunst, Sitten und des Gemeinen Lebens* 8 (1801): 21–22; and "Der Brasilienholzbaum," *Neue Bilder-Gallerie für Junge Söhne und Töchter* 3 (1796): 162–163; Jean-Étienne Guettard, "Beobachtung, von den brasilianischen Topasen," *Hamburgisches Magazin, oder Gesammelte Schriften, zum Unterricht und Vergnügen* 12.6 (1754): 666–673; Johann Friedrich Blumenbach's notes, "Nachricht von einigen Naturseltenheiten (Aus einem Briefe des Hrn. Dr. Langsdorf, vom 9. Jan. 1798)," *Magazin für den Neuesten Zustand der Naturkunde mit Rücksicht auf die Dazu Gehörigen Hülfswissenschaften* 1.2 (1798): 52–53; "Ueber einige brasilische Fossilien. Aus einem Briefe des Hn. Dr. Langsdorf aus Lissabon vom 7. Jun. 1798," *Magazin für den Neuesten Zustand der Naturkunde mit Rücksicht auf die Dazu Gehörigen Hülfswissenschaften* 2.1 (1800): 32–33; and "Fernere Reisenachrichten vom Hrn. D. Langsdorff von der Insel St. Catharina an der Küste von Brasilien den 15ten Januar 1804," *Magazin für den Neuesten Zustand der Naturkunde mit Rücksicht auf die Dazu Gehörigen Hülfswissenschaften* 9.3 (1805): 220–223; Koch, "Nachricht von einer sehr einfachen Maschine, Brasilienholz klein zu schneiden," *Neues Hannoversches Magazin* 3 (1793): 511–512; Johann Bernhard Wilhelm Lindenberg, "Beschreibung eines Brasilischen Rüßelkäfers," *Der Naturforscher* 10 (1777): 86–87 and "Ausführlichere Beschreibung des Brasilischen Rüsselkäfers, nebst einigen Betrachtungen," *Der Naturforscher* 14 (1780): 211–220; Friedrich Heinrich Wilhelm Martini, "Der Amerikanische oder Brasilianische Einhornteufel. Die Seefledermaus," *Neue Mannigfaltigkeiten* 3 (1776): 193–195; Peter Simon Pallas, "Beschreibung zweyer südamerikanischer merkwürdiger Vögel," *Neue Nordische Beyträge zur Physikalischen und Geographischen Erd- und Völkerbeschreibung, Naturgeschichte und Oekonomie* 3 (1782): 1–7; Georg Wilhelm Steller, "Beschreibung der Meerotter, und ob sie Marggrafs Icya oder die Carigveibein der Brasilienser sey?," *Hamburgisches Magazin, oder Gesammelte Schriften, Aus der Naturforschung und den Angenehmen Wissenschaften Überhaupt* 11 (1753): 460–500; Guillaume Thomas François Raynal, "Geschichte der Goldminen in Brasilien, und von der Art, sie zu bearbeiten; imgleichen der Diamantenminen, die man daselbst entdeckt hat. Betrachtungen über die Beschaffenheit dieses Edelsteines," *Hannoverisches Magazin* 20 (1782): 1249–1264; and finally Georg Friedrich Wehrs, "Etwas von den Brasilianischen Thieren, Bäumen, Früchten und andern Pflanzen," *Hannoverisches Magazin* 17 (1779): 801–812. Although long, this list should not be considered exhaustive.

However, a closer examination of some of these texts shows that there is now a much more complex network of topics and interests than the one presented by the early-nineteenth-century German works on Brazil, which were almost exclusively engaged in scientifically describing, classifying, and cataloging the land. Indeed, besides the expected nature/nation scenery there is now a set of texts that focuses exclusively on religious and political matters,[9] another set of important translations, preprints, and reviews of books and of (historical) travel accounts of different epochs,[10] and finally a background image that appears to

---

[8] See the anonymously published "Anmerkungen über ein Paar Stellen in dem Vorbericht des Herrn Hofraths Lessings zu der von ihm herausgegebenen Beschreibung Brasiliens, betreffend die vermeinte Person eines Spanischen Hauptmanns, der mit seinem Geschlechtsnamen Marannon y Gran Para geheißen haben soll," *Hannoverisches Magazin* 21 (1783): 801–814; and "Handelsnachrichten von der Stadt Rio de Janeiro in Brasilien (mit Tabelle)," *Magazin der Handels- und Gewerbskunde* 3.2 (1805): 568–571; H., "Streitigkeiten der Portugiesen und Holländer wegen Brasiliens im vorigen Jahrhundert," *Hannoverisches Magazin* 6 (1768): 1249–1264, 1265–1278; Thomas Lindley, "Die Palmareser. Ein ehemaliger Neger-Staat in Brasilien," *Minerva. Ein Journal für Geschichte Politik und Literatur* 3 (1805): 343–356 and *Thomas Lindley's Reise nach Brasilien und Aufenthalt daselbst in den Jahren 1802 und 1803. Nebst einer beschreibung der Städte und Provinzen Porto-Seguro und San Salvador* (Weimar: Landes-Industrie-Comptoir, 1806); C. F. Lüning, "Einige Notizen über Brasilien, in statistischer und naturhistorischer Hinsicht," *Neues Hannoversches Magazin* 18 (1808): 785–810; James Hingston Tuckey, "Heroismus eines Neger-Sclaven. Eine Anecdote," *Minerva. Ein Journal Historischen und Politischen Inhalts* 3 (1805): 412–420; and Georg Friedrich Wehrs, "Von der Religion der wilden Brasilianer, ihren Heyrathen und übrigen Gebräuchen," *Hannoverisches Magazin* 17 (1779): 921–934.

[9] J. B., "Varia de Vita P. Gabrielis Malagrida," *Journal zur Kunstgeschichte und zur Allgemeinen Litteratur* 16 (1788): 41–54; [Anselm Franz Dominik von Eckart], "Animadversiones cujusdam plures per annos in Brasilia Missionarii in librum, Lipsiae, 1782, 8. editum, qui inscribitur *Briefe über Portugal, nebst einem Anhang über Brasilien. Aus dem Französischen. Mit Anmerkungen herausgegeben von Matthias Christian Sprengel, Professor der Geschichte in Halle*," *Journal zur Kunstgeschichte und zur Allgemeinen Litteratur* 14 (1787): 192–291; Benedictus de Fonseca, "*Litterae P. Benedicti de Fonseca, Soc. Iesu Procuratoris quondam Generalis Prov. Maraguonensis, datae 11 Aug. 1779 Annadiae ad R.P. Anselmum Eckart*," *Journal zur Kunstgeschichte und zur Allgemeinen Litteratur* 16 (1788): 54–75; Franz Xavier Veigl, *Franz Xavier Veigl vormaliger Mißionar der Gesellschaft Jesu. Gründliche Nachrichten über die Verfassung der Landschaft von Maynas in Süd-Amerika bis zum Jahre 1768 nebst des Herrn P. Anselm Eckarts Zusätze zu Pedro Cudenas Beschreibung der Länder von Brasilien* (Nürnberg: Zeh, 1798).

[10] See the anonymously published "[Review of] Cudena, *Beschreibung des portugiesischen Amerika*," *Allgemeine Deutsche Bibliothek* 43.1 (1780): 211–214, "[Review of] *Briefe über Portugall*. Leipzig: Weygand 1782," *Ephemeriden der Menschheit oder Bibliothek der Sittenlehre, der Politik und der Gesetzgebung* 1 (1783): 162–188, and "[Review of] des Herrn Johann von Lery Reise in Brasilien," *Neue Allgemeine Deutsche Bibliothek* 4 (1799): 462–466; Christian Wilhelm Dohm, "[Review of] Stephens, P. [=Blankett, John]: *Briefe über Portugal*," *Allgemeine Deutsche Bibliothek* 53.2 (1783): 462–468; [Anselm Franz Dominik von Eckart], "Historia persecutionis Societatis Iesu

be transversal and ubiquitous to most of the texts, an image that cannot simply be avoided or overlooked in the current framework of analysis, that of European Portugal.

The fact that the role played by this image of European Portugal in shaping the image of Brazil has been generally neglected by scholarly research has complex origins. On one hand, it is the result of the methodological procedure traditionally used by this kind of "imagological" literary and cultural analysis, a procedure that tends to neutralize discourse and its production of contexts and conditions, concentrating its central focus of attention on either the author or the object of study (i.e., the "images" of Brazil created by the texts). On the other hand, it is also a consequence of the characteristic analytical bipolarity put forward by this kind of comparative studies (where the main thematic core usually spins around two national entities, e.g., Brazil and France or Brazil and the Netherlands). This bipolarity becomes especially obvious when one looks at most of the products of the so-called imagological studies,[11] but it is not completely absent (though in a revised and upgraded version) from the postcolonial studies as well. Indeed, by insisting on a text interpretation that tends to stress the oppositions (i.e., the disruptions, the conflicts, the differences) between the colonizer and the colonized, postcolonial perspectives eventually end up overlooking the similarities and the common traits that both identities can share in their dynamic interactions.

A passage from Seixo's essay, published in the aforementioned issue of the *Revista da Universidade de São Paulo*, could be considered emblematic of the way these perspectives tend to disregard explicit similitudes, namely when the author quotes a long excerpt of Pero Vaz de Caminha's letter without a comment

---

in Lusitania," *Journal zur Kunstgeschichte und zur Allgemeinen Litteratur* 7: 293–320; C.M. de La Condamine, "Nachricht von einer Reise in das Innerste von Südamerika, von der Küste des Südmeeres an, bis zu den Küsten von Brasilien und Guiana, längst dem Amazonenstrome (mit Karte)," *Hamburgisches Magazin, oder Gesammelte Schriften, zum Unterricht und Vergnügen* 6.1 (1750): 3–70; Amerigo Vespucci, "Reisen nach Brasilien von 1501 bis 1504," *Neue Beiträge zur Völker- und Länderkunde* 10 (1792): 245–272.

11 See several of the titles published in the series *Studia Imagologica* of the Dutch academic publishing house Rodopi, especially the volume edited by Manfred Beller and Joseph T. Leerssen, *Imagology. The Cultural Construction and Literary Representation of National Characters. A Critical Survey* (Amsterdam: Rodopi, 2007); regarding the "images" of Brazil in Germany see Celeste H. M. Ribeiro de Sousa, "A imagologia no Brasil: primeira tentativa de sistematização," *Revista Brasileira de Literatura Comparada* 14 (2009): 37–55 and many of the publications of the research group "Rellibra": "Relações Lingüísticas e Literárias Brasil-Alemanha" (http://www.rellibra.com.br, 19 June 2014).

or note about the important role played by the comparison between the described Brazilian landscape and the Portuguese one:

> All the coastal country from one point to the other is very flat and very beautiful. As to the jungle it seemed very large to us seen from the sea; for, look as we would, we could see nothing but land and woods, and the land seemed very extensive. Till now we have been unable to learn if there is gold or silver or any kind of metal or iron there; we have seen none. However, the air of the country is very healthful, fresh, and as temperate *as that of Entre Douro e Minho*, we have found the two climates alike at this season. There is a great plenty, an infinitude of waters. The country is so well-favoured that if it were rightly cultivated it would yield everything, because of its waters.[12]

Even though Seixo recognizes in this and other contemporary texts of this kind a typical oscillation between the unknown and strange on one side and the known and comparable on the other, the fact is that her further analysis is exclusively interested and determined by concepts such as alterity (*alteridade*) and strangeness (*estranheza*).[13]

What is interesting about the way the comparison is made in this excerpt is that it is introduced by an adversative conjunction, "However" (*Porém*), which marks a central turning point in discourse and in the description. The comparison, namely the similarities between the Brazilian and the Portuguese landscapes that it brings forth, seems to compensate for the fact that the travelers did not find any gold, silver, or other metals, but it also expands itself semantically in the "infinitude of waters" and the "well-favoured," fertile land – that is, a land "as that of Entre Douro e Minho" – so that eventually the comparison ends up by playing a decisive role in the text, operating as a recurrent background idea against which the whole discourse must be reread and reinterpreted. Metaphors and comparisons are powerful epistemological devices that make the unknown understandable, readable, comparable, as it is here. And the power of this comparison between the Portuguese and the Brazilian landscapes is certainly well attested by the fact that it finds itself reproduced in the most variegated forms during the centuries that followed.

Three brief passages from the article "Brasilien" of Zedler's encyclopedia present a good starting point for an analysis that does not lose sight of Portugal as an important background reference to the shaping of European discourse on Brazil.

---

12 Maria Alzira Seixo, "Entre Cultura e Natureza. Ambigüidades do olhar do viajante," *Revista USP* 30 (1996), 124, emphasis mine; English translation from Charles David Ley (ed.), *Portuguese Voyages, 1498–1663* (London: J.M. Dent; New York: E.P. Dutton, 1947), 59.
13 Seixo, "Entre Cultura e Natureza," 124, 125, and passim.

It [Brazil] lies below the *Zona Torrida*, but has a rather temperate climate and excellent water, so that the inhabitants often live 90 to 100 years.[14]

The people think highly of sorcery, soothsayers and fortune-tellers, and are very scared of evil spirits, as well as of thunder and lightning. They take so many wives as they want, but they easily leave them. [...] They are interested in nothing but war and vengeance, and they are used to eating the enemies that get captured.[15]

Two things in Brazil are remarkable such as 1) that the *Inquisition* was not introduced over there and 2) that no beggars are tolerated, but the poor are fed by those in rich houses.[16]

Besides introducing *in nuce* many of the themes – in fact many of the stereotypes – about Brazil that have lasted to the present day (or at least some of them and in a somehow modified and updated form), what is worth noting in these excerpts is that both the "temperate" climate and the "long life" of its natives, not forgetting the two (and for the author apparently unexpected) "remarkable things" about Brazil, show traces of what could be called a matrix image of the colonizing power that seems to lie in the background. And although the differences of its inhabitants and customs, that is, their "more exotic" features such as polygamy and cannibalism, already have a central place in Zedler's discourse, occupying most of the article, the truth is that one still cannot help asking, "What nature, which nation, and to some extent also what people are being depicted in these texts?" This is especially so when one considers some of the geographic descriptions found in the entry "Portugal" of the same encyclopedia, where the country is described as a land that "has many beautiful rivers and is therefore called the *Mesopotamia Europæ*"[17] and where "the climate is in Portugal still relatively moderate, therefore there is an abundance of wine, olive oil, oranges, lemons and other kinds of fruit, as well as of honey."[18] As for the population, it should be noted that the two "remarkable things" about Brazil – the absence of both Inquisition and beggars in the streets – are remarkable only because they are unexpected, thus making perfectly clear the viewpoint and expectations of

---

14 "Brasilien," in *Grosses Vollständiges Universal-Lexicon Aller Wissenschaften und Künste, Welche bißero durch menschlichen Verstand und Witz erfunden worden*, Vol. 4 (Leipzig: Zedler, 1733), 1098–1100, 1098.
15 "Brasilien," in *Grosses Vollständiges Universal-Lexicon Aller Wissenschaften und Künste, Welche bißero durch menschlichen Verstand und Witz erfunden worden*, Vol. 4 (Leipzig: Zedler, 1733), 1099.
16 "Brasilien," in *Grosses Vollständiges Universal-Lexicon Aller Wissenschaften und Künste, Welche bißero durch menschlichen Verstand und Witz erfunden worden*, Vol. 4 (Leipzig: Zedler, 1733), 1100.
17 "Portugall," in *Grosses Vollständiges Universal-Lexicon*, Vol. 28 (Leipzig: Zedler, 1741), 1659.
18 "Portugall," in *Grosses Vollständiges Universal-Lexicon*, Vol. 28 (Leipzig: Zedler, 1741), 1659.

the author: Being a colony of Portugal, Brazil would "naturally" share most of its features with its Motherland and one would "of course" expect to discover traces of both the Inquisition and beggars.

Furthermore, the two short notes on some Brazilian "natural curiosities" left by Blumenbach in his *Magazin für den Neuesten Zustand der Naturkunde* could well be considered paradigmatic of how information about Brazil circulated in late-eighteenth-century Germany and of the central role – either as a fundamental source of information or as an essential mediator – assigned to Portugal in this communication network. Both notes were significantly triggered by two letters sent from Lisbon by Georg Heinrich von Langsdorff, who was by then living and working in Portugal as the personal physician (*Leibarzt*) of Prince Christian von Waldeck.[19]

The role played by Portugal in these eighteenth-century German texts on Brazil is therefore decisive, though not always self-evident: Either as an explicit metaphor, a term of comparison, a counterpoint, or the central node of an European network of information on Brazil, the representations of Portugal are a touchstone for German representations of Brazil.

Europe overseas: politics and religion

Another set of German eighteenth-century texts on Brazil deals much more explicitly with contemporary Portuguese and European themes. Particularly noteworthy in this set are the translations of Vieira's texts,[20] which manifestly have to be read as pamphlets produced by Catholic southern Germany against the suppression of the Society of Jesus by the Marquis of Pombal in 1759. Moreover, in this same context of religious and political controversy that admittedly had im-

---

[19] Blumenbach, "Nachricht von einigen Naturseltenheiten (Aus einem Briefe des Hrn. Dr. Langsdorf, vom 9. Jan. 1798)" and "Ueber einige brasilische Fossilien. Aus einem Briefe des Hn. Dr. Langsdorf aus Lissabon vom 7. Jun. 1798."

[20] António Vieira, *Hundertjährige Trost-Rede aus Brasilien für die schweigende Gesellschaft Jesu in Europa, oder Rede des ehrwürdigen Vatters Antonius Viejra [...] in der königlichen Capelle zu Lisabon im Jahre 1662*. Trans. Goßwin Theodor von Dille (Augsburg: Wagner, 1762), *Zwote hundert-jährige Trost-Rede aus Brasilien für die schweigende Gesellschaft Jesu in Europa, oder zwote Rede des ehrwürdigen Vaters Antonius Viejra [...] drey Tage vor seiner geheimen Ab- und Zurück-Reise nach dem portugiesischen königlichen Hof: gehalten 1654*. Trans. Goßwin Theodor von Dille (Augsburg: Wagner, 1763); and Guillaume Thomas François Raynal and António Vieira, "Klagen eines portugiesischen Predigers zu Gott, über das Glück einer ketzerischen Nation," *Ephemeriden der Menschheit oder Bibliothek der Sittenlehre, der Politik und der Gesetzgebung* 1 (1783): 103–114.

portant repercussions both in South America and in Europe,[21] a series of several other occasional texts (essays, reviews of books, letters) also stands out.[22] They were published in Latin by Christoph Gottlieb von Murr, most of them in his *Journal zur Kunstgeschichte und zur Allgemeinen Litteratur,* and their author (as well as the main source of the information von Murr conveys on these matters) is Anselm von Eckart, a German Jesuit who was expelled from Brazil by Pombal in 1758 and spent almost the next 20 years of his life in Portuguese prisons. Von Murr, a polymath jurist from Nuremberg, was himself a controversial character as he was simultaneously an enlightened Protestant in Catholic southern Germany and a defender of the Jesuits, whose trust he had won in a *peregrinatio academica* that took him to Strasbourg, where he was granted access to the library of the Jesuit College.[23]

Among the many texts related to Brazil that von Murr published in his crusade for the Jesuits, it is worth mentioning the very extensive – one hundred pages long – critical review by Eckart[24] of the German translation of a small (66 pages) book first published anonymously in London in 1777.[25] The *Letters*

---

21 See the extensive essays by Stefan Gatzhammer, "Antijesuitismo Europeu. Relações político-diplomáticas e culturais entre a Baviera e Portugal (1750–1780)," *Lusitânia Sacra* 5 (1993): 159–250 and "Politisch-diplomatische Beziehungen zwischen Portugal und Österreich im 18. Jahrhundert vor dem Hintergrund der Jesuitenfrage," *Mitteilungen des Instituts für Österreichische Geschichtsforschung* 102.1–4 (1994): 359–408.

22 Besides the texts listed in note 8 see also Christoph Gottlieb von Murr and Anselm Franz Dominik von Eckart, "Nachrichten von den Sprachen in Brasilien," *Journal zur Kunstgeschichte und zur Allgemeinen Litteratur* 6 (1778): 195–213 and "Zusätze zum Specimine Linguae Brasilicae vulgaris," *Journal zur Kunstgeschichte und zur Allgemeinen Litteratur* 7 (1779): 121–122.

23 On Murr's life and works see Renate Jürgensen, "Ein Leben: Christoph Gottlieb von Murr (1733–1811)," *Bibliotheca Norica. Patrizier und Gelehrtenbibliotheken in Nürnberg Zwischen Mittelalter und Aufklärung* 2 (2001): 1310–1324; Christoph Nebgen, "Christoph Gottlieb von Murr: ein Protestant erhebt die Stimme gegen die Aufhebung der Gesellschaft Jesu," *Archivum Historicum Societatis Iesu* 73.145 (2004): 121–147; and Peter Wolf, "Protestantischer 'Jesuitismus' im Zeitalter der Aufklärung. Christoph Gottlieb von Murr (1733–1811) und die Jesuiten," *Zeitschrift für Bayerische Landesgeschichte* 62 (1999): 99–137; on Murr's publishing activity related to Portugal see Fernando Clara, *Mundos de palavras. Viagem, história, ciência, literatura: Portugal no espaço de língua alemã (1770–1810)* (Bern, Switzerland: Peter Lang, 2007), 170–188.

24 [Eckart], "Animadversiones." See also other reviews of the German translation of the book, among them the one published by historian and political writer Christian Wilhelm Dohm, "[Review of] Stephens, P. [=Blankett, John]: *Briefe über Portugal*" and the anonymous "[Review of] *Briefe über Portugall*. Leipzig: Weygand 1782," *Ephemeriden der Menschheit oder Bibliothek der Sittenlehre, der Politik und der Gesetzgebung* 1 (1783): 162–188.

25 [Blankett, John], *Briefe über Portugal, nebst einem Anhang über Brasilien* (Leipzig: Weygand, 1782) [English original: *Letters from Portugal, on the Late and Present State of That Kingdom* (London: J. Almon, 1777); French translation: *Lettres écrites du Portugal, sur l'état ancien et actuel de*

from Portugal was translated into German from the French version (which appeared in 1780 in Paris) by Matthias Christian Sprengel, son-in-law of Johann Reinhold Forster and history professor at the University of Halle, whose main research interests were the European discoveries and the history of the British, Spanish, and Portuguese colonies.

The 17 original letters, an apparent firsthand systematic account of the situation in Portugal after the death of D. José I and the downfall of Pombal (1777), written by British naval captain John Blankett, awakened natural curiosity and interest in contemporary European political settings. Germany was no exception, and the death of Pombal in 1782 was probably the key event that made Sprengel translate the *Letters* that same year. But what is striking about the German edition of Blankett's letters is that to the French translation used by Sprengel was added a portrait of the Marquis of Pombal, which Sprengel did not translate at all. Instead, following his research and probably also his public's interests, he replaced it by an appendix on Brazil.

The fact that Sprengel introduces Brazil as an appendix to his translation is in many ways emblematic: It is of course an unmistakable sign of the still supplemental and thus secondary role played by Brazil in the European public sphere of the mid-eighteenth century, but it is also emblematic of an emerging interest for Brazil (and generally for the non-European world) in Germany. The same could be said about another series of texts, clearly motivated by contemporary European politics, that deal with Brazil from a lateral perspective, where the typical Aufklärung critique of colonialism[26] together with discussions about slavery come forth. This is the case of the long essay about the conflict of the Portuguese and the Dutch in Brazil, published in the *Hannoverisches Maga-*

---

ce Royaume. Traduites de l'Anglois. Suivies d'un portrait historique de M. le Marquis de Pombal (Paris: Cellot, 1780)].

26 A passage from the aforementioned entry "Portugall" in Zedler's encyclopedia may be a good example of how colonialism was considered to collide with the eighteenth-century German ideal of a demographically, culturally, and economically rich society: "In ancient times it [Portugal] had a considerable population, but ever since it has lost a large number of people due to the numerous Indian colonies and the long distance sea voyages, and also many thousands of people have been executed or persecuted by the Inquisition, a large decrease in population has been registered." "Portugall," in *Grosses Vollständiges Universal-Lexicon*, 1659. As for Brazil, the consequences of colonialism were much more devastating. Some decades later, the author of possibly the first history of Brazil ever published in Germany could hardly be more explicit: "The natives of Brazil have almost suffered the same fate as the natives of all other American countries. Where the devastating foot of the European trod, life died; fanaticism choked ruthlessly the remains left by war wrath and greed." Ernst Münch, *Geschichte von Brasilien* (Dresden: Hilscher, 1829), 6.

zin,[27] the heroic anecdote reproduced by Tuckey,[28] or, eventually, the allegorical, moral story about slavery, freedom, and independence published in Archenholz's *Minerva*.[29]

This last article and the network of people, texts, and interests it unveils could again be considered paradigmatic of the way Germany perceived and gathered information about Brazil by the end of the eighteenth century: As Archenholz mentions in a small introductory note to the text, the story was found in a recently published travel account by Thomas Lindley, who had read it in Pitta's book on the *History of Portuguese America*.[30] As for the German translation of Lindley's travelogue, an abridged version of it was published the next year (*Thomas Lindley's Reise nach Brasilien*) by Theophil Friedrich Ehrmann, co-editor, together with Matthias Christian Sprengel, of an extensive collection of travels – *Bibliothek der neuesten und wichtigsten Reisebeschreibungen zur Erweiterung der Erdkunde* – where Lindley's account appeared as part 2 of volume 29. In spite of the supplemental role assigned to Brazil in these texts and in spite of the fact that the stories told are complex intertextual exercises (fundamentally mediated by English or French texts, which may or may not have emanated from a Portuguese source), it is important to point out that a network of specific German interests in Brazil is already noticeable.

Getting there

Most of the German texts that have been considered so far share an interesting feature: their intertextuality. In fact, they are what one would call third-hand or second-hand texts, that is, they are texts *on* texts and *about* texts, leaving in the German public sphere an impressive void space of firsthand testimonial experience, which the many French and British translations along with their critical re-

---

[27] H., "Streitigkeiten der Portugiesen und Holländer wegen Brasiliens im vorigen Jahrhundert," *Hannoverisches Magazin* 6 (1768).
[28] James Hingston Tuckey, "Heroismus eines Neger-Sclaven. Eine Anecdote," *Minerva. Ein Journal Historischen und Politischen Inhalts* 3 (1805).
[29] Thomas Lindley, "Die Palmareser. Ein ehemaliger Neger-Staat in Brasilien," *Minerva. Ein Journal für Geschichte Politik und Literatur* 3 (1805).
[30] Sebastião da Rocha Pitta, *História da América portugueza: desde o anno de mil e quinhentos do seu descobrimento até o de mil e setecentos e vinte e quatro* (Lisbon: Joseph Antonio da Sylva, 1730).

views[31] or the more rare Portuguese sources are certainly not in the position of completely replacing.

Nevertheless, there are exceptions. The set of texts resulting from a one-month stopover in Rio de Janeiro of the Fifteenth and Sixteenth Infantry Regiments of Hannover (which were on their way to Madras, India, participating in the British East India Expedition), for instance, offers some of the most curious and impressive firsthand German testimonies about Brazil that were published in eighteenth-century Germany.[32]

Besides the travelogue by Friedrich Ludwig Langstedt,[33] military chaplain of the Fifteenth Regiment, there were an unusual number of miscellaneous letters and diaries written during the voyage (from Langstedt and from other anonymous German officers) that appeared in several German magazines.[34] Among

---

[31] Besides the texts and translations mentioned in the preceding section of this chapter, see the anonymous "[Review of] des Herrn Johann von Lery Reise in Brasilien"; C.M. de La Condamine, "Nachricht von einer Reise in das Innerste von Südamerika, von der Küste des Südmeeres an, bis zu den Küsten von Brasilien und Guiana, längst dem Amazonenstrome (mit Karte)," *Hamburgisches Magazin, oder Gesammelte Schriften, zum Unterricht und Vergnügen* 6.1 (1750): 3–70; Guillaume Thomas François Raynal, "Geschichte der Goldminen in Brasilien, und von der Art, sie zu bearbeiten; imgleichen der Diamantenminen, die man daselbst entdeckt hat. Betrachtungen über die Beschaffenheit dieses Edelsteines," *Hannoverisches Magazin* 20 (1782): 1249–1264; or Amerigo Vespucci, "Reisen nach Brasilien von 1501 bis 1504," *Neue Beiträge zur Völker- und Länderkunde* 10 (1792): 245–272.

[32] Details on this expedition in Chen Tzoref-Ashkenazi, "German Voices from India: Officers of the Hanoverian Regiments in East India Company Service," *South Asia: Journal of South Asian Studies* 32:2 (2009): 189–211, and "The Experienced Traveller as a Professional Author: Friedrich Ludwig Langstedt, Georg Forster and Colonialism Discourse in Eighteenth-Century Germany," *History* 95.317 (2010): 8–15 and passim; a list of the published works by officers of the Fifteenth and Sixteenth Hanoverian Regiments is provided by Tzoref-Ashkenazi, "The Experienced Traveller," 208–211; for the present chapter only the texts dealing with Brazil were considered.

[33] *Reisen nach Südamerika, Asien und Afrika, nebst Geographischen, Historischen und das Kommerzium betreffenden Anmerkungen* (Hildesheim: Tuchtfeld, 1789); on Langstedt in Brazil see also Luiz Barros Montez, "O Brasil para os europeus. Três narrativas de viajantes germânicos no Rio de Janeiro entre os séculos XVIII e XIX," in *200 Anos da chegada da família real portuguesa ao Brasil: da abertura dos portos às nações amigas e seus reflexos na arquitetura e no espaço brasileiro*, ed. Luiz Manoel Cavalcanti Gazzaneo, Vol. 3: *Espacialização patrimônio e sociedade* (Rio de Janeiro: Four Print Editora, 2007), 107–123.

[34] See the anonymous letters "Rio Janeiro in Brasilien, 21 Mai 1782," *Stats-Anzeigen* 2 (1782): 216–218, "Auszug aus einem Briefe eines teutschen Officiers auf einem englisch-ostindischen Schiffe. In Hafen von Rio Janeiro. Den 8ten May, 1782," *Politisches Journal Nebst Anzeige von Gelehrten und Andern Sachen* 2 (1782): 208–217, "Briefe eines Hannov. Offiziers vom 15ten nach Ostindien eingeschifften Regiment, am Bord des Nottingham vom 30ten März 1782," *Hanauisches Magazin* 6 (1783): 253–264, and "Schreiben eines Officiers bei dem 15ten Churbraunschweig-Lüneburgischen Regiment, am Bord Europa, in der Bay der Allerheiligen zu St. Salvador," *Hanno-*

these, the very synthetic letter from Rio de Janeiro that was published anonymously in the *Stats-Anzeigen*[35] – and whose author was probably Langstedt because its style, projected views, and observations are very similar to those of his other writings on Brazil – could be considered exemplary of the travelers' perspectives. Dated 21 May 1782, it reproduces some of the idyllic features that were also found in other eighteenth-century German texts, but something has evidently changed, for discourse becomes enthusiastic and the style apologetic. The author does not hesitate to describe Brazil as a "paradise with black angels," a paradisiac nature that is also reflected in the friendliness of the locals, whether indigenous or not: "In general, you can not praise enough the politeness of the Inhabitants, and even their *Negres*."[36]

The references to the Catholic Church in Brazil also deserve special reference in this context, to the extent that they make it clear (as happened with Zedler's encyclopedia) that discourse on Brazil is built against a background global picture of Portugal, which sometimes operates as a comparison factor, sometimes as a counterpoint, and always as a horizon of expectations. In this case it is again the dark image that the Portuguese church had in Protestant Germany by that time that serves as an obvious counterpoint to Brazilian clergy: "Also you can think of nothing more tolerant, obliging, and pleasant, as the local Catholic clergy." And the same goes eventually for the references to the military in Brazil: "The *Militaire* is on German heels, in the best discipline: their exercises, maneuvers, uniform, Propreté, and what comes with it, and the particular polite and modest nature of Officers and others, is remarkable, and stirs admiration that people could have been brought to this degree of perfection."[37] These last, unexpected observations are undoubtedly due to the fact that the Brazilian Army was then commanded by General Johann Heinrich Böhm, a Prussian officer from Bremen who had been in Portugal with Count Schaumburg-Lippe during the Seven

---

verisches Magazin 21 (1783): 923–926, as well as extracts from Friedrich Ludwig Langstedt's letters, "Auszüge einiger Briefe des Herrn Langstedts, Feldpredigers bei dem fünfzehnten Churfüstl. Braunschweig-Lüneburgischen nach Ostindien gegangenen Infanterie-Regiment. Nebst einem Extract aus dessen Tagebuche," *Hannoverisches Magazin* 21 (1783): 353–366, and "Verfolg der Reise eines Theils nach Ostindien gegangenen Chur-Braunschweig-Lüneburgische Truppen, von Rio de Janeiro bis Madras," *Hannoverisches Magazin* 21 (1783): 593–608.

35 "Rio Janeiro in Brasilien, 21 Mai 1782," 216–218.
36 "Rio Janeiro in Brasilien, 21 Mai 1782," 216, 218. Several passages of Langstedt's travelogue published later on introduce very similar idyllic views; see Langstedt, *Reisen nach Südamerika*, 50–81.
37 "Rio Janeiro in Brasilien, 21 Mai 1782," 218.

Years' War and had been appointed to organize the Brazilian Army by the Marquis of Pombal in 1767.[38]

Despite the more local motivations of this encomium, with these texts a new Brazil seemed about to emerge from empirical direct observation, one with a paradisiac nature, friendly natives, a tolerant church, and a disciplined army, all of them painted with vivid colors. Yet one cannot help noticing that not only do these positive attributes still depend largely on European established values, expectations, and stereotypes (Portuguese and German in this case), but also Langstedt's and the other anonymous texts remain de facto an exception in a otherwise empirical void of direct firsthand German testimonies. As has been argued before, this empirical void might explain the researchers' evident lack of interest in this epoch of German-Brazilian intercultural relations, but this silence, which blatantly contrasts with the exuberance of the linguistic and pictorial discourses of the mid-nineteenth century, is unequivocally very loud and meaningful, therefore calling for some examination.

From a methodological point of view it might be useful to distinguish two silences during this period. One is certainly the silence enforced by Portuguese imperial policies that simply did not allow foreign travelers to go to Brazil (the case of Alexander von Humboldt is possibly the best-known product of this silence, always regretted and mourned by research in these areas). But there is also a second kind of silence, one created by the absence or omission of discourse, yet not by the lack of firsthand experience, a silence produced by travelers and explorers who actually went to Brazil and returned to Europe but apparently never shared their experiences with the European public (or at least not in the expected and usual form of a travel account or a diary).

This is the case of Friedrich Wilhelm Sieber, a naturalist who went to Brazil in the winter of 1800–1801 and returned to Germany more than 10 years later, in June 1812, "bringing with him not only what he had collected in the State of Pará during the last years, but also a good many bird skins from New South Wales and the United States."[39] The materials collected were deposited at the Zoological Museum of the recently founded University of Berlin.[40]

---

38 See Karl Heinrich Oberacker Jr., "Johann Heinrich Boehm, der Gründer der ersten brasilianischen Armee," *Staden-Jahrbuch* 4 (1956): 101–117.
39 Erwin Stresemann, "On a Collection of Birds from Georgia and Carolina Made About 1810 by John Abbot," *The Auk. A Quarterly Journal of Ornithology* 70.2 (1953): here 113.
40 See "Vermehrung des Berlinischen Museums der Naturgeschichte," *Repertorium des Neuesten und Wissenswürdigsten aus der Gesammten Naturkunde* 4 (1812): 93–94. On Sieber's voyages and on the history of the Zoological Museum of the University of Berlin, see Nelson Papavero, *Essays on the History of Neotropical Dipterology, with Special Reference to Collectors (1750–1905)*,

The context of this voyage to Brazil is interesting enough to deserve, finally, some attention here. Sieber was actually a preparator who had accompanied Count Johann Centurius von Hoffmannsegg and Heinrich Friedrich Link (at the time professor at the University of Rostock) on a multiyear journey through Portugal that began in 1797 with the goal of making a Portuguese flora.[41] While in Portugal, the Catholic count managed to obtain permission to travel to Brazil, certainly because of his good relationships with the local authorities. In one of his letters to his family, sent from Lisbon in March 1798, he refers to the voyage to Brazil in the following terms: "I have certain hope to fulfill one of my favorite wishes: to make a voyage to Brazil. I have already received permission for this voyage and in the coming Spring I will be sending my instruments over there."[42]

Vol. I (São Paulo: Museu de Zoologia, Universidade de Sa~o Paulo, 1971); Olivério Mário de Oliveira Pinto, *A ornitologia do Brasil através das idades: século XVI a século XIX* (São Paulo: Revista dos Tribunais, 1979); Günther Hartmann, "Die Sammlungen südamerikanischer Naturvölker im Museum für Völkerkunde Berlin," *Zeitschrift für Ethnologie* 100.1/2 (1975): 307–322; Stresemann, "Die brasilianischen Vogelsamlungen des Grafen von Hoffmannsegg aus den Jahren 1800–1812," *Bonner Zoologische Beiträge* 1 (1950): 43–51, 126–143, "On a Collection of Birds" and "Aus dem Briefwechsel von C.J. Temminck mit dem Grafen von Hoffmannsegg und C. Illiger 1810–1814," *ARDEA* 44.4 (1956): 253–263; and Hinrich Lichtenstein, *Das zoologische Museum der Universität zu Berlin* (Berlin: Dümmler, 1816); at least one letter from Sieber was published in English translation in *The Philosophical Magazine*; see "Natural History," *The Philosophical Magazine Comprehending the Various Branches of Science, the Liberal and Fine Arts, Agriculture, Manufactures and Commerce* XXI (1805): 91–93. Wilhelm von Eschwege, "Allgemeine Bemerkungen über Brasilien," *Geist der Zeit. Ein Journal für Geschichte, Politik, Geographie, Staaten- und Kriegskunde und Literatur* 4 (1818): 170–192; Martius, *Herbarium Florae Brasiliensis*. Monachii 1837 [*Beiblätter zur allgemeinen botanischen Zeitung*, II/1837], 26–27; Étienne Geoffroy Saint-Hilaire, "Description de deux singes d'Amérique, sous les noms d'*Ateles arachnoides* et d'*Ateles marginatus*," *Annales du Muséum d'Histoire Naturelle* 13 (1809): 89–97; and Hoffmannsegg, "Beschreibung vier affenartiger Thiere aus Brasilien," *Magazin für die Neuesten Entdeckungen in der Gesamten Naturkunde* 1 (1807): 83–104 also give interesting information on Sieber's activities in Brazil. The foreword by Theophil Friedrich Ehrmann to the German version of Lindley's voyage (*Thomas Lindley's Reise nach Brasilien*, III–XIV) is particularly revealing about the difficulties of obtaining permission to travel to Brazil; on this last subject see also Anita Hermannstädter's "*Deutsche am Amazonas: Forscher oder Abenteurer? Expeditionen in Brasilien 1800–1914. Auseinandersetzung mit fremden Lebenswelten. Sonderausstellung im Ethnologischen Museum Berlin vom 18.4.–10.11.2002*," *Tópicos* 3 (2002): 22–25, among others.

41 Details in Fernando Clara, *Mundos de palavras*, 228–253 and "Deutsche Wissenschaft – Portugiesische Natur: die Entstehung einer Flore portugaise," in *Wissen im Netz: Botanik und Pflanzentransfer in europäischen Korrespondenznetzen des 18. Jahrhunderts*, ed. Regina Dauser et al. (Berlin: Oldenbourg Akademieverlag, 2008), 65–78, among others.

42 Johann Centurius Graf von Hoffmannsegg, "Fortsetzung der Briefe des Herrn Grafen von Hoffmannsegg," *Lausizische Monatsschrift* 2.8 (1798): 99. However, according to a letter from Georg Heinrich Nöhden, "[Brief] Von dem Herrn Dr. Nöhden. London, den 1. Aug. 1799," *Journal*

By the late eighteenth century, these dreams and expectations were certainly far from being unique to Hoffmannsegg. His "favorite wish" was increasingly becoming the lifetime dream of every natural scientist in Europe – Humboldt's too, of course. Clearly, Brazil was already becoming the "El Dorado for naturalists."[43] However, Hoffmannsegg fulfilled his dream only partially; he never went to Brazil, although he managed to send the instruments along with Friedrich Wilhelm Sieber. And Sieber's journeys produced an important informational shift as far as the perception of Brazil in eighteenth-century Germany goes, for the outcome of his travels was radically different from what the German public had been used to. In fact, there was no Brazil mediated by Portugal, England, or France; there were no words, travel accounts, letters, or diaries, but objects and products of nature that were to be analyzed in laboratories and displayed in museums, thus feeding new and more tangible Brazilian dreams. And these were getting stronger in Europe precisely because of the success of this kind of scientific enterprise[44] and the concomitant growing recognition of the power of science in the

---

für die Botanik 2 (1799): 173–181, the count is unlikely to have received official permission from the Portuguese authorities to travel to Brazil. Interestingly enough, Nöhden's information source was his "old friend" Georg Heinrich von Langsdorff, whom he accidentally ran across in London when the latter was returning from Portugal, where he had been with Hoffmannsegg and Link. It is worth noting that this network of scientists does not seem to have many contacts (if any at all) with the closed network of Portuguese scientists who were (or had been) also exploring Brazil's nature by that time (see Ângela Domingues, "Para um melhor conhecimento dos domínios coloniais: a constituição de redes de informação no Império Português em finais do setecentos," *História, Ciências, Saúde: Manguinhos* 8 (suppl) (2001): 823–838).
43 "Nachrichten aus Brasilien," *Morgenblatt für Gebildete Stände* 120 (20 May 1818): 477; these "Nachrichten" are actually excerpts of the correspondence between Spix, Martius, and Franz Paula von Schrank, the editor of the *Flora oder Botanische Zeitung*, who originally published them in his journal (see Schrank, "Correspondenz. Nachrichten über die Reise der beiden Akademisten, der Herren DD. Spix und Martius, nach Brasilien, aus ihren Berichten gesammelt," *Flora oder Botanische Zeitung* 1.5 (18 February 1818): 65–84).
44 See the significantly increasing number of more specific scientific essays on the fauna, flora, and mineralogy of Brazil published in Germany in the second half of the eighteenth century (listed in note 6). Along with these scientific publications were several other kinds of books that clearly fed this Brazilian dream in Germany, namely Robinsonade, adventure or history books specially designed for younger readers. For reasons of space I cannot go here into details about this prolific German pedagogic literature but would nevertheless like to mention Johann Eberhard Zeh (ed.), *Historisch-geographische Beschreibung von Amerika für Jünglinge* (Nürnberg: Zeh, 1784); Karl Hammerdörfer and Christian T. Kosche, "Brasilien," *Amerika: ein geographisch-historisches Lesebuch zum Nutzen der Jugend und ihrer Erzieher*, vol. 5.2 (Leipzig: Weidmann, 1788): 173–250; and Joseph Müller, *Der Steyerische Robinson, oder Reisen und besondere merkwürdige Begebenheiten des Joseph Müller an den Brasilianischen Küsten von Amerika* (Frankfurt

public sphere. The voyages of Langsdorff, Spix and Martius, and Maximilian zu Wied-Neuwied were in the pipeline. The nineteenth century had somehow already begun.

Europe's dreams

The texts briefly examined here bear witness to the process of identity and nation building in Brazil and are at the same time, directly or indirectly, part of that same process. They unveil a complex and variegated network of themes, interests, and people that is very different from the one laid out by the dominant scientific travel discourse of the mid-nineteenth century on Brazil.

In the eighteenth century, the representations of Brazil in Germany reveal a three-stage evolution. The first stage, lasting until about 1780, is clearly dominated by a European framework of themes and interests and by an image of Portugal that lies in the background. The Jesuits in South America, the critique of European colonialism, and the discussions about slavery are the main pretexts that bring Brazil to the foreground. But even when it reaches the foreground, this image of Brazil appears unfocused and blurred. The reason is obvious: There are no German firsthand testimonial texts published during this period. Most of these texts are products of well-known intertextual games: As texts *of* texts and *about* texts, they are grounded, ultimately, in ancient classical topic and rhetoric. Their discourse obeys the rules established by the panegyric style, and the images projected are variations of a catalog that has well-defined, stable attributes.[45]

To some extent, then, one might say that this Brazil *is not*. It does not exist except *by comparison* and *within the framework* of the formal and stylistic catalogs made available by classical topic and rhetoric (Zedler). It does not exist except *as mediated* by English, French, and Portuguese texts or as an *appendix* to Europe's – and above all Portugal's – political landscape (Sprengel, Blankett).

Along with the increasing number of scientific reports and descriptions of Brazilian products of nature, published in German periodicals in the last two decades of the eighteenth century, the set of texts left by the officers of the Fifteenth and Sixteenth Infantry Regiments of Hannover (Langstedt, among others) function as an important part of a transitional second stage. Direct empirical

---

and Leizpig, 1793) as three examples of a much larger number of works that surely deserve some attention in this area.
45 See Ernst Robert Curtius, *Europäische Literatur und lateinisches Mittelalter*, 11th ed. (Tübingen: Francke, 1993 [1948]), 163–168.

contact with the land did have an effect on a discourse that became undoubtedly more colorful, but it was not powerful enough to change the horizon of expectations of the travelers, still almost fully determined by European references, values, and views. As for the scientific news and descriptions, though also the result of empirical observation of the land, for the German reader they were texts of texts, that is, copies, digests, or translations of English and French sources. For most of the German eighteenth century, Brazil remained an "undetermined new land"[46] or, perhaps better, a land determined *in* Europe and *by* Europe in a political as well as a more metaphorical way: It is a Portuguese colony that shares its nature and people with the Motherland and serves as a "projection screen"[47] for Europe's (that is, also Germany's) fantasies (Hoffmannsegg, Humboldt, among many others).

By the turn to the nineteenth century, however, as science began to crystallize much of Europe's dreams of knowledge and power, the picture underwent significant changes. It was no longer mediated by Portugal, England, or France, and the important background image of Portugal began to fade way, along with many of the European national and political themes that, until then, played a modeling role in it. Sieber's voyages in Brazil could well be considered to mark the beginning of this third stage, which later enthroned the names of Langsdorff, Spix, Martius, Wied-Neuwied, and Eschwege in the context of German-Brazilian intercultural relations. Considering the dynamics of this eighteenth-century German Brazil, one would certainly be tempted to conclude that, after a rhetorical, political, and supplemental existence, the land from then on led a new life of independence, focused almost exclusively on nature. But the truth is that this new existence was mediated by European science; Europe was still mediating Brazil, and this time not at a national political level but at a rational, much more effective one.

Indeed, to fully grasp the overwhelming power of this European science in the identity and nation building of Brazil, it is worth recalling that when in 1840 the Instituto Histórico e Geográfico do Brasil announced a prize for a "plan to write the ancient and modern History of Brazil," the winner was a well-known naturalist, Karl Friedrich Philipp von Martius, and his answer did

---

46 Georg Wink, "Brasilien als "vorgestellte Gemeinschaft"? Eine kulturwissenschaftliche Untersuchung der Erzählung Brasiliens vom Reich zur Nation im lateinamerikanischen Kontrast" (PhD diss., Mainz, 2008), 269.
47 Georg Wink, "Brasilien als "vorgestellte Gemeinschaft"? Eine kulturwissenschaftliche Untersuchung der Erzählung Brasiliens vom Reich zur Nation im lateinamerikanischen Kontrast" (PhD diss., Mainz, 2008), 269.

not address historical, political, religious, or cultural issues or events but, significantly, only scientific matters: the human races.

> Whoever may be in charge of writing the History of Brazil, a land that promises so much, should never lose sight of which elements have contributed there to the development of man. These elements are however very different in nature, and three races converged in a particular way for the development of man, namely: the copper-colored or American, the white or Caucasian, and finally the black or Ethiopian. Out of the encounter, the mixing, the mutual relations and changes of these three races, formed the current population, whose history, on this account, has a very particular slant.[48]

The land "that promises so much," the "land of the future" (as Stefan Zweig put it a century later) would not have a past but a present and above all a future (like science itself). Brazil would then not have a (national) history – at least in European terms – but a natural history. In other words, the nation was the nature. After Brazilian nature had been explored, described, classified, and cataloged, Europe's dreams were forging Brazil's history too. The process of colonization was thus completed.

References

Andrada e Silva, José Bonifácio d'. "Ueber die brasilianischen Diamanten." *Magazin für das Neueste aus der Physik und Naturgeschichte* 9.2 (1794): 47–54.
"Anmerkungen über ein Paar Stellen in dem Vorbericht des Herrn Hofraths Lessings zu der von ihm herausgegebenen Beschreibung Brasiliens, betreffend die vermeinte Person eines Spanischen Hauptmanns, der mit seinem Geschlechtsnamen Marannon y Gran Para geheißen haben soll." *Hannoverisches Magazin* 21 (1783): 801–814.
"Aus Brasilien." *Gartenkalender* 3 (1784): 136–138.
"Auszug aus einem Briefe eines teutschen Officiers auf einem englisch-ostindischen Schiffe. In Hafen von Rio Janeiro. Den 8ten May, 1782." *Politisches Journal Nebst Anzeige von Gelehrten und Andern Sachen* 2 (1782): 208–217.
Beller, Manfred, and Joep Leerssen, eds. *Imagology. The Cultural Construction and Literary Representation of National Characters. A Critical Survey* (Amsterdam: Rodopi, 2007).
Berger, Paulo. *Bibliografia do Rio de Janeiro de viajantes e autores estrangeiros 1531–1900*, 2nd ed. (Rio de Janeiro: Secretaria de Estado de Educaça͂o e Cultura, RJ, 1980).
Blankett, John. *Briefe über Portugal, nebst einem Anhang über Brasilien* (Leipzig: Weygand, 1782). [English original: *Letters from Portugal, on the Late and Present State of that Kingdom* (London: J. Almon, 1777); French translation: *Lettres écrites du Portugal, Sur l'état ancien et actuel de ce Royaume. Traduites de l'anglois. Suivies d'un portrait*

---

[48] Martius, "Como se deve escrever a História do Brazil," *Revista Trimensal de Historia e Geographia, ou Jornal do Instituto Historico e Geographico Brazileiro* 24 (January 1845): 381–382.

historique de M. le Marquis de Pombal (Paris: Cellot, 1780); Portuguese translation: *Cartas sobre o estado presente e passado do Reyno de Portugal* (Ms. 1777, Lisbon, 1822)]

Blumenbach, Johann Friedrich. "Fernere Reisenachrichten vom Hrn. D. Langsdorff von der Insel St. Catharina an der Küste von Brasilien den 15ten Januar 1804." *Magazin für den Neuesten Zustand der Naturkunde mit Rücksicht auf die Dazu Gehörigen Hülfswissenschaften* 9.3 (1805): 220–223.

Blumenbach, Johann Friedrich. "Nachricht von einigen Naturseltenheiten (aus einem Briefe des Hrn. Dr. Langsdorf, vom 9. Jan. 1798)." *Magazin für den Neuesten Zustand der Naturkunde mit Rücksicht auf die Dazu Gehörigen Hülfswissenschaften* 1.2 (1798): 52–53.

Blumenbach, Johann Friedrich. "Ueber einige brasilische Fossilien. Aus einem Briefe des Hn. Dr. Langsdorf aus Lissabon vom 7. Jun. 1798." *Magazin für den Neuesten Zustand der Naturkunde mit Rücksicht auf die Dazu Gehörigen Hülfswissenschaften* 2.1 (1800): 32–33.

"Brasilien," in *Grosses Vollständiges Universal-Lexicon Aller Wissenschaften und Künste, Welche bißero durch menschlichen Verstand und Witz erfunden worden*, Vol. 4 (Leipzig: Zedler, 1733), 1098–1100.

"Briefe eines Hannov. Offiziers vom 15ten nach Ostindien eingeschifften Regiment, am Bord des Nottingham vom 30ten März 1782." *Hanauisches Magazin* 6 (1783): 253–264.

Canstatt, Oscar. *Kritisches Repertorium der deutsch-brasilianischen Literatur* (Berlin: Reimer, 1902–1906).

Certeau, Michel de. "Travel Narratives of the French to Brazil: Sixteenth to Eighteenth Centuries." *Representations* 33 (1991): 221–226.

Clara, Fernando. "Deutsche Wissenschaft – Portugiesische Natur: Die Entstehung einer *Flore portugaise*," in *Wissen im Netz: Botanik und Pflanzentransfer in europäischen Korrespondenznetzen des 18. Jahrhunderts*, ed. Regina Dauser et al. (Berlin: Oldenbourg Akademieverlag, 2008), 65–78.

Clara, Fernando. *Mundos de palavras. Viagem, história, ciência, literatura: Portugal no espaço de língua alemã (1770–1810)* (Bern, Switzerland: Peter Lang, 2007).

Curtius, Ernst Robert. *Europäische Literatur und lateinisches Mittelalter*, 11th ed. (Tübingen: Francke, 1993 [1948]).

"Der Brasilianische Großkopf." *Neue Bilder-Gallerie für Junge Söhne und Töchter zur Angenehmen und Nützlichen Selbstbeschäftigung aus dem Reiche der Natur, Kunst, Sitten und des Gemeinen Lebens* 8 (1801): 21–22.

"Der Brasilienholzbaum." *Neue Bilder-Gallerie für Junge Söhne und Töchter zur Angenehmen und Nützlichen Selbstbeschäftigung aus dem Reiche der Natur, Kunst, Sitten und des Gemeinen Lebens* 3 (1796): 162–163.

Dohm, Christian Wilhelm. "[Review of] Stephens, P. [= Blankett, John]: *Briefe über Portugal*." *Allgemeine Deutsche Bibliothek* 53.2 (1783): 462–468.

Domingues, Ângela. "Para um melhor conhecimento dos domínios coloniais: a constituição de redes de informação no Império português em finais do setecentos." *História, Ciências, Saúde: Manguinhos* 8 (suppl) (2001): 823–838.

Eckart, Anselm Franz Dominik von. "Animadversiones cujusdam plures per annos in Brasilia Missionarii in librum, Lipsiae, 1782, 8. editum, qui inscribitur *Briefe über Portugal, nebst einem Anhang über Brasilien. Aus dem Französischen. Mit Anmerkungen herausgegeben* von Matthias Christian Sprengel, Professor der Geschichte in Halle." *Journal zur Kunstgeschichte und zur Allgemeinen Litteratur* 14 (1787): 192–291.

Eckart, Anselm Franz Dominik von. "Historia persecutionis Societatis Iesu in Lusitania." *Journal zur Kunstgeschichte und zur Allgemeinen Litteratur* 7 (1779): 293–320. [Portuguese translation: *Memórias de um Jesuíta prisioneiro de Pombal*. Trans. Joaquim Abranches and Ana M. L. da Silva (São Paulo: Braga, 1987)]

Eschwege, Wilhelm Ludwig von. "Allgemeine Bemerkungen über Brasilien." *Geist der Zeit. Ein Journal für Geschichte, Politik, Geographie, Staaten- und Kriegskunde und Literatur* 4 (1818): 170–192.

Estermann, Alfred Adolph. *Die deutschen Literatur-Zeitschriften 1815–1850: Bibliographien, Programme, Autoren*, Vol. 1: *Zeitschriften mit Erscheinungsbeginn 1645–1814* (Munich: Saur, 1991).

Estermann, Alfred Adolph. *Kontextverarbeitung. Buchwissenschaftliche Studien*, ed. Klaus-Dieter Lehmann and Klaus G. Saur (Munich: Saur, 1998).

Fonseca, Benedictus de. "*Litterae P. Benedicti de Fonseca, Soc. Iesu Procuratoris quondam Generalis Prov. Maraguonensis, datae 11 Aug. 1779 Annadiae ad R.P. Anselmum Eckart.*" *Journal zur Kunstgeschichte und zur Allgemeinen Litteratur* 16 (1788): 54–75.

Franzbach, Martin. "Versuch einer chronologischen Bibliographie der Reisebeschreibungen, geographischen, historischen und theologischen Spezialwerke über Brasilien im deutschen Sprachraum 1504–1800." *Jahrbuch für Geschichte Lateinamerikas/Anuario de Historia de América Latina* 7 (1970): 146–156.

Gatzhammer, Stefan. "Antijesuitismo Europeu. Relações político-diplomáticas e culturais entre a Baviera e Portugal (1750–1780)." *Lusitânia Sacra* 5 (1993): 159–250.

Gatzhammer, Stefan. "Politisch-diplomatische Beziehungen zwischen Portugal und Österreich im 18. Jahrhundert vor dem Hintergrund der Jesuitenfrage." *Mitteilungen des Instituts für Österreichische Geschichtsforschung* 102.1–4 (1994): 359–408.

Guettard, Jean-Étienne. "Beobachtung, von den brasilianischen Topasen." *Hamburgisches Magazin, oder Gesammelte Schriften, zum Unterricht und Vergnügen* 12.6 (1754): 666–673.

H. "Streitigkeiten der Portugiesen und Holländer wegen Brasiliens im vorigen Jahrhundert." *Hannoverisches Magazin* 6 (1768): 1249–1264, 1265–1278.

Hammerdörfer, Karl, and Christian T. Kosche. "Brasilien," in *Amerika: ein geographisch-historisches Lesebuch zum Nutzen der Jugend und ihrer Erzieher*, Vol. 5.2 (Leipzig: Weidmann, 1788), 173–250.

"Handelsnachrichten von der Stadt Rio de Janeiro in Brasilien (mit Tabelle)." *Magazin der Handels- und Gewerbskunde* 3.2 (1805): 568–571.

Hartmann, Günther. "Die Sammlungen südamerikanischer Naturvölker im Museum für Völkerkunde Berlin." *Zeitschrift für Ethnologie* 100.1/2 (1975): 307–322.

Hermannstädter, Anita. "*Deutsche am Amazonas: Forscher oder Abenteurer? Expeditionen in Brasilien 1800–1914*. Auseinandersetzung mit fremden Lebenswelten. Sonderausstellung im Ethnologischen Museum Berlin vom 18.4.–10.11.2002." *Tópicos* 3 (2002): 22–25.

Hocks, Paul, and Peter Schmidt. *Index zu deutschen Zeitschriften der Jahre 1773–1830*. (Nendeln, Liechtenstein: KTO Press, 1979).

Hocks, Paul, and Peter Schmidt. *Literarische und politische Zeitschriften 1789–1805. Von der politischen Revolution zur Literaturrevolution* (Stuttgart: Metzler, 1975).

Hoffmannsegg, Johann Centurius Graf von. "Beschreibung vier affenartiger Thiere aus Brasilien." *Magazin für die Neuesten Entdeckungen in der Gesamten Naturkunde* 1 (1807): 83–104.

Hoffmannsegg, Johann Centurius Graf von. "Fortsetzung der Briefe des Herrn Grafen von Hoffmannsegg." *Lausizische Monatsschrift* 2.8 (1798): 89–99.

J. B. "Varia de Vita P. Gabrielis Malagrida." *Journal zur Kunstgeschichte und zur Allgemeinen Litteratur* 16 (1788): 41–54.

Jürgensen, Renate. "Ein Leben: Christoph Gottlieb von Murr (1733–1811)." *Bibliotheca Norica. Patrizier und Gelehrtenbibliotheken in Nürnberg Zwischen Mittelalter und Aufklärung* 2 (2001): 1310–1324.

Koch. "Nachricht von einer sehr einfachen Maschine, Brasilienholz klein zu schneiden." *Neues Hannoversches Magazin* 3 (1793): 511–512.

La Condamine, C. M. de. "Nachricht von einer Reise in das Innerste von Südamerika, von der Küste des Südmeeres an, bis zu den Küsten von Brasilien und Guiana, längst dem Amazonenstrome (mit Karte)." *Hamburgisches Magazin, oder Gesammelte Schriften, zum Unterricht und Vergnügen* 6.1 (1750): 3–70.

Langstedt, Friedrich Ludwig. "Auszüge einiger Briefe des Herrn Langstedts, Feldpredigers bei dem fünfzehnten Churfüstl. Braunschweig-Lüneburgischen nach Ostindien gegangenen Infanterie-Regiment. Nebst einem Extract aus dessen Tagebuche." *Hannoverisches Magazin* 21 (1783): 353–366.

Langstedt, Friedrich Ludwig. *Reisen nach Südamerika, Asien und Afrika, nebst Geographischen, Historischen und das Kommerzium betreffenden Anmerkungen* (Hildesheim: Tuchtfeld, 1789).

Langstedt, Friedrich Ludwig. "Verfolg der Reise eines Theils nach Ostindien gegangenen Chur-Braunschweig-Lüneburgische Truppen, von Rio de Janeiro bis Madras." *Hannoverisches Magazin* 21 (1783): 593–608.

Ley, Charles David, ed. *Portuguese Voyages, 1498–1663* (London: J.M. Dent; New York: E.P. Dutton, 1947).

Lichtenstein, Hinrich. *Das zoologische Museum der Universität zu Berlin* (Berlin: Dümmler, 1816).

Lindenberg, Johann Bernhard Wilhelm. "Ausführlichere Beschreibung des Brasilischen Rüsselkäfers, nebst einigen Betrachtungen." *Der Naturforscher* 14 (1780): 211–220.

Lindenberg, Johann Bernhard Wilhelm. "Beschreibung eines Brasilischen Rüßellkäfers." *Der Naturforscher* 10 (1777): 86–87.

Lindley, Thomas. "Die Palmareser. Ein ehemaliger Neger-Staat in Brasilien." *Minerva. Ein Journal für Geschichte Politik und Literatur* 3 (1805): 343–356.

Lindley, Thomas. *Thomas Lindley's Reise nach Brasilien und Aufenthalt daselbst in den Jahren 1802 und 1803. Nebst einer beschreibung der Städte und Provinzen Porto-Seguro und San Salvador* (Weimar: Landes-Industrie-Comptoir, 1806). [English original: *Narrative of a Voyage to Brasil, Terminating in the Seizure of a British Vessel and the Imprisonment of the Author and the Ships Crew, by the Portuguese. With General Sketches of the Country, Its Natural Productions, Colonial Inhabitants etc. and a Description of the City and Provinces of St. Salvador and Porto Seguro* (London: J. Johnson, 1805)]

Lüning, C. F. "Einige Notizen über Brasilien, in statistischer und naturhistorischer Hinsicht." *Neues Hannoversches Magazin* 18 (1808): 785–810.

Martini, Friedrich Heinrich Wilhelm. "Der Amerikanische oder Brasilianische Einhornteufel. Die Seefledermaus." *Neue Mannigfaltigkeiten* 3 (1776): 193–195.
Martius, Karl Friedrich Philipp von. "Como se deve escrever a história do Brazil." *Revista Trimensal de Historia e Geographia, ou Jornal do Instituto Historico e Geographico Brazileiro* 24 (January 1845): 381–411.
Martius, Karl Friedrich Philipp von. *Herbarium Florae Brasiliensis* (Monachii, 1837). [*Beiblätter zur Allgemeinen Botanischen Zeitung*, II/1837]
Montez, Luiz Barros, "O Brasil para os europeus. Três narrativas de viajantes germânicos no Rio de Janeiro entre os séculos XVIII e XIX," in *200 Anos da chegada da família real portuguesa ao Brasil: da abertura dos portos às nações amigas e seus reflexos na arquitetura e no espaço brasileiro*, ed. Luiz Manoel Cavalcanti Gazzaneo, Vol. 3: *Espacialização patrimônio e sociedade* (Rio de Janeiro: Four Print Editora, 2007), 107–123.
Müller, Joseph. *Der Steyerische Robinson, oder Reisen und besondere merkwürdige Begebenheiten des Joseph Müller an den Brasilianischen Küsten von Amerika* (Frankfurt and Leipzig, 1793).
Münch, Ernst. *Geschichte von Brasilien* (Dresden: Hilscher, 1829).
Murr, Christoph Gottlieb von, and Anselm Franz Dominik von Eckart. "Nachrichten von den Sprachen in Brasilien." *Journal zur Kunstgeschichte und zur Allgemeinen Literatur* 6 (1778): 195–213.
Murr, Christoph Gottlieb von, and Anselm Franz Dominik von Eckart. "Zusätze zum *Specimine Linguae Brasilicae vulgaris*." *Journal zur Kunstgeschichte und zur Allgemeinen Litteratur* 7 (1779): 121–122.
"Nachrichten aus Brasilien." *Morgenblatt für Gebildete Stände* 120 (20 May 1818): 477–479.
"Natural History." *The Philosophical Magazine Comprehending the Various Branches of Science, the Liberal and Fine Arts, Agriculture, Manufactures and Commerce* XXI (1805): 91–93.
"Naturgeschichte der brasilischen Spinne." *Berlinische Sammlungen zur Beförderung der Arzneywissenschaft, der Naturgeschichte, der Haushaltungskunst, Kameralwissenschaft und der Dahin Einschlagenden Litteratur* 5 (1773): 66–68.
Nebgen, Christoph. "Christoph Gottlieb von Murr: Ein Protestant erhebt die Stimme gegen die Aufhebung der Gesellschaft Jesu." *Archivum Historicum Societatis Iesu* 73.145 (2004): 121–147.
Nöhden, Georg Heinrich. "[Brief] Von dem Herrn Dr. Nöhden. London, den 1. Aug. 1799." *Journal für die Botanik* 2 (1799): 173–181.
Oberacker, Karl Heinrich Jr. "Johann Heinrich Boehm, der Gründer der ersten brasilianischen Armee." *Staden-Jahrbuch* 4 (1956): 101–117.
Obermeier, Franz. "Brasilien in der englischen Reiseliteratur der Kolonialzeit." *Jahrbuch für Geschichte Lateinamerikas/Anuario de Historia de América Latina* 41 (2004): 373–398.
Obermeier, Franz. "Die französischen Aufklärer und Brasilien, Brasilien in Raynals Histoire philosophique des deux Indes." *Literaturwissenschaftliches Jahrbuch* 50 (2009): 81–113.
Pallas, Peter Simon. "Beschreibung zweyer südamerikanischer merkwürdiger Vögel." *Neue Nordische Beyträge zur Physikalischen und Geographischen Erd- und Völkerbeschreibung, Naturgeschichte und Oekonomie* 3 (1782): 1–7.

Papavero, Nelson. *Essays on the History of Neotropical Dipterology, with Special Reference to Collectors (1750–1905)*, Vol. I (São Paulo: Museu de Zoologia, Universidade de Sãʳo Paulo, 1971).

Pinto, Olivério Mário de Oliveira. *A ornitologia do Brasil através das idades: século XVI a século XIX* (São Paulo: Revista dos Tribunais, 1979).

Pitta, Sebastião da Rocha. *História da América portugueza: desde o anno de mil e quinhentos do seu descobrimento até o de mil e setecentos e vinte e quatro* (Lisbon: Joseph Antonio da Sylva, 1730).

"Portugall." in *Grosses Vollständiges Universal-Lexicon Aller Wissenschaften und Künste, Welche bißero durch menschlichen Verstand und Witz erfunden worden*, Vol. 28 (Leipzig: Zedler, 1741), 1658–1663.

Raynal, Guillaume Thomas François, and António Vieira. "Klagen eines portugiesischen Predigers zu Gott, über das Glück einer ketzerischen Nation." *Ephemeriden der Menschheit oder Bibliothek der Sittenlehre, der Politik und der Gesetzgebung* 1 (1783): 103–114.

Raynal, Guillaume Thomas François. "Geschichte der Goldminen in Brasilien, und von der Art, sie zu bearbeiten; imgleichen der Diamantenminen, die man daselbst entdeckt hat. Betrachtungen über die Beschaffenheit dieses Edelsteines." *Hannoverisches Magazin* 20 (1782): 1249–1264.

Rescher, Hubertus. *Die deutschsprachige Literatur zu Brasilien von 1789–1850: Widerspiegelung brasilianischer Sozial- und Wirtschaftsstrukturen von 1789–1850 in der deutschsprachigen Literatur desselben Zeitraums* (Bern, Switzerland: Peter Lang, 1979).

Revista USP 30 (1996). http://www.usp.br/revistausp/30/SUMARIO-30.htm, 19 June 2014.

"[Review of] *Briefe über Portugall*. Leipzig: Weygand 1782." *Ephemeriden der Menschheit oder Bibliothek der Sittenlehre, der Politik und der Gesetzgebung* 1 (1783): 162–188.

"[Review of] Cudena, *Beschreibung des portugiesischen Amerika*." *Allgemeine Deutsche Bibliothek* 43.1 (1780): 211–214.

"[Review of] des Herrn Johann von Lery Reise in Brasilien." *Neue Allgemeine Deutsche Bibliothek* 4 (1799): 462–466.

"Rio Janeiro in Brasilien, 21 Mai 1782." *Stats-Anzeigen* 2 (1782): 216–218.

Saint-Hilaire, Étienne Geoffroy. "Description de deux singes d'Amérique, sous les noms d'*Ateles arachnoides* et d'*Ateles marginatus*." *Annales du Muséum d'Histoire Naturelle* 13 (1809): 89–97.

Schneider, Ulrich Johannes, ed. *Kulturen des Wissens im 18. Jahrhundert* (Berlin: De Gruyter, 2008).

Schrank, Franz Paula von. "Correspondenz. Nachrichten über die Reise der beiden Akademisten, der Herren DD. Spix und Martius, nach Brasilien, aus ihren Berichten gesammelt." *Flora oder Botanische Zeitung* 1.5 (18 February 1818): 65–84.

"Schreiben eines Officiers bei dem 15ten Churbraunschweig-Lüneburgischen Regiment, am Bord Europa, in der Bay der Allerheiligen zu st. Salvador." *Hannoverisches Magazin* 21 (1783): 923–926.

Seixo, Maria Alzira. "Entre Cultura e Natureza. Ambigüidades do olhar do viajante." *Revista USP* 30 (1996): 120–133. http://www.usp.br/revistausp/30/11-seixo.pdf, 19 June 2014.

Sousa, Celeste H. M. Ribeiro de. "A imagologia no Brasil: primeira tentativa de sistematização." *Revista Brasileira de Literatura Comparada* 14 (2009): 37–55.

Steller, Georg Wilhelm. "Beschreibung der Meerotter, und ob sie Marggrafs Icya oder die Carigveibein der Brasilienser sey?" *Hamburgisches Magazin, oder Gesammelte Schriften, Aus der Naturforschung und den Angenehmen Wissenschaften Überhaupt* 11 (1753): 460–500.

Stresemann, Erwin. "Aus dem Briefwechsel von C.J. Temminck mit dem Grafen von Hoffmannsegg und C. Illiger 1810–1814." *ARDEA* 44.4 (1956): 253–263.

Stresemann, Erwin. "Die brasilianischen Vogelsamlungen des Grafen von Hoffmannsegg aus den Jahren 1800–1812." *Bonner Zoologische Beiträge* 1 (1950): 43–51, 126–143.

Stresemann, Erwin. "On a Collection of Birds from Georgia and Carolina Made About 1810 by John Abbot." *The Auk. A Quarterly Journal of Ornithology* 70.2 (1953): 113–117.

Tuckey, James Hingston. "Heroismus eines Neger-Sclaven. Eine Anecdote." *Minerva. Ein Journal Historischen und Politischen Inhalts* 3 (1805): 412–420.

Tzoref-Ashkenazi, Chen. "The Experienced Traveller as a Professional Author: Friedrich Ludwig Langstedt, Georg Forster and Colonialism Discourse in Eighteenth-Century Germany." *History* 95:317 (2010): 2–42.

Tzoref-Ashkenazi, Chen. "German Voices from India: Officers of the Hanoverian Regiments in East India Company Service." *South Asia: Journal of South Asian Studies* 32:2 (2009): 189–211.

Veigl, Franz Xavier. *Franz Xavier Veigl vormaliger Mißionar der Gesellschaft Jesu. Gründliche Nachrichten über die Verfassung der Landschaft von Maynas in Süd-Amerika bis zum Jahre 1768 nebst des Herrn P. Anselm Eckarts Zusätze zu Pedro Cudenas Beschreibung der Länder von Brasilien* (Nürnberg: Zeh, 1798).

"Vermehrung des Berlinischen Museums der Naturgeschichte." *Repertorium des Neuesten und Wissenswürdigsten aus der Gesammten Naturkunde* 4 (1812): 93–94.

Vespucci, Amerigo. "Reisen nach Brasilien von 1501 bis 1504." *Neue Beiträge zur Völker- und Länderkunde* 10 (1792): 245–272.

Vieira, António. *Hundertjährige Trost-Rede aus Brasilien für die schweigende Gesellschaft Jesu in Europa, oder Rede des ehrwürdigen Vatters Antonius Viejra [...] in der königlichen Capelle zu Lisabon im Jahre 1662*. Trans. Goßwin Theodor von Dille (Augsburg: Wagner, 1762).

Vieira, António. *Zwote hundert-jährige Trost-Rede aus Brasilien für die schweigende Gesellschaft Jesu in Europa, oder zwote Rede des ehrwürdigen Vaters Antonius Viejra [...] drey Tage vor seiner geheimen Ab- und Zurück-Reise nach dem portugiesischen königlichen Hof: gehalten 1654*. Trans. Goßwin Theodor von Dille (Augsburg: Wagner, 1763).

Wehrs, Georg Friedrich. "Etwas von den Brasilianischen Thieren, Bäumen, Früchten und andern Pflanzen." *Hannoverisches Magazin* 17 (1779): 801–812.

Wehrs, Georg Friedrich. "Von der Religion der wilden Brasilianer, ihren Heyrathen und übrigen Gebräuchen." *Hannoverisches Magazin* 17 (1779): 921–934.

Wilke, Jürgen. *Literarischen Zeitschriften des 18. Jahrhunderts (1688–1789)*. (Stuttgart: Metzler, 1978).

Wink, Georg. "Brasilien als 'vorgestellte Gemeinschaft'? Eine kulturwissenschaftliche Untersuchung der Erzählung Brasiliens vom Reich zur Nation im lateinamerikanischen Kontrast" (PhD diss., Mainz, 2008).

Wolf, Peter. "Protestantischer 'Jesuitismus' im Zeitalter der Aufklärung. Christoph Gottlieb von Murr (1733–1811) und die Jesuiten." *Zeitschrift für Bayerische Landesgeschichte* 62 (1999): 99–137.

Zeh, Johann Eberhard, ed. *Historisch-geographische Beschreibung von Amerika für Jünglinge* (Nürnberg: Zeh, 1784).

Gabi Kathöfer
Devouring Culture: Cannibalism, National Identity, and Nineteenth-Century German Emigration to Brazil

South America's relevance for German identity construction and for political decision-making has long been ignored in the field of German studies. It was Susanne Zantop's groundbreaking study on *Colonial Fantasies* (1997)[1] in precolonial Germany that disclosed the eighteenth- and nineteenth-century German fixation on South America and revealed the interrelation of Germans' subconscious desire for colonies and their anxiety about loss of racial, cultural, and political identity.[2] However, Zantop's innovative study of nineteenth-century German colonial imagination did not address the German interest in Brazil, and it failed to consider the *existing* German immigrant communities and their influence on German precolonial fantasies and German emigration politics. The impact of German settlements in Brazil on cultural identity constructions in both countries and their cultural interrelations remains to be explored.

This chapter centers on the German presence in Brazil and undertakes an analysis of nineteenth-century German-Brazilian interculturalities pertaining to German colonization in Brazil. German emigration to Brazil was of great importance for nineteenth-century German and Brazilian cultural identity. In the German states, Brazil was imagined as either a utopian or a dystopian model for

---

1 Susanne Zantop, *Colonial Fantasies. Conquest, Family, and Nation in Precolonial Germany, 1770–1870* (Durham, NC: Duke University Press, 1997). Zantop pointed out that South America served a special function for Germans; reports on the foreign continent triggered and satisfied the German curiosity in exotic lands, thereby providing the people with an intellectual control of the uncivilized Other; South America became "an imaginary testing ground for colonial action" (6) in precolonial Germany: "As readers of travelogues and accounts of South America, German *Hausväter* and *Hausmütter* are becoming active participants in this great civilizing enterprise: they approve, disapprove, suffer, rejoice, with every step man takes toward greater control of nature and the natural universe. [...] By providing readers with a measuring stick to assess their own superiority vis-à-vis other cultures, travelogues and other 'scientific' writings engaged in what one might call intellectual colonialism" (41). Like the writings on other areas in South America, scientific explorations and travelogues on Brazil, its nature, and its native tribes, were essential sources for the "civilizing enterprise."
2 For this common feature of "colonial anxiety" (in relation to the British Empire), see also David Spurr, *The Rhetoric of Empire: Colonial Discourse in Journalism, Travel Writing, and Imperial Administration The Rhetoric of Empire: Colonial Discourse in Journalism, Travel Writing, and Imperial Administration* (Durham, NC: Duke University Press, 1993).

German communal identity. In Brazil, Germans were portrayed either as the bearers of (white) civilization or as a peril for national safety. The discussions in both countries were based on cultural essentialism and influenced one another through travel writing, letters, political propaganda, and human interaction. In this chapter, I analyze the cultural identity constructions on both sides and focus on their interrelation as a reciprocal process of intercultural negotiation and creation of meaning, knowledge, and power.

In my analysis of nineteenth-century German-Brazilian interculturalities, the concept of cannibalism will serve as the *tertium comparationis*. Read as a cipher for intercultural influence and conflict, the discussions of cannibalism reveal the translational dynamics between the two cultures in the nineteenth century and can therefore provide insights into Brazilian and German identity politics. When thinking about cannibalism in the German-Brazilian context, two texts immediately come to mind: Hans Staden's famous report *Wahrhaftige Historia und Beschreibung einer Landschaft der wilden, nackten, grimmigen Menschenfresser, in der Neuen Welt Amerika gelegen* (1557) and Oswaldo de Andrade's *Manifesto Antropófago* (1928). Both texts played a critical role in the history of Brazil and, more importantly, in the history of German-Brazilian interrelations. Using the texts by Staden and Andrade as a framework, I position nineteenth-century German emigration in the intersection of German colonial desire and its subversion by Brazilian modernists and evaluate the nineteenth century as one of the most essential times in the history of German-Brazilian interculturalities.

Cannibalism: a trope of identity

The concept of cannibalism offers an innovative framework for the study of German emigration to Brazil, when understood not as an action but as a trope of intercultural encounter. I follow Peter Hulme's distinction between the fantasy of being eaten by the Other (cannibalism) and the actual consumption of human beings (anthropophagy) and focus on the former to analyze German and Brazilian identity politics and their interrelations in the nineteenth century.[3] Moreover, I rely on William Arens's study *Man-Eating Myth* (1979) and the many, mostly postcolonial studies following his account that define cannibalism as a myth constructed about other cultures in order to justify identity construction and be-

---

[3] Peter Hulme, *Colonial Encounters: Europe and the Native Caribbean, 1492–1797* (London: Routledge, 1986), 86.

havior toward the Other.⁴ Arens was among the first scholars who questioned the credibility of eyewitness reports on cannibalism as historical, objective documentation; furthermore, he argued that the definition of non-Western "savages" as cannibals was not only a Western obsession but also an important prerequisite for colonial conquest. According to Arens, cannibalism is an invention, a product of European imperialism and a justification of colonialism.⁵ Arens's historical skepticism initiated a postcolonial reevaluation of the "appropriation of the cannibal in terms of Europe's own preexisting values and prejudgments stemming from its past,"⁶ which in itself has been interpreted as the "cultural cannibalism of colonialism, [...] the projection of western imperialist appetites onto the cultures they then subsumed."⁷ From this perspective, cannibalism becomes a trope of identity for the creation of alterity.

It is the fantasy of a cultural cannibalism on which my approach to nineteenth-century German emigration centers. It has been shown how the imagination of the cannibal facilitated the definition of Brazilian identity on both the German and the Brazilian side: For Brazilian modernists, the desire to liberate oneself from nineteenth-century Western influence resulted in the reclamation of the country's cultural, cannibalistic roots, expressed most explicitly in Oswaldo de Andrade's infamous *Manifesto Antropófago*. On the German side, the imagination of Brazil had centered around the image of the cannibal since the sixteenth century: "Cannibalism was used from the earliest colonial moment to 'define, qualify, name, and classify' the Brazilians who were otherwise unknown to Europeans."⁸ The most important sources for the German fascination with Brazil were the travel reports by Columbus and Hans Staden. Whereas Columbus created the term and concept of the "modern" cannibal, it was Staden's famous *Historia* that gave Brazil reality and presence in the German mind.⁹

---

4 William Arens, *The Man-Eating Myth: Anthropology & Anthropophagy* (New York: Oxford University Press, 1979).
5 His position has initiated heated debates on the reality of cannibalism, and his argument has been highly criticized and misinterpreted, especially in its association with Holocaust denial.
6 Gananath Obeyesekere, *Cannibal Talk. The Man-Eating Myth and Human Sacrifice in the South Seas* (Berkeley: University of California Press, 2005), 4.
7 Maggie Kilgour, *From Communion to Cannibalism. An Anatomy of Metaphors of Incorporation* (Princeton, NJ: Princeton University Press, 1990), VII.
8 Carole Myscofski, "Imagining Cannibals: European Encounters with Native Brazilian Women," *History of Religions* 47.2/3 (2007–2008): 150.
9 For the history of the idea of the cannibal beginning from the Greeks of Homer and for the geographic confusion that equated the Caribs of the Antilles, Guyana, and western Venezuela with the equally unknown Tupinambás of the Brazilian coast, see Frank Lestringant, *Cannibals. The Discovery and Representation of the Cannibal from Columbus to Jules Verne* (Berkeley: Uni-

What is less discussed, though, is the fact that the German cannibalistic imagination influenced German self-definition, too, and that nineteenth-century German and Brazilian identity construction are intertwined. The *Manifesto* refers to Staden's *Wahrhaftige Historia* as one of the essential sources about Brazilian cannibalism. This reference points toward the German influence on Brazilian cultural identity construction and calls for a closer analysis of nineteenth-century German emigration in the context of European imperialist appetite. Furthermore, recent research on the famous *Historia* emphasizes not only that it is "a fundamental text in the history and discovery of Brazil"[10] but also, and more importantly, that it is an *invention* of Brazil with political overtones. In this vein, scholars such as Richard John Ascárate move beyond the question of authenticity and place Brazil and Brazilian cannibalism in the context of German history.[11] From this perspective, an interpretation of cannibalism ought to include a reflection of German identity construction, especially with regard to the German obsession with Brazil as part of a general fixation on South America in the nineteenth century. Analyzing the fantasy of cannibalism can therefore disclose the translational dialogue between the two cultures in the nineteenth century and allow us to reevaluate German emigration to Brazil as a key event that linked German and Brazilian identity politics in the nineteenth and early twentieth century.

---

versity of California Press, 1997). For detailed information of Staden's *Historia*, see Donald Forsyth, "Three Cheers for Hans Staden: The Case for Brazilian Cannibalism," *Ethnohistory* 32.1 (1985): 17–36; Annerose Menninger, "Hans Stadens *Warhaftige Historia*. Zur Geschichte eines Bestsellers der Reiseliteratur," *Geschichte in Wissenschaft und Unterricht* 9 (1984): 509–523; Michaela Schmölz-Häberlein and Mark Häberlein, "Hans Staden, Neil L. Whitehead, and the Cultural Politics of Scholarly Publishing," *The Hispanic American Historical Review* 81 (2001): 745–751; Neil Whitehead, "Hans Staden and the Cultural Politics of Cannibalism," *Hispanic American Historical Review* 80 (2000): 721–751.
10 Neil Whitehead, "Hans Staden and the Cultural Politics of Cannibalism," *Hispanic American Historical Review* 80 (2000): 721.
11 Ascárate interprets the text as Protestant propaganda with a rhetorical purpose as well as political and theological implications "that may not have eluded contemporaneous readers." Richard John Ascárate, "Translating Cannibalism, or the Possible Politics of Representation in Hans Staden's *Warhaftig Historia* (1557)," *Interdisciplinary Journal for Germanic Linguistics and Semiotic Analysis* 9.2 (2004): 304.

A perfect match? Push and pull factors of nineteenth-century German emigration to Brazil

Nineteenth-century German mass emigration was a response to the unsatisfying conditions in the homeland. Deeply disappointed by the outcome of the French Revolution, the German people had been defeated by Napoleon and were frustrated by the continuing fragmentation of their fatherland. Many had been repressed by political censorship and weakened by the economic depression. Even before the failed revolution of 1848, many Germans decided to swap their homeland for political and intellectual freedom, or, more often, they left in order to survive.[12] Although the majority of emigrants (about 90 percent) settled in North America, many Germans hoped for a better life in South America, and Brazil became the third most popular emigration destination for Germans.

Brazil's popularity among German emigrants in the nineteenth century originated from a long history of travel reports and fantasies about the South American country. The German interest in Brazil awoke in the sixteenth century when the first German travelers began to explore the country and to write about its exotic animals, beautiful wilderness, and dangerous, cannibalistic indigenous tribes. Various accounts of Brazil followed in the seventeenth and eighteenth centuries.[13] At that point in German history, the German interest in Brazil was part of a general interest in travel reports in Europe; travel writing had "become the most important medium of information on foreign countries."[14] At the turn of the nineteenth century, then, it was Alexander von Humboldt's travel account

---

[12] Horst Rößler, "Massenexodus: die Neue Welt des 19. Jahrhunderts," in *Deutsche im Ausland – Fremde in Deutschland. Migration in Geschichte und Gegenwart.* Ed. Klaus Bade (Munich: Beck, 1992), 149. For more information on the sociopolitical background of nineteenth-century German emigration, see David Blackbourn, *The Long Nineteenth Century. A History of Germany, 1780 – 1918* (Oxford: Oxford University Press, 1998); Peter Marschalck, *Deutsche Überseewanderung im 19. Jahrhundert* (Stuttgart: Klett, 1973); or Mack Walker, *Germany and the Emigration 1816 – 1885* (Cambridge, MA: Harvard University Press, 1964).

[13] To name a few: Straubinger Ulrich Schmiedel traveled to the *Presillg Landt* in 1534. In 1627, Johann Gregor Aldenburgk published his *Westindianische Reiße*. Jesuit Pater Samuel Fritz created the first map of Brazil: *Mappa geografico del Rio Maranhão hecha por el padre Samuel Fritz de al Compania de Jesus, Missionero in este mismo Rio Amazonas – El anno 1691.* Pater Franz X. Veigl published *Gründliche Nachrichten über Verfassung und Landschaft von Maynas in Südamerika bis zum Jahre 1768* (1785) in Nürnberg.

[14] Thomas Grosser, "Der mediengeschichtliche Funktionswandel der Reiselektüre in den Berichten deutscher Reisender aus dem Frankreich des 18. Jahrhunderts," in *Europäisches Reisen im Zeitalter der Aufklärung.* Ed. Hans-Wolf Jäger (Heidelberg: Winter, 1992), 275.

that further intensified the German fascination with South America.[15] This new German obsession with South America increasingly concentrated on Brazil, as Christian August Fischer observed in 1819: "So it seems that collecting natural specimens in Brazil has become a speculative venture."[16]

Numerous nineteenth-century adventurous travelers explored the South American country and described Brazil "enthusiastically and with the use of superlatives, underscoring how exotic the sight of such opulent greenery and teeming life was to European travelers."[17] Prince Maximilian of Wied-Neuwied, for example, wrote in *Reise nach Brasilien* (1820–1821), "The European who finds himself for the first time in these tropical regions will be drawn to the beauty of nature from everywhere, especially to the opulent and rich vegetation."[18] Descriptions by travelers such as Wied-Neuwied created the imagery and vocabulary that influenced the evaluation of Brazil as a popular emigration destination in subsequent centuries: The South American country was defined as a space where Germans could establish a new German society in private peace and in harmony with nature. In that vein, the first literary text on German emigration to Brazil to appear in German-speaking Europe, Amalia Schoppe's *Die Auswanderer nach Brasilien oder die Hütte am Gigitonhonha* (1828), depicted Brazil as an exotic version of the *Heimat:* "A stately cottage, or rather a comfortable house, furnished with all of the European comforts rises above the banks of the beautiful, crystal clear river; next to the cottage lies a large, well-appointed garden filled with the most precious and rare fruits, and beyond the garden are splendid acres that provide them with all of life's necessities."[19]

The positive travel reports became an important political instrument in the turbulent nineteenth century as German politicians and economists used them

---

[15] Brigitte Hoppe's article "Nach dem Vorbild Humboldts in Südamerika: Erweiterung der Kenntnisse und Erkenntnisse durch deutsche Naturforscher" includes a list of German scientists in the eighteenth and nineteenth centuries (in *Ansichten Amerikas: neuere Studien zu Alexander von Humboldt*. Ed. Ottomar Ette and Walther Bernecker (Frankfurt am Main: Vervuert, 2001), 195–218). Hubertus Rescher's monograph on *Die deutschsprachige Literatur zu Brasilien von 1789–1850* (Frankfurt am Main: Lang, 1979) also provides valuable and detailed information.
[16] Christian August Fischer, *Neueste Gemälde von Brasilien* (Leipzig: Hartleben, 1819), 116. All German quotations in this article were translated by Christen Sohnholz.
[17] Cerue Diggs, "Brazil After Humboldt: Triangular Perceptions and the Colonial Gaze in Nineteenth-Century German Travel Narratives" (PhD diss., University of Maryland, 2008), 151.
[18] Maximilian von Wied-Neuwied, *Reise nach Brasilien in den Jahren 1815 bis 1817* (Frankfurt am Main: H.L. Brönner, 1820), 28.
[19] Amalia Schoppe, *Die Auswanderer nach Brasilien oder die Hütte am Gigitonhonha; nebst noch andern moralischen und unterhaltenden Erzählungen für die geliebte Jugend von 10 bis 14 Jahren* (Berlin: Amelang, 1828), 132.

to promote Brazil as a solution for the social crisis in the German states. They evaluated emigration in terms of its impact on domestic policies and claimed that colonies in Brazil would lead to better living conditions in the German states. The majority of emigrating Germans belonged to the lower social stratum (rural peasantry and village artisans), and the relocation of the excess masses ("überflüssige Masse") and lazy people ("müßiges Volk") was considered the best remedy against revolution ("Heilmittel gegen Revolutionen"): "Only emigration can change the unnatural situation in the German states. The excess masses have to leave in order to restore the past repose and lost happiness for the ones left behind."[20] The establishment of agrarian communities in foreign territory was to counteract the overpopulation and lack of resources in the German states. Thus, Brazil emerged as "a mythical site for the recreation of the nation."[21]

The benefits of German-Brazilian relations was not just promoted by German politicians, however; the Brazilian government, too, wanted to raise the popularity of its country among Europeans, especially Germans. After Brazil's independence in 1822, the founder and first ruler of the Empire of Brazil, Dom Pedro I (1798–1834), tried to attract European settlers by promising free passage, free land, and state subsidies for seeds, tools, and other needs. He also invested in recruitment agents and advertisements in German newspapers and reports that portrayed Brazil as an ideal place for German settlements.[22] The establishment of European settlements in southern Brazil was intended to populate uninhabited areas and to prevent military encroachments by neighboring countries. Thus, German immigration was not a spontaneous movement but an endeavor organized and encouraged by the Brazilian government.

---

20 Franz Xavier Ackermann, *Das Kaiserreich Brasilien. Beobachtung und praktische Bemerkung für deutsche Auswanderer* (Heidelberg, 1834), 16. Moreover, there was an economic motivation behind the positive evaluation of German emigration to Brazil as the entry on "Colonien" in the *Conversationslexikon der neuesten Zeit und Literatur* (1832) indicates: "In general, the world is meant to feed humankind, and no one people has the right to exclude other people from a land which it does not need, at least if it is not interested in the kind of progress that the transition to agriculture means" (473).
21 Sebastian Conrad, *Globalisation and the Nation in Imperial Germany* (New York: Cambridge University Press, 2010), 291.
22 For further information, see Ana-Isabel Aliaga-Buchenau, "German Immigrants in Blumenau, Brazil: National Identity in Gertrud Gross-Hering's Novels," *The Latin Americanist* 50.2 (2007): 5–21; Débora Bendocchi Alves, *Das Brasilienbild der deutschen Auswanderungswerbung im 19. Jahrhundert* (Berlin: Wissenschaftlicher Verlag Berlin, 2000); Klaus Bade, *Europa in Bewegung. Migration vom späten 18. Jahrhundert bis zur Gegenwart* (Munich: Beck, 2002); Fritz Sudhaus, *Deutschland und die Auswanderung nach Brasilien im 19. Jahrhundert* (Hamburg: Hans Christians Verlag, 1940); or Mack Walker, *Germany and the Emigration 1816–1885* (Cambridge, MA: Harvard University Press, 1964).

German emigration was also connected to the discussion on Brazil's labor shortage and the increasing international pressure on Brazil to abolish slavery. The emperor's goal to replace slaves with immigrant labor initiated a discussion on the genotypical and phenotypical characteristics of the worker and citizen that would make a significant contribution to Brazil's development and future, and Brazilian propaganda centered on the myth of the diligent German colonist. Visconde de Abrantes, a Brazilian diplomat in Berlin and an important figure in the debate on the Brazilian future in the nineteenth century, was among the many intellectuals who strongly supported the recruitment of Germans because "the aptitude of these settlers for agricultural work, for arts and crafts, and their peaceful and conservative spirit are proven by the most authentic testimony. [...] Love of work and of family, temperance, resignation, respect for authority are qualities which generally distinguish German settlers from those of other origins."[23] Although German immigration was numerically insignificant in comparison to other immigrant groups (Italians, Spaniards, and Portuguese), the German colonist was often depicted as the ideal settler to fill Brazil's cultural and geographic emptiness.[24]

In the beginning, German emigration to Brazil seemed to serve both countries well; both sides believed that it would help solve their national crisis and improve the situation of their nation. Nineteenth-century German-Brazilian relations were characterized by a mutual interest in the other; while Germans hoped that Brazilian land would provide a new German home, the Brazilian government believed in German virtues, values, and whiteness for the improvement of its society. However, the hopes on both sides emanated from an invention,

---

23 Visconde de Abrantes, "Memória sobre os meios de promover a colonização," *Revista de Imigração e Colonização* II (1941): 833.

24 "In spite of the numerical insignificance of these numbers vis-à-vis the three main immigrant groups – Italians, Spaniards, and Portuguese – that represented more than 70 percent of the total immigration to Brazil, German immigration was fundamental in the articulation of the colonization system. Until the middle of the 1870s, the majority of the colonies established in the South were German. Colonization policy during the empire held Germans to be the ideal colonists." Giralda Seyferth, "German Immigration and Brazil's Colonization Policy," in *Mass Migration to Modern Latin America*. Ed. Samuel Baily and Eduardo José Míguez (Wilmington, DE: Scholarly Resources Inc., 2003), 229. The abolishment of slavery was mainly the result of international pressure (especially from England) and racist theory apparent in the writings of prominent figures of the abolition movement, such as Jaoquim Nabuco. In his speeches, Nabuco distinguished between the superior, white race and the inferior, black and yellow ones. He called for a flow of European immigration bearing human and universal values. Like Nabuco, many so-called social reformers of the nineteenth century expressed the desire of whites' omnipresence and omnipotence in Brazil.

a myth of the other culture, and soon after the first intercultural encounters had taken place, anticipation and attraction turned into disappointment and aversion. As the result of a mutual fear of cultural identity loss, both sides began to define and protect their identity against the other culture's "devouring" nature.

Brasilianische Menschenjagd [Brazilian man hunt]

Despite the numerous positive descriptions of its exotic nature, a plethora of warnings against Brazil's untamed, dangerous wilderness circulated in Europe throughout the nineteenth century. As Frederick Luebke points out, "Many emigration pamphlets, books, and periodicals published in Germany [...] described Brazil as undesirable or unattractive for Germans."[25] Traveler Ida Pfeiffer, for example, expressed her disappointment in her travelogue as follows:

> In Europe, I had heard and read much about the splendor and lushness of Brazil's nature, and about the perpetually bright and smiling sky. About the wonderful appeal of eternal spring. It is true that the vegetation here is so opulent, the growth is strong and luxuriant, maybe like in no other country in the world, and that everyone who wants to see nature's work in its full power and in its ceaseless activity, has to come to Brazil. However, no one should believe that everything will be beautiful here, that everything will be good, that there will be nothing that could diminish the magic of the first impression. We all celebrate nature's everlasting Green at first and spring's endless magnificence, but we willingly admit in the end that all of this loses its attraction with time.[26]

The demotion of Brazilian nature was often influenced by negative descriptions of the German colonies. Soon after the first colonies had been established in Brazil, German emigrants, scientists, and travelers increasingly started to report on the horrific situation on the ships, Brazil's unbearably hot climate, the terrible living and working conditions in the German colonies, and the settlers' isolation in remote areas of the tropical forests. Fervent opponents of emigration to Brazil deployed the image of the "thoroughly rough, violent and untamed nature still

---

[25] Frederick Luebke, *Germans in the New World: Essays in the History of Immigration* (Urbana: University of Illinois Press, 1990), 11. The positive observations held true for some colonies, but only for a few successful settlements such as Blumenau and Joinville: "These were exceptional success stories and were heralded as such in numerous German articles." Ute Ritz-Deutch, "Alberto Vojtech Fric, the German Diaspora, and Indian Protection in Southern Brazil, 1900–1920: A Transatlantic Ethno-Historical Case Study" (PhD diss., Binghamton University, 2008), 96.
[26] Ida Pfeiffer, *Eine Frau reist um die Welt. Die Reise 1846 nach Südamerika, China, Ostindien, Persien und Kleinasien* (Vienna: Promedia, 2005), 27.

everywhere"[27] to counteract the positive advertisements about Brazil and to discourage Germans from emigrating to Brazil.

The discussions of Brazilian wilderness in the context of German settlements abroad revealed another important component of Germans' imagination of nineteenth-century Brazil: Despite European efforts to define the South American country scientifically, the myth and fear of Brazilian cannibalism lived on in the nineteenth century as Ina von Binzer's descriptions of her experience with German explorers in Brazil humorously illustrate:

> He lunged forward, breathless, soiled from head to toe, one boot covered with a layer of slime, the other one completely replaced by slime, no glasses or hat, [...] holding the empty butterfly net like a flag – the scraps of a German scholar who had left to research nature! Panting, he sat down on the bank; the doctor looked at him, horrified, and then looked at me imploringly, right as I blurted out: "What happened?!" "Happened?! Ach! Oh! I'm being chased! Someone wants to kill me! Murder! Whew! Oh, my precious plants – such an orchid! And these interesting sand fleas [...] ah, I had a magnificent specimen under my magnifying glass [...]!" "But then who in the world is chasing you?" "Who? The wild, the cannibals, the – ack!" [...] At that moment, the black man approached, completely breathless. He held a field manual of botany in his left hand, and in the right hand, he held a field manual of entomology. [...] "*Sim, sim Senhor*," said the black man, "the German man visiting *Senhor* is crazy." Neither of us could choke down our laughter.[28]

Although Binzer's text emphasizes the absurdity of the scientist's behavior, it documents the complex meshing of old imagery of Brazil and the nineteenth-century debate on German emigration; passed-on images of Brazilian cannibalistic destruction entered the discussion of German national future. In their endeavor to influence Germans not to leave their homeland, nineteenth-century writers resorted to the set of imagery and vocabulary of Brazil that early travel writings had introduced: It was argued that Germans merely served as human fertilizer ("Völkerdünger")[29] and "nutriment" to reinvigorate and strengthen the foreign nation while losing their own cultural identity. In that vein, the "Brasilianische Menschenjagd" (1858) [Brazilian man hunt], a series of articles in the *Illustrirte Zeitung*, described the emigration process and especially the recruitment methods as a hunt for humans that started in the German states with

---

27 Carl Friedrich Philip Martius and Johann B. von Spix, *Reise nach Brasilien in den Jahren 1817–1820* (Munich: M. Lindauer, 1823), I/90.
28 Ina von Binzer, *Leid und Freud einer Erzieherin in Brasilien*. Ed. Ray-Güde Mertin (Frankfurt am Main: Teo Ferrer de Mesquita, 1994), 42.
29 H. Schentke, *Mahnruf gegen die Auswanderung nach Brasilien* (Berlin, 1873). Cit. Fritz Sudhaus, *Deutschland und die Auswanderung nach Brasilien im 19. Jahrhundert* (Hamburg: Hans Christians Verlag, 1940),152.

the capture of emigrants by recruiting agents and often ended with the settlers' exploitation, if not death in Brazil. The nineteenth-century Brazilian "human hunters" were presented as a "civilized" version of Staden's naked, wild, ferocious cannibals ("wilden, nackten, grimmigen Menschenfresser"), for both groups seemed to belong to the same "proud people, very cunning and always ready to persecute and devour their enemies."[30]

Besides the exploitation of German workers, the German fear of Brazilian devouring nature centered on cultural identity loss. It was argued that German settlers would be lost for the German nation because their essential German cultural values and virtues would not be preserved. In that vein, Therese of Bavaria observed, "These people lose their family traditions so fast, and the immigrants make very little effort to transmit even the slightest knowledge about their homeland to their offspring."[31] The fictional stories by German settler Therese Stutzer present another good example of Germans' fear of losing their cultural values in Brazil: In "Vor fünfzig Jahren," Stutzer depicts a dystopia of German *Gemütlichkeit* (coziness):

> Seelbach opened the front door which, as usual, was slightly ajar, and he and his companions entered a room which looked like a venda. Dirt was on the table and on the benches, cockroaches ran around, the air smelled like schnapps. From a side door, a woman appeared, just as filthy as her surroundings. She shook hands with the men. As she wanted to greet Elise in the same manner, she could not help going back a few steps.[32]

Germans in the fatherland mourned the loss of their fellow citizens in Brazil that fell victim to the barbaric nature of Brazil and its citizens. The concern about the destiny of Germans in Brazil grew so strong that German politicians decided to intervene in the second half of the century. Although the situation of German settlers in Brazil was not addressed on a federal level, governments such as Bavaria and Prussia decided to tighten measures against the settlers' exploitation in Brazil.[33] Bavaria temporarily prohibited emigration to Brazil in 1852, and after Prus-

---

30 Hans Staden, *Wahrhaftige Historia und Beschreibung einer Landschaft der wilden, nackten, grimmigen Menschenfresser, in der Neuen Welt Amerika gelegen* (Marburg 1557), 213.
31 Therese von Bayern, *Meine Reise in den brasilianischen Tropen* (Berlin: Verlag von Dietrich Reimen, 1897), 419.
32 Therese Stutzer, *Am Rande des brasilianischen Urwaldes* (Braunschweig: Hellmuth Wollermann Verlagsbuchhandlung, 1889), 112.
33 From the beginning, there was a strong opposition to German colonies in the underdeveloped, dangerous country Brazil. However, the southern states Baden and Bavaria, the first states affected by German emigration, were among the few governments that actively reacted to the increasing numbers of emigrants to South America. Because of negative reports on Brazil from German travelers and after alarming news about the situation in Swiss colonies, the

sia had tried to discourage emigration by forbidding advertisements in the 1820s, it introduced the *Heydtsche Reskript* (1859–1895), which "officially discouraged emigration to Brazil [...] [and] also curtailed the recruitment activities of agents and ship owners."[34] Overall, Brazil became the most contested destination for emigrating Germans: "Germans debated and opposed Brazil as an emigration destination more than any other country."[35] This ongoing debate on German settlements in Brazil provided a platform for the discussion and definition of German identity, and the focus on the preservation of authentic German culture and civilization – that was at risk of being swallowed up in the maw of Brazilian barbarism – contributed to the rise of German nationalism and the pan-German movement toward the end of the century.

A questão do perigoso allemanismo [The question of the dangerous "Germanness"]

It was not only the German view on Brazil that took a turn for the worse in the nineteenth century. The Brazilian attitude toward its German immigrant communities changed drastically in the second half of the century, too, and discussions on the future of the country began to center on *o perigo alemão* ("the German danger"), Germans' colonial appetite. Thus, Brazilian identity politics also began to center on the imagination of a "devouring Other."

In the second half of the nineteenth century, Brazil underwent significant social and political changes, and these changes influenced the view on its immigrant communities. During the empire, the "elite thought more about slavery

---

Baden government forbade emigration to Brazil in 1824. From 1826 on, Baden, like Württemberg, tolerated emigration under the condition that the emigrants would have enough financial savings to conclude the journey. In Prussia a law was introduced in 1820 that penalized advertisements for emigration ("Verleitung zur Auswanderung"); see Agnes Bretting and Hartmut Bickelmann, *Auswanderungsagenturen und Auswanderungsvereine im 19. und 20. Jahrhundert* (Stuttgart: Steiner, 1991), 56.

34 Frederick Luebke, *Germans in the New World: Essays in the History of Immigration* (Urbana: University of Illinois Press, 1990), 11. For further information, see also Fritz Sudhaus, *Deutschland und die Auswanderung nach Brasilien im 19. Jahrhundert* (Hamburg: Hans Christians Verlag, 1940), 76.

35 Fritz Sudhaus, *Deutschland und die Auswanderung nach Brasilien im 19. Jahrhundert* (Hamburg: Hans Christians Verlag, 1940), 3. For detailed information on the states' regulations, see p. 27.

than about either color or race."[36] After slavery was abolished in 1888 and Pedro II was deposed by a Republican military coup in 1889, immigration became an important issue again, as Frederick Luebke explains:

> The republic had to demonstrate its authority and its ability to govern, a task made more difficult by the diffusion of political power among the states and the development of political parties on a state basis. The abolition of slavery had its own repercussions as many thousands of new immigrants were recruited [...] to supplement the labor supply. At the same time, the modernization of the economic structure of Brazil was under way, especially in the South.[37]

In Brazil's modernization process, the encouragement of European immigration became national policy; furthermore, all immigrants present in the country were given Brazilian nationality as the politicians of the República Velha (the Old Republic) focused on the definition of Brazil's unique racial future and saw immigration from Europe as a contribution to *embranquecimento,* the endeavor to whiten Brazil's population. In the words of famous literary critic Sílvio Romero,

> the white type will continue to predominate by natural selection until it emerges pure and beautiful as in the old world. That will come when it has totally acclimatized on this continent. Two factors will greatly contribute to this process: on the one hand the abolition of the slave trade and the continuous disappearance of the Indians, and on the other hand European immigration![38]

As Thomas Skidmore has analyzed in detail, the whitening theory was a compromise with racist determinism: "Instead of two exclusive ethnic categories, it presupposed a miraculous movement from black *into the direction of* white."[39] Although the theory centered on the belief that the white race was superior, the improvement of Brazilian society was envisioned as a continuous process of racial mixing. Therefore, what the Brazilian government had celebrated at the beginning of the nineteenth century became a thorn in Brazil's side toward the end

---

36 Thomas Skidmore, "Brazilian Intellectuals and the Problem of Race, 1870–1930," *The Graduate Center for Latin American Studies, Vanderbilt University. Occasional Paper* 6 (1969): 2.
37 Frederick Luebke, *Germans in the New World: Essays in the History of Immigration* (Urbana: University of Illinois Press, 1990), 124.
38 Sílvio Romero, *A Literatura brasileira e a crítica moderna* (Rio de Janeiro, 1880), 53. Cit. Thomas Skidmore, *Black into White. Race and Nationality in Brazilian Thought* (New York: Oxford University Press, 1974), 37.
39 Thomas Skidmore, "Brazilian Intellectuals and the Problem of Race, 1870–1930," *The Graduate Center for Latin American Studies, Vanderbilt University. Occasional Paper* 6 (1969): 4.

of the century: Germans' adherence to their distinct cultural values, virtues, and traditions.

Most German colonies in southern Brazil were established in remote rural areas, they remained in isolation and tended to exclude other ethnic groups for centuries: "Formalized ethnic boundaries included the daily use of the language and the creation of institutions to preserve the culture – in elementary schools that taught the German language, in the German-Brazilian press, and in German recreational, sporting, and cultural associations."[40] Furthermore, by the end of the nineteenth century the Teuto-Brazilians had became the most dominant minority in the southern provinces; "After seventy-five years the Germans had multiplied and prospered until they numbered nearly four hundred thousand persons, mostly Brazilian-born and German-speaking. [...] [T]hey created a society within a society – a large, isolated, diverse, structured community with its own values, attitudes, language, and folkways."[41] Therefore, a discussion of Brazil's racial future had to include a reflection on the country's German immigrant population and its cultural ties to the homeland.

Brazilian intellectuals pondered the role of the German immigrant community for Brazil's future. It is worth mentioning a few examples of Brazilian authors that incorporated German characters into their literary texts: Similar to previously cited descriptions in Ina von Binzer's diary, we find a caricature of a German scientist in Visconte Alfredo d'Escragnolle Taunay's *Inocência* (1872), with a "scientific rigor" ("rigorismo cientifico") and a "perfectly German diligence" ("minuciosidade perfeitamente germânica") but with the social, emotional, and intercultural intelligence of a child.[42] Mário de Andrade's *Amar, verbo intransitivo* (1927) introduces the character of a German governess "whose main charge is to give young Brazilian men their sexual initiation."[43] The most prominent example, however, is the novel *Canaã* (1902), by José Pereira da Graça Aranha. In *Canaã*, Aranha broached the issue of Brazil's cultural identity by presenting two German immigrants who discuss their opposing world views and attitudes (e. g., cosmopolitanism versus nationalism; racial mixing versus racial purity).

---

40 Giralda Seyferth, "German Immigration and Brazil's Colonization Policy," in *Mass Migration to Modern Latin America*. Ed. Samuel Baily and Eduardo José Míguez (Wilmington, DE: Scholarly Resources Inc., 2003), 238.
41 Frederick Luebke, *Germans in the New World: Essays in the History of Immigration* (Urbana: University of Illinois Press, 1990), 111.
42 Visconte Alfredo d'Escragnolle Taunay, *Inocência* (São Paulo: Atica, 1966 [1972]), 92, 215.
43 Mary Daniel, "Brazilian Fiction from 1900 to 1945," in *Cambridge History of Latin American Literature*. Ed. Roberto Gonzalez Echevarria and Enrique Pupo-Walker (Cambridge, England: Cambridge University Press, 1996), 169.

Canaã became one of the most popular books in Brazil.[44] However, it also provoked controversy among the country's intellectuals because the book's message was not directly spelled out: "Aranha seems to sympathize with Milkau, who rejects Lentz's racist theories. But the novel's moral was ambiguous enough for Aranha to arouse the fury of journalists and Congressmen, who attacked him of impugning Brazil's reputation."[45] Given the anti-German sentiment at the time, it can be suspected that it was not only the ambiguous moral of the book that caused such fury but also (and maybe more so) Aranha's choice of his protagonists' nationality.

Although Brazilian literary discussions on the German immigrant present very different German characters, they all address the German influence on Brazilian society as a potential problem for Brazil's future. In the words of Wolfgang Bader, "The German himself is of no interest to the authors [...]; rather, they cast their gaze on him only in as much as these stated clichéd characteristics distort into a foreignness that exists on Brazilian soil – a foreignness that directly affects the country itself. The treatment of the German is part of Brazil's self-definition."[46] Thus, it was not just their seclusion that made German immigrants suspicious in the eyes of the Brazilian elite but also, and more importantly, their otherness, their *Fremdheit*. German strangeness was said to increasingly threaten the equilibrium of Brazilian society because it could not be integrated into Brazilian society.

One of the most influential political texts in the debate of the German "danger" in Brazil is Sílvio Romero's *O Allemanismo no sul do Brasil* (The Germanism in the South of Brazil) (1906). In his pamphlet, Romero compares the German immigration movement to the barbarian invasion of the Roman Empire and warns against the continuing isolation and separation of German settlers in southern Brazil: "They are tight to us only through territorial bonds; because

---

44 "Along with *Os sertões*, *Canaã* was one of the most widely read and discussed books in Brazil in the early part of the century. *Canaã* is a work of ideas rather than actions, and one of the central ideas that Graça Aranha promotes is that culture in the broadest sense (*cultura*) is the ultimate answer to society's ills." Raymond Leslie Williams, *The Twentieth-Century Spanish American Novel* (Austin: University of Texas Press, 2003), 5.
45 Thomas Skidmore, "Brazilian Intellectuals and the Problem of Race, 1870–1930," *The Graduate Center for Latin American Studies, Vanderbilt University. Occasional Paper* 6 (1969): 4.
46 Wolfgang Bader, "Zwischen Metaphysik und Arbeit: Die Deutschen in der brasilianischen Literatur," *Komparatistische Hefte* 2.1 (1980): 67. For more information on the depiction of Germans in Brazilian literature, see also Erwin Theodor Rosenthal, "Die Deutschen in der brasilianischen Literatur," in *Brückenschlag. Lengua y cultura alemanas: un puente entre dos continentes*. Ed. Renate Koroschetz de Maragno (Caracas: Universidad Central de Venezuela, 2002), 103–121.

we can not talk about effective political bonds as we all know, they do not participate in our life in that respect."⁴⁷ Romero emphasized the need to address the question of the dangerous "Germanness" in the South of Brazil ("questão do perigoso allemanismo do Sul do Brasil") and to forcibly assimilate German immigrants by forbidding the use of the German language and relocating the population.

In Romero's text it becomes obvious that the German *Fremdheit* was not only a disruptive but also threatening element in Brazilian society. Germans' lack of interest in integrating themselves into Brazilian society on one hand and their strong ties to the German homeland on the other hand deeply concerned Brazilian politicians and intellectuals. Behind this concern was an even deeper concern: It was German colonial appetite that caused the strong anti-German sentiment at the end of the nineteenth century. Whereas Brazilian colonization policy during the empire had held Germans to be the ideal colonists, Brazilian politicians and theorists of the republic began to speak of the German "danger" to the Brazilian nation as they became suspicious of the political developments in Germany and of Germans' colonial ambition with regard to their presence in Brazil. This concern was well founded. In his analysis of *Globalisation and the Nation in Imperial Germany* (2010), Sebastian Conrad explains the relationship between nineteenth-century German emigration and colonial desire. Conrad distinguishes between two main phases of discussion about emigration in nineteenth-century Germany. Whereas the debates in the German states until 1870 focused on the advantages and disadvantages of emigration for the German nation, the debate from the 1870s onward "became a question of geography."⁴⁸ After German unification, the dismissal of Otto von Bismarck, and the adoption of the foreign policy of *Weltpolitik* by Wilhelm II, the topos of recreating Germanness gained currency in Germany, and southern Brazil became the destination of choice. Wilhelm II, along with conservative politicians and members of the Pan-German League, declared Brazil an ideal space for the establishment of a German cultural community.

Thus, although Brazil had become a thorn in the side of many German nationalists and politicians in the nineteenth century, Brazil's popularity peaked toward the turn of the century.⁴⁹ Nancy Mitchell explains the German predilection for Brazil toward the end of the nineteenth century as follows:

---

47 Sílvio Romero, *O Allemanismo no sul do Brasil* (Rio de Janeiro: Heitor Ribeiro, 1906).
48 Sebastian Conrad, *Globalisation and the Nation in Imperial Germany* (New York: Cambridge University Press, 2010), 277.
49 Friedrich Fabri was one of the representative propagandists for colonization in Brazil at the end of the nineteenth century. In his famous report *Bedarf Deutschland der Kolonien?* (Does Ger-

When pan-Germans [...] scanned the globe for places to build a New Germany, southern Brazil beckoned. There, the climate was pleasant, the land fertile, the natives friendly, and thousands of Germans already lived there. Moreover, the three southern states, particularly Rio Grande do Sul, were demographically congenial to the pan-Germans, imbued as their worldview was with racism: few indigenous people remained, few Africans had been brought there, whites were dominant, and among the whites, the Germans were preeminent.[50]

As the German politicians' focus switched from domestic affairs to the establishment of a global German community, the debate on Brazil returned to the previous celebration of the splendor and virginity of Brazil's nature, only this time with regard to pan-Germans' ideology on racial purity. Political measures followed toward the end of the century. In 1896, the *Heydtsche Reskript* was lifted, and the most important provisions of the 1897 Emigration Act focused on redirecting emigration: The preamble to the law stated, "[In Brazil] not only will the German preserve his nationality, but he will find [...] all the conditions favorable to a prosperous existence."[51] Furthermore, Wilhelmine policies supported Germanness abroad in numerous ways, for example by funding German schools, lecture tours, and performances by German theaters and by establishing embassies. Thus, for the newly established German Empire, emigration to Brazil was no longer a domestic issue but rather related to German imperial desires and the search for a "place in the sun."[52]

---

many need colonies?) (1879), Fabri considered South America an ideal region for a targeted emigration policy. He also advocated vigorously for German emigration to Brazil at the third general assembly of the German colonial society in 1886. For further information on Fabri, see Klaus Bade, *Friedrich Fabri und der Imperialismus in der Bismarckzeit: Revolution – Depression – Expansion* (Freiburg: Atlantis, 1975).
50 Nancy Mitchell, *The Danger of Dreams. German and American Imperialism in Latin America* (Chapel Hill: University of North Carolina Press, 1999), 113.
51 "The Significance of German Expansion," *Review of Reviews* 32 (January 1905): 116. Cit. Nancy Mitchell, *The Danger of Dreams. German and American Imperialism in Latin America* (Chapel Hill: University of North Carolina Press, 1999), 115.
52 Brazil seemed to offer the "place in the sun" for which the Germans longed, as German foreign secretary Bernhard von Bülow stated during a Reichstag debate in 1897: "In one word: we do not want to place anyone into the shadow, but we also claim our place in the sun." Johannes Penzler, ed., *Fürst Bülows Reden nebst urkundlichen Beiträgen zu seiner Politik* (Berlin: Georg Reimer, 1907). As Conrad points out, the fascination with Brazil was also related to a nostalgia for a premodern, preindustrial society: "When, confronted with Germanness of the South American settlements, visitors from Germany found themselves almost unable to believe that they were [...] 'not in Germany'; it was not Wilhelmine Germany they were reminded of, but the Germany 'of fifty or seventy-five years previously'. Here the past did not carry any sense of lacking or backwardness, but abundance: 'prosperity and sufficiency wherever one looks.'" (*Globalisation and*

It was this kind of "cultural cannibalism of colonialism"[53] which Brazilians in the Old Republic fought; they feared that Germany would try to establish a German protectorate and state in southern Brazil. Thus, toward the end of the nineteenth century, Germans' reputation in Brazil had changed from that of a role model to that of a disturbing, foreign element in society that, in the opinion of many, needed to be "tamed," removed, or even destroyed. The German immigrant had become a bogeyman for the young republic, a cultural cannibal that threatened to "devour" the southern part of the country. This development led to two different reactions in the early twentieth century. On one hand, the new perception of the German presence from the end of the nineteenth century on fueled nationalist sentiments, and after Brazil declared war on Germany in 1917, anti-German sentiment hit its peak; a series of destructive riots occurred, and numerous bans on German-language publications, schools, church services, and clubs were enacted.[54]

On the other hand, the conflict with the German immigrant community, Brazil's largest single minority group, accelerated the effort to construct a Brazilian national identity in the new republic, and this self-definition was asserted in opposition to the German Other: "The conflict acted as a catalyst, bringing the other nationalities in the country together."[55] The endeavor to define the Brazilian self in opposition to the German Other hit its peak in the modernists' subversion of European cultural cannibalism: the famous *Manifesto Antropófago* (1928) proclaimed cannibalism as the core of Brazilian cultural identity. And by referring to a German text, to Hans Staden's account on Brazil, as one of its main

---

the Nation 331). For information on Germans' hope for a New Germany in Brazil and U.S. perceptions of a German threat to the Monroe Doctrine, see Nancy Mitchell, *The Danger of Dreams. German and American Imperialism in Latin America* (Chapel Hill: University of North Carolina Press, 1999), 108.

53 Maggie Kilgour, *From Communion to Cannibalism. An Anatomy of Metaphors of Incorporation* (Princeton, NJ: Princeton University Press, 1990), VII.

54 "During the German emigration and colonization discussions of the 1880s and early 1890s, circulating, long-standing traditional nationalistic beliefs about a deviation from the German mass emigration from North America to South America, about a 'teutonization' of South American target areas through 'organized' immigration to establish a 'New Germany in South American,' and especially in Brazil, greatly underestimated the integrative power of the Brazilian nation state. They remained not only illusory, but also were counterproductive because at the beginning of the 1890s, they aroused long-lasting skepticism about the German immigration." Walther Bernecker and Thomas Fischer, "Deutsche in Lateinamerika," in *Deutsche im Ausland – Fremde in Deutschland. Migration in Geschichte und Gegenwart*. Ed. Klaus Bade (Munich: Beck, 1992), 205.

55 Sebastian Conrad, *Globalisation and the Nation in Imperial Germany* (New York: Cambridge University Press, 2010), 315.

sources, the *Manifesto* returned to the beginning of German-Brazilian interculturalities, and the German-Brazilian cannibalistic imagination had come full circle.

Da kommt unser Essen angehoppelt / ali vem a nossa comida pulando: devouring culture

"Brazil is not far from here": As the popular nineteenth-century folk song indicates, Brazil played an important role in nineteenth-century German life and imagination. The South American country had attracted Germans for centuries, but in the nineteenth century, when the faraway place was close to many people in the German states, more and more Germans decided to leave their homeland for Brazil. To a degree, this fascination was part of the Western obsession with South America, which Susanne Zantop's study on precolonial Germany addressed in detail. However, German-Brazilian interrelations deserve special attention as they are distinguished from the German interest in other South American countries for the following reasons:

- Nineteenth- and early twentieth-century German-Brazilian interrelations can be characterized as a mutual preoccupation with the other culture; the attraction was reciprocal as both countries shared an obsession for the other. Brazil was envisioned as a natural, virgin space where German culture would flourish, spread, and be preserved without any influence from other cultural communities, and German colonists were often seen as the ideal settlers to fill Brazil's cultural and geographic emptiness.
- What made the nineteenth-century German preoccupation with Brazil unique was the complex combination of *imaginative* power and *real* occupation of Brazilian land by German immigrants. Consequently, the image of the other country was based on a complex meshing of stereotypes and myths with actual intercultural experiences on both sides.
- For both German and Brazilian identity construction in the nineteenth century, German emigration played an important role, and the encouragement of German migration to Brazil at different times during the century was closely related to the cultural identity politics in both countries. Interestingly, as the interrelations progressed, both cultures began to feel threatened by the other culture; the hope that the other culture would enhance each nation's economic and cultural prosperity turned into the fear of being exploited by the other culture. Both cultures' continuous fluctuation between attraction and aversion toward the other culture manifests an ongoing process of intercultural negotiation of identity.

In this transatlantic discourse, the metaphor of the cannibal can help reveal the complexity of German-Brazilian interculturalities. The threat of cultural cannibalism was used to create images of alterity and define the Other as a danger to the own nation, thereby expressing and defending a certain racial, cultural, or national model of collective identity. On the German side, Brazil became a discussion forum for Germans' endangered national identity. While Brazil was celebrated as the ideal space to preserve authentic German culture, it was also condemned as a cannibalistic force that would devour German cultural identity; both perspectives on the South American country allowed the definition of authentic German cultural identity. The Brazilian government in turn was fascinated with German presumed essential cultural values and virtues, but at the same time it was concerned about German cultural separatism and, more importantly, colonial appetite. Thus, on both sides the cannibal metaphor served as a cipher for cultural repression as well as self-assertion.

The analysis of German-Brazilian interculturalities in the context of cultural cannibalism to Brazil allows us to challenge the dualities of civilization and barbarism and to supersede static oppositions in order to disclose the translational dynamics between the two cultures in the nineteenth century, and to focus on the reciprocal process of intercultural negotiation and creation of identity that German emigration to Brazil precipitated. Thus, the first sentence of Andrade's *Manifesto* could be applied to the cultures' complex interrelations and interdependencies and read as a definition of nineteenth-century German-Brazilian interculturalities:

> [A] Antropofagia nos une. Socialmente. Economicamente. Filosoficamente. [Cannibalism unites us. Socially. Economically. Philosophically.]

References

Abrantes, Visconde de. "Memória sobre os meios de promover a colonização." *Revista de Imigração e Colonização* II (1941): 833.
Ackermann, Franz Xavier. *Das Kaiserreich Brasilien. Beobachtung und praktische Bemerkung für deutsche Auswanderer* (Heidelberg, 1834).
Aliaga-Buchenau, Ana-Isabel. "German Immigrants in Blumenau, Brazil: National Identity in Gertrud Gross-Hering's Novels." *The Latin Americanist* 50.2 (2007): 5–21.
Alves, Débora Bendocchi. *Das Brasilienbild der deutschen Auswanderungswerbung im 19. Jahrhundert* (Berlin: Wissenschaftlicher Verlag Berlin, 2000).
Andrade, Oswaldo de. *Manifesto Antropófago* (1928).
Arens, William. *The Man-Eating Myth: Anthropology & Anthropophagy* (New York: Oxford University Press, 1979).

Ascárate, Richard John. "Translating Cannibalism, or the Possible Politics of Representation in Hans Staden's *Warhaftig Historia* (1557)." *Interdisciplinary Journal for Germanic Linguistics and Semiotic Analysis* 9.2 (2004): 304.

Bade, Klaus. *Europa in Bewegung. Migration vom späten 18. Jahrhundert bis zur Gegenwart* (Munich: Beck, 2002).

Bade, Klaus. *Friedrich Fabri und der Imperialismus in der Bismarckzeit: Revolution – Depression – Expansion* (Freiburg: Atlantis, 1975).

Bader, Wolfgang. "Zwischen Metaphysik und Arbeit: Die Deutschen in der brasilianischen Literatur." *Komparatistische Hefte* 2.1 (1980): 53–71.

Bernecker, Walther, and Thomas Fischer. "Deutsche in Lateinamerika," in *Deutsche im Ausland – Fremde in Deutschland. Migration in Geschichte und Gegenwart*. Ed. Klaus Bade (Munich: Beck, 1992).

Binzer, Ina von. *Leid und Freud einer Erzieherin in Brasilien*. Ed. Ray-Güde Mertin (Frankfurt am Main: Teo Ferrer de Mesquita, 1994).

Blackbourn, David. *The Long Nineteenth Century. A History of Germany, 1780–1918* (Oxford: Oxford University Press, 1998).

Bretting, Agnes, and Hartmut Bickelmann. *Auswanderungsagenturen und Auswanderungsvereine im 19. und 20. Jahrhundert* (Stuttgart: Steiner, 1991).

Conrad, Sebastian. *Globalisation and the Nation in Imperial Germany* (New York: Cambridge University Press, 2010).

Daniel, Mary. "Brazilian Fiction from 1900 to 1945," in *Cambridge History of Latin American Literature*. Ed. Roberto Gonzalez Echevarria and Enrique Pupo-Walker (Cambridge, England: Cambridge University Press, 1996).

Diggs, Cerue. "Brazil After Humboldt: Triangular Perceptions and the Colonial Gaze in Nineteenth-Century German Travel Narratives" (PhD diss., University of Maryland, 2008).

Fabri, Friedrich. *Bedarf Deutschland der Colonien?* Ed. Muriel Evelyn Chamberlain and E. C. M. Breuning (Lewiston, NY: Edwin Mellon Press, 1998). (Originally published 1879)

Fischer, Christian August. *Neueste Gemälde von Brasilien* (Leipzig: Hartleben, 1819).

Forsyth, Donald. "Three Cheers for Hans Staden: The Case for Brazilian Cannibalism," *Ethnohistory* 32.1 (1985): 17–36.

Grosser, Thomas. "Der mediengeschichtliche Funktionswandel der Reiselektüre in den Berichten deutscher Reisender aus dem Frankreich des 18. Jahrhunderts," in *Europäisches Reisen im Zeitalter der Aufklärung*. Ed. Hans-Wolf Jäger (Heidelberg: Winter, 1992).

Hoppe, Brigitte. "Nach dem Vorbild Humboldts in Südamerika: Erweiterung der Kenntnisse und Erkenntnisse durch deutsche Naturforscher," in *Ansichten Amerikas: neuere Studien zu Alexander von Humboldt*. Ed. Ottomar Ette and Walther Bernecker (Frankfurt am Main: Vervuert, 2001), 195–218.

Hulme, Peter. *Colonial Encounters: Europe and the Native Caribbean, 1492–1797* (London: Routledge, 1986).

Kilgour, Maggie. *From Communion to Cannibalism. An Anatomy of Metaphors of Incorporation* (Princeton, NJ: Princeton University Press, 1990).

Lestringant, Frank. *Cannibals. The Discovery and Representation of the Cannibal from Columbus to Jules Verne* (Berkeley: University of California Press, 1997).

Luebke, Frederick. *Germans in the New World: essays in the history of immigration* (Urbana: University of Illinois Press, 1990).

Marschalck, Peter. *Deutsche Überseewanderung im 19. Jahrhundert* (Stuttgart: Klett, 1973).
Martius, Carl Friedrich Philip, and Johann B. von Spix. *Reise nach Brasilien in den Jahren 1817–1820* (Munich: M. Lindauer, 1823), I/90.
Menninger, Annerose. "Hans Stadens *Warhaftige Historia*. Zur Geschichte eines Bestsellers der Reiseliteratur." *Geschichte in Wissenschaft und Unterricht* 9 (1984): 509–523.
Mitchell, Nancy. *The Danger of Dreams. German and American Imperialism in Latin America* (Chapel Hill: University of North Carolina Press, 1999).
Myscofski, Carole. "Imagining Cannibals: European Encounters with Native Brazilian Women." *History of Religions* 47.2/3 (2007–2008): 150.
Obeyesekere, Gananath. *Cannibal Talk. The Man-Eating Myth and Human Sacrifice in the South Seas* (Berkeley: University of California Press, 2005).
Penzler, Johannes, ed. *Fürst Bülows Reden nebst urkundlichen Beiträgen zu seiner Politik.* (Berlin: Georg Reimer, 1907).
Pfeiffer, Ida. *Eine Frau reist um die Welt. Die Reise 1846 nach Südamerika, China, Ostindien, Persien und Kleinasien* (Vienna: Promedia, 2005).
Rescher, Hubert. *Die deutschsprachige Literatur zu Brasilien von 1789–1850* (Frankfurt am Main: Lang, 1979).
Ritz-Deutch, Ute. "Alberto Vojtech Fric, the German Diaspora, and Indian Protection in Southern Brazil, 1900–1920: A Transatlantic Ethno-Historical Case Study" (PhD diss., Binghamton University, 2008).
Romero, Sílvio. *O Allemanismo no sul do Brasil* (Rio de Janeiro, 1906).
Romero, Sílvio. *A Literatura brasileira e a crítica moderna* (Rio de Janeiro, 1880).
Rosenthal, Erwin Theodor. "Die Deutschen in der brasilianischen Literatur," in *Brückenschlag. Lengua y cultura alemanas: un puente entre dos continents.* Ed. Renate Koroschetz de Maragno (Caracas: Universidad Central de Venezuela, 2002), 103–121.
Rößler, Horst. "Massenexodus: die Neue Welt des 19. Jahrhunderts," in *Deutsche im Ausland – Fremde in Deutschland. Migration in Geschichte und Gegenwart.* Ed. Klaus Bade (Munich: Beck, 1992).
Schentke, H. *Mahnruf gegen die Auswanderung nach Brasilien* (Berlin, 1873).
Schmölz-Häberlein, Michaela, and Mark Häberlein. "Hans Staden, Neil L. Whitehead, and the Cultural Politics of Scholarly Publishing." *The Hispanic American Historical Review* 81 (2001): 745–751.
Schoppe, Amalia. *Die Auswanderer nach Brasilien oder die Hütte am Gigitonhonha; nebst noch andern moralischen und unterhaltenden Erzählungen für die geliebte Jugend von 10 bis 14 Jahren* (Berlin: Amelang, 1828).
Seyferth, Giralda. "German Immigration and Brazil's Colonization Policy," in *Mass Migration to Modern Latin America.* Ed. Samuel Baily and Eduardo José Míguez (Wilmington, DE: Scholarly Resources Inc., 2003), 227–244.
Skidmore, Thomas. *Black into White. Race and Nationality in Brazilian Thought* (New York: Oxford University Press, 1974).
Skidmore, Thomas. "Brazilian Intellectuals and the Problem of Race, 1870–1930." *The Graduate Center for Latin American Studies, Vanderbilt University. Occasional Paper* 6 (1969).
Spurr, David. *The Rhetoric of Empire: Colonial Discourse in Journalism, Travel Writing, and Imperial Administration* (Durham, NC: Duke University Press, 1993).

Staden, Hans. *Wahrhaftige Historia und Beschreibung einer Landschaft der wilden, nackten, grimmigen Menschenfresser, in der Neuen Welt Amerika gelegen* (Marburg 1557).
Stutzer, Therese. *Am Rande des brasilianischen Urwaldes* (Braunschweig: Hellmuth Wollermann Verlagsbuchhandlung, 1889).
Sudhaus, Fritz. *Deutschland und die Auswanderung nach Brasilien im 19. Jahrhundert* (Hamburg: Hans Christians Verlag, 1940).
Taunay, Visconte Alfredo d'Escragnolle. *Inocência* (São Paulo: Atica, 1966).
Therese von Bayern. *Meine Reise in den brasilianischen Tropen* (Berlin: Verlag von Dietrich Reimen, 1897).
Walker, Mack. *Germany and the Emigration 1816–1885* (Cambridge, MA: Harvard University Press, 1964).
Whitehead, Neil. "Hans Staden and the Cultural Politics of Cannibalism." *Hispanic American Historical Review* 80 (2000): 721–751.
Wied-Neuwied, Maximilian von. *Reise nach Brasilien in den Jahren 1815 bis 1817* (Frankfurt am Main: H.L. Brönner, 1820).
Williams, Raymond Leslie. *The Twentieth-Century Spanish American Novel* (Austin: University of Texas Press, 2003).
Zantop, Susanne. *Colonial Fantasies. Conquest, Family, and Nation in Precolonial Germany, 1770–1870* (Durham, NC: Duke University Press, 1997).

Thomas O. Beebee
Cultural Entanglements and Ethnographic Refractions: Theodor Koch-Grünberg in Brazil

> It is certain that Brazilian civilization is not connected to the Indian element, and has not received any influence from it; and this should suffice for us not to go looking for the titles of our literary identity among defeated tribes.
> – Machado de Assis, Notícia da atual literatura brasileira. Instinto de nacionalidade, 1873

> Who says that Brazilians aren't monkeys (*macacos*)?
> – Theodor Koch-Grünberg, *Die Xingú-Expedition*, 28 November 1899

What Brazilians were supposedly not interested in looking for among "defeated tribes" at the end of the nineteenth century, some Germans were. Not among defeated tribes, exactly – an anthropology of hybridity and accommodation, of trauma, or even of collaboration had not yet come into being – but among so-called "Peoples of Nature" (*Naturvölker*). Not in the sense of cultural entanglement that Machado de Assis warns against in the epigraph, but in the opposite direction, using analysis to isolate the peoples of nature from the culture that surrounds and interacts with them. Comparison and contrast of these anthropological objects was for the purpose of better confirming and clarifying for Germans and Europeans their own status as *Kulturvölker* ("Peoples of Culture"). If the Greeks had been the premier *Kulturvolk* for the Germans, the First Nations of the Americas became their premier *Naturvolk*. One of the most important of these German seekers after "defeated" tribes was Theodor Koch-Grünberg (1872–1924), who undertook four Amazon expeditions in 1899, 1903–1905, 1911–1913, and 1924, the first of these being more of an apprentice voyage under the leadership of Hermann Meyer, the last curtailed by his death from malaria. The writings of Koch-Grünberg hold a special place in Brazilian literature as the source of Mário de Andrade's myth-novel *Macunaíma* (1928), a literary work that, along with Oswald de Andrade's *Antropofagismo*, deliberately countered Machado's dictum.[1]

The three groups discussed so far – Indians, Brazilians, and Germans – all appear in Koch-Grünberg's narratives, despite (or at times because of) his desire to bracket or exclude Brazilians as creators of a "pseudocivilization," a space

---

[1] Machado's comments, in turn, were aimed indirectly at the first "popular" Brazilian author, José de Alencar (1829–1877), whose idealized Indian characters such as Peri and Iracema had become icons of Brazilian identity. "Iracema," a name Alencar invented by scrambling the letters of "America," remains a popular name for women in Brazil.

that belongs neither to nature nor to culture. Yet Koch-Grünberg's vision of the presumably unspoiled Indians necessarily takes place within the actual panorama of the "contact zone" of Brazilian "pseudocivilized" reality that makes his research possible, a zone of cultural entanglements between Brazilian, European, and Indian. Koch-Grünberg's ethnographic writings, at least as one reads them today, reveal as much about the threats to these peoples and about their connections to the larger Brazilian and world economy (e. g., to the rubber trade) as they do about their isolation and pristine nature. This chapter emphasizes this aspect of Koch-Grünberg's writings as a refracted ethnography of Brazil, one where the intended single, focused gaze is split so that it strikes a variety of objects rather than being confined to the Indians of Roraima or of other regions. The two works that I consider in some detail, the unpublished Xingu notebooks and the published, two-volume account of his travels in the Rio Negro region, complement each other in this regard. I will read them against one another after placing Koch-Grünberg in the context of German exploration and ethnographic writing at the turn of the century.

The genres of German ethnography

Koch-Grünberg's refracted ethnographic gaze was produced out of the indefinite methods and incoherent objectives at the birth of German *Völkerkunde* to the extent that these were supplemented by the ethnographer's own sense of authorship and of a moral mission. Germany's colonial aspirations in the late nineteenth century were intended to bring into reality what Suzanne Zantop calls the country's "colonial fantasies" for a "place in the sun." They also continued the already very real intra-European colonization (e. g., of eastern Slavic Europe) that had been carried out through the centuries: Germany, when it united in 1871, did so under the rubric of "Reich" or empire.[2] The German Reich's newest colonies were in Africa and Asia. In the case of Latin America, where Germany had no prospects of overt colonization, there remained the fact of significant German emigration to the region (including about 300,000 to southern Brazil be-

---

[2] Suzanne Zantop, *Colonial Fantasies: Conquest, Family, and Nation in Precolonial Germany* (Durham, NC: Duke University Press, 1997). The complex imbrication of anthropological investigation with racial theories and with European colonial undertakings has received a thorough airing in the secondary literature. See, for example, James Clifford, *The Predicament of Culture* (Cambridge, MA: Harvard University Press, 1988); Michael Taussig, *Mimesis and Alterity* (New York: Routledge, 1992); and Mary Louise Pratt, *Imperial Eyes: Travel Writing and Transculturation* (New York: Routledge, 1992).

tween 1890 and 1914), as well as commercial and capital exchanges typical of North–South relations. Gerhard Brunn concludes at the end of his study of German ambitions in Brazil that the German immigrants were largely immune to ideological control from their country of origin, and attempts at the diplomatic level were like ships passing in the night. The overall result was a "world politics [on the part of Germany] without knowledge of the world."[3]

In the case of Brazil, then, the series of ethnographic expeditions in this period remained a symbolic compensation for an absence of other mechanisms of control, Zantop's colonial fantasies redux. Back in Europe, the specific complex of power-knowledge acquired in expeditions of collection and observation was to join chemistry, physics, engineering, and other disciplines in the panorama of German science that the newly formed nation saw as necessary complements to its economic, political, and military importance. As a result, Germany joined France, England, and the United States as a North Atlantic practitioner of a "hegemonic anthropology" thoroughly imbricated in imperial ambitions and colonial practices.[4] In its educated middle classes (*Bildungsbürgertum*), Germany possessed a pool of talent for carrying out field research in the tropics. Its research was guided both by the preceding scientific explorations, such as those of Alexander von Humboldt, and by the exotic-ethnographic adventure novels of popular authors such as Karl May, whose most memorable works, including the *Winnetou* series (1893), featured natives of North America as prominent characters. South America was also soon to have its novelist: Oskar Weber wrote *Letters of a Coffee Planter* (1913; *Briefe eines Kaffeepflanzers*) and *The Sugar Baron* (1914; *Der Zuckerbaron*), among others.

Given that they were in the process of founding the discipline, none of the field researchers who traveled to South America could be rigorously trained in anthropology; instead they learned the discipline mostly by doing it. Karl von den Steinen (1855–1929), for example, was trained as a doctor and psychiatrist, and he undertook his first colonial tourism ostensibly to compare how psychiatric institutions operated in various parts of the world, before it morphed into two expeditions to the Xingu River in Brazil.[5] Von den Steinen's account of the sec-

---

3 Gerhard Brunn, *Deutschland und Brasilien (1889–1914)* (Vienna: Böhlau, 1971), 285.
4 On the concept of hegemonic anthropology and its alternatives, see Gustavo Lins Ribeiro and Arturo Escobar, eds., *World Anthropologies* (New York: Berg, 2006), 1–25.
5 Karl Von den Steinen, *Unter den Naturvölkern Zentral-Brasiliens. Reiseschilderung und Ergebnisse der zweiten Schingú-Expedition* (Berlin: Dietrich Reimer, 1894; rpt. New York: Johnson Reprint Corporation, 1968).

ond expedition became something of a bestseller in Germany.⁶ Perhaps the most famous of all German ethnographers to report on South America, Curt Unckel Nimuendajú (1883–1945), had no university training at all. The subject of this chapter, Theodor Koch-Grünberg, had studied classical philology, German, history, and geography in Giessen and Tübingen and had begun his career as a teacher of those subjects in a high school (*Gymnasium*) before giving up his position to work at the nascent Museum für Völkerkunde in Berlin. What the varied backgrounds of the researchers added up to was first of all a rapid evolution of and improvisation in the methods of collection, and second a high level of literary engagement with the material, increased by the fact that books about South American Indians based on their travels could become bestsellers, to the extent that they were often reprinted in cheaper (shortened) editions in order to reach a wider reading public.⁷ Sales of books provided some of the income to support museums and their expeditions. At the same time, most of these researchers were publishing more scholarly and narrowly focused articles in scholarly journals or in limited-edition books aimed at a more specialized readership.

The varied training and lack of a fixed methodology for these ethnographers, as well as the different audiences for their publications, resulted in writing that did not consistently exhibit the objectivity of academically styled ethnography, an unstable and confusing genre that at times resembled travel memoirs, at others novels. Michael Kraus finds the admixture of details in much of this early writing to be irrelevant: "Most [of these details] have disappeared from [later] scholarly writings and are not missed. Indeed, it is no longer relevant to know the price of a hotel room in Rio Hacha in 1914, or what time the train arrived at Uberaba in 1908. [...] What these details meant [...] was the attempt at giving subsequent researchers practical directions along with the scientific results."⁸ Yet these details, as Kraus admits, also lend a literary quality to the supposedly scientific writing, contributing to the "effect of the real" deployed by novelists. In the introduction to their translation of Koch-Grünberg's Roraima expedition, Nádia Farage and Paulo Santilli say something similar about Koch-Grünberg's Roraima book, based on his 1908–1910 sojourn: "Data are recorded in almost excessive detail, as though Koch-Grünberg had the goal of capturing life-in-mo-

---

6 Karl Von den Steinen, *Unter den Naturvölkern Zentral-Brasiliens* (Berlin: Dietrich Reimer, 1894).
7 For a comprehensive overview of the German ethnographers in Brazil, see Michael Kraus, *Bildungsbürger im Urwald* (Marburg: Curupira, 2004), 25–46, and the exhibition catalog *Deutsche am Amazonas. Forscher oder Abenteurer? Expeditionen in Brasilien 1800 bis 1914*. Ed. Anita Hermannstadter (Münster: LIT Verlag, 2002).
8 Michael Kraus, *Bildungsbürger im Urwald* (Marburg: Curupira, 2004), 216. My translation.

tion, the color of days of seasons."⁹ They note how these scintillating data refract, blurring the focus of his ethnography, which "seeks to be comprehensive, but is not delimited by the thematic focus that would render it systematic and totalizing."¹⁰ Reading these two appraisals in conjunction, one gets the impression that the "intrusion" of details into Koch-Grünberg's work ends up expanding the boundaries of anthropology and providing a view of northwestern Brazil as a whole. In spite of his own desire to focus on Indians as people of nature, Koch-Grünberg ends up portraying them as affected by the whole of Brazilian culture. Rather than defining the subject–object relationship established in the more specialized scientific literature, Koch-Grünberg constantly lays bare the mediation and triangulation through which one arrives at – and for him it is still an arrival at rather than a construction of – the object of ethnographic investigation.

Despite their supposed focus on the "untouched" natives of the Amazon region, Koch-Grünberg's refracted writings acquaint readers with various levels of Brazilian society, from the officials of Belém and Manaus to the missionaries and soldiers manning their outposts, to the traders who speak the *lingoa geral*, to the remote Indians who speak only their own languages and have never before seen a European.¹¹ His descriptions of these various groups are often satirical and relate the groups to each other – and to himself as a European – in complex ways. Koch-Grünberg's writing about Brazil can be divided into various concentric circles of interest, admiration, and attention: Taking first place are the unspoiled First Nations; then the common people, nearly always racially mixed; then the local economic and political powers, often international in composition and outlook; and finally the national government, distant and ineffective, entering the scene mostly to deny or delay visas or to extort outrageous duties on imported equipment. The history of Brazil as a nation or analysis of its present political configurations is addressed by Koch-Grünberg only when the consequences directly threaten him or his expedition. Thus, the political unrest surrounding

---

9 Nádia Farage and Paulo Santilli, "Introdução," in *Do Roraima ao Orinoco, Vol. 1*, by Theodor Koch-Grünberg. Trans. Cristina Alberts-Franco (São Paulo: UNESP, 2005), 11–12. This Portuguese edition is prepared from the German of Theodor Koch-Grünberg, *Vom Roraima zum Orinoco. Ergebnisse einer Reise in Nordbrasilien und Venezuela in den Jahren 1911–1913*. 5 vols. (Berlin: Reimer, 1917–1927).
10 Farage and Santilli, "Introdução," 11–12.
11 *Lingua geral* (spelled by Koch-Grünberg as *lingoa geral*), also known as Nheengatu, was a *lingua franca* of the Amazon region based on Tupinambá. It was once the most widely spoken language in colonial Brazil, including by Europeans, but its use has declined precipitously since Koch-Grünberg's time.

the elections of 1899 finds frequent mention in the Xingu notebooks, but only because Koch-Grünberg directly observes the stockpiling of weapons and eventually the desertion of some of the Brazilian *Kameraden* who return to Cuiabá to protect their property and families in the event of revolution. Koch-Grünberg's view of the common Brazilian has been summarized accurately by Michael Kraus: "In various passages he presents the common people of Brazil as a negative contrast to the Indians,"[12] that is, as *macacos* or "monkeys," to quote his outburst in the epigraph. In Brazil, the trip out of nature into culture has inverted evolutionary ascent. Combining personal experience with theory and with prejudice, and availing himself of a variety of writing techniques, Koch-Grünberg produces his own negative vision of Brazilianness as pseudocivilization. Let us now explore that personal experience in more detail.

Enter Koch-Grünberg

Christian Theodor Koch was born in 1872 in Grünberg, a small town of upper Hessen. He studied classical philology at the universities of Giessen and Tübingen and taught *Gymnasium* for several years. He conducted his first field research in Brazil in 1898–1899 under Hermann Meyer in the Xingu region, where he caught malaria for the first time. His extensive notebooks from that expedition were published in German more than a century later, in 2004. Koch-Grünberg returned to Germany to resume high school teaching, until his colleagues Adolf Bastian and Karl von den Steinen persuaded him to become the curator of the South American collection of the Royal Museum for Völkerkunde in Berlin. He completed his PhD in 1902 with a thesis on the relationships between various tribes in the Pantanal/Gran Chaco region. The museum financed Koch-Grünberg's expedition to the Rio Negro region that began in April 1903. Koch-Grünberg explored that river and its many tributaries, including the Içana, Uaupés and Curicuriari, Apaporis and Japurá, purchasing crafts from the various Indians that he met and often photographing them. He brought his goods back to Germany in June 1905 and published his findings in two volumes in 1909–1910 under the title *Zwei Jahre unter den Indianern* (Two Years Among the Indians), with a single-volume, condensed edition for the trade market in 1921. Also in 1909, Koch-Grünberg delivered his inaugural lecture at the University of Freiburg,

---

[12] Michael Kraus, "Von der Theorie zum Indianer," *Deutsche am Amazonas. Forscher oder Abenteurer? Expeditionen in Brasilien 1800 bis 1914.* Ed. Anita Hermannstädter (Münster: LIT Verlag, 2002), 95.

on masks and masked dancing of indigenous peoples. Koch-Grünberg's third trip was to the Roraima region of Brazil, Venezuela, and Guyana, along the Uraricoera River to the upper Orinoco. He published a five-volume account of this trip, *Vom Roraima zum Orinoco,* which resulted in his being offered a chair at the University of Freiburg. Koch-Grünberg also directed the Stuttgarter Museum für Völkerkunde until 1924. His fatal, final trip to Brazil was undertaken in that year, under direction of the American scholar Hamilton Rice. Held up in Vista Alegre on the Rio Branco, Koch-Grünberg suffered a severe attack of malaria to which he succumbed on 8 October.

Koch-Grünberg's tasks among the Indians were varied: He was expected to arrange as many acquisitions of the material cultures of the people he visited as could be managed; he also made linguistic notations and published articles on the languages of the regions visited. Finally, he collected the nonmaterial cultural products of the tribes he visited, including their rituals and dances. His major impact on Brazilian culture came from a volume he published in Berlin in 1916, *Myths and Legends of the Taulipang and Arekuna Indians* (*Mythen und Legenden der Taulipáng- und Arekuna-Indianer*), based on legends he had collected between 1911 and 1913. The native informants for these myths and legends were Akúli for the Arekuná, and Mayuluaípu for the Taulipáng peoples. The latter also translated for the former, who did not know Portuguese. An extraordinary cycle of translation was thus set up in this volume, from indigenous languages into Portuguese by Mayuluaípu, then from Portuguese into German by Koch-Grünberg, and then transadapted back from German into Portuguese by Mário de Andrade in his *Macunaíma,* and much later, more literally by Henrique Roenick for the *Revista do Museu Paulista* 7 (1953).

Mário de Andrade was delighted to find in the myth of Macunaíma, as told by Koch-Grünberg, a hero "with no character" whom he could use as the symbol of Brazilianness.[13] I will not explore here whether this supposed lack of character was inherent to the myth itself or a product of the cultural bleaching that occurs whenever myths are removed from their original contexts, or whether it came about as a translation effect or simply as a figment of Andrade's imagination. Curious is the apparent consonance between Andrade's assessment of lack of character as the chief characteristic needing embodiment in Brazilian literature and Koch-Grünberg's notion of "pseudocivilization" with which he constantly dismisses everything in Brazil that is not "unspoiled" and authentically Indian.

---

13 Mário de Andrade, *Macunaíma o herói sem nenhum caráter* [1928]. Ed. Telê Porto Ancona Lopez (Florianópolis: Universidade Federal de Santa Catarina, 1988). In a letter to Alceu Amoroso Lima, Andrade writes of the "lyrical ecstasy" he experienced on finding Macunaíma's lack of character specifically in Koch-Grünberg's version (cited in Andrade, *Macunaíma,* 401).

Also symptomatic, as we shall see shortly, is the set of mediated perspectives whereby one culture observes another culture observing. On the other hand, although *Zwei Jahre* was translated into Spanish, to this day it has still not found its way into Portuguese. (The Roraima book, as noted earlier, was finally translated in the first decade of the twenty-first century.)

Sérgio Medeiros reminds us of what we might consider to be a contradiction in Koch-Grünberg's position vis-à-vis the Indians he encountered, an attitude that combined a defense of Indians' right to their way of life in the face of civilization with the paternalistic attitude toward their culture and mentality typical of late-nineteenth-century Europe. Medeiros notes that "Koch-Grünberg's scientific contribution as an ethnographer (collector of materials) seems to surpass by far his analyses and interpretations as an anthropologist who, in contrast with the former, did not venture to open new pathways, although perhaps he did point out or suggest these to those who came after him."[14] Thus, although it has been repeatedly remarked that Koch-Grünberg approached his subjects largely free of the blinders of theory, nevertheless, as in any other type of research or observation, a deep, unmentioned structure of theoretical presuppositions determined what was to count as data and what success would look like.[15] Specifically, Koch-Grünberg's writings are imbued with recapitulation theory and with the racial and hereditary typology theories prevalent in his day. We shall examine some examples shortly.

In the opposite direction, and another predilection that freed him from the bonds of theory, Koch-Grünberg's writing from his Xingu notebooks onwards exhibits a concern for capturing every detail and observation. It is this compulsive aspect to record everything that takes Koch-Grünberg beyond the confines of ethnography and makes him a writer. Koch-Grünberg's urge to capture every detail entails a writing-to-the-moment style that stretches the reader's credulity, much in the way a novel does. One of the most striking examples reports on the absolute low point of the troubled Xingu expedition, when every single one of the Europeans – including Koch-Grünberg himself – had fallen prey to malaria: "My own exhaustion is reaching its limit, I am staggering around and often fall on the ground. Have partially lost my hearing, buzzing in my ears. [...] Significant

---

14 Sérgio Medeiros, "A Mitologia do Viajante Solitário," in *Makunaíma e Jurupari: Cosmogonias Ameríndias*. Ed. Sérgio Medeiros (São Paulo: Perspectiva, 2002), 17. My translation.
15 The chapter devoted to his work in the catalog of an exhibition on the German ethnographers is even titled "From Theory to the Indian," with the idea of "from" meaning that he discard theory in favor of direct observation. See Michael Kraus, "Von der Theorie zum Indianer," in *Deutsche am Amazonas. Forscher oder Abenteurer? Expeditionen in Brasilien 1800 bis 1914*. Ed. Anita Hermannstädter (Münster: LIT Verlag, 2002), 86–105.

loss of memory, which Meyer and Mansfeld blame me for in spite of my miserable condition."[16] Does Koch-Grünberg's malarial forgetfulness extend to what he enters in his notebook? He is able to report on his own abject condition at the same moment he is struck down by it. Nor does one suspect Koch-Grünberg of overdramatizing his situation, because the notebooks were not intended for publication. Instead, writing and reporting – and satirizing – appear here as the last handhold on sanity, and perhaps on life.

Perspectives

A brief sample of the pictorial record that Koch-Grünberg included in *Two Years* can (literally) illustrate the themes of mutual cultural reflection discussed earlier. The pictographic record produced by Koch-Grünberg, including approximately 1,000 photographs, formed a substantial part of his material collection activities. The transportation of heavy photographic equipment and preservation of the negative plates were among his more difficult travel tasks. In a thorough study of Koch-Grünberg's visual record, Paul Hempel notes that his general approach to photography remained very much in line with his overall turn to participant–observer anthropology. Numerous photographs taken by Koch-Grünberg's assistant Schmidt in *Two Years,* for example, show Koch-Grünberg working, conversing, reading to, or playing with his "friends" (*Freunde*), thus setting up scenes like that in Figure 1, with a focus on process and a content more related to the semiotics of cultural encounter than to the recording of positivist ethnographic data. Figure 1 shows Koch-Grünberg sharing his photographs with the anthropological subjects who are, at the same time, being photographed. A *mise en abyme* structure is set up in this photo of Indians looking at pictures. (Although this photo appears to be posed – slow film speed being yet another technological hindrance to capturing life's flux – others showing, for example, the process of Koch-Grünberg trading goods with locals appear to be more spontaneously composed.) Our gaze is refracted, unsure whether to focus on the profiled group on the right, to decipher the interaction between native and ethnographer in the center, or to drift over to the pair of viewers on the right.

---

16 Theodor Koch-Grünberg, *Die Xingu-Expedition (1898–1900). Ein Forschungstagebuch.* Ed. Michael Kraus (Cologne: Böhlau, 2004), 195. Dated 23 June 1899.

Figure 1. "The Author Shows [His] Pictures."[17]

This highly self-referential meta-image contrasts greatly with the many others in the book that are determined by dominant racial theories of the nineteenth century. Photographs of individuals tend to use a standard frontal–profile pairing that shows Koch-Grünberg's continuing loyalty to the positivist classification of racial types. In *Two Years,* such photographs often accompany text that summarizes the physical features of the photographed subject, with a view toward his or her typicality. Figure 2 shows one such picture from this book, which Koch-Grünberg hopes will convey the following information about the Bará tribe: "Even though they had not been contaminated by European influence, and in contrast with the open, honest, always likeable Tuyúka, most of these Bará showed a closed, almost somber character type. [...] Some of them had sinister faces with squinting eyes, attributable in part to the prominent brows. In most of them the forehead is well-rounded and not sloping. All of them possess a prominent, well-formed nose."[18] Description of facial features, and especially of mouth, eyes, eyebrows, and forehead, are almost obligatory anthropological descriptions of the time, as is the profile–frontal double picture in Figure 2,

---

17 Theodor Koch-Grünberg, *Zwei Jahre Unter den Indianern. Reisen in Nordwest-Brasilien 1903–1905.* 2 vols. (Berlin: Wasmuth, 1910), 2: 69. The English translation would be: *Two Years Among the Indians. Travels in Northwest Brazil 1903–1905.* Referred to in the text as *Two Years.*
18 Theodor Koch-Grünberg, *Zwei Jahre,* 1: 333–334.

which one finds in *Two Years* by the hundreds. In the connection of physical features to dubious moral qualities one detects the premises of the most successful anthropometric theory of the century, Cesare Lombroso's famous typology of delinquency. The adjectives *düster* ("gloomy") and *finster* ("sinister"), which share the same basic semantic meaning of "dark," are used here ambiguously, pointing either to introversion or to shadiness, or to some combination of the two. The impression of moral delinquency is increased by the squinty eyes, though presumably alleviated by the "well-formed" nose. Not surprisingly, in the next paragraph Koch-Grünberg describes the disappearance of his camp knife during trading activities, which he was able to recover only through energetic inquiries. Here, then, is the positivist perspective of Koch-Grünberg and an objectification of the subject according to the scientific models of his time.

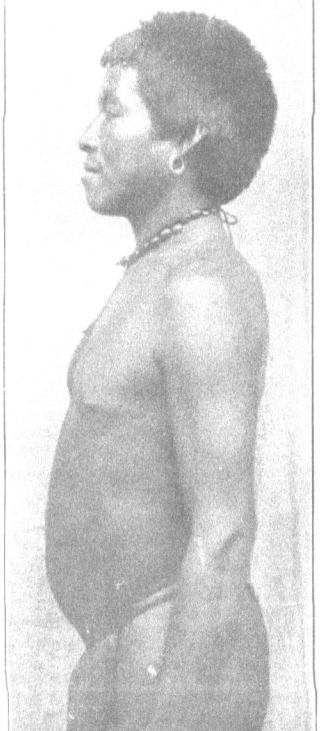 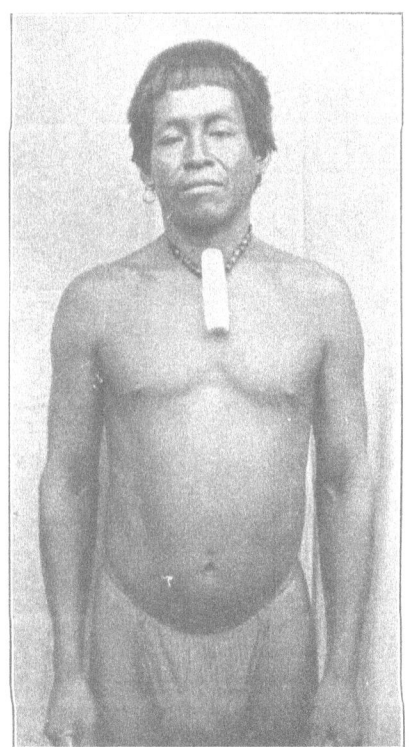

Figure 2. Bará, Tiquié River.[19]

---

[19] Theodor Koch-Grünberg, *Zwei Jahre*, 1: 333.

Hempel concludes in the same bifurcating language that Medeiros uses to distinguish these two aspects of Koch-Grünberg's efforts: "one set of [Koch-Grünberg] images [as in Figure 2] contributed to the construction of ethnographic data and the other [as in Figure 1] to the constitution of the ethnographic field as an intersubjective space of method and communication."[20] In the overall pictographic record, however, there is yet a third category to be added to these two: ethnographer as self-contained ethnographic object. And just as an image captured in the first category is meant to represent "the primitive," so too the images in the third category are meant to represent "civilization," a term Koch-Grünberg nearly always uses in a pejorative and ironic sense. One example can be found in his commentary on this drawing by a Siusí boy of Koch-Grünberg himself, complete with pants and notebook (Figure 3):

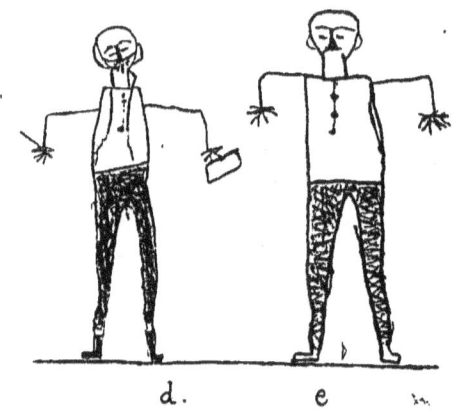

Figure 3. Koch-Grünberg as drawn by a Siusí boy.[21]

Koch-Grünberg explains the drawing as follows:

A highly intelligent Siusí boy was a very skilled and accurate sketch artist. At my request, he sketched my characteristic profile. I was required to sit, or rather stand, for the little artist. He carefully observed and felt out my slippers and the stockings that I had put on over my pants due to the horrendous plague of mosquitoes. He did this as well for my suspend-

---

20 Paul Hempel, "Theodor Koch-Grünberg and Visual Anthropology in Early Twentieth-Century German Anthropology," in *Photography, Anthropology and History: Expanding the Frame*. Ed. Christopher Morton and Elizabeth Edwards (Farnham UK: Ashgate, 2009), 206.
21 Theodor Koch-Grünberg, *Zwei Jahre*, 1: 126.

ers, useless splendors of civilization, which I had still been glad to possess at the beginning of my journey.[22]

Untrained in ethnography, the boy neglects recording Koch-Grünberg's profile, but he does detail the notebook and pencil used to record everything around him, and the unusual clothing. He records Koch-Grünberg recording. What caused Koch-Grünberg to make this experiment in reversing the ethnographic viewpoint? From his remarks, he seemed to want to use his native informants to capture in miniature his own project, that of looking past the layers of civilization to the truly human. His self-deprecatory comments about the uselessness of his civilized clothing indicate the often awkward position he occupied in carrying out his project. He made sure that his book would show Germans alongside other Amazonian folk.

The pseudocivilized exotic

The level of self-reflection exemplified in the Siusí boy's drawing rests uneasily against the search for the purely Indian. *Unverdorben* ("unspoiled") is an adjective that occurs with great frequency in Koch-Grünberg's writings, such as the following passage from *Two Years:* "The next two weeks I experienced here, alone with the Indians, were peaceful and full of fun. Soon I was on such friendly footing with these magnificent, unspoiled people that it seemed as though we had known each other for years."[23]

Just as often, however, native life is found in the midst of civilization. In all, the word *civilization* occurs more often in scare-quotes, or negated by the prefix *pseudo-* or *so-called*, in the writing of Koch-Grünberg than it does as a straightforward marker of material and technological advancement. For Koch-Grünberg, "civilized" is the opposite of "unspoiled." For example, he writes to Wilhelm Sievers, a professor of geography: "Here, too, the primordial has been forced to yield to the advancing so-called 'Civilization,' the lively steamer commerce and the rubber-gatherers who penetrate into even the smallest igarapés."[24] With "here" Koch-Grünberg seems to mean the whole of the Brazilian northwest. It is interesting to note the side-by-side appearance of general improvements in transportation and communication that could be seen as positive or at least neu-

---

[22] Theodor Koch-Grünberg, *Zwei Jahre*, 1: 122. Getting natives to draw was not an unusual practice among ethnographers. Unusual is Koch-Grünberg's use of the picture as the basis of self-criticism.
[23] Theodor Koch-Grünberg, *Zwei Jahre*, 1: 244.

tral but which bring with them the exploitative rubber traders. But Koch-Grünberg is speaking here of the loss of the primordial (*ursprünglich*), not necessarily of what is most beneficial or harmful to the people he is studying. In any case, the result is the frequent appearance of the unspoiled and exotic in the midst of the quotidian structures of pseudocivilization.

To give one example, Koch-Grünberg's most significant collection from the failed Xingu expedition was achieved on his return via an advanced travel technology, when the river steamer from Cuiabá to Corumbá made a stop in Porto Murtinho, a factory town for the production of maté herb, run by the former governor of Mato Grosso. Here Koch-Grünberg finally has the time and relative health to sit down with Cadioéos, who are "sitting around in front of the custom house" and to write down some vocabulary of their language and a bit of its grammar, which he thinks will be enough data for him to prepare a scholarly article on the language.[25] Consequently, the journal entry for the day (not including the data, which were recorded separately) is one of the longest of the Xingu notebooks, four and a half printed pages. Far more information is gathered in this situation of pseudocivilization than when he is among the remote peoples who have never before seen a white man.

An analogous event happens at the beginning of Koch-Grünberg's 1903–1905 journey. He is able to collect a large amount of linguistic data from Ipuriná Indians, not in their homeland, but in the city of Manaus. And this situation of having linguistic informants available is a product of the nefarious forces of pseudocivilization:

> Their patron, a mestizo, had brought them to Manaus from their home on the Ituxy river, a tributary of the Puru, in order to present them to the Governor and thus receive financial support from him for their "catechism": a Christian word that resounds splendidly. Unfortunately, it is often used in Brazil to mask the exploitation of the Indians. In addition, their patron was seeking a concession that would give him economic control of rubber cultivation in the Indians' homeland – this was of course his main objective. In the patron's words, his people should "learn civilization, in order to spread it among their fellow tribesmen when they return." A fine experiment![26]

Koch-Grünberg takes care to point out that this exploiter of the Indians is a "mestizo." His attention to this detail alerts us to the possible existence of another

---

24 Theodor Koch-Grünberg to Wilhelm Sievers, 29 January 1904. Cited in Michael Kraus, "'Und wann ich endlich weiterkomme, das wissen die Götter.' Theodor Koch-Grünberg und die Erforschung des oberen Rio Negro," in *Amazonas Indianer. LebensRäume, LebensRituale, LebensRechte*. Ed. Doris Kurella and Dietmar Neitzke (Berlin: Reimer, 2002), 118.
25 Theodor Koch-Grünberg, *Die Xingu-Expedition*, 370. Dated 24 November 1899.

theoretical presumption in his work, that of hybridity, which I explore in greater detail later. Because the word *civilization* occurs here in the mouth of a Brazilian mestizo, Koch-Grünberg sees no need to attach his usual *pseudo-* prefix to the word: The situation says it for him, and the reader is meant to understand the context. The mention of rubber reminds us that Koch-Grünberg's expeditions coincided, as did nearly all the German undertakings beginning with Karl von den Steinen's second expedition to the Xingu River in 1887–1888, with the high point of Brazilian participation in the international rubber trade. The extractive trade provided an economic motivation for Brazilian authorities to allow and provide some assistance to ethnographic expeditions by foreigners, in the hope that they would open new pathways for economic exploitation.

If we look ahead to the scathing last section of *Two Years*, we encounter the same idea as in the previous quotation, formulated on a grander scale:

> A mere five years have passed since my sojourn on the Caiarý-Uaupés River. Those who travel there today will no longer find my idyll. The contagious air of a pseudo-civilization visits the brown people unprotected by law. Like a plague of locusts devouring everything in its path, the inhuman hordes of rubber-gatherers invade ever further. In this manner, a dynamic race, a people with magnificent intellectual and moral endowments will be destroyed. Human material capable of development is being ruined by the brutalities of these modern cultural barbarians.[27]

This passage is typical of the method and attitude of Koch-Grünberg. He has a tripartite schema for human development: European civilization; the "unspoiled," indigenous raw state of nature; and Brazilian pseudocivilization. The second is capable of development into the first, but the third does not rise to the level of the human. To a greater extent than his predecessors, Koch-Grünberg placed a high priority on living with and becoming friends with the peoples he was observing and collecting. Koch-Grünberg's genuine affection for the people he was observing did not preclude his subscription to the prevalent Darwinian view of cultural development and the theory of recapitulation, that peoples currently living in nature necessarily represent the earliest stages of human development and will eventually "grow up" the way children do. The Indians thus represent "human material" that exhibits a "capacity for development." This seems to contradict the ideas of "pseudocivilization" and "cultured barbarians" that run through the passage: What does Koch-Grünberg expect the peoples he visited to develop into? Apparently not into Brazilians, as so many of them have

---

26 Theodor Koch-Grünberg, *Zwei Jahre*, 1: 5.
27 Theodor Koch-Grünberg, *Zwei Jahre*, 2: 319.

done. Apparently, Koch-Grünberg conducts a thought experiment here, a work of science fiction that imagines the Indians, left on their own, developing into a civilization parallel to Europe.

Koch-Grünberg summarizes here what a careful reader of *Two Years* would have noticed throughout the text: In between the idylls that the explorer encounters from time to time are villages that have been terrorized by the rubber traders, by the armed forces of one or more of the nations disputing territory in the region, or by corrupt Brazilian officials. But taking the quotations in this section together, we perceive a double focus on two different topographies for the location of the primordiality Koch-Grünberg seeks: In one, the "quotidian exotic" lies within the civil society of Brazil, and the Indians he seeks walk the streets of Manaus on their way to catechism or work in maté factories along the Paraguay River; in the other, the idyll of the unspoiled, they are to be found only beyond the reach of the steamers and the constraints of the law.

The Brazilians

To what extent is Koch-Grünberg's idea of pseudocivilization congruent with Brazil and Brazilians? True to his nontheoretical approach to observation, Koch-Grünberg is ready to change his assessment of Brazilians at any moment, and there are typologies within typologies. His very first recorded remark on Brazilians concerns the women on board the steamer going up the Paraguay River to Corumbá: "Brazilian women are the dullest creatures on earth. They sit there all day without saying a word: only their small fans are in motion, with machine-like regularity."[28] However, in exploring the environs of Cuiabá, the starting point for reaching the unexplored areas, he notes, "Half-naked or entirely naked brown washerwomen sit in the hollows where rain water has pooled. What friendly, polite people these Brazilians are! Not a single one of them forgets to call out his 'como pasou' [How's it going?]."[29]

Once the trip begins, however, depending as it does on the participation of the *Kameraden* (hired native guides), the comments turn mostly negative once again. Even one of the more dependable of them, Federico, breaks his contract, as it were, to return home after just fourteen days: "There is just no depending on Brazilians, however useful Federico has been in other respects."[30] Similarly, as the expedition is deep in the jungle, the failure to plan and to save food is

---

28 Theodor Koch-Grünberg, *Die Xingu-Expedition*, 59–60. Dated 5 February 1899.
29 Theodor Koch-Grünberg, *Die Xingu-Expedition*, 68. Dated 22 February 1899.

marked as a cultural failing: "This people [Volk] has no concept of planning for the next day – from hand to mouth!"[31] From here, as we saw in the epigraph, the judgments on Brazilians descend even further. But an earlier entry, made while the expedition is gathering forces in Cuiabá, provides the most striking and extensive view of what Koch-Grünberg will dismiss ever afterwards as "pseudocivilization."

I have mentioned that the longest single entry of the Xingu notebooks reports on Koch-Grünberg's linguistic activities among Indians whom he encountered on his return trip from Cuiabá. The second-longest recounts Cuiabá's festivities on 24 February 1899, in celebration of the anniversary of the proclamation of the Brazilian Constitution. The high point is a pageant and concert by students in schools run by the Salesians. Koch-Grünberg's detailed description of the scenery painted on the curtain gives another dimension to his leitmotif of "pseudocivilization." The designers of the panorama had made a deliberate attempt to represent various streams of European culture and then to translate them into a tropical landscape:

> During intermission we make atrocious comments on the theater curtain, which has been painted up like the scenery for a murder ballad. In the background, a tropical rivering landscape with high mountains; palm trees, a city on the left with high, crenellated towers and a tent camp before its walls. In the foreground a Roman solider sitting on a pile of weapons beneath a tree and grabbing his head with a desperate face, to the right of him a Greek hero leaning on his lyre, meditatively gazing at the soldier with an ironical expression. To the left a few figures with large turbans, long beards and gowns, evidently rabbis engaged in lively conversation, one of them expressing regret with his hands. Outside, a black military band is playing most ineptly on flutes that are out of tune.[32]

The painting reminds Koch-Grünberg of the kind made in Germany to illustrate *Bänkelsängerlieder,* literally "bench-singer songs," so called because the singer stood on a small bench, to be seen above the crowd, and pointed at a large painting illustrating the murder or other lurid event that was the song's subject. The story was often broken down into a series of scenes. This predecessor of today's comic books and reality TV was despised by elites. After the reminder of genre, Koch-Grünberg points out every incongruity he can think of in the painting, starting with the overall transculturation of the origins of Europe into a "tropical riverine landscape" ("tropische Flusslandschaft"). There follows the historical commingling of medieval castles, Roman soldiers, Greek heroes, and Jewish rab-

---

30 Theodor Koch-Grünberg, *Die Xingu- Expedition,* 123. Dated 11 April 1899.
31 Theodor Koch-Grünberg, *Die Xingu-Expedition,* 177. Dated 7 June 1899.
32 Theodor Koch-Grünberg, *Die Xingú-Expedition,* 70. Dated 24 February 1899.

bis. Notably missing from the picture are Indians and Africans: The Salesian fathers who run the school seem determined to produce perfect colonial subjects and not to have their charges look for their origins among "defeated tribes."

The long description of the painting that Koch-Grünberg appears eager to remember and to record at length in his notebook is followed by descriptions of a *tableau vivant*, of the singing of the Brazilian national anthem and of a recital of classical music that exceeds the capabilities of the children as much as the tunes do those of the military band. Koch-Grünberg remarks repeatedly that the teachers of the Salesian school responsible for the pageant resemble German schoolteachers, who like the Romans, Greeks, Jews, and the Afro-Brazilians of the band have been transculturated into Amazonian folk in the very act of miming Europeanness. As in Koch-Grünberg's descriptions of Indians, one can surmise an underlying theory of civilization at work in his simultaneous fascination with and repulsion by this display of Brazilian pseudoculture. His view of Brazilian hybridity seems to be the familiar one, which posited cultural and biological mixing as analogous and interdependent. Hybridity was seen as a deviation from, rather than the creative force behind, racial types: "In the different theoretical positions woven out of this intercourse, the races and their intermixture circulate around an ambivalent axis of desire and aversion: a structure of attraction, where people and cultures intermix and merge, transforming themselves as a result; and a structure of repulsion, where the different elements remain distinct and are set against each other dialogically."[33] Renata Wassermann summarizes the hybridity specific to the Americas: "New World populations call into question all definitions of identity that rest on clear oppositions between those recognizably like and those unlike a predefined European self. That self is shattered and combined with other fragments into identities whose heterogeneity precludes complete acceptance as well as complete rejection and who are both self and other, kin and stranger."[34] This fragmentary, refracted cultural identity, it seems to me, is precisely what Koch-Grünberg finds in the pageant of the Brazilian Republic and is a major contributor to his idea of pseudocivilization. The hybrid picture he describes shatters and fragments the European while painting over and making invisible the racially pure, "unspoiled" Indian that he seeks. One suspects that Koch-Grünberg's exaggerated and uncharitable irritation (mixed with a certain fascination, or else why write so extensively on it?) stems from a realization that his own writing will be unable to purify

---

[33] J. C. Young, *Colonial Desire: Hybridity in Theory, Culture and Race* (New York: Routledge, 1995), 19.

[34] Renata R. Mautner Wasserman, "Mario Vargas Llosa, Euclides da Cunha, and the Strategy of Intertextuality," *PMLA* 108.3 (1993): 466.

away the refracted qualities of the culture. One could also speculate that Koch-Grünberg's later delight with the Siusí boy's straightforward, "Occidentalist" drawing effort, to the extent that he reproduces it in *Two Years* alongside his scientific photos, is fueled by a distant memory of and implicit comparison to the hybridized Brazilian bricolage that the European satirizes here.

Conclusion

The untheoretical Koch-Grünberg did not explicitly use the pageant he observed as a metaphor for Brazilianness, to the extent that I drew inferences from his description in the concluding sentence of the preceding section. It is up to us as readers to connect the various descriptions to each other in order to fill out Koch-Grünberg's notion of Brazilian pseudocivilization. To repeat a point made earlier, there is a strong consonance between Koch-Grünberg's perceptions and those of Brazilian author Euclides da Cunha, who was at work on his *Os Sertões* in São Paulo state while Koch-Grünberg took in the town of Cuiabá. *Os Sertões* (*The Backlands*, 1902) became the definitive statement on Brazilian identity, and it agrees with Koch-Grünberg that European models and paradigms fit uneasily on Brazilian reality. Other ideas must be sought, for example among the first inhabitants of the continent. When Mário de Andrade finds these in reading Koch-Grünberg's version of native myths, the German participates in the construction of Brazilian identity in a way he never anticipated.

Koch-Grünberg's writings thus show the features of what Andrew Zimmerman has identified as the middle ground in which neither ethnographer nor native fully dominated:

> While anthropologists could usually exercise overwhelming power over their subjects, this power, like all power, was never so absolute as to subordinate reality itself. [...] To overlook the actions and perspectives of anthropology's colonized subjects [...] would allow a myth of objective distance, originally constructed by anthropologists themselves, to obscure a more historically accurate account of anthropology. German anthropology was not the rarefied product of an isolated German intellectual history but rather an active participant in world history.[35]

Koch-Grünberg's verbal texts – at least the ones considered here – show shifting perspectives analogous to those of his graphic images. Koch-Grünberg's honesty as a writer contradicts his overarching, idealized ethnographic goal of describing peoples of nature who are still unspoiled by the encroachments and admixtures of pseudocivilization. Overall, his writing instead shows the refraction of the ethnographic gaze through the presence of a third party, who is neither Indian nor European but Brazilian.

References

Andrade, Mário de. *Macunaíma o herói sem nenhum caráter*. Ed. Telê Porto Ancona Lopez (Florianópolis: Universidade Federal de Santa Catarina, 1988). (Original work published 1928)

Andrade, Oswald de. "Manifesto Antropófago." *Revista de Antropofagia* 1.1 (1928): 3, 7.

Machado de Assis, Joaquim Maria. "Notícia da atual literatura brasileira: instinto de nacionalidade," in *Obra Completa*. 4 vols. (Rio de Janeiro: Nova Aguilar, 1973): 3:801–809. (Original work published 1873)

Brunn, Gerhard. *Deutschland und Brasilien (1889–1914)* (Vienna: Böhlau, 1971).

Clifford, James. *The Predicament of Culture* (Cambridge, MA: Harvard University Press, 1988).

Cunha, Euclides da. *Os Sertões: Campanha de Canudos (The Backlands)*. Ed. Leopoldo M. Bernucci. (São Paulo: Arquivo do Estado, 2002). (Original work published 1902)

Farage, Nádia, and Paulo Santilli. "Introdução," in *Do Roraima ao Orinoco, Vol. 1*. By Theodor Koch-Grünberg. Trans. Cristina Alberts-Franco. (São Paulo: UNESP, 2005), 1–26.

Hempel, Paul. "Theodor Koch-Grünberg and Visual Anthropology in Early Twentieth-Century German Anthropology," in *Photography, Anthropology and History: Expanding the Frame*. Ed. Christopher Morton and Elizabeth Edwards (Farnham UK: Ashgate, 2009), 193–219.

Koch-Grünberg, Theodor. *Myths and Legends of the Taulipang and Arekuna Indians (Mythen und Legenden der Taulipáng- und Arekuna-Indianer)* (Berlin: Dietrich Reimer, 1916).

Koch-Grünberg, Theodor. *Vom Roraima zum Orinoco. Ergebnisse einer Reise in Nordbrasilien und Venezuela in den Jahren 1911–1913*. 5 vols. (Berlin: Reimer, 1917–1927).

Koch-Grünberg, Theodor. *Die Xingu-Expedition (1898–1900). Ein Forschungstagebuch*. Ed. Michael Kraus (Cologne: Böhlau, 2004).

Koch-Grünberg, Theodor. *Zwei Jahre Unter den Indianern. Reisen in Nordwest-Brasilien 1903–1905*. 2 vols. (Berlin: Wasmuth, 1910).

Kraus, Michael. *Bildungsbürger im Urwald* (Marburg: Curupira, 2004).

Kraus, Michael. "'Und wann ich endlich weiterkomme, das wissen die Götter.' Theodor Koch-Grünberg und die Erforschung des oberen Rio Negro," in *Amazonas Indianer. LebensRäume, LebensRituale, LebensRechte*. Ed. Doris Kurella and Dietmar Neitzke (Berlin: Reimer, 2002), 113–128.

Kraus, Michael. "Von der Theorie zum Indianer," in *Deutsche am Amazonas. Forscher oder Abenteurer? Expeditionen in Brasilien 1800 bis 1914*. Ed. Anita Hermannstädter (Münster: LIT Verlag, 2002), 87–106.

Lins Ribeiro, Gustavo, and Arturo Escobar, eds. *World Anthropologies* (New York: Berg, 2006).

---

[35] Andrew Zimmerman, *Anthropology and Antihumanism in Imperial Germany* (Chicago: University of Chicago Press, 2001), 8–9.

Medeiros, Sérgio. "A Mitologia do Viajante Solitário," in *Makunaíma e Jurupari: Cosmogonias Ameríndias*. Ed. Sérgio Medeiros (São Paulo: Perspectiva, 2002), 13–28.
Pratt, Mary Louise. *Imperial Eyes: Travel Writing and Transculturation* (New York: Routledge, 1992).
Roenick, Henrique, trans. *Mitos e lendas dos indios Taulipáng e Arekuná*. By Theodor Koch-Grünberg. *Separata da Revista do Museu Paulista* 7 (1953).
Taussig, Michael. *Mimesis and Alterity* (New York: Routledge, 1992).
Von den Steinen, Karl. *Unter den Naturvölkern Zentral-Brasiliens. Reiseschilderung und Ergebnisse der zweiten Schingú-Expedition* (Berlin: Dietrich Reimer, 1894; rpt. New York: Johnson Reprint Corporation, 1968).
Wasserman, Renata R. Mautner. "Mario Vargas Llosa, Euclides da Cunha, and the Strategy of Intertextuality." *PMLA* 108.3 (1993): 460–473.
Weber, Oskar. *Letters of a Coffee Planter (Briefe eines Kaffeepflanzers. Zwei Jahrzehnte deutscher Arbeit in Zentral-Amerika)* (Cologne: Hermann & Friedrich Schaffstein, 1913).
Weber, Oskar. *The Sugar Baron (Der Zuckerbaron: Schicksale eines ehemaligen deutschen Offiziers in Südamerika)*. (Cologne: Hermann & Friedrich Schaffstein, 1914).
Young, J. C. *Colonial Desire: Hybridity in Theory, Culture and Race* (New York: Routledge, 1995).
Zantop, Suzanne. *Colonial Fantasies: Conquest, Family, and Nation in Precolonial Germany* (Durham, NC: Duke University Press, 1997).
Zimmerman, Andrew. *Anthropology and Antihumanism in Imperial Germany* (Chicago: University of Chicago Press, 2001).

Everyday Cultures and Media

Ricarda Musser
German-Brazilian Cultural Exchange in the Times of the Dictatorship: The Cultural Magazine *Intercâmbio**

"Yet another magazine? ... Are not name, explanation and justification enough? Two really great countries can only win when they get to know each other better and better, and they intensify their 'exchange' [*Intercâmbio*] in the different fields of the sciences, the fine arts, the measures for the welfare of the people, the technological progress, the exaltation of the intellect."[1] These are the words chosen by the editors in June 1935 to open the first issue of the new bilingual magazine that was intended to become a bridge between Brazil and Germany, between Brazilians and Germans.

With this declaration of intent, the magazine *Intercâmbio* positions itself in the tradition of eighteenth-century European cultural magazines that were published periodically and focused on progress in the sciences as well as in the arts, literature, and culture. It was the educated middle class in particular that traditionally belonged to the subscribers and readers of this kind of periodical. Nevertheless, although art and culture were considered from a national, unifying perspective by most of these magazines, the editors proclaimed that *Intercâmbio* aimed to mediate between Germany and Brazil, to give each other's nation an understanding of the self and the other, and to perhaps discover common ground and learning potentials in the process.

The editors of *Intercâmbio* identified language as the vehicle that would make the intended lively exchange possible. The magazine was also particularly committed to language teaching:

> It is obvious that such an ambitious task is much easier to fulfill if there is a mutual language knowledge. Hundreds of thousands of the sons of Germany and the Teuto-Brazilians speak Portuguese and seek to understand better and better the thinking, the orientation, the activity and the idealism of the sons of Terra de Santa Cruz. Then again, for the latter, who never leave Brazil, it is not as easy to familiarize themselves with the German language, both intimidating and difficult.[2]

---

* Translated by Rocío Vázquez Pérez.
1 R. J., "Intercambio," *Intercâmbio* I.1 (1935): n.p.
2 R. J., "Intercambio," *Intercâmbio* I.1 (1935): n.p.

This chapter deals with the first publication period of the magazine from 1935 to 1941[3] in an attempt to find answers to the following questions: To what topics was the magazine especially committed, and how did it go about the mediation of culture? Why do the fields of music and medicine serve as good examples for the way cultural and scientific themes, respectively, were presented in the magazine? How much value did the magazine attribute to language learning, and how did it emphasize the necessity of language acquisition? And to what extent did the magazine achieve its goal of a cultural exchange between Brazil and Germany? In order to carry out an analysis of the magazine and its communication goals, I first critically read all the issues available and evaluated their contents. A text interpretation follows, done by means of hermeneutics, on the basis of the aforementioned thematic fields. In this process, I pay attention to the fact that the cultural and educational policies both in National Socialist Germany and the Brazil of the Vargas era were particularly attuned to the definition, spreading, and anchoring of presumed "national" cultural aspects.

The "enforced conformity" or *Gleichschaltung* of administrative and cultural life in Nazi Germany started as early as spring 1933. A particularly important aspect of this process was the standardization of the mass media, especially newspapers and magazines, and the abolition of the freedom of the press. Consequently, only printed products that affirmed the National Socialist ideology were officially permitted. In 1937, Getúlio Vargas, who had been governing Brazil since 1930, instituted the *Estado Novo*, in which the National Congress and the political parties were dismissed. Furthermore, there was a shift of power from the federal states to the capital. As in Germany, press censorship was introduced, which allowed the ban of unwanted media. An aggressive nationalization policy was implemented during the *Estado Novo*. The objective of this *campanha de nacionalização* was to push back the influence of immigrant groups. Among others, the measures taken for this purpose included, initially, the requirement to teach in Portuguese and the prohibition of teaching languages to children under the age of 14. Of course, this new policy affected the foreign-language mass media as well. In the early phase, bilingual magazines with a Brazilian editor were still authorized. In 1941, these periodicals were banned, too. It goes without saying that this political constellation also affected the selection of topics and the promotion of a magazine whose stated goal was cultural exchange between both countries. The potential political influences will therefore be taken into consideration in this analysis.

---

[3] Issues 4.1939, 7–12; 5.1940, 1–3 and 7–9; and 6.1941, 4–9 were not available for analysis.

Editors, mode of publication, and audience of the magazine

Three institutions took part in the foundation of the magazine: two from Brazil, the Instituto Teuto-Brasileiro de Alta Cultura and Pro Arte; and one from Germany, the Deutsche Akademie in Munich. The three institutions already had wide-ranging experience in the area of cultural mediation. The Instituto Teuto-Brasileiro de Alta Cultura was founded in April 1930 by Brazilian academics to promote the exchange of professors and students between Brazil and Germany. It gave Brazilian students and scientists the possibility to expand and improve their knowledge in Germany. The appointment of German scholars to Brazil – preferably those who through the nature of their academic field and the time at their disposal were able to give lectures and workshops – was equally a goal. Moreover, tasks such as the opening of a public library, the promotion of translations from German to Portuguese and vice versa, and the organization of exhibitions were popular ways to facilitate a mutual cultural exchange, for the benefit of both countries.

Book translations in both countries, magazines and public lectures, and German language courses in Brazil and Portuguese courses in Germany deepened the mutual understanding and the consequent friendship between the two countries.[4] At the beginning of 1932, the association for art, literature, and science Pro Arte moved into its quarters in the Avenida Rio Branco, where it organized literary, musical, and artistic events with and by artists from Latin America and Germany. In the same year, it started to offer language courses as well.

The Deutsche Akademie in Munich was officially founded on 5 May 1925, and in 1924 it had already been entered in the register of associations in Munich under the name "Akademie zur Wissenschaftlichen Forschung und Pflege des Deutschtums/Deutsche Akademie" (Academy for the Scientific Study and for the Cultivation of Germanness/German Academy).[5] It soon included the foreign German expatriates in its activities, and from 1929 on it focused its attention on promoting German language studies abroad. In this context, a milestone of this development was the foundation of the Goethe-Institut für Fortbildung Ausländischer Deutschlehrer (Goethe Institute for Further Training for Teachers of Ger-

---

[4] Henrique Schueler, "Rundfunkübertragung durch das 'Brasilianische Propaganda-Amt,'" *Boletim do Instituto Teuto-Brasileiro de Alta Cultura* 1 (1937): 17–18.
[5] Cf. Eckard Michels, *Von der Deutschen Akademie zum Goethe-Institut. Sprache und auswärtige Kulturpolitik 1923–1960* (Munich: Oldenbourg, 2005), 28.

man as a Foreign Language) on 22 March 1932.[6] Furthermore, the Akademie was strongly involved in the development of up-to-date approaches to the teaching of German. The Akademie's first outpost in South America was established in Brazil.

Unfortunately, nothing about *Intercâmbio*'s circulation figures can be inferred from the magazine itself. The frequency of publication was monthly in the first quarter of its existence (June–August 1935), then it appeared bimonthly until the end of 1935 and every three months from that point on until the end of 1941, and it was not published again until 1949. The magazine's editorial department was headquartered in the Avenida Rio Branco 118/120 in Rio de Janeiro. The *Impressum* (masthead) listed Amelia de Rezende Martins as chief editor, Theodor Heuberger as managing director, and Otto Cziersky as editor. The initial price per unit amounted to 3 milreis, but the students attending language courses at the Deutsche Akademie were given a discount of 1 milreis. By the end of 1941, a single issue cost 7 milreis. The subscription rate fell from 36 milreis per year for twelve monthly issues to 20 milreis per year for four quarterly issues. The magazine was sold in bookshops in Rio de Janeiro, São Paulo, Belo Horizonte, Curitiba, Porto Alegre, Campos, Vitória, Bahia, and Recife. In Germany, it was available through the Deutsche Akademie Munich.

The target audience included the German immigrant population residing in Brazil and their descendants as well as Brazilians interested in German art and culture, especially if they wanted to learn German, and also Germans who lived in Brazil temporarily and wanted to get to know their host country better. The magazine was also read in Germany, where the number of subscribers was admittedly quite small. Today, the issues from 1935 to 1941 are completely or partially available in seven German libraries.[7]

Range of topics in *Intercâmbio*

In accordance with the aspirations of the magazine, the contributions covered a wide range of topics. The central cultural topics were literature, visual arts, and music. The magazine was also committed to the sciences, although these were covered less than culture. Within the sciences, medicine, pharmacy, and engineering were of central importance. Other articles appeared under the heading

---

[6] Eckard Michels, *Von der Deutschen Akademie zum Goethe-Institut. Sprache und auswärtige Kulturpolitik 1923–1960* (Munich: Oldenbourg, 2005), 82.

[7] Cf. research in the German journal database (*Zeitschriftendatenbank*) on 29 April 2011. Unfortunately, such research is not possible for Brazil.

"Generalities" and could address topics as diverse as Christmas traditions and handicrafts, the effects of the Treaty of Versailles on Germany, and the establishment of kindergartens according to Friedrich Fröbel's educational principles. The contributions were occasionally illustrated with photographs, drawings, and paintings, but the overall number of images was limited. The German and Portuguese language courses remained especially important, and they will be closely examined later in this chapter.

The contributions were written partly in German and partly in Portuguese. In some cases, they were published in both languages or at least with an extract in the other language. However, the topics about Germany were not written principally in Portuguese for the benefit of Brazilian readers, nor were Brazilian contents written in German for readers in Germany. The very definition of the magazine as an organ for the promotion of culture through language teaching argued against such practices. For Brazilians who attended German courses and for Germans who enrolled in Portuguese courses, the magazine was also supposed to serve as an incentive to apply their recently acquired knowledge when reading the articles.

Accordingly, the literature of both countries took up a big part of every issue of the magazine. After all, it was the one cultural area that could be transmitted exclusively through language, whereas other branches of culture, such as sculpture and painting, could be comprehended without language skills. The magazine's very first issue contained the beginning of the serial publication of the Brazilian novel *Bugrinha* (1922) by Afrânio Peixoto, translated into German by consul R. Hieber. A poem by Mário de Andrade was also published for the first time, both in the original and in German translation. To give the readers deep insight into the literature of the respective countries, the first issue in 1936 featured two series of articles, both composed by Amelia de Rezende Martins: "For the German Friends. Facts About Brazilian Literature" (Für die deutschen Freunde. Daten über brasilianische Literatur) and "For Brazilians. Visiting the Wonderful Field of German Literature" (Para os Brasileiros. Respigando no campo maravilhoso da litteratura allemã); however, the former opens with the writings of Father Anchieta and the latter with medieval courtly romances.

Only a few articles were devoted exclusively to the politics of both countries. Disguised as cultural themes, the political undertones were very often evident, particularly in the choice of words. For example, when addressing the topic "The Song of the Time," Heinrich Verlé wrote,

> Of particular value is the corpus of current folk songs whose creative approach, for instance its battle songs, offers a material that due to the force of its effect and the simple popular language stands next to the best German tradition of all cultural periods. Thus it is nothing

but incorporation, coupling of blood and earth, homeland and folklore, with form and expression turned into a song of the time.[8]

The promotion of new books provided another opportunity to spread the ideologies of National Socialist politics abroad. Issues 6 and 7 (1935) announced a new series of publications on politics, culture, and economy under the title "Das neue Reich" (The new Reich). These articles were published by the Deutsche Akademie in Munich, whose concern it was to define the fundamentals of Germany's "renovation," the intellectual and ethical impulses of the "New Reich's" political and cultural objectives. At the same time, the series aimed to enlighten the non-German world with regard to the intellectual foundation of the new Germany and to contribute to the historical "truth" that, according to National Socialist ideology, the German nation's enemies kept distorting. The series' special importance, compared with similar publications, lies in the fact that, for the first time, National Socialism was represented as an intellectual manifestation and a creative force.[9]

To convey the desired impression of the sociopolitical situation in Germany and Brazil, *Intercâmbio* bet primarily on the power of images. Under the title "O Brasil de hoje" (Today's Brazil), Getúlio Vargas was portrayed inspecting a formation of cadets of the Escola Naval (Maritime Academy); on the magazine's next page, devoted to "A Allemanha de hoje" (Today's Germany), four pictures show a group of the Hitler Youth, young drummers in the Nuremberg Rally (Nazi party convention), a column of the Reich Labor Services, and Adolf Hitler with a child. It can definitely be assumed that the magazine aimed to emphasize more than just the linguistic similarity of the pictures' titles.[10] The German-Brazilian friendship was also displayed in pictures of the new German ambassador Karl Ritter's inaugural visit with the Brazilian president,[11] as well as by an article on the chief press officer of the Brazilian Foreign Office and his visit to Nuremberg under the supervision of the German Ministry of Public Enlightenment and Propaganda, which was accompanied by a photograph of the Nuremberg Rally.[12]

An important component of the magazine was the advertising of German or German-Brazilian companies at the end of every issue. The ads were written both

---

8 Heinrich Verlé, "Das Lied der Zeit," *Intercâmbio* I.4–5 (1935): 200.
9 Anonymous, "Das Neue Reich," *Intercâmbio* I.6–7 (1935): 315.
10 Cf. Anonymous (Fotographs), "O Brasil de hoje. A Allemanha de hoje," *Intercâmbio* I.4–5 (1935): 183–185.
11 Cf. Anonymous (Fotograph), "Der neue deutsche Botschafter," *Intercâmbio* II.10–12 (1937): 278.
12 Renato Almeida, "O Encantamento de Nuremberg!," *Intercâmbio* II.7–9 (1937): 181–182.

in Portuguese and in German. The central focus was on the areas of finance, health, and pharmacy as well as technology, machines, and devices. In turn, the magazine's ads were directed to the advertising clients. Already in the magazine's very first issue, a page titled "German Businessman!" gives the following hint: "Remember that you are called to fulfill a cultural mission. When designing plans in your office [...], do not forget the weapon available to you in the modern economic struggle; the spreading of the German language! The modern businessman is a cultural carrier who knows how to put spiritual values in the service of material benefits."[13] Some pages later, the Brazilian businessman is addressed:

> This magazine for the cultural exchange between Brazil and Germany is also worth of your interest, of your support. [...] It will promote your products through its pages, that will be read in millions of homes on both sides of the Atlantic. It will increase your number of trade relations and it will help you conquer new markets.[14]

As the readers' letters indicate, readers in both countries and beyond liked the content orientation and the presentation of the particular issues.

In the following, I will take a closer look at one complex theme from each of the areas of culture, science and organization, and language acquisition. In the first area (culture), I selected music because musical themes were culturally easy to convey regardless of the readers' language skills. Besides, longstanding close relationships already existed between Brazil and Germany in this field. From the field of science, I chose medicine because it was the topic most widely dealt with in the magazine. Finally, I analyze the magazine's coverage of language acquisition, because the promotion of language courses was considered an essential centerpiece of the magazine and was included in each issue.

Music: cultural transfer or exchange?

By the nineteenth century, European music had become important for Brazil's cultural life. Numerous Brazilian musicians studied in Italy, France, or Germany and brought their experiences back to Brazil. In turn, the local audiences got to know some Brazilian compositions, such as the opera *O Guarani* by Antônio Carlos Gomes, which was premiered in Milan's La Scala on 17 March 1870. The cultural exchange in music seemed to be unproblematic, because it did not depend on the knowledge of a particular language, or, to be more precise, music already

---

13 Anonymous, "Deutscher Kaufmann!," *Intercâmbio* I.1 (1935): n.p.
14 Anonymous, "Ao comerciante brasileiro," *Intercâmbio* I.1 (1935): n.p.

had its own international language. However, the magazine contained quite a few commentaries by German students of the Instituto Nacional de Música of the University of Rio de Janeiro who were learning the language "because the best masters of music were German; [...] I want to be able to read and understand what they wrote about their art."[15]

Intercâmbio focused mainly on classical music. Some issues showed photographs or pictures of composers on their front cover. In 1936, for example, Carlos Gomes was portrayed in the January to March issues. Commemorating the hundredth anniversary of his birth, the magazine dedicated several articles to the composer, including an interview with his daughter, Itala Gomes Vaz de Carvalho, who was asked what encounters with German music her father might have had.[16] But Carlos Gomes had never collaborated closely with German musicians, nor had he ever been to Germany. In contrast, pianist Charley Lachmund studied for almost six years at the Leipzig Conservatory of Music. He wrote an article for the magazine describing, among other things, his first concert in Brazil, which took place in front of 350 guests in his uncle's house in Belo Horizonte and unexpectedly turned into a patriotic event:

> It had been impossible to find a grand piano, but uncle Steckel's Blüthner upright piano was brand new and in order to intensify the sound I had the front board removed and the mechanism, that was now exposed, covered with a cloth. Since we could not find a suitable cloth, the piano was draped with a Brazilian flag. Thus the concert was turned into an unforeseen patriotic demonstration.[17]

The concerts of Brazilian musicians in Germany were also mentioned. In 1938, issues 4–6 included a review of Brazilian singer Cristina Maristany's song recital evening, which had taken place in Berlin with a program consisting primarily of recent Brazilian songs. Both the singer and her lecture clearly made a positive impression; moreover, her "exotic" appearance and performance fascinated the German audience:

> Cristina Maristany's very appearance reveals that she comes from a different nation, a different country. She shows herself playful and casual in her performance, in a way unknown to us here in the harsh North. The sound of her voice betrays a different race too. [...] But this was for me the most interesting thing: a whole string of modern Brazilian compositions accompanied personally by the very composer Francisco Mignone, which guaranteed a re-

---

15 Lisette de Oliveira, "Porque estudas a lingua allemã?," *Intercâmbio* I.1 (1935): 46.
16 Cf. Otto Cziersky, "Mein Vater. Gespräch mit Itala Gomes Vaz de Carvalho," *Intercâmbio* I.8–10 (1936): 343.
17 Charley Lachmund, "Erinnerungen an Belo Horizontes Kinderjahre," *Intercâmbio* III.10–12 (1938): 418.

liable rendition. Apart from Mignone, the program also included pieces by Camargo Guarnieri, Villa Lobos and Frutuoso Vianna. Have we Germans ever even known about the existence of modern Brazilian compositions? The music from Brazil is completely unknown to us and in my opinion it is absolutely essential that we discover something about it here in Germany.[18]

The exoticizing description of Maristany discloses the author's racial prejudice and reminds today's reader of the (pseudo)ethnological portrayals of indigenous people by Europeans who traveled to the presumed "uncivilized" parts of the world in the nineteenth and twentieth centuries.

Aside from the disconcerting lack of critique, the article shows how, at that time, Brazilian music was practically unknown in Germany, even among German musicians. A cultural transfer from Germany to Brazil had definitely taken place in the field of music, but it was not at all possible to call it a cultural exchange yet. However, because of the concert's success, the reviewer looked forward to such an exchange in the future: "I very much hope that the cultural exchange between Brazil and Germany is still further promoted so that we get to recognize and respect each other."[19]

In contrast, the works by German composers was very much present in Brazil. *Intercâmbio*, too, regularly reported on the composers and their work. Issues 7–9 (1937), for example, featured Christoph Willibald Gluck on its cover. A short contribution acknowledged the composer on the occasion of the 150th anniversary of his death. In issue 2 (1935), an employee of the Reichsmusikkammer (Reich Music Chamber) reported on the Bach-Händel-Schütz-Celebration in Germany.[20] The same issue dedicated an article to "Beethoven as a Linguistic Purist."[21]

As a rule, anniversaries and commemoration days served as a welcome occasion to write about individual musicians. Furthermore, guest performances offered the opportunity to present ensembles or choirs in the magazine. For Germans in Brazil, such musical events also presented a possibility to keep in touch with the (old) homeland. After a concert of the Regensburger Domspatzen (Regensburg Cathedral Choir) in the Brazilian capital, *Intercâmbio* reported, "While the Regensburger Domspatzen were singing up there in the marvellous

---

[18] Adele Harmsen, "Eine deutsche Sängerin erlebt brasilianische Musik," *Intercâmbio* III.4–6 (1938): 190.
[19] Adele Harmsen, "Eine deutsche Sängerin erlebt brasilianische Musik," *Intercâmbio* III.4–6 (1938): 190.
[20] Cf. Heinz Ihlert, "Deutsche Bach-Händel-Schützfeier 1935," *Intercâmbio* I.2 (1935): 90–93.
[21] Cf. Hermann Seeliger, "Beethoven als Sprachreiniger," *Intercâmbio* I.2 (1935): 99–101.

monastery of São Bento in Rio de Janeiro, many of us who are living out here far away from the German homeland might have had a vision of the German land, the German churches, the German cities, the German forest."[22] German composers also played a major role in the concerts that Pro Arte or the German music association of Rio de Janeiro, for example, organized in Brazil. Furthermore, Germans and German speakers living in Brazil wrote new compositions. *Intercâmbio* reported on the "first German opera in Brazil," written by Otto Adolf Nohel. The libretto was based on an old Indian legend. The music was composed by Josef Pratl, who conducted an orchestra in Joinville. The poet and the composer, both Austrians, had settled in Santa Catarina. The premiere of the opera *Yara* took place on 17 January 1935 in Joinville.[23]

German composer Richard Wagner garnered particular attention in the magazine. The first three issues (1938) started a series of articles on the composer, whose 125th birthday anniversary was commemorated that same year. Issues 4–6 (1938) contained an anecdotal description of his life story, written in Portuguese and accompanied by illustrations.[24] Issues 10–12 (1938) reported on a Bayreuth farewell walk after the 1938 annual festival.[25] Another article in issues 7–9 (1937) focused on the influence of Wagner's and Verdi's œuvre on Carlos Gomes.[26]

Apparently, the Brazilian theaters did not take advantage of his anniversary year and did not schedule any performances of Wagner's works. When Wagner's opera *Lohengrin,* the first opera by Wagner ever performed in Brazil, had been staged in Rio de Janeiro in 1883, it had not received particularly positive critiques. However, according to Theodor Heuberger,

> Here the theatre and all that belongs to it [...] is always under a very strong Italian influence. Any cleaner of boots whistles all the schmaltzy arias to himself, since they have all been heard here to the point of satiety. Any Brazilian person learns the essential from this musical tradition and has long since been inwardly desperate for a change. [...] A large Brazilian community would be thankful for that. And what better way to beautifully express our German thinking and feeling than through Wagner's great dramatic creations.[27]

---

22 Anonymous, "Regensburger Domspatzen," *Intercâmbio* II.7–9 (1937): n.p.
23 Anonymous, "Yara," *Intercâmbio* I.6–7 (1935): 366.
24 Cf. Anonymous, "Esse é Richard Wagner," *Intercâmbio* III.4–6 (1938): 124–132.
25 Cf. Rudolf Becker, "Bayreuther Abschiedsspaziergang," *Intercâmbio* III.10–12 (1938): 380.
26 Cf. Anonymous, "Richard Wagner – Giuseppe Verdi – Carlos Gomes – Tres gigantes de arte internacional," *Intercâmbio* II.7–9 (1937): 226–227.
27 Theodor Heuberger, "Immer noch fehlt Richard Wagner im offiziellen Spielplan in Brasilien," *Intercâmbio* III.1–3 (1938): 3.

The quote's obvious chauvinism is very typical for the magazine's articles on German music in general.

All in all, it seems clear that all issues of *Intercâmbio* incorporated musical themes. Music was considered particularly appropriate for the cultural exchange between Brazil and Germany, which became especially clear in the form of concerts and guest performances by German musicians in Brazil and Brazilian musicians in Germany. Whereas the importance of the works by German composers was never called into question (on the contrary, they were always regarded as very advanced cultural expressions), the Brazilian compositions were almost entirely unknown in Germany, and their quality was noticed with astonishment. Nevertheless, the magazine provided its readers with much more information about German music than about Brazilian compositions.

Medicine: German science for Brazil

Within the range of the sciences, medicine was the most often addressed field in *Intercâmbio*. Closely related to this area was the Instituto Teuto-Brasileiro de Alta Cultura, which devoted itself to the exchange of scientists from both countries. Thus, for the fifth anniversary of the institute's existence, Brazilian doctor Rodolpho Josetti gave a lecture titled "Today's German Surgery," which was based on his visit to Germany; the lecture was printed in the first issue of *Intercâmbio*.[28] The magazine also published comments on visits to Brazil by German doctors. This is how the readers learned that two Berlin professors of medicine, Walter Unverricht and H. Ulrici, presented a lecture in São Paulo on their way back home from the Congresso Panamericano de Tuberculose (Pan-American Congress on Tuberculosis) in Santiago de Chile.[29] In view of the dissemination of medical knowledge, *Intercâmbio* also published translations from the *Münchner Medizinische Wochenschrift* (Munich's weekly medical journal). In the article titled "Médico e doente" (Doctor and patient), the questions raised included why medical treatments did not infrequently fail[30] and how the sick can be treated at home.[31] The column was established upon readers' request, and the articles were addressed to laymen, medical students, and physicians equally. In addi-

---

28 Cf. Rodolpho Josetti, "Die heutige deutsche Chirurgie," *Intercâmbio* I.1 (1935): 15–19.
29 Cf. Anonymous, "Lumes da sciencia medica da Allemanha na America do Sul," *Intercâmbio* III.1–3 (1938): 42.
30 Cf. C. B. Herrligkoffer, "Porque fracassam não raras vezes as prescripções medicas?," *Intercâmbio* I.11–12 (1936): 464–465.
31 Cf. Eduard Mader, "Tratamento domestico de doente," *Intercâmbio* II.1–3 (1937): 58–59.

tion, some readers seemed to be interested in the history of medicine. For example, a short biography of Konrad Röntgen included information on the discovery of X-rays.[32] On the 50th anniversary of the discovery of the vaccines against diphtheria and tetanus, the work of Emil von Behring was remembered in a richly illustrated article.[33] The Sociedade Brasileira de Tuberculose (Brazilian Tuberculosis Society) in Rio de Janeiro dedicated a ceremony to Robert Koch and his discovery of tuberculin in 1890.[34] That same year, the magazine also referred to the movie *Robert Koch: Bekämpfer des Todes* (Robert Koch, fighter against death). Starring Emil Jannings in the role of a German doctor, the movie received several film awards in Germany.[35] The article "Meio século de luta contra a doença e a morte" (Half a century of fighting against illness and death) portrayed Bayer Leverkusen's pharmaceutical success.[36] Although *Intercâmbio* also commemorated outstanding Brazilian physicians, such as Adolpho Lutz,[37] articles on German medicine and German doctors predominated. Ethnomedical contributions also found their way into *Intercâmbio* but to a much lesser extent, such as in the article "Os curandeiros indígenas" (The indigenous healers),[38] which was based on the book *Índios, História de uma grande nação* (Indians, the history of a great nation) by Otto Willi Ulrich and described different medicinal plants and their effects.

However, the little amount of information on Brazilian medicine did not necessarily reflect the perception that Brazilian medicine was inferior to the medical studies and practices in Germany. But it could also be understood as another symptom of German chauvinism.

> With regard to teaching, the young Brazilian physician who graduated school is surely not less prepared for his profession than the young physician who graduates from university in Germany. It might be that the German student has looked deeper into certain scientific issues, but the Brazilian student, in turn, is decidedly superior to him as far as the practical medical training at the patient's bedside is concerned. This had to do with the intensive training of the students as so-called "internos" in the practical work of the different serv-

---

[32] Cf. Anonymous, "Cuidado: Raios X," *Intercâmbio* I.4–5 (1935): 192–196.
[33] Cf. Anonymous, "Salvador das creanças: Retter der Kinder: Emil von Behring," *Intercâmbio* VI.1–3 (1941): 1–4.
[34] Cf. Anonymous, "Roberto Koch. Meio Centenario da descoberta da tuberculina," *Intercâmbio* V.10–12 (1940): 263.
[35] Cf Anonymous, "Robert Koch e Rudolf Virchow. Dois grandes cientistas focalisados para o film," *Intercâmbio* V.4–6 (1940): 121.
[36] Cf. Anonymous, "Meio século de luta contra a doença e a morte," *Intercâmbio* III.10–12 (1938): 375–377.
[37] Cf. Anonymous, "Dr. Adolpho Lutz," *Intercâmbio* V.10–12 (1940): 259–260.
[38] Cf. Otto Willi Ulrich, "Os curandeiros indígenas," *Intercâmbio* IV.1–3 (1939): 23–35.

ices of the hospitals, and not just during some weeks or months during the holidays, as was the case in Germany.[39]

The lack of interest in Brazilian medicine might be related to the fact that since the Constitution of 1934, immigrating physicians without a Brazilian diploma were no longer allowed to practice their profession in Brazil,[40] and therefore there was less need for information on the part of German doctors. Then again, the language problem stood in the way of an intensive exchange between German and Brazilian physicians: Only a few physicians in Germany were ready to take on the task of learning Portuguese, which severely hindered study and research stays in Brazil, for example, in tropical medicine. In contrast, numerous physicians in Brazil were fluent in German, and not all of them were of German descent. A directory of German-speaking doctors in Rio de Janeiro published in *Intercâmbio* listed 128 addresses.[41]

Language courses: the centerpiece of the magazine

In the very first issue, *Intercâmbio* presented a German course for Brazilians. This seemed to be the logical consequence of the magazine's regularly repeated philosophy that access to a different culture would take place through language.

All the institutions involved in the magazine had practical experience in organizing language courses. According to the statistics of Pro Arte for 1933, the association offered three beginners' courses, two intermediate training courses, and an advanced course, which amounted to a total of 560 hours, taught by five instructors of German and one of Portuguese. At the beginning of 1933, the number of participants increased to 624 attendees of Brazilian or German nationality. Rotermund's *Fibel für deutsche Schulen* (Primer for German schools) and the *Schulgrammatik der deutschen Sprache* (School grammar of the German language) by Martin Vorbrodt served as textbooks.[42] In the Instituto Teuto-Brasileiro

---

[39] Erich Bethke, "Zur Problematik des deutschen Arztes in Brasilien," *Intercâmbio* I.3 (1935): 147.
[40] The new legal situation did not limit the exercise of the profession by physicians who had taken an examination at a medical faculty in Brazil in order to validate their degree before the Constitution of 1934 came into effect.
[41] Cf. Anonymous, "Deutschsprechende Aerzte in Rio de Janeiro," *Intercâmbio* I.3 (1935): 179.
[42] Anonymous, "Unsere Sprachkurse," *Pro Arte. Sociedade de Artistas e Amigos das Bellas Artes* October–November (1933): 13.

de Alta, five teachers offered German language lessons for approximately 500 officers, physicians, engineers, jurists, and merchants. An exam was scheduled after six semesters.[43] The branch office of the Deutsche Akademie Munich also focused on language teaching.

Although many German courses had already been offered, their methods and successes became scrutinized. Father Pedro Sinzig developed a course for *Intercâmbio* that was first published in the magazine. He incorporated new methods used in Germany, such as learning by singing (*singendes Lernen*).[44] As in the Deutsche Akademie in Munich, the main focus of the German course was on speaking with the objective of "being able to speak, sing, in short, participate in this language, so that those who are intellectually more ambitious, more demanding, are encouraged to immerse themselves even more thoroughly in the grammatical structures, the history, in short, in the whole richness of the German language."[45]

Every issue included several lessons. The first one started with a Rhine tour during which the song "Die Loreley" (The Loreley) by Heinrich Heine, with music composed by Friedrich Gilcher, was performed. The notes were enclosed with the text in Fraktur script. The second lesson dealt with the first grammatical lesson on the three genders of German nouns, followed by the present tense and an introduction to pronunciation in lesson 3. In the fourth lesson, course participants found out that the family on the Rhine tour was accompanied by a cousin from Brazil who, like them, was in the process of learning German. Therefore, the course alluded to the situation of many learners who were still in contact with their relatives in Germany but had not yet had the opportunity to learn the language systematically. Each lesson was two pages or less and therefore appropriate for an hourly class. After a year, the first course finished with lesson 45. To further improve their knowledge, students were encouraged to read the magazine as well as the book *Wir lesen deutsch* (We read German) by the Deutsche Akademie in Munich. The *Supplemento Linguístico* (Linguistic supplement) started anew with lesson 1, and the language course, entitled *Ich, der Brasilianer reise nach Deutschland* (I, Brazilian, travel to Germany), built on students' experience from their first year of classes. To further intensify "learning by singing," lesson 43 announced the foundation of a choir that would sing German folk songs at

---

[43] Henrique Schueler, "Rundfunkübertragung durch das 'Brasilianische Propaganda-Amt,'" *Boletim do Instituto Teuto-Brasileiro de Alta Cultura* 1 (1937): 18–19.
[44] Cf. Anonymous, "Eine fremde Sprache zu verstehen, ist verhältnismäßig leicht, sie zu sprechen viel schwerer. Woher kommt das?," *Intercâmbio* I.3 (1935): 165.
[45] Theodor Heuberger, "Der neue Weg," *Intercâmbio* I.1 (1935): 2.

Pro Arte once a week. Furthermore, as a complement to language classes, German plays were performed.

In 1936, a Portuguese language course for Germans started in the January–March issue. The language course supplement of *Intercâmbio* presented both courses under the motto "Estuda a minha língua, que estudarei também a tua – Lernst Du meine, Lern ich Deine Sprache" (Learn my language, and I'll learn yours). In this case, the beginning of the course was not preceded by any methodological discussion. The course followed the same goal as the German course: to communicate immediately applicable knowledge. Once more the texts' chapters were designed as a travel story, this time featuring Germans traveling to Brazil. From the very first lesson on, grammatical rules were conveyed. Therefore, the Portuguese course was designed for Germans living in Germany, but very often the participants were living in Brazil temporarily or had only recently settled in Brazil. None of the analyzed issues contained any reports by course participants on their experiences and their progress with the teaching material, nor on their motivations to learn Portuguese.

In contrast, Brazilian students got a chance to express themselves in the magazine and provided many reasons why they were applying themselves to the German language: They wanted to maintain contact with Germans, be that in Brazil or in Germany; there were also professional reasons for their interest in German; and, finally, they repeatedly mentioned an interest in culture, especially literature and music. The method of the language courses was addressed only in the margins, but overall students seemed satisfied with the lessons. Given the experiences of Pro Arte and the Instituto Teuto-Brasileiro de Alta Cultura, one can assume that people from very different professional groups and social classes followed this language course, although it focused on students and graduates.

Intercâmbio: an authentic cultural exchange?

"It is without doubt an excellent idea to cultivate the cultural relations between Germany and Brazil through a magazine,"[46] and "The bilingual, richly illustrated magazine is particularly original in its advertising of German culture."[47] These two enthusiastic voices from Germany introduce the final question I will discuss:

---

46 Horn, "Der Widerhall. Aus den vielen Zuschriften an die Schriftleitung des Intercambio," *Intercâmbio* I.4–5 (1935): 237.
47 Alfons Paquet, "Der Widerhall. Aus den vielen Zuschriften an die Schriftleitung des Intercambio," *Intercâmbio* I.4–5 (1935): 237.

Did *Intercâmbio,* as intended by the editors, devote itself to the cultural exchange between Brazil and Germany, or did the magazine consist predominantly of publicity for German culture or, more precisely, for the objectives of National Socialist cultural policy?

Undoubtedly, the magazine embraced a wide range of cultural and scientific topics from Germany and Brazil. Apparently, between 1935 and 1941, sports was considered a theme only marginally belonging to culture and inappropriate for an exchange, even though the 1936 Olympics in Berlin would have been an excellent occasion for it. On the whole, German culture and science were addressed more often and in a more comprehensive way than Brazilian culture and science. The focus was generally not on current art and culture but on the cultural production of past epochs. The magazine did not dissociate itself from German cultural policy of the 1930s and 1940s; this was in accordance with the fact that neither the art banned in Germany as "degenerate" nor the cultural creations of German Jews were included. Apparently, the editors were equally uncritical toward – or welcoming of – German politics in general, which was frequently mirrored in the unreflected choice of words. Just as absent was a critical approach to current Brazilian politics and cultural policy. The cultural achievements of indigenous and Afro-Brazilian peoples were almost completely ignored. The presentation suggests that it was the magazine's main goal to emphasize the existing bond between German and Brazilian culture.

According to the information that can be gathered about its means of distribution, the reception of the magazine was substantially greater in Brazil than in Germany. Therefore, one can assume that the magazine's marketing of German culture targeted German-speaking citizens and that the German community living in Brazil was of central importance. It is also possible to assume that, because of the immigration of numerous Germans to Brazil, readers' interest in Germany and its culture and science was substantially more significant in Brazil than Germans' interest in Brazil. Germans who had family ties or professional contacts in Brazil were interested in the culture of the Latin American country as well. It was not possible to analyze the reception and impact of the magazine using the available materials. In this respect, only the readers' letters printed in *Intercâmbio* provided information on the magazine's popularity, but one can assume that they were specifically chosen for publication because of their thoroughly positive feedback. However, the magazine also regularly provided Germans with information on cultural topics from Brazil, which by other means would have definitely involved a bigger effort, especially for readers without any knowledge of Portuguese. A better balance between information on Brazil and Germany would have definitely enriched the magazine's modes of expression and diversity of topics. The thematic orientation and presentation, together with the choice of vocabulary, undoubtedly indicate that the magazine followed and affirmed National Socialist Germany's cultural policy and propaganda and did not act independently from it.

References

Almeida, Renato. "O Encantamento de Nuremberg!" *Intercâmbio* II.7–9 (1937): 181–182.
Anonymous. "Ao comerciante brasileiro." *Intercâmbio* I.1 (1935): n.p.
Anonymous. "Cuidado: Raios X." *Intercâmbio* I.4–5 (1935): 192–196.
Anonymous. "Deutscher Kaufmann!" *Intercâmbio* I.1 (1935): n.p.
Anonymous. "Deutschsprechende Aerzte in Rio de Janeiro." *Intercâmbio* I.3 (1935): 179.
Anonymous. "Dr. Adolpho Lutz." *Intercâmbio* V.10–12 (1940): 259–260.
Anonymous. "Eine fremde Sprache zu verstehen, ist verhältnismäßig leicht, sie zu sprechen viel schwerer. Woher kommt das?" *Intercâmbio* I.3 (1935): 164–165.
Anonymous. "Esse é Richard Wagner." *Intercâmbio* III.4–6 (1938): 124–132.
Anonymous. "Lumes da sciencia medica da Allemanha na America do Sul." *Intercâmbio* III.1–3 (1938): 42.
Anonymous. "Meio século de luta contra a doença e a morte." *Intercâmbio* III.10–12 (1938): 375–377.
Anonymous. "Der neue deutsche Botschafter." *Intercâmbio* II.10–12 (1937): 278.
Anonymous. "Das Neue Reich." *Intercâmbio* I.6–7 (1935): 315–316.
Anonymous. "O Brasil de hoje. A Allemanha de hoje." *Intercâmbio* I.4–5 (1935): 183–185.
Anonymous. "Regensburger Domspatzen." *Intercâmbio* II.7–9 (1937): n.p.
Anonymous. "Richard Wagner – Giuseppe Verdi – Carlos Gomes – Tres gigantes de arte internacional." *Intercâmbio* II.7–9 (1937): 226–227.
Anonymous. "Roberto Koch. Meio Centenario da descoberta da tuberculina." *Intercâmbio* V.10–12 (1940): 263.
Anonymous. "Robert Koch e Rudolf Virchow. Dois grandes cientistas focalisados para o film." *Intercâmbio* V.4–6 (1940): 121.
Anonymous. "Salvador das creanças: Retter der Kinder: Emil von Behring." *Intercâmbio* VI.1–3 (1941): 1–4.
Anonymous. "Unsere Sprachkurse." *Pro Arte. Sociedade de Artistas e Amigos das Bellas Artes* October–November (1933): 13.
Anonymous. "Yara." *Intercâmbio* I.6–7 (1935): 366.
Becker, Rudolf. "Bayreuther Abschiedsspaziergang." *Intercâmbio* III.10–12 (1938): 380.
Bethke, Erich. "Zur Problematik des deutschen Arztes in Brasilien." *Intercâmbio* I.3 (1935): 146–149.
Cziersky, Otto. "Mein Vater. Gespräch mit Itala Gomes Vaz de Carvalho." *Intercâmbio* I.8–10 (1936): 342–343.
Harmsen, Adele. "Eine deutsche Sängerin erlebt brasilianische Musik." *Intercâmbio* III.4–6 (1938): 190.
Herrligkoffer, C. B. "Porque fracassam não raras vezes as prescripções médicas?" *Intercâmbio* I.11–12 (1936): 464–465.

Heuberger, Theodor. "Immer noch fehlt Richard Wagner im offiziellen Spielplan in Brasilien." *Intercâmbio* III.1–3 (1938): 3.
Heuberger, Theodor. "Der neue Weg." *Intercâmbio* I.1 (1935): 2–4.
Horn. "Der Widerhall. Aus den vielen Zuschriften an die Schriftleitung des Intercambio." *Intercâmbio* I.4–5 (1935): 237.
Ihlert, Heinz. "Deutsche Bach-Händel-Schützfeier 1935." *Intercâmbio* I.2 (1935): 90–93.
Josetti, Rodolpho. "Die heutige deutsche Chirurgie." *Intercâmbio* I.1 (1935): 15–19.
Lachmund, Charley. "Erinnerungen an Belo Horizontes Kinderjahre." *Intercâmbio* III.10–12 (1938): 414–419.
Mader, Eduard. "Tratamento dómestico de doente." *Intercâmbio* II.1–3 (1937): 58–59.
Michels, Eckard. *Von der Deutschen Akademie zum Goethe-Institut. Sprache und auswärtige Kulturpolitik 1923–1960* (Munich: Oldenbourg, 2005).
Oliveira, Lisette de. "Porque estudas a lingua allemã?" *Intercâmbio* I.1 (1935): 46.
Paquet, Alfons. "Der Widerhall. Aus den vielen Zuschriften an die Schriftleitung des Intercambio." *Intercâmbio* I.4–5 (1935): 237.
R. J. "Intercambio." *Intercâmbio* I.1 (1935): n.p.
Schueler, Henrique. "Rundfunkübertagung durch das 'Brasilianische Propaganda-Amt.'" *Boletim do Instituto Teuto-Brasileiro de Alta Cultura* 1 (1937): 17–19.
Seeliger, Hermann. "Beethoven als Sprachreiniger." *Intercâmbio* I.2 (1935): 99–101.
Ulrich, Otto Willi. "Os curandeiros indígenas." *Intercâmbio* IV.1–3 (1939): 23–35.
Verlé, Heinrich. "Das Lied der Zeit." *Intercâmbio* I.4–5 (1935).

Andrew W. Hurley
From Documentation to Dialogue: On Bringing Brazilian Popular Music and Jazz to West Germany*

In 1963, West Germany's "Jazz Pope," Joachim-Ernst Berendt, agonized over what to make of the bossa nova, one of the latest developments in global popular music and jazz. Was it an exciting impetus and breath of fresh air in a context where jazz was losing some of its public? Was it a commercialized fad? Or was it some combination of the two? It was a question that he never answered unambiguously. Fifteen years after the precarious beginning, however, German jazz musicians could look back on a long-running and fruitful love affair with Brazilian music, which had manifested itself, among other things, in a series of dialogic partnerships with Brazilian musicians.

This chapter examines some of the ways that West German jazz critics and impresarios, including Berendt, Horst Lippmann and Fritz Rau, and Claus Schreiner mediated Brazilian popular music to German audiences, especially in the 1960s and 1970s.[1] I demonstrate how their mediation of art forms such as the bossa nova was driven partly by pedagogical zeal about reforming Germany's post–National Socialist "national" culture and by an exoticizing enthusiasm, both of which cast Brazil as an Other to undesirable aspects of German culture. However, Brazilian popular music also represented a problem for certain parts of the German music press. It was one important site at which music journalists and writers first began to think about intercultural appropriation and the hybridization of popular music and to query the limits thereof. More importantly, though, these discursive activities did not occur in a vacuum. Institutions such as the Berlin Jazz Days and the Goethe-Institut's jazz tours presented practical opportunities for German and Brazilian musicians to perform together, both in Germany and in Brazil, and gave rise to a productive substratum for a series of genuine intercultural meetings that, to some extent, took place regardless of the theories that men such as Berendt expounded. These "meetings" will

---

* Thanks to Claus Schreiner and Christopher Larkosh and to the DeGruyter-appointed readers for their constructive comments on an earlier draft of this chapter.
1 In this chapter I will not examine the reception of the bossa nova and Brazilian popular music in East Germany at the time. This is a matter that is, to my knowledge, underilluminated and needing of a specific analysis that unpacks the ways in which the German Democratic Republic politicized popular music production, mediation, and reception.

set the scene for my examination of some of the ways in the 1980s that both "anxious" and "celebratory" German accounts of the international dissemination of popular music, and of "world music," called on Brazilian popular music and its development to make their case.

"Schuld war nur der Bossa Nova?" The bossa as a problem for the German jazz press

Emerging in Rio de Janeiro in the late 1950s, the bossa nova has been described as "the first truly pan-hemispheric music of the Americas."[2] Although its first manifestations were in Antônio Carlos Jobim and Vinicius de Moraes's music for the 1956 stage play *Black Orpheus*, the "classic phase of bossa nova," which ran to 1962, commenced with guitarist João Gilberto's 1958 recordings of "Chega de Saudade" and "Desafinado."[3] Generically speaking, the bossa nova is regarded as a "slower, cooler samba" with a simplified rhythm.[4] There is considerable dispute as to the heritage of this innovation, however. Some of the genre's prime movers, such as João Gilberto, were clearly influenced by the West Coast, or "cool," jazz of North American musicians including Chet Baker and Gerry Mulligan. However, this was not the case for all, including for the central figure of Jobim.[5] Moreover, the "influência do jazz," and any putative "Americanization" of Brazilian musical culture became a highly charged matter in Brazil.[6] If the bossa nova was just such an "Americanized" form for some Brazilians, then for others it was an expression of a "dare-to-be-different aspect of the Brazilian

---

[2] Ed Morales, *The Latin Beat: The Rhythms and Roots of Latin Music from Bossa Nova to Salsa and Beyond* (Cambridge, MA: Da Capo, 2003), 205.
[3] David Treece, "Guns and Roses: Bossa Nova and Brazil's Music of Popular Protest, 1958–68," *Popular Music* 16.1 (1997), 6.
[4] Ed Morales, *The Latin Beat: The Rhythms and Roots of Latin Music from Bossa Nova to Salsa and Beyond* (Cambridge, MA: Da Capo, 2003), 205. See also Chris McGowan and Ricardo Pessanha, *The Brazilian Sound* (Philadelphia: Temple University Press, 1998), 55.
[5] John S. Roberts, *Latin Jazz* (New York: Schirmer, 1999), 93, 119; Charles A. Perrone and Christopher Dunn, *Brazilian Popular Music and Globalization* (Gainesville: University of Florida Press, 2001), 17; Ed Morales, *The Latin Beat: The Rhythms and Roots of Latin Music from Bossa Nova to Salsa and Beyond* (Cambridge, MA: Da Capo, 2003), 205.
[6] Chris McGowan and Ricardo Pessanha, *The Brazilian Sound* (Philadelphia: Temple University Press, 1998), 65–66; Claus Schreiner, *Musica Brasileira*. Trans. M. Weinstein (London: Marion Boyars, 1993), 135.

psyche" and a bid to "become a cultural peer of the United States."[7] Claus Schreiner suggests that the North American music industry also stressed the "influência do jazz" notion so as to authorize its own expropriation of Brazilian music, which began in earnest in 1962 and 1963.[8] Ed Morales points out that the bossa nova "traveled well outside of Brazil."[9] Indeed, by the early 1960 s "bossa novas" were being recorded by North American musicians practicing in a range of genres, from jazz to pop. The bossa nova became a veritable boom after the success of Stan Getz's recording of "The Girl from Ipanema," included on the 1963 recording *Getz/Gilberto* and featuring vocals by Astrud Gilberto, a Brazilian of partly German extraction.[10]

When the bossa nova began to be received in West Germany in the early 1960s, it was something of a guilty pleasure for the jazz and jazz-related press. Foremost among West German jazz critics by this time was the "Jazz Pope," Joachim-Ernst Berendt (1922–2000), a broadcaster, music writer, and producer based at the Südwestfunk (Southwest Radio, or SWF), the public radio station based in Baden Baden.[11] Berendt was a complex man who was doubly scarred by the Nazi era. During the war he fought on the Eastern front, but his father, a Protestant minister, had been incarcerated by the Nazi regime and subsequently died. This background profoundly influenced his postwar cultural politics, as we will see. Berendt felt himself pulled in several directions by the bossa nova, which he first encountered during a short trip to Buenos Aires in 1960.[12] Berendt had a long-standing interest in all sorts of "exotic" musics. An ardent fan of jazz, he adhered to the notion of jazz as the "sound of surprise" (Whitney Balliett) and was always keen to hear new sounds. The open-eared Be-

---

7 Ed Morales, *The Latin Beat: The Rhythms and Roots of Latin Music from Bossa Nova to Salsa and Beyond* (Cambridge, MA: Da Capo, 2003), 207; see also Charles A. Perrone, *Masters of Contemporary Brazilian Song: MPB, 1965–1985* (Austin: University of Texas Press, 1989), xxv; David Treece, "Guns and Roses: Bossa Nova and Brazil's Music of Popular Protest, 1958–68," *Popular Music* 16.1 (1997), 16; Charles A. Perrone and Christopher Dunn, *Brazilian Popular Music and Globalization* (Gainesville: University of Florida Press, 2001), 18–19.
8 Claus Schreiner, *Música Brasileira*. Trans. M. Weinstein (London: Marion Boyars, 1993), 146.
9 Ed Morales, *The Latin Beat: The Rhythms and Roots of Latin Music from Bossa Nova to Salsa and Beyond* (Cambridge, MA: Da Capo, 2003), 208.
10 See, generally, Claus Schreiner, *Música Brasileira*. Trans. M. Weinstein (London: Marion Boyars, 1993); Chris McGowan and Ricardo Pessanha, *The Brazilian Sound* (Philadelphia: Temple University Press, 1998); Charles A. Perrone and Christopher Dunn, *Brazilian Popular Music and Globalization* (Gainesville: University of Florida Press, 2001).
11 For a critical biography of Berendt, see Andrew W. Hurley, *The Return of Jazz: Joachim-Ernst Berendt and West German Cultural Change* (New York: Berghahn Books, 2009).
12 Joachim-Ernst Berendt, "Die Bossa Nova Story," *Twen* (May 1963): 36–41.

rendt was clearly intrigued by and attracted to bossa nova when he heard it.[13] And yet he was not alone, which was where his problems started. In West Germany, too, something of a bossa nova fad had broken out in the early 1960s. For example, the *Schlager* singer Manuela had a hit with the 1963 song "Schuld war nur der Bossa Nova," a German version of the Mann/Weil song "Blame It on the Bossa Nova," made famous by U.S. singer Eydie Gorme in the same year.

Berendt wrote about the bossa nova several times in the 1960s and 1970s, and he frequently changed his mind about it. We need to read his overdetermined flip-flopping not just in line with the prerogative of the critic to change her or his mind but especially in the context of his long-running attempts to "legitimate" jazz in postwar West Germany, as well as in the context of his desire to endure as Germany's primary jazz authority. The latter was an almost impossible task in the 1960s, when fronts opened up in the Federal Republic between the adherents of "pop jazz" – jazz versions of the bossa nova were located here – and of avant-garde free jazz.[14] By the mid-1960s, Berendt was wearing several caps. He continued to broadcast and write books and articles about jazz. He advised the Goethe-Institut about which jazz musicians it should send abroad as part of its cultural outreach program. He was responsible for the artistic programming of the Berlin Jazz Days, Europe's most handsomely funded jazz festival at the time, where he attempted to satisfy all jazz fans by presenting all sorts of jazz, past and present. He was responsible for producing jazz records released by the important German independent label Saba/MPS and was associated with Hamburg's *twen* magazine, which released its own record series.[15] In other words, he was intimately involved with all aspects of the music market, even if that position was occasionally in open conflict with his discourse about jazz *as art*.

In a context where the distinction between *ernste Musik* ("serious music") and *Unterhaltungsmusik* ("entertainment music") was ossified and a great deal of German opposition to jazz existed, some of it a carryover from National Socialist antijazz ideology, Berendt had spent much of the late 1940s and 1950s attempting to legitimate jazz as an art music and to fence off "true" jazz from popular music, especially the *Schlager*. This included doing so in the journal *Merkur* in mid-1953 in a public debate with Theodor W. Adorno, the prominent Frankfurt

---

13 See also Joachim-Ernst Berendt, *Ein Fenster aus Jazz* (Frankfurt am Main: Fischer, 1977), 351.
14 See Siegfried Schmidt-Joos, "Ein Votum für populären Jazz," *Jazz Podium* (December 1965): 320–321; Siegfried Schmidt-Joos and Felix Schmidt, "Reisst die Barrieren nieder," *Der Spiegel* (27 January 1969): 118–120.
15 See Jens Mueller, ed., *Philips-Twen: Der Tonangebende Realismus* (Baden: Lars Mueller Publishers, 2009).

School critical theorist and a notorious leftist opponent of jazz.[16] In the early 1960s, the bossa nova fad and its popularity in Germany seemed as if it might undo that hard work. In his first major printed piece on the bossa nova, in the May 1963 edition of *twen,* Berendt walked a difficult line; essentially, he praised Brazilian bossa nova while damning (with faint praise) the majority of North American bossa novas. According to Berendt, Brazilian protagonists such as Gilberto and Jobim made a jazzlike music and had no interest in the commercial music industry. On the other hand, in North America the bossa had become "a business [proposition] such as there had not been for a long time in jazz."[17] While defending "true" jazz, he could afford to be slightly charitable toward the bossa nova:

> As a listener and critic of jazz you can certainly have reservations about the bossa nova, but the musical listener who has an interest in something being played on the *Schlager* programs from which (s)he doesn't have to immediately flee in disgust has no reservations.[18]

How then to deal with the respectable jazz musicians such as Stan Getz – or in the German context saxophonists Hans Koller and Klaus Doldinger – who were involved in this fad?[19] Here was a case of musicians doing what they liked, independent of the Jazz Pope's opinions. Berendt was initially inclined to see in musicians like these a certain opportunism at a time when jazz sales were not healthy. However, he had changed his mind, suggesting that they were simply attracted to the charms of the bossa nova.[20] And so he could, with a clean conscience, promote the record that *twen* was then marketing: a recording of protobossa made by North American jazz guitarist Charlie Byrd in the mid-1950s. The title of this record, *Brasilien. Jazz und Poesie – so begann Bossa Nova* (Brazil. Jazz and Poetry – thus began the bossa nova) hinted at the "influência do jazz" stance he would take in 1966, when he returned to appropriations of the bossa nova. On the whole, however, Berendt maintained arm's length from these activities in the early 1960s.

---

16 Theodor Adorno, "Für und wider den Jazz," *Merkur* (July 1953): 890–893; Joachim-Ernst Berendt, "Für und wider den Jazz," *Merkur* (July 1953): 887–890. On this debate see Christian Broecking, "Adorno vs Berendt Revisited," in *Jazz und Gesellschaft.* Ed. Wolfram Knauer (Hofheim: Wolke Verlag, 2002), 41–53.
17 Translations are the author's.
18 Joachim-Ernst Berendt, "Die Bossa Nova Story," *Twen* (May 1963): 36–41.
19 Doldinger, for example, had recorded the song "Blue Note Samba" on his 1963 album *Live at Blue Note Berlin.*
20 Joachim-Ernst Berendt, "Die Bossa Nova Story," *Twen* (May 1963): 36–41.

By contrast, 1965–1967 represents a new watershed in the German reception of Brazilian popular music, which also heralded a new approach to the bossa nova on Berendt's part. The reasons for this were several; funded by the Goethe-Institut, German jazz musicians traveled to Brazil for the first time and engaged with the music *in situ*.[21] Second, Brazilian popular music would be performed live in Germany in a new "documentary" context. Third, German-instigated recordings of Brazilian music would begin to be made, both in Germany and in Brazil itself. Finally, Stan Getz and the Teuto-Brazilian Astrud Gilberto would perform live at the Berlin Jazz Days. Berendt was actively involved in these activities and had a vested interest in them, which doubtless had an impact on his discourse about Brazilian music and its appropriation, which now softened a little.

Returning to the bossa: a model and a warning

In 1966, Berendt was instrumental in the presentation of a troupe of Brazilian musicians and dancers at a range of locations in Germany, including at the Berlin Jazz Days, where they shared the bill with the Stan Getz Quartet and Astrud Gilberto. In Berlin, the Folklore e Bossa Nova do Brasil troupe and Getz's group were supposed to demonstrate how jazz was capable of engaging with folklore, a guiding theme of the Jazz Days that year.[22] (Later in this chapter I return to this important theme and the ideological freight Berendt invested in it.) Presenting Getz's commercially successful quartet was also a function of Berendt's desire, in increasingly polarized times, of presenting the "whole jazz" at the Jazz Days. Thus, Getz's pop jazz would be a counterbalance for the more uncompromising free jazz that he was also presenting that year.

Horst Lippmann and Fritz Rau, two Frankfurt-based jazz enthusiasts who had recently diversified from organizing jazz concerts to presenting a range of "authentic folklore documentations" were responsible for mounting the Folklore e Bossa Nova do Brasil tour.[23] Lippmann and Rau had commenced their "authentic documentations" of folk music and folklore in 1962 with an American Folk

---

21 German jazz musicians were not the only ones to visit Brazil in this period. The popular *Schlager* singer Caterina Valente also visited the country and took part in a Globo TV popular song competition in 1965, winning a Globo award for the best foreign interpreter of Latin American music. Thanks to Claus Schreiner for pointing this out.
22 Joachim-Ernst Berendt, Programme notes for the 1966 Berlin Jazz Days.
23 This account of Lippmann and Rau's activities is from Kathrin Brigl and Siegfried Schmidt-Joos, *Fritz Rau: Buchhalter der Träume* (Berlin: Quadriga, 1985).

Blues Festival and continued with festivals of flamenco (1965–1970) and Musica Folklórica Argentina (1967). Lippmann's and Rau's motivations were as multiple as Berendt's. On one hand, they wanted to advocate for various types of music, that, like jazz, Germans misunderstood, undervalued, or were oblivious to. Therefore, they presented music that was a "precursor" to jazz (as in the "folk blues") or that had artistic merit in its "authentic" form or was otherwise similar to "true" jazz. Their efforts were not without significance, including in Brazil. For example, the Brazilian daily *Jornal do Brasil* claimed that so representative a troupe as Folklore e Bossa Nova do Brasil had not yet been assembled even in Brazil.[24] But if Lippmann's and Rau's motives were partly documentary and pedagogical, they were also commercial. At a time when the market for jazz was shrinking, they wanted to capitalize on the emerging folk revival, which in Germany had a distinctly "international" hue given the way in which German *Volksmusik* had been instrumentalized under National Socialism.[25]

Berendt and Lippmann made trips to Brazil in the summer of 1966 to scout for "authentic" Brazilian folklore and bossa nova singers. This marked the first of Berendt's several trips to Brazil, and he used it extremely productively. Not only did he assist Lippmann in locating musicians for the tour, he also tracked down guitarist Baden Powell and collaborated with Brazilian producer Wadi Gebara Neto on the German release of one of Powell's recordings.[26] The resulting album, titled *Tristeza on Guitar,* was commercially successful and inaugurated a relationship with the guitarist that endured for several widely released albums and live concerts and until well into the 1970s. In contrast, the Folklore e Bossa Nova do Brasil concerts were not a success, which Fritz Rau attributes to the failure of the mainstream German media to take notice of them.[27] Claus Schreiner notes that the live music competition in Germany that year, including from the Rolling Stones, Bob Dylan, Franz Josef Degenhardt, and Hannes Wader, was simply too great (1997). This commercial failure explains why Lippmann and Rau staged only one festival of Folklore e Bossa Nova do Brasil. By the late 1960s,

---

24 Joachim-Ernst Berendt, Cover notes for Various musicians, *Folklore e Bossa Nova do Brasil,* 1966. See also Joachim-Ernst Berendt, "Berendts September Jazz," *Twen* (September 1966): 114–115.
25 See Andrew W. Hurley, *The Return of Jazz: Joachim-Ernst Berendt and West German Cultural Change* (New York: Berghahn Books, 2009), 94.
26 It is not clear exactly what role Berendt played in the recording. He is listed as coproducer of the album, but Schreiner suspects that he may have simply purchased for Saba the rights to an already recorded album (Schreiner, e-mail to the author, 2011).
27 Kathrin Brigl and Siegfried Schmidt-Joos, *Fritz Rau: Buchhalter der Träume* (Berlin: Quadriga, 1985), 150.

they had moved away from the poorly remunerating "authentic documentations" and rebadged themselves as rock and pop concert agents.[28]

Despite the 1966 tour's limited commercial success and the lack of attention paid by the mainstream media, the critical and audience reception was not insignificant. The reaction in Berlin, for example, was rapturous. Heinz Ohff, writing in the *Berliner Tagespiegel*, noted that "the enthusiasm was great: Brazil fascinated."[29] Other specialist reviewers singled out for comment two features of this concert. First, there was the so-called "nest-warmth" or "vitality" the Brazilian musicians displayed.[30] Second, there was scantily clad dancer Marly Tavares, whom Rainer Blome memorably described as a "glowing ball of passion and fire. She brought something of South America's sun into a cold and foggy Berlin. [...] The skin, blood and heartbeat of a warm and lively continent, from which one [can] only dream, lay within reach."[31]

This exoticist and clearly eroticized reception reflected both the history of Germany's reception of Brazilian popular culture and the fact that, pedagogical impulses notwithstanding, Lippmann and Rau actually had an interest in the exoticization and eroticization of Brazilian culture, or what Rau later called the "touristic aspect."[32] As they had discovered from their experience with the flamenco festivals, these "authentic documentations" might attract die-hard folklore fans, but they also attracted Germans who were beginning to discover international travel and tourism, and this latter segment boosted concert attendances noticeably.[33] (It is of course an artificial exercise to distinguish, as Fritz Rau does, between the serious music enthusiasts and the tourists. Music enthusiasts travel, and tourists listen to music.) Deciding to include the dancer Ta-

---

[28] Kathrin Brigl and Siegfried Schmidt-Joos, *Fritz Rau: Buchhalter der Träume* (Berlin: Quadriga, 1985), 150.

[29] Heinz Ohff, "Faszinierendes Brasilien," *Berliner Tagespiegel* (November 1966). Included in D. Rein, ed. *Berliner Jazztage Documentation* (Berlin: Hochschule der Künste, n.d.).

[30] Heinz Ohff, "Faszinierendes Brasilien," *Berliner Tagespiegel* (November 1966). Included in D. Rein, ed. *Berliner Jazztage Documentation* (Berlin: Hochschule der Künste, n.d.); Manfred Miller, "Berliner Jazztage 1966," *Jazz Podium* (December 1966): 324–328.

[31] Rainer Blome, "Berliner Jazztage 1966," *Sounds* (Winter 1966–1967): 9–10.

[32] Fritz Rau noted that up until the point of their tour, Brazilian musical culture had been represented by "revue groups like 'Carnival in Rio'" (Kathrin Brigl and Siegfried Schmidt-Joos, *Fritz Rau: Buchhalter der Träume* [Berlin: Quadriga, 1985], 151). On the genealogy of the German reception of Brazil, see the introduction to this volume and the various contributions to it.

[33] On the increase in international tourism among young West Germans during the "long 1960s," see Axel Schildt, "Across the Border: West German Youth Travel to Western Europe," in *Between Marx and Coca-Cola*. Eds. A. Schildt and Detlef Siegfried (New York: Berghahn Books, 2006), 149–160.

vares, and depicting her on the cover of the accompanying Saba recording, was not innocent either.[34] Other German showcases of Brazilian popular music from the period, including a 1965 recording for *twen* by Klaus Doldinger (*Doldinger in Südamerika*) and Baden Powell's *Tristeza on Guitar*, were marketed in ways that also featured the female form.[35]

The feminization and sexualization of Brazil by way of cover art may or may not have reflected producer Berendt's influence, nor was it inconsistent with the "cheesecake" way in which other non-Brazilian recordings were marketed by Saba/MPS and other German labels at the time.[36] However, it was also not inconsistent with what Michael Ruesenberg has called Berendt's "erotomania,"[37] including in relation to dark-skinned and mixed-race women. Berendt's 1996 autobiography reveals that he believed interracial sexual encounters had an antiracist value and that they were invested in a project of "creating" a postracial world, far removed from the racial thinking of the Nazi era.[38] This discourse was clearly influenced by his family's own experience of the Nazi era, by his experiences in Brazil, and by his positive interpretation of Brazil's race mixing and "racial democracy."[39] Berendt advanced a similarly naive and self-justifying argument in the 1980s in relation to *Weltmusik*, where he suggested that "the god Eros and Lady Music" had done much to break down racial thinking.[40]

In the 1960s Berendt's discourse had not yet taken on this overtly sexualized tone, although he was very much committed to the idea of using music as a way of transcending categories such as the nation and race. Indeed, he was interested in the way jazz and the musical "encounters" it allowed might offer a platform on which to engage in symbolic internationalism and thereby contribute

---

34 Berendt produced the record for the Saba/MPS label.
35 A 1970 recording of Egberto Gismonti, produced by Berendt for the MPS label, likewise featured an erotic silhouette of a female face.
36 Cf. Klaus-Gotthard Fischer, *Jazzin' The Black Forest* (Berlin: Crippled Library, 1999); Jens Mueller, ed., *Philips-Twen: Der Tonangebende Realismus* (Baden: Lars Mueller Publishers, 2009). Curiously, the cover for *Tristeza on Guitar* was designed by Berendt's second wife, Gigi.
37 Michael Ruesenberg, personal interview with the author, 22 October 2004.
38 Joachim-Ernst Berendt, *Das Leben ein Klang* (Munich: Droemersche Verlagsanstalt, 1996): 106.
39 See, for example, Joachim-Ernst Berendt, *Ein Fenster aus Jazz* (Frankfurt am Main: Fischer, 1977), 338–340. On the popular survival of Gilberto Freyre's notion of Brazil as a racial democracy, first introduced in the 1930s, and on its masking effect on the real inequality between races, see Barbara Browning, *Samba: Resistance in Motion* (Bloomington: Indiana University Press, 1995), 3–34; Ed Morales, *The Latin Beat: The Rhythms and Roots of Latin Music from Bossa Nova to Salsa and Beyond* (Cambridge, MA: Da Capo, 2003), 199–200.
40 Joachim-Ernst Berendt, "Über Weltmusik." *Jazz Podium* (March 1985): 8.

to banishing the evils of the recent German past. This ideological dimension was an important one for Berendt, perhaps as important as the musical dimension. Seizing especially on what he saw as the democratic, international, and cosmopolitan aspects of jazz but thereby appropriating the music from African America, Berendt tenaciously promoted jazz in postwar Germany, putting it into service for a German post-Nazi project, aimed at liberalizing German hearts and minds.[41] By the early 1960s he was beginning to incorporate other musics into that project too. In 1962, Berendt coproduced an encounter between a Japanese jazz group and a koto ensemble, and he further developed this idea in 1965 at the Berlin Jazz Days.[42] He soon began to conceive of other such meetings that would eventually take their place in the important "Jazz Meets the World" series, one of the early cornerstones of world music in Germany.[43]

Berendt's conceptualization of jazz as symbolically international and of the importance of the musical "encounter" provides another crucial reason why he returned to the "problem" of the bossa nova in 1966. As Berendt now explained, the bossa nova had a singular value to him as an *international* form of music: It represented the first true hybridization of jazz with folk music outside the United States.[44] Whereas other attempts to hybridize jazz had remained jazz, the bossa nova was something quite new and different.[45] By extrapolation, it could offer a model for other such hybrids and for a type of collegial, international music making, such as he was contemplating with "Jazz Meets the World." Berendt's recourse to cool jazzer Stan Getz expanded his argument. If Brazil's musical innovators had borrowed from cool jazz – a proposition that, as we have seen, was actually very contentious in Brazil – then Getz was merely reborrowing something that had been borrowed from him and his colleagues in the first place. This was not an end to the matter, however, because for Berendt the most important thing was what the non-Brazilian musician did with the bossa nova; straight copies were not enough. A respectable musician such as Getz rendered the bossa nova in his or her own individual way; it was this process of artistic transformation that redeemed a few exceptions to the general rule that the non-Brazilian

---

[41] Joachim-Ernst Berendt, *Das Leben ein Klang* (Munich: Droemersche Verlagsanstalt, 1996): 314.
[42] See Andrew W. Hurley, "Beyond the *Sakura Waltz*: Reflections on the Encounter Between German and Japanese Jazz, 1962–1985," *Perfect Beat: The Pacific Journal of Research into Contemporary Music and Popular Culture* 8.4 (2008): 25–43.
[43] For more on this series, see Andrew W. Hurley, *The Return of Jazz: Joachim-Ernst Berendt and West German Cultural Change* (New York: Berghahn Books, 2009), 147–217.
[44] Joachim-Ernst Berendt, Programme notes for the 1966 Berlin Jazz Days, 20.
[45] Joachim-Ernst Berendt, *Ein Fenster aus Jazz* (Frankfurt am Main: Fischer, 1977), 349.

appropriation of the bossa nova involved a "perversion, commercialization and watering down" of the original form.⁴⁶ Getz, for example, had developed an "artistic product that [had been] alienated in multiple ways [and was a] refined derivative."⁴⁷ This tortured logic revealed several things. First, the Brazilian bossa nova delineated how a valuable new hybrid might arise. Rather than plumping for a chauvinist line – only Brazilians can perform "authentic" bossa nova – Berendt was very much interested in a model of international collegiality, but one where standards of individual artistic vision were paramount. Only under these ill-defined circumstances might the categories of jazz (i.e., art) and commerce be kept apart. On the whole, Berendt continued to display a distinct discomfort with the commercial success of the bossa nova, even as he presented in Berlin one of its most successful North American purveyors. A decade later, when the broad success of the bossa nova was a distant memory and jazz musicians engaged with Brazilian music in more complex, and less "popular" ways, Berendt could relax a little and suggest that jazz and Brazilian folk music stood "as intimate equals": "It is precisely because the trend is now over that a true 'integration' of Brazilian music into the mainstream of Western popular music could come to pass."⁴⁸ Yet he still could not resist a snipe; earlier activities had been "basically just a commercial fad."⁴⁹ Hence, when one was looking for ways of conceiving of intercultural music making, the bossa nova might have offered a model, but in a context where hardened distinctions between *ernste Musik* and *Unterhaltungsmusik* persisted, it also served as a warning.

Although Berendt's discourse and the broader German reception of Brazilian popular music at this time were not without their problems, one ought not to dismiss his efforts. As Claus Schreiner notes, Berendt's activities in presenting Baden Powell in concert and in producing a string of records with him in the late 1960s and 1970s promoted Powell's career at a time when musical fashions in his native Brazil had outmoded his playing.⁵⁰ If Brazilian musicians such as Powell could benefit from Berendt's efforts, then his activities also inaugurated a new type of collegial experimentation between German and Brazilian musicians too. This occurred not so much in the hasty recording dates he called in the Saba/MPS studios but rather in the context of the Goethe-Institut's activities.

---

46 Joachim-Ernst Berendt, "Berendts September Jazz," *Twen* (September 1966): 114–115.
47 Joachim-Ernst Berendt, Programme notes for the 1966 Berlin Jazz Days, 18.
48 Joachim-Ernst Berendt, *Ein Fenster aus Jazz* (Frankfurt am Main: Fischer, 1977), 350–351.
49 Joachim-Ernst Berendt, *Ein Fenster aus Jazz* (Frankfurt am Main: Fischer, 1977), 95.
50 Claus Schreiner, *Música Brasileira*. Trans. M. Weinstein (London: Marion Boyars, 1993), 251.

From "jazz ambassadors" to dialogic encounters

As I have shown elsewhere, Berendt persuaded the Goethe-Institut in the early 1960s that it should not, when representing German culture abroad, forget German jazz.[51] Beginning in 1963, the West German government sent jazz musicians to a wide range of locations to perform concerts. This was intended to demonstrate how up-to-date West German culture had become and to speak to a younger audience. Brazil was an early destination, which is not surprising given that composer Hans-Joachim Koellreutter was the Goethe-Institut's music director at the time, and he had spent many years as an expatriate in Brazil.[52] In April 1965, the Klaus Doldinger Quartet performed five live and two TV concerts in Brazil while undertaking a broader tour of South America, then in September 1968 an All-Star German group visited Brazil, also in the context of a South America tour. Doldinger in particular used jazz adaptations of local folklore as "greetings" to the countries on the itinerary,[53] yet the model of "musical diplomacy" was one-sided. Typically, the Germans' adaptations of musical forms such as the bossa nova were conceived and rehearsed well in advance of the tours.

Nevertheless, the Goethe tours were welcomed by some Brazilian audiences and critics at the time. For example, the *Jornal do Bahia* considered the Dolding-

---

[51] Andrew W. Hurley, "West German Government–Sponsored Jazz Tours During the 1960s: Revising 'Outdated Imaginations of West Germany' or Participating in Western 'Cultural Penetration,'" *Melbourne University School of Languages Postgraduate Research Papers on Language and Literature* 4 (2004): 117–140.

[52] The German-born Koellreutter is a key figure in several respects. Born 1915 in Freiburg, the flautist and composer studied at the Berlin State Academy in the mid-1930s, including with Hindemith. Between 1937 and 1962 he lived in Brazil, teaching at the conservatories in Rio and São Paulo and finally joining the music department at the University of Bahia. He was considered the "forerunner of modern music in Brazil" (Claus Schreiner, Cover notes for Various musicians, *Jazz Meets Brazil*, 1997, 2), and bossa nova pioneer Antônio Carlos Jobim and many others studied under him. Between 1963 and 1965 he was the head of the music division at the Goethe-Institut in Munich. (It was he who persuaded the German government to finance Goethe-Institut tours by jazz musicians [Anonymous, "Jazz aus Deutschland für Südamerika," *Jazz Podium* (September 1968): 277]). Stints with the Goethe-Institut in New Delhi and Tokyo followed. He returned to São Paulo in 1984, where he remained until his death in 2005. Koellreutter was also no opponent to the idea of intercultural musical borrowings; for example, a 1970 composition of his featured sitar and chamber orchestra (Michael Kennedy, *The Concise Oxford Dictionary of Music* [Oxford: Oxford University Press, 1988], 350).

[53] On this model, see Joachim-Ernst Berendt, "Jazz für den fernen Osten," *Jazz Podium* (June 1964): 138–140. Compare the 1965 album *Doldinger in Südamerika*. A subsequent (1969) album of Doldinger's was duly titled *The Ambassador*. The album was partly financed by the Goethe-Institut and was used by it to advertise its "Jazz Ambassadors."

er Quartet's Rio concert to be "a wonderful opportunity for cultural exchange."[54] There were various jam-session encounters between Doldinger and Brazil's jazz musicians. Hömberg notes that the musicians "jammed to the 'bossa nova' and talked about the latest musical developments."[55] Similar activities occurred with the "German All-Stars" in 1968, yet the hectic timetabling during these early tours prevented any in-depth engagement between the tourists and local Brazilian musicians, however desirable such encounters might be from the perspective of the institute.[56] German pianist Wolfgang Dauner also noted in his review of the 1968 tour that there had been an unhappy mismatch between the Germans and their Brazilian counterparts during these short encounters. This was because of what he perceived as a lack of common rhythmic sensibility and general feeling between the participants. In Dauner's view, the Germans could not perform proper bossa novas and grew tired of attempting to do so.[57] It was only subsequently after a change in institute policy in the early 1970s that more in-depth encounters became possible and a new focus on dialogic cultural work bore fruit.[58]

Of particular note is the 1972 collaboration between the German-based Dave Pike Set and the Bahian Grupo Baiafro, which came about as a result of a coincidence in the gardens of the Goethe-Institut in Salvador do Bahia the previous year. The Bahian location was not coincidental; Bahia has a strong Afro-Brazilian musical culture and had been a cradle to the Tropicalismo movement in the late 1960s. The Dave Pike Set was in the middle of a two-month Goethe-Institut tour of South America, and their concert in Bahia took place at the same time that the Grupo Baiafro were using the local institute for rehearsals.[59] What fol-

---

54 Quoted in Hans Herrmann Köper, Cover notes for Klaus Doldinger, *Doldinger in Südamerika*, 1965; see also Johannes Hömberg, "Musikreferat," *Goethe Institut Jahrbuch* (1965), 50.
55 Johannes Hömberg, "Musikreferat," *Goethe Institut Jahrbuch* (1965), 50; see also Anonymous, "Doldinger füllt Titelseiten," *Jazz Podium* (July 1965): 175–176.
56 See Volker Kriegel, *Manchmal ist es besser, man sagt gar nichts* (Zurich: Haffmanns Verlag, 1998), 169–170.
57 Wolfgang Dauner, "Mit Jazz in Südamerika I," *Jazz Podium* (December 1968): 383–385; Wolfgang Dauner, "Mit Jazz in Südamerika II," *Jazz Podium* (January 1969): 16–17.
58 On this change, see Andrew W. Hurley, "West German Government–Sponsored Jazz Tours During the 1960s: Revising 'Outdated Imaginations of West Germany' or Participating in Western 'Cultural Penetration,'" *Melbourne University School of Languages Postgraduate Research Papers on Language and Literature* 4 (2004): 117–140.
59 The group was an initiative of the local institute. Percussionist and composition student Djalma Correa (also a former student of Koellreutter) was employed by the institute as a technician. When the local institute director, Roland Schaffner, became aware of Correa's musical background, he encouraged him to form a group and use the institute facilities and resources for rehearsals. The forming of the Afrocentric Baiafro percussion ensemble was also consistent

lowed was a chance encounter that might have been envisaged by the institute's new policy of creating a space where intercultural dialogue could take place but was still remarkable given the tight schedule.[60] The two groups found themselves on the same stage, performing together in an impromptu and thoroughly unrehearsed manner a performance that apparently went down very well with the local audience.[61] This chance encounter led to a collaborative tour the next year, with live and television concerts, and a joint MPS recording titled *Salomão*. At the initiative of Roland Schaffner, the Goethe-Institut's local director in Bahia and a man who went out of his way to promote the practice of intercultural dialogue, a house was rented for two weeks, so as to give the musicians time to get to know each other and to rehearse their music before setting out on tour.[62] German music journalist and concert agent Claus Schreiner was also in attendance to produce the resulting album for MPS.

Claus Schreiner was about to succeed where Lippmann and Rau had failed. With his concert agency (established 1967), and especially the "Tropical Music" publishing house and record label (established 1976), Schreiner went on to consolidate a long-running career as a niche promoter of world music in Germany.[63] Unlike Berendt, whose interest was sporadic and always part of a much larger whole, Schreiner dedicated himself in the longer term to world musics, including Brazilian music. This dedication manifested itself over the years not only in numerous tours and recordings with and by Brazilian musicians but also in a book on Brazilian popular music, which has since been translated into English.[64]

The collaborative process, undertaken by Baiafro and the Dave Pike Set in 1972, with its melding of "the form and content of pop-jazz on one hand and Bra-

---

with another of the institute's fostering activities. For some time, it had hosted a series of seminars by the Nucleo Cultural Afro-Brasileiro, a group of Brazilian leftist musicologists and sociologists who were interested in researching and reimagining African cultural roots in Bahia (Roland Schaffner, *Denkwürdige transkulturelle Fremdgänge* [Schweinfurt: Wiesenburg Verlag, 2009], 114). In these ways the Bahian Goethe-Institut played a small role in the Afro-Brazilian musical renaissance of the 1970s.

60 Volker Kriegel, *Manchmal ist es besser, man sagt gar nichts* (Zurich: Haffmanns Verlag, 1998), 169–170.

61 Claus Schreiner, Cover notes for The Dave Pike Set and Grupo Baiafro, *Salomao*, 1972; Volker Kriegel, *Manchmal ist es besser, man sagt gar nichts* (Zurich: Haffmanns Verlag, 1998), 169–170.

62 On Schaffner and his pioneering work in Brazil, see his memoir: *Denkwürdige transkulturelle Fremdgänge* (Schweinfurt: Wiesenburg Verlag, 2009).

63 On Schreiner's career and the Tropical Music business, see http://www.tropical-music.com/index1.html.

64 Schreiner, Claus. *Musica Brasileira*. Trans. M. Weinstein (London: Marion Boyars, 1993).

sileiro-Afro rhythm required a certain degree of compromise on both sides," as Schreiner revealed:

> The concept was debated at length: We didn't want a Dave Pike Set with an enlarged, exotic-sounding rhythm section. The German musicians, superior in certain respects in the eyes of the Baiafros, must not interfere with the originality of the Grupo Baiafro, not force any prepared arrangements on them. While the Set's music is changing from rigid structure to free parts, one musician of Baiafro may cause with his drumming a different beat played by his fellow drummer.[65]

Despite the imperative to compromise, it was important, as Schreiner also pointed out, "that none of the two groups sacrificed its own music to what was after all only a temporary fusion; however not without having come closer together during the time of communal rehearsing and on tour – both on a musical and human level."[66] On the strength of this tour and recording, an impressed Berendt could claim that "it was thus far the most intensive and longest collaboration between Western and Brazilian musicians," only to be outstripped some time later by the collaborations between jazz musicians and U.S.-based Brazilian expatriates such as Airto Moreira and Flora Purim.[67]

Thanks to this initial exposure in 1971 and 1972, the Dave Pike Set's guitarist Volker Kriegel continued to engage in an in-depth way with Brazilian music, especially with Baiafro percussionist Djalma Correa, many times over the coming years.[68] Indeed, writing in 1977, Berendt considered Kriegel to have been the German musician who had most engaged with Brazilian music.[69] For Kriegel, several things stuck from the experience with the Grupo Baiafro and with Brazilian music more generally. Looking back more than twenty years later, he first mentioned the admiration he gained for "the melancholy hybrid mood of the simultaneously joyous and deeply sad music of the Certao [sic]." Just as important as inner musical inspiration, or the refreshing notion of happy–sad emotional hybridity, was the sense Kriegel gained of what the music represented about Brazil-

---

[65] Claus Schreiner, Cover notes for The Dave Pike Set and Grupo Baiafro, *Salomao*, 1972.
[66] Claus Schreiner, Cover notes for The Dave Pike Set and Grupo Baiafro, *Salomao*, 1972.
[67] Joachim-Ernst Berendt, *Ein Fenster aus Jazz* (Frankfurt am Main: Fischer, 1977), 234. This may well be a case of boosterism. Even on Berendt's own account, Moreira had established Brazilian percussion as a feature of jazz in the 1970s by way of his performance on the 1970 album *Miles Davis Live at the Fillmore East* (pp. 94–95).
[68] See, generally, Klaus-Gotthard Fischer, *Jazzin' The Black Forest* (Berlin: Crippled Library, 1999); Roland Schaffner, *Denkwürdige transkulturelle Fremdgänge* (Schweinfurt: Wiesenburg Verlag, 2009), 116–117; Schreiner 2011.
[69] Joachim-Ernst Berendt, *Ein Fenster aus Jazz* (Frankfurt am Main: Fischer, 1977), 233.

ian life: "This music has something uncramped [to it], it is relaxed in spite of all its liveliness. It is the expression of a life-feeling where values such as achievement, efficiency and power do not play first string."[70] For Kriegel too, Brazil was partly an Other to Germany, then. He may have been exoticizing Brazil, and Bahia especially, but his was a very productive exoticization in terms of the insights and more importantly the music making it enabled, both for Kriegel and for his co-musicians, German and Brazilian.

Brazilian music and the *Weltmusik* debates of the 1980s and 1990s

As this chapter has shown so far, particularly in the 1960s and 1970s, a range of German jazz musicians, writers, impresarios, and producers engaged with Brazilian culture. Indeed, insofar as German jazz musicians engaged with other musical cultures – and many did – Brazilian music was a very popular choice.[71] These engagements developed as time progressed. Initially there was a superficial copying of forms such as the bossa nova; however, as time went by, and as bodies such as the Goethe-Institut began to enable more in-depth, "dialogic" cultural encounters, the engagement became more substantial. As Volker Kriegel's case illustrates, the multiple benefits that such an engagement might bring ought not to be undervalued. Yet not all the musicians profited equally. Wolfgang Dauner, for example, took little from his short-term encounter with Brazilian music in 1968. For him, the "German" and the "Brazilian" remained quite separate entities.

Several factors drove this German encounter with Brazilian music. One was jazz's ideology, especially as promoted in postwar Germany. Jazz was seen as an inherently "universal" music.[72] The emphasis on improvisation and practices such as the jam session allowed openness to experimentation, particularly in the modern jazz era. By the mid-1960s, several other factors coincided. First, there was a widespread reach among modern jazz musicians for "exotic" musics, in ways that replicated what was understood to have been the "jazz + samba" genesis of the bossa nova in Brazil. Often, the outreach to exotic music took

---

[70] Volker Kriegel, *Manchmal ist es besser, man sagt gar nichts* (Zurich: Haffmanns Verlag, 1998), 170.

[71] Joachim-Ernst Berendt, *Ein Fenster aus Jazz* (Frankfurt am Main: Fischer, 1977), 233. The other popular choices Berendt mentioned were Asian (and especially Indian) musics and North African musics.

[72] Joachim-Ernst Berendt, "Teutonic Tour," *Down Beat* (10 September 1964): 15.

place in the context of avant-garde free jazz. However, recourse to the bossa nova and to other Brazilian musics was a countermovement to free jazz. The bossa nova represented "the possibility of a gentler way, in an increasingly noisy world."[73] Both Klaus Doldinger, and later Volker Kriegel, aligned themselves with a type of pop-jazz that was largely opposed to free jazz, and they approached Brazilian musics in that context.

Another important impetus for these musical engagements was the changing brief of the Goethe-Institut. Without the Goethe-Institut, Germany's jazz engagement with Brazilian musical culture might have been much slighter and more a matter of individual musicians' fantasies. Especially in the wake of 1968, the Goethe-Institut's policy shifted from the idea of representing German culture as a thing to exploring the idea of culture as process.[74] The Goethe-Institut had for some years been interested in sending jazz musicians abroad, including to Brazil. Now, however, it began to reach out more and to provide the basis for collaborative, dialogic projects. Jazz, already understood as being international and capable of engaging with other musics and as being as much about process as about the final product, was the ideal vehicle for such projects.[75] This policy especially bore fruit in Salvador do Bahia, where the Goethe-Institut provided not only a location for concerts by German jazzers but also significant, ongoing support for local musicians such as Djalma Correa and the Grupo Baiafro.[76] It also leapt at the opportunity to bring the two groups together and move beyond the jam session model by providing valuable time and space for more thoroughgoing musical encounters.

These musical encounters did not always necessarily work for all the partners. As the discussion of *Salomão* indicated, even at the time there were long debates about how much each of the partners shared, how much they differed, and how much they could and should accommodate the other. However, this was necessarily the case with any such experimental process. Some meetings were ill-fated from the beginning, in part because of the attitude of the Germans.

---

[73] North American saxophonist Paul Winter, quoted in Pedro van der Lee, "Sitars and Bossa: World Music Influences," *Popular Music* 17.1 (1998): 52.
[74] Andrew W. Hurley, "West German Government–Sponsored Jazz Tours During the 1960s: Revising 'Outdated Imaginations of West Germany' or Participating in Western 'Cultural Penetration,'" *Melbourne University School of Languages Postgraduate Research Papers on Language and Literature* 4 (2004): 117–140.
[75] On jazz as process, see Ted Gioia, *Jazz: The Imperfect Art* (New York: Oxford University Press, 1988).
[76] Other, less well documented activities were promoted by the Goethe-Institut elsewhere in Brazil, including by the São Paulo Goethe-Institut's director, Dr Schwierskott. Thanks to Claus Schreiner for pointing this out.

When Klaus Doldinger returned to Brazil in 1978, for example, he simply employed Brazilian percussionists to add color to an otherwise unchanged musical concept.[77] A 2004 tour of South America by another German All-Star group was also problematic. In Schreiner's opinion, this was another case of "the Brazilians [making] background music for the German stars."[78]

Whereas freer passages provided some space for a more equal meeting between the Dave Pike Set and the Grupo Baiafro in 1972,[79] free jazz and its ideology could also be inimical to these sorts of encounters. Indeed, by the late 1970s the model of "musical diplomacy" was beginning to fall out of favor because of the German discourse of "emancipation." Many free jazzers had spent the 1960s and 1970s emancipating themselves from the pattern of slavishly copying American jazz innovators.[80] For them, the idea of borrowing too heavily from elsewhere – including from Brazil – was anathema. In the mid-1970s, bassist Eberhard Weber, a veteran of recording sessions with Baden Powell in 1967 and of a Goethe-Institut tour to Brazil in 1972, was reported as saying that the idea of visitors adapting local musics was as absurd as insisting that a Chinese group play "My Bonnie Lies Over the Ocean" if it were to visit Scotland.[81] In 1981, pianist Alexander von Schlippenbach argued that touring German jazzers should dedicate themselves to their *own* concept.[82] This type of attitude was the logical conclusion of a mature artist, but it could be interpreted another way too. For his part, Roland Schaffner was exasperated by the German jazzers who were sent by the Goethe-Institut to Brazil but who did not at all engage with Brazilian music before their arrival in the country.[83]

By the 1980s, some German discourse about Western engagement with Brazilian music was also beginning to harden. This was partly a result of the emergence of *Weltmusik* (world music) as a commercially successful marketing category. It was also a result of the increasingly ideological freight that Berendt, in particular, was imposing on *Weltmusik*. In the wake of a "New Age" conversion, he began to stress ideas of musical universalism. He produced *Weltmusik* sum-

---

77 Schreiner 2011.
78 Schreiner, e-mail to the author, 2011.
79 Claus Schreiner, Cover notes for The Dave Pike Set and Grupo Baiafro, *Salomao*, 1972.
80 Ekkehard Jost, *Europas Jazz* (Frankfurt am Main: Fischer, 1987); Wolfram Knauer, "Emanzipation wovon?," in *Jazz in Deutschland*. Ed. W. Knauer (Hofheim: Wolke Verlag, 1996), 141–157.
81 Quoted in Joachim-Ernst Berendt, *Ein Fenster aus Jazz* (Frankfurt am Main: Fischer, 1977), 235.
82 Alexander von Schlippenbach, "Jazz mit Berendt: reaktionär," *Jazz Podium* (March 1981): 32.
83 Rolands Schaffner, *Denkwürdige transkulturelle Fremdgänge* (Schweinfurt: Wiesenburg Verlag, 2009), 92. For a like argument, see also Joachim-Ernst Berendt, "Jazz mit Goethe und Fragezeichen," *Stereo* (March 1981): 10–11; Schreiner 2011.

mits that attempted to demonstrate a successful fusion of many different types of music and musicians,[84] which culminated in one such summit at the 1985 Donaueschingen Musiktage, which gathered on one stage musicians from Europe, North America, India, and, of course, Brazil. Concurrently, Berendt also published a controversial article on *Weltmusik* where he stressed not only intercultural dialogue but also universalism and the idea of an unerringly harmonious communication between widely disparate musicians.[85] Unlike his 1960s discourse about the bossa nova, with its laboring over "commercialization," Berendt's 1980s *Weltmusik* discourse exhibited a curious blind spot for the way the global music industry capitalized on musical alterity. This provoked a sharp rebuke from leftist critics such as Stephan Voswinkel and Peter Niklas Wilson, who now called on precisely the example of the bossa nova to illustrate the Western music industry's neocolonial plundering of the Third World.[86] In fact, the *Weltmusik* controversy reentered the decades-old bossa nova debates. Yet if Berendt had, in the 1960s and 1970s, been able to draw a line (however vague or problematic) between commercial exploitation and artistic legitimacy, some of the more anxious critics of *Weltmusik* now saw it all as a First World ripoff and unfortunately seemed unable, or unwilling, to reserve a place for the possibility of intercultural dialogue. In the polarized terms of the discourse, there was no place for a differentiated position that combined both "celebratory" and "anxious" aspects.[87] Stripped of their more extreme ideological overburden, however, there remains something quite valuable to these musical encounters, like that which occurred between the Dave Pike Set and the Gruppo Baiafro in 1972, which had their genesis in an interpretation of the bossa nova and in an interest in musical cosmopolitanism spawned as a reaction to the experience of National

---

84 I use the German term here to distinguish between Berendt's spiritually inflected notion of *Weltmusik* as fusion from the term *world music*, which I use to designate musics of the non-Western world marketed in the West.
85 Joachim-Ernst Berendt, "Über Weltmusik," *Jazz Podium* (March 1985): 8–13.
86 See Stephan Voswinkel, "Über die Vielfalt der Musik," *Jazz Podium* (May 1985): 10–11; Peter N. Wilson, "Zwischen Ethnopop und Weltmusik," *Neue Zeitschrift für Musik* 148.5 (1987): 5–8.
87 As David Bennett, following Steven Feld, notes, debates about world music, especially in the 1990s, were divided between celebrators who saw world music as a postmodern sign of hybridity, one that contributed to undermining constructs such as nation and culture, and the more anxious voices who saw it as a repeat of colonialism, whereby it was the First World that profited from materials sourced in the Third World (David Bennett, "Postmodern Eclecticism and the World Music Debate: The Politics of the Kronos Quartet," *Context: A Journal of Music Research* 29, 30 (2005): 5–15). For more on these debates in a German context, see Andrew W. Hurley, "Postnationalism, Postmodernism and the German Discourse(s) of *Weltmusik*," *New Formations* 66 (2009): 100–117.

Socialism. They sparked a contemplation of the nature of intercultural encounters, of cultural boundedness, and of the musical and ethical limits to such activities.

References

Adorno, Theodor. "Für und wider den Jazz." *Merkur* (July 1953): 890–893.
Anonymous. "Doldinger füllt Titelseiten." *Jazz Podium* (July 1965): 175–176.
Anonymous. "Jazz aus Deutschland für Südamerika." *Jazz Podium* (September 1968): 277.
Bennett, David, "Postmodern Eclecticism and the World Music Debate: The Politics of the Kronos Quartet." *Context: A Journal of Music Research* 29, 30 (2005): 5–15.
Berendt, Joachim-Ernst. "Berendts September Jazz." *Twen* (September 1966): 114–115.
Berendt, Joachim-Ernst. Cover notes for Various musicians, *Folklore e Bossa Nova do Brasil*.
Berendt, Joachim-Ernst. "Die Bossa Nova Story." *Twen* (May 1963): 36–41.
Berendt, Joachim-Ernst. *Ein Fenster aus Jazz* (Frankfurt am Main: Fischer, 1977). Refs to 1978 paperback edition.
Berendt, Joachim-Ernst. "Für und wider den Jazz." *Merkur* (July 1953): 887–890.
Berendt, Joachim-Ernst. "Jazz für den fernen Osten." *Jazz Podium* (June 1964): 138–140.
Berendt, Joachim-Ernst. "Jazz mit Goethe und Fragezeichen." *Stereo* (March 1981): 10–11.
Berendt, Joachim-Ernst. *Das Leben ein Klang* (Munich: Droemersche Verlagsanstalt, 1996).
Berendt, Joachim-Ernst. Programme notes for the 1966 Berlin Jazz Days.
Berendt, Joachim-Ernst. "Teutonic Tour." *Down Beat* (10 September 1964): 13–15.
Berendt, Joachim-Ernst. "Über Weltmusik." *Jazz Podium* (March 1985): 8–13.
Blome, Rainer. "Berliner Jazztage 1966." *Sounds* (Winter 1966–1967): 9–10.
Brigl, Kathrin, and Siegfried Schmidt-Joos. *Fritz Rau: Buchhalter der Träume* (Berlin: Quadriga, 1985).
Broecking, Christian. "Adorno vs Berendt Revisited," in *Jazz und Gesellschaft*. Ed. Wolfram Knauer (Hofheim: Wolke Verlag, 2002), 41–53.
Browning, Barbara. *Samba: Resistance in Motion* (Bloomington: Indiana University Press, 1995).
Dauner, Wolfgang. "Mit Jazz in Südamerika I." *Jazz Podium* (December 1968): 383–385.
Dauner, Wolfgang. "Mit Jazz in Südamerika II." *Jazz Podium* (January 1969): 16–17.
Fischer, Klaus-Gotthard. *Jazzin' The Black Forest* (Berlin: Crippled Library, 1999).
Gioia, Ted. *Jazz: The Imperfect Art* (New York: Oxford University Press, 1988).
Hömberg, Johannes. "Musikreferat." *Goethe Institut Jahrbuch* (1965): 49–51.
Hurley, Andrew W. "Beyond the *Sakura Waltz*: Reflections on the Encounter Between German and Japanese Jazz, 1962–1985." *Perfect Beat: The Pacific Journal of Research into Contemporary Music and Popular Culture* 8.4 (2008): 25–43.
Hurley, Andrew W. "Postnationalism, Postmodernism and the German Discourse(s) of Weltmusik." *New Formations* 66 (2009):100–117.
Hurley, Andrew W. *The Return of Jazz: Joachim-Ernst Berendt and West German Cultural Change* (New York: Berghahn Books, 2009).
Hurley, Andrew W. "West German Government–Sponsored Jazz Tours During the 1960s: Revising 'Outdated Imaginations of West Germany' or Participating in Western 'Cultural

Penetration.'" *Melbourne University School of Languages Postgraduate Research Papers on Language and Literature* 4 (2004): 117–140.
Jost, Ekkehard. *Europas Jazz* (Frankfurt am Main: Fischer, 1987).
Kennedy, Michael. *The Concise Oxford Dictionary of Music* (Oxford: Oxford University Press, 1988).
Knauer, Wolfram. "Emanzipation wovon?," in *Jazz in Deutschland*. Ed. W. Knauer (Hofheim: Wolke Verlag, 1996), 141–157.
Köper, Hans Herrmann. Cover notes for Klaus Doldinger, *Doldinger in Südamerika*, 1965.
Kriegel, Volker. *Manchmal ist es besser, man sagt gar nichts* (Zurich: Haffmanns Verlag, 1998).
McGowan, Chris, and Ricardo Pessanha. *The Brazilian Sound* (Philadelphia: Temple University Press, 1998).
Miller, Manfred. "Berliner Jazztage 1966." *Jazz Podium* (December 1966): 324–328.
Morales, Ed. *The Latin Beat: The Rhythms and Roots of Latin Music from Bossa Nova to Salsa and Beyond* (Cambridge, MA: Da Capo, 2003).
Mueller, Jens, ed. *Philips-Twen: Der Tonangebende Realismus* (Baden: Lars Mueller Publishers, 2009).
Ohff, Heinz. "Faszinierendes Brasilien." *Berliner Tagespiegel* (November 1966). Included in D. Rein, ed. *Berliner Jazztage Documentation* (Berlin: Hochschule der Künste, n.d.).
Perrone, Charles A. *Masters of Contemporary Brazilian Song: MPB, 1965–1985* (Austin: University of Texas Press, 1989).
Perrone, Charles A., and Christopher Dunn. *Brazilian Popular Music and Globalization* (Gainesville: University of Florida Press, 2001).
Roberts, John S. *Latin Jazz* (New York: Schirmer, 1999).
Ruesenberg, Michael. Personal interview with the author, 22 October 2004.
Schaffner, Roland. *Denkwürdige transkulturelle Fremdgänge* (Schweinfurt: Wiesenburg Verlag, 2009).
Schildt, Axel. "Across the Border: West German Youth Travel to Western Europe," in *Between Marx and Coca-Cola*. Eds. A. Schildt and Detlef Siegfried (New York: Berghahn Books, 2006), 149–160.
Schmidt-Joos, Siegfried. "Ein Votum für populären Jazz." *Jazz Podium* (December 1965): 320–321.
Schmidt-Joos, Siegfried, and Felix Schmidt. "Reisst die Barrieren nieder." *Der Spiegel* (27 January 1969): 118–120.
Schreiner, Claus. Cover notes for The Dave Pike Set and Grupo Baiafro, *Salomao*, 1972.
Schreiner, Claus. Cover notes for Various musicians, *Jazz Meets Brazil*, 1997.
Schreiner, Claus. *Música Brasileira*. Trans. M. Weinstein (London: Marion Boyars, 1993).
Treece, David. "Guns and Roses: Bossa Nova and Brazil's Music of Popular Protest, 1958–68." *Popular Music* 16.1 (1997): 1–29.
van der Lee, Pedro. "Sitars and Bossa: World Music Influences." *Popular Music* 17.1 (1998): 45–69.
von Schlippenbach, Alexander. "Jazz mit Berendt: reaktionär." *Jazz Podium* (March 1981): 32.
Voswinkel, Stephan. "Über die Vielfalt der Musik." *Jazz Podium* (May 1985): 10–11.
Wilson, Peter N. "Zwischen Ethnopop und Weltmusik." *Neue Zeitschrift für Musik* 148.5 (1987): 5–8.

Discography

Davis, Miles. *Miles Davis Live at the Fillmore East.* Columbia, 61539, 1970.
Doldinger, Klaus. *The Ambassador.* Liberty, 83317 & 83318, 1969.
Doldinger, Klaus. *Doldinger in Südamerika.* Philips Twen, 843728 PY, 1965.
Doldinger, Klaus. *Live at Blue Note Berlin.* Philips, P 48 067 L, 1963.
Getz, Stan, and João Gilberto. *Getz/Gilberto.* Verve, 11173, 1963.
Pike, Dave (as The New Dave Pike Set) and Grupo Baiafro. *Salomao.* MPS, 15370, 1972.
Powell, Baden. *Tristeza on Guitar.* Saba, 15090, 1966.
Various musicians. *Folklore e Bossa Nova do Brasil.* Saba, 15102, 1966.
Various musicians. *Jazz Meets Brasil.* Motor Music, 5333 133–2, 1997.

Ulrike Schröder*
Conceptual Metaphors: A Culture-Specific Construction of Meaning Using the "Life Is War" Metaphor in Brazilian and German Rap Lyrics

The globalization of cultural styles does not lead to a mere imitation of the original in particular regions but rather to the formation of local style variants that result in a reciprocal relationship between global circulation and local adaptation, a phenomenon already described by Roland Robertson as "glocalization."[1] To put it another way, certain elements of global culture and economy are translated according to the specific local contexts of appropriation and reinterpretation. In line with this bipolar mechanism, the way in which homogenizing and heterogenizing tendencies are mutually implicative is an extraordinary characteristic of hip-hop, where local context plays an important role in the localization process, which cannot be seen as a consensual transition but rather one "fraught with tensions and contradictions, as young people attempt to reconcile the issues of musical and stylistic authenticity with those of locality, identity and everyday life."[2] From this perspective, local culture indeed depends on the cultural styles conveyed by the mass media, although in the end it is the local culture itself that decides how the global product will be recontextualized within the new environment. As Deleuze and Guattari put it in their analysis of pop formations as centrifugal forces, such processes of "deterritorialization" and "decodification" represent a creative emancipation practice because they go beyond the binary capitalistic logic of inclusion and exclusion by replacing such obsolete dichotomies with their infinite facets of reproduction.[3] Following a framework proposed by James Lull, such a perspective includes a less pessimistic view with regard to the effects of the media and rejects the idea of the disinformation and

---

* I want to thank the program Capes-Humboldt Research Fellowship for experienced researchers for the financial support of my postdoctoral stay at the University of Münster, Germany, for the period of 12 months.
1 Roland Robertson, *Globalization. Social Theory and Global Culture* (London: Savage Publications, 1992), 173–174.
2 Andy Bennett, "Hip-Hop am Main, Rappin' on the Tyne: Hip-Hop Culture as a Local Construct in Two European Cities," in *That's the Joint!: The Hip-Hop Studies Reader*. Ed. Murray Forman and Mark Anthony Neal (New York: Routledge, 2004), 180.
3 Gilles Deleuze and Félix Guattari, *A Thousand Plateaus: Capitalism and Schizophrenia* (London: Continuum, 1987).

standardization of cultural diversity by assuming a much deeper process in the "deterritorialization" and "reterritorialization" of cultural styles.[4] There are three mechanisms involved: First, by a process of "transculturation," the initial cultural form obtains a new contour through the crossing of temporal and spatial borders. In the second stage, a process of "hybridization" by means of a fusion of different cultural patterns may be observed. Finally, the process of "indigenization" refers to the absorption of local singularities, which are then integrated into the new cultural style.

The focus of the present study is on the globally circulating hip-hop culture and its local forms of reterritorialization, with regard to German and Brazilian speech communities, and is based on the assumption that divergent forms of reterritorialization also produce different rap styles in the two cultures in question. The decision to compare these two cultures with respect to a specific metaphor originates from the results of a pilot study, conducted in 2005, which revealed significant differences in Brazilian and German rap style tendencies.[5] In summary, in a historical comparison of Brazilian and German hip-hop culture development, their particular key subjects, social backgrounds, and the preferred speech styles already singled out were in opposition to preferences concerning the selection and development of the original model's multiple facets; that is, there was a more collective and social orientation in the Brazilian case and a more individualistic and competitive orientation in the German case. Despite all the contrasts found between Brazilian and German rap lyrics, the conceptual metaphor "Life Is War" prevailed in both corpora as the most significant metaphor in use. Therefore, it seemed an interesting undertaking to analyze this apparently ubiquitous metaphor in detail and to investigate possible varieties of particular mappings in terms of the relative cultural frame.[6] Theoretically speaking, doubt is also cast concurrently on whether the simple formula "x is y," as understood in conceptual metaphor theory (CMT) and proposed by Lakoff and Johnson,[7] is actually able to integrate and explain the decisive cultural divergences that are embedded in the particular discourse contexts being considered.

---

4 James Lull, *Media, Communication, Culture. A Global Approach* (Cambridge, England: Polity, 1995).
5 Ulrike Schröder, "Tendenzen gegenläufiger Reterritorialisierungen in brasilianischen und deutschen Rap-Texten," *Lusorama* 71–72 (2007): 217–243.
6 Zoltán Kövecses, *Language, Mind, and Culture. A Practical Introduction* (Oxford, England: Oxford University Press, 2006).
7 George Lakoff and Mark Johnson, *Metaphors We Live By* (Chicago: University of Chicago Press, 1980).

The development of rap music in its original and reterritorialized contexts

Hip-hop emerged as a component of black culture from the South Bronx at the end of the 1970s. It synthesized language, music, dance, and image and encompassed the four elements: rap, D.J.ing, breakdance, and graffiti. Initially, the new style was expressed as street culture in which battles between different crews of breakdancers were accompanied by the music of ghetto blasters. Thus was the background for the development of hip-hop.[8] After a time, this original scenario was augmented by a new style of singing, the "rap," performed by the master of ceremonies (MC). Rap itself as rhymed and rhythmic spoken words is rooted in the tradition of verbal dueling found in more orally based cultures. In the context of the growth of American cities, it evolved into the language game variant dozens adopted by peer groups from the ghettos. It came to be viewed as an insult contest in which the exchanges between speaker and hearer proceed by means of conventionalized offenses that have in turn to be outdone by the other. Hence, an insult as a *rap* is followed by an answer as a *cap*, and so on.[9] Furthermore, other influences can be found in the emergence of rap: the poetry of the black art movement of the sixties, the tradition of the boasting songs as a subgenre of the 1950s blues, jive talk as an element of vernacular Black English, and toasting, traced back to the slugfests of Jamaican mountebanks promoting their reggae records.[10]

Whereas in the beginning old-school rappers such as Kurtis Blow, the Sugarhill Gang, or Busy Bee represented a style aimed at dancing and partying, as from the 1980s, more and more political rap groups such as Public Enemy and Boogie Down Production came to the fore and, with them, critical messages referring to the black power movement or the Nation of Islam. Thus was introduced a new stage of hip-hop culture. In contrast, at the end of the 1980s gangsta rap arose in Compton and South Central, the black ghettos of Los Angeles, and new topics such as romanticizing everyday gangster life in the ghetto and glorifying violence, drugs, and sexual excess were introduced. Icons such as NWA, Ice-T, and Above the Law set their nihilistic and fatalistic point of view

---

8 The neologism is composed of the constituents *hip* (= to be crazy about something) and *hop* (= dance) and also refers to the black music style doo-wop (David Toop, *Rap Attack 2. African Rap To Global Hip Hop* [London: Serpent's Tail, 1991], 22–23).
9 Cf. Roger D. Abrahams, "Playing the Dozens," *Journal of American Folklore* 75 (1962): 209–213; Thomas Kochman, "Rapping in the Black Ghetto," *Trans-Action* 2 (1969): 26–28.
10 Cf. David Dufresne, *Rap Revolution. Geschichte, Gruppen, Bewegung* (Zürich: Atlantis Musikbuch-Verlag, 1997), 19.

against the rap style dominant in New York, which opened out into the "war" between East and West Coast hip-hop. With the advent of the 1990s, hip-hop began to fragment and globalize.

With respect to the initial geographic reference points, Germany is an exception to the general rule in comparison to other cultures because the local centers of hip-hop have been created against the background of American soldiers stationed in towns such as Heidelberg, Frankfurt, Stuttgart, and Mannheim after World War II, so that these early centers hardly can be linked to the original myth of the "metropolis experience." Through this consequent direct American input, contact with hip-hop culture was already established very early: The American version of *Yo! MTV Raps!* was already broadcast in Germany in 1988; in 1993, the program *Freestyle* went on the air, and for the first time German hip-hop was discussed in the media. In contrast to these developments, *Yo! Raps!* was broadcast for the first time on the Brazilian MTV channel only at the end of the 1990s. Here, in 1992 the first hip-hop magazine, *Pode Crê!*, became available, but it ceased publication only two years later. Today, there is one nationally distributed magazine, *Rap Brasil*. In contrast to this development, until the beginning of the 1990s only the American magazine *Source* and the British *Hip Hop Connection* were distributed in Germany; it was not until the mid-1990s that the German-language magazines *Mzee*, *MK Zwo* (today named *MIK'x news*), and *Juice* were published for the first time. This singular German trajectory, which is strongly tied to developments after World War II, perhaps could also explain the dominant presence of Anglicism in the whole lexis of the hip-hop domain.

Unlike the Brazilian rap scene, the German scene comprises all social classes and ethnicities. Everyday reality is hardly marked by exclusion. The first rap lyrics arose from the middle class and reflected a highly self-referential content, as showcased by the famous group Die Fantastischen Vier. With the advent of the 1990s, rap music divided into a more aggressive and confrontational Oriental hip-hop of Turkish origin and German rap, which is now described as "upper stage" or "student" hip-hop because of its lack of "authenticity." Against this background, at the end of the 1990s a new variant of gangsta rap was founded by youngsters from German and Turkish backgrounds, which for its part is often disqualified as "rap of the underclass"[11] or glorified as "real."[12] Although

---

11 Falk aka Hawkeye, "Das letzte Wort: Unterschichten-Rap," *Juice* 8 (2005): 162.
12 Cf. Gabriele Klein and Malte Friedrich, *Is This Real? Die Kultur des Hip Hop* (Frankfurt am Main: Suhrkamp, 2003), 77–80.

the origins seem to be clearly different, what these two directions have in common is the high degree of self-referentiality, as we will see later in this chapter.

In Brazil, the initial conditions were quite different: In the mid-1970s, American funk and soul music started to enter the night life of the lower-class black quarters of Rio de Janeiro, where the first national funk music groups such as Banda Black Rio, Tim Maia, and Toni Tornado emerged. When these tendencies became mixed up with rap, the new style was first called *funk balanço* or *funk pesado*. So whereas in German culture the deployment of U.S. soldiers, the high level of education and consequent sophisticated command of English, and the medial density of imported products originating from American culture afforded direct access to American hip-hop culture, in Brazil the distribution of hip-hop had to overcome several impediments: the lack of material and technical conditions, language barriers, the military dictatorship until the mid-1908 s, and the simple fact that the potential audience represented by the excluded side of Brazilian society was also excluded in a medial sense. These shortcomings led to a highly locally coined recontextualization of hip-hop on the musical level, where sound elements of the Afro-Brazilian religion *candomblé* and the northeastern music style ilê aiê have been absorbed. Through the mixture of these hybrid influences, Rio funk, as a style similar to the American Miami bass, began to develop independently while the advance of hip-hop shifted increasingly to São Paulo, where the so-called *movimento hip hop* had its origins: "While in Rio the content and the rhythm were transformed into a climate in which music is more danceable, cheerful and not necessarily political, in São Paulo, and within several circles, hip-hop became an important political discourse revitalizing a part of the recovery of the black movement. [...] Funkeiros and b-boys dissociate from one another; it has created the dichotomy between the alienated and the engaged ones."[13]

"Movimento hip-hop" was the slogan under which this new sociocritical context was displayed in São Paulo and where associations and posses were founded, offering workshops to mediate techniques using graffiti, breakdance, D.J.ing, and rapping to the youngsters of the ghettos. Through this kind of involvement the rapper quickly became the mouthpiece of the forgotten black majority of the urban regions. As a consequence, unlike in German hip-hop culture, in Brazil the difference between "authentic" and "fake" is connected primarily to skin color.

---

13 Micael Herschmann, *O Funk e o Hip-Hop invadem a cena* (Rio de Janeiro: Editora UFRJ, 2005), 27–28.

Theoretical and methodological framework

According to the philosophical position of experientialism and embodied realism,[14] the basic idea of conceptual metaphor is rooted in the conviction that "any adequate account of meaning and rationality must give a central place to embodied and imaginative structures of understanding by which we grasp our world."[15] Correspondingly, metaphor is no longer conceived as an isolated linguistic phenomenon but as an expression of embodied conceptual structures. Hence, a large part of our everyday experience is made coherent to us only by means of establishing correspondences between an already known source domain and a still shapeless target domain through a cross-domain mapping of a set of counterparts in the conceptual system. By doing so, linguistic expressions turn out to be merely a superficial device for the deep cognitive structure behind them: "In short, the locus of metaphor is not in language at all, but in the ways we conceptualize one mental domain in terms of another."[16] Thus, in the first chapter of their famous publication, Lakoff and Johnson resort to war as the source domain for argument reflected in expressions such as "Your claims are indefensible," "He attacked every weak point in my argument," or "He shot down all of my arguments."[17]

Besides successful proliferation in the course of the next three decades, the CMT has also objected to criticism that contends that their analysis is limited to the individual-corporal level, following the unidirectional way from conceptual metaphor to linguistic expression, that is, from concrete sensorimotor experience to image schemas and then to abstract concepts. One approach striving to overcome these flaws has been embarked on by the research group Pragglejaz,[18] a project searching for metaphor identification procedures in actual discourse.

---

[14] Mark Johnson, *The Body in the Mind: The Bodily Basis of Meaning, Imagination, and Reason* (Chicago: University of Chicago Press, 1987); George Lakoff, *Women, Fire and Dangerous Things: What Categories Reveal About the Mind* (Chicago: University of Chicago Press, 1987); George Lakoff and Mark Johnson, *Philosophy in the Flesh. The Embodied Mind and Its Challenge to Western Thought* (New York: Basic Books, 1999).
[15] Mark Johnson, *The Body in the Mind: The Bodily Basis of Meaning, Imagination, and Reason* (Chicago: University of Chicago Press, 1987), XIII.
[16] George Lakoff, "The Contemporary Theory of Metaphor," in *Metaphor and Thought*. Ed. Andrew Ortony (Cambridge, England: Cambridge University Press, 1995), 203.
[17] George Lakoff and Mark Johnson, *Metaphors We Live By* (Chicago: University of Chicago Press, 1980).
[18] The name of this group is composed by the first letters of the first names of its participants Lynne Cameron, Alan Cienki, Peter Crisp, Alice Deignan, Ray Gibbs, Joe Grady, Zoltan Kövecses, Graham Low, Elena Semino, and Gerard Steen.

The proposal is a more process-oriented approach where metaphor is understood in the context of the "dialogic nature of most language in use" as a process of "talking-and-thinking"[19] as opposed to the idealized conceptual metaphors of Lakoff and Johnson. Gerard Steen describes the shortcomings of the conceptual metaphor theory in the following way: "One paradoxical effect of the cognitive turn in metaphor studies has been the neglect of the linguistic analysis of metaphorical language. Many metaphor scholars have concentrated on fleshing out the presumed conceptual connections between related metaphorical expressions, but they have not really turned back to examine how and why which conceptual metaphors are expressed in the way they are in which contexts of language use."[20] As a more cultural extension of CMT, but without breaking with its basic assumptions, Kövecses focuses on metaphor understood at the same time as a linguistic, conceptual, neurological, embodied, social, and cultural phenomenon.[21] In striving for an integration of universalistic and relativistic components, he draws a distinction between "primary metaphors" and "congruent metaphors": Whereas primary metaphors might be imagined as products of correlations of different dimensions of basic embodied experience, congruent or complex metaphors give a vivid structure to these scaffolds like concrete scenes and images. Thus, for instance, Kövecses shows that the metaphor "The angry person is a pressurized container" can have a near-universal status because it is present in many different languages such as English, Chinese, German, Japanese, Hungarian, Polish, Wolof, and Zulu.[22] Nevertheless, at this generic level the metaphor does not specify many things that de facto are specified in the respective cultures, such as what kind of container is used, how the pressure arises, whether the container is heated, what kind of substance fills the container, and what consequences the explosion has. Therefore, the generic-level conceptual metaphor is instantiated in culture-specific ways at a particular level.

In each culture, 150 rap lyrics were analyzed.[23] In fact, this corpus served for a study realized in 2006, the aim of which was to reveal the differences in con-

---

19 Lynne Cameron, "Confrontation or Complementarity? Metaphor in Language Use and Cognitive Metaphor Theory," *Annual Review of Cognitive Linguistics* 5 (2007): 110.
20 Gerard Steen, "Identifying Metaphor in Language: A Cognitive Approach," *Style* 36.3 (2002): 386.
21 Zoltán Kövecses, *Metaphor in Culture. Universality and Variation* (Cambridge, England: Cambridge University Press, 2005), 293.
22 Zoltán Kövecses, *Metaphor in Culture. Universality and Variation* (Cambridge, England: Cambridge University Press, 2005), 67–69.
23 The Brazilian lyrics were accessed from the site http://www.letrasdemusicas.com.br/generos/rap.html, (9 July 2013) and the German lyrics from http://www.hiphoplyrics.de/ (9 July 2013).

tent and speech style of German and Brazilian rap lyrics.[24] In the course of the analysis I became more and more aware that there is an interesting detail worthy of more in-depth research: the discovery that in both corpora, the German and the Brazilian, one can observe the strong presence of the "Life Is War" metaphor. However, the mappings and the communicative functions related to the use of this metaphor in discourse seemed to vary to a significant degree. Thus, all the data were reviewed in order to systematize the material linked to the source domain. As the analysis set out to investigate the target domains of the source war, the method corresponded to a semasiological and deductive approach. Thus, the wide range of findings offered by the literature on conceptual metaphor theory built up the background and starting point of the analysis by providing evidence for the ubiquitous existence of the source "war"[25] and also for the general conceptual metaphor "Life Is War."[26] However, what had to be defined in detail was the specific cultural mapping involved in the application of the war metaphor.

Therefore, the first step of the analysis implied the grouping of all instances of the war metaphor by the identification of lexical items that stand out against the background of a literal frame forming disparate or incongruent semantic fields. To identify the lexical units as being metaphorical, the Pragglejaz procedure[27] was adopted with respect to determining whether the lexical unit in question has a more basic contemporary meaning in other contexts than the one in the given context, that is, a more concrete, precise, and historically older meaning, often related to bodily action. In this case, the decision had to be made as to whether the contextual meaning contrasts with the basic meaning but can be understood in comparison with it. If this was indeed the case, the lexical unit was marked as metaphorical. The pivotal issue was to find out how the linguistic met-

---

24 Ulrike Schröder, "Tendenzen gegenläufiger Reterritorialisierungen in brasilianischen und deutschen Rap-Texten," *Lusorama* 71–72 (2007): 217–243.
25 George Lakoff and Mark Johnson, *Metaphors We Live By* (Chicago: University of Chicago Press, 1980); Veronika Koller, *Metaphor and Gender in Business Media Discourse: A Critical Cognitive Study* (Basingstoke, England: Palgrave Macmillan, 2004); Frank Boers and Murielle Demecheleer, "A Few Metaphorical Models in (Western) Economic Discourse," in *Discourse and Perspectives in Cognitive Linguistics*. Ed. Wolf-Andreas Liebert (Amsterdam: Benjamins, 1997), 115–129.
26 Nikoletta Köves, "Hungarian and American Dreamworks of Life" (Term paper, Eötvös Loránd University, 2002); Abdulsalam Al-Zahrani, "Darwin's Metaphors Revisited: Conceptual Metaphors, Conceptual Blends, and Idealized Cognitive Models in the Theory of Evolution," *Metaphor and Symbol* 23.1 (2008): 50–82; Maria Dolores López Maestre, "War in the News: Fight in Cognitive Stylistics Research," *Resla* 14 (2000–2001): 217–243.
27 Steen 2007, pp. 88–91.

aphors were spread across the rap lyrics and how density of metaphor use emerges. In the second stage, a subsequent conceptual analysis established the two distinct domains that were linked by a cross-domain mapping connecting the linguistic material to conceptual structures. That is, within the domain of war, a decision was made about what were the actual foci of the concrete image mapped by the particular expression, for example, whether the expression *adversary*, applied in a specific context, corresponds to other MCs, society in general, politicians, police, or criminals, so that a complete metaphorical mapping could be defined by generating a detailed target, setting out a list of correspondences.

Findings

Initial findings revealed that from the 150 lyrics in the German corpus, 35 included the war metaphor, whereas in the Brazilian one, the war metaphor could be found in 44 lyrics. One surprising result is that although there were more Brazilian lyrics containing the war metaphor, the lexical items were more limited and more spread over the whole corpus than in the German one. In the latter, it was more common to find that if there were any expressions related to the war concept, often the whole track was constructed around that metaphor. As a consequence of these results, we can conclude that the density of the metaphor bundles is much higher in the German as opposed to the Brazilian corpus. In the following, I draw attention primarily to the differences concerning the occurrence of lexical items connected to the war metaphor in both corpora.

Most common lexical units in the German corpus	No.	Most common lexical units in the Brazilian corpus	No.
battle/Kampf (battle)	49	*guerreiero/soldado* (warrior/soldier)	36
Bombe (bomb)	27	*guerra* (war)	24
Krieg (war)	23	*luta* (battle)	19
schießen (shoot)	21	*arma* (weapon)	13
Feind/Gegner (adversary/enemy)	17	*revolução* (revolution)	12

There are three striking points in this list that we should address: First, the idea of the MC himself as soldier or warrior seems to be more stressed in the Brazilian corpus, whereas the adversary/enemy topic is more explicit in the German one. Second, there is a noticeable occurrence of the lexical item *revolution* in the Brazilian corpus, whereas this term, in a metaphorical sense, is not used once in the

German corpus. Finally, the overwhelming number of the lexical item *battle* in the German corpus is highly significant, especially as it occurs in English in 20 out of the 49 times it is used. We will return to this peculiarity later.

To move one step deeper in the analysis, the most interesting finding refers to the mapping itself. Although in both corpora, on a superordinate level there is evidence for the same conceptual metaphor (MC's) "Life Is War," the correspondences and entailments are in some respect different in that they allude to different speech acts and functions and to different contexts in which the rap lyrics are incorporated. Thus, the prototypical German mapping can be sketched out as the following:

Source domain: War		Target domain: (MC's) Life
soldier, killer, warrior, mercenary, winner, legionnaire, partisan, 1-man-army, rifleman	⇨	MC (ego)
tribe, elite troop, troops, army, riot squad	⇨	MC's group
adversary, enemy, dead man, loser	⇨	other MC (alter ego)
shots, bombs, detonation, explosion, ammunition, gun, armor plate, fire, blasting composition, grenade	⇨	rhyme, style, beats, words
to battle, to bomb, to fire, to attack, to shoot, to affront somebody, to shell, to knife, to spark a missile	⇨	to rap
to burn down, to conquer, to kill, to occupy	⇨	to rap better, to win the battle
catacombs, bunker	⇨	studio

The following instances provide an illustration of this basic mapping:

(1) Azad: 1 Mann Armee

Explosionen wenn ich komme / mit dem Mic *einreite* und Biter *zerbombe* /
Explosions when I come / riding in by my mic and bombing biters /
bewaffnet mit Kanonen / erschaffen in *Katakomben* /
armed with cannons / built in catacombs /
Eliteeinheit, die in der Tiefe Rhymes schreibt / und für jeden *Krieg* bereit bleibt /
special force writing rhymes in the depth / and being prepared for any war /
Beats verteilt und aufs Mieseste die *Weakburg einreißt* / die besten *Fighter* erblassen /
distributing beats *ripping down the "weakburg"* / the best *fighters* turn pale /
neben dem Meister aller Klassen / ihr schiebt 'n krassen /
abreast the master of all classes / [untranslatable]/
aber eure Styles sind Scheiße und *verpaffen*
but your styles are shit and *fulminate*

(2) Die Firma: Kampf der Titanen
Wir wurden *gestürzt* doch der Blitzmob hat es *überlebt* /
We were *overthrown* but the Blitzmob *survived* /
finden erneut zusammen und *ziehen* nun wieder *in den Krieg* /
get together again and *go to war* /
legen die Welt in Flammen mit der Macht, die in den Liedern liegt /
let the *world burst into flames* by the power laying in the songs /
von Rick Ski der Firma die *Armee*, die immer wieder *siegt* /
by Rick Ski The Firm the *army* that *triumphs* again and again /
damit das dritte Auge sieht und Gott dann vor uns niederkniet
so that the third eye perceives and God will kneel down in front of us

(3) Scopemann: Toy Terminator
Terminiert Toys! Ab jetzt wird *scharf geschossen* /
Terminate toys![28] From now on it will be a *sharp shot* /
Keine *Pistolen*, Kein *Blut* wird *vergossen* / Niemand will dir was antun /
No *pistols*, no *blood* will be *shed* / Nobody wants to do any harm to you /
Hör einfach nur zu – das ist Scopemann /
Just listen to me – it's Scopemann speakin' /
zur Lage der deutschen Hip Hop Nation /
About the situation of the German Hip Hop nation /
Wie ein *Heckenschütze* in den eigenen *Reihen* /
Like a *sniper* behind in *his own lines* /
Konstruktiv nicht besserwisserisch Kritik verteilen [...] /
Givin' criticism constructively not smart-alecky [...] /
Terminiert Toys, egal wo immer ihr sie findet /
Terminate toys wherever you find them /
der *Gegner* verschwindet, wenn ihr Innovation *zündet* /
The *enemy* disappears when you *detonate* innovation /
wie 'ne *Bombe*, 'ne *Rakete*, 'ne *Granate*, *die explodiert* /
Like a *bomb*, a *rocket*, a *grenade exploding* /
Toys werden *terminiert*, wenn man vorexerziert.
Toys are *terminated* when shown how to do it.

By contrast, the Brazilian rap lyrics map a different set of correspondences based on the same superordinate concept metaphor MC's "Life Is War":

---

[28] The term means "fake MCs" who do not possess their own style.

Source domain: War	Target domain: MC's Life
soldier, revolutionary, bomb, knife, invader, guerilla, victor, rifleman, fighter	⇨ MC (ego)
tribe, troop, army, riot squad	⇨ MC's group
fellow, ally, victor	⇨ other MCs (alter ego)
adversary	⇨ society, politicians, police, middle class
adversary	⇨ playboys,[29] criminals
shots, bombs, weapons, terror, arsenal, ammunition, gun, fire, nine millimeters of steel	⇨ rhyme, style, words, national rap
transfer news from war, war, battle, conquer, defense, to stand on the front	⇨ to rap
revolution, burn down, comply a mission, revenge, recovery, reward, victory	⇨ the aim of rap

The following examples portray these correspondences mapped by the Brazilian rap lyrics:

(4) GOG: O terror
Rap Nacional é o *terror* que chegou [...] é o *terror* meu estilo meus *planos de guerra* /
Brazilian Rap is the arriving *terror* [...] *terror* and *war plans* are my style /
comunidade do morro que não *se rende a lei da selva* /
Ghetto community which doesn't *surrender to the law of the jungle* /
eu sou mais um parceiro desse submundo /
I'm one more partner of this underworld /
trazendo à tona notícias só por alguns segundos / [...] / aí político eu sou a *faca* /
Bearing news only for some seconds / [...] / I'm the *knife*, politician /
que *arranca a sua pele* / a *gaveta gelada o rabeção* do IML /
That *tears up your skin* / The freezing chamber, the hearse of the IML /
a CPI da favela / a *luta* do vinil contra a alienação da novela [...] /
The CPI of the ghetto / The *combat* of the vinyl against the alienation of soap-operas /
sou *revolucionário* sou nova forma de pensar / [...] / a *bomba que explode* /
I'm a *revolutionary* with a new way of thinking / [...] / The *bomb that explodes* /

---

[29] The term *playboy* is used to refer to rich kids but also to youngsters of the ghettos who want to be rich and behave in this way.

o *batalhão* inteiro.
The whole *battle*.
(5) Thaíde & DJ Hum: Revolução
    Temos que *vencer, tomar o poder,* de uma vez por todas /
    We have to *win,* to *seize power* once and for all /
    revolução é o que é preciso e eu tô nessa lista /
    revolution is what we need and I'm on the list /
    precisamos com coragem *unir as nossas forças* /
    we need to *unify our forces* with courage /
    e acabar com esse flagelo capitalista [...] se você não acredita em uma *salvação* /
    and finish with this capitalistic flagellum [...] if you don't believe in *liberation* /
    está chegando a minha, a sua, a nossa *revolução.*
    it is coming my, your, our *revolution.*
(6) Mano Brown: Capítulo 4, Versículo 3
    A primeira faz "Bum!," a segunda faz "Tá!" /
    The first goes "Bum!," the second goes "Bang!" /
    Eu tenho uma *missão* e não vou parar! /
    I have a *mission* and I won't stop! /
    Meu estilo é pesado e faz *tremer o chão!* /
    My style is heavy and makes the *ground tremble!* /
    Minha palavra vale um *tiro* / eu tenho muita *munição!*
    My word has the value of a *shot* / I got a lot of *ammunition!*

In summary, what follows from these depictions is that we can actually confirm the hypothesis of Kövecses, that is, both specific-level metaphors explored here are instantiations of the generic-level one in the sense that they exhibit the same general structure. Where they differ is in the specific content that they give to the metaphor. As a consequence, we can maintain that the crucial point in the Brazilian rap lyrics seems to be that the target "life" can be concretized as the "collective survival of an excluded majority living on the periphery of Brazilian cities" and includes two principal mappings. In the first, the soldier is the rapper; the adversary is a more abstract entity such as a politician, society, or the police; the weapon is the word that reveals the unfairness; and the victory is found in overcoming this exclusion by dignified participation in society as a kind of revolution. In the second mapping, again the soldier is the rapper, but now the adversary is the fatalistic or criminal self as a lost or weak person; the weapon is the word in its educating and persuasive function; the victory is another way of life geared toward peaceful and self-conscious life conduct. In terms such as *revolucionário, ativista, guirelheiro, camarada, tomar o poder, missão, revolução,* and *salvação* (revolutionary, activist, guerilla, comrade, seize power, mission, revolution, and liberation) war is conceptualized more forcibly as civil war, which corresponds to the starting point of the metaphorical concept itself. This can be conceived as originating in the precarious situation in the Brazilian ghettos. In other words, we get a certain overlap of source and target domains because some elements of war in the everyday life of Brazilian people living in ghettos can be found. This consequently results in some expressions having indistinct boundaries and thus makes it hard to decide whether these are used in a metaphorical or literal sense.

Contrastingly, in the German rap lyrics, the target builds on the interplay of two underlying metaphors: "Life Is a Game," which forms together with the "Life Is War" metaphor. More specifically, "the good life is being the winner / living the good life is having a victory over another individual (the rival)." Thus, we get a mapping where the soldier is the rapper in a battle, the adversary is the competitor, and the weapon is the word. Hence, in the German case we may also talk about a starting point motivating the metaphorical expressions in question represented by the concept of "battle." As pointed out in the first paragraph, this is of fundamental importance for the birth of hip-hop culture and rap lyrics. Consequently, because the German war metaphor originates in a specific hip-hop culture and theme rather than in a specific social context in the German speech community, the metaphor tends to allude to the idea of a prototypical war between two countries as specific linguistic expressions such as *sergeant, colonel, legionnaire, cavalry, dugout, catacombs, bunker, military hospital, armor plate, jet airplane,* and *battleship* (*Feldwebel, Oberst, Legionär, Kavallerie, Schützengraben, Katakomben, Bunker, Lazarett, Panzer, Düsenflieger,* and *Schlachtschiff*) testify. In addition to this, the war referred to is often set in former eras, probably to exploit, for instance, the vocabulary of medieval times. Take the track "Der flammende Ring" (The flamed ring) by Torch, where the whole lyrics refer to historical figures, weapons, and famous battles of this period. In these kinds of lyrics, lexical items allied to the semantic field "weapon" such as *sword, rapier, lance, scalpel, axe,* and *torch* (*Schwert, Degen, Lanze, Skalpell, Axt,* and *Fackel*) give rise to a high density of metaphor bundles.

Discussion

As outlined earlier in this chapter, unlike in the Brazilian corpus, in the German one the competitive-dialogic language use of rap lyrics is represented by the discourse type "verbal dueling"[30] and, traced back to the ritualization of confrontation, provides the most dominant motivation for the war metaphor. Correspondingly, the content consists of self-presentation where the speech act of boasting – the praise of their own skills – is ubiquitous and implies a strong emphasis on sophisticated and challenging rhymes over a coherent content. During the first stage, these tendencies afford a more intellectualized means of self-presence. However, the second stage, especially the so-called pimp, showbiz, and gangsta rap, produced by the label Aggro-Berlin, is characterized by verbal transformation and takes a more provocative acrobatic rap style, one that integrates more and more elements of violence and sexist language combined with "*Everyone's crap except me*-attitudes."[31]

Another aspect that probably contributes to the high self-reference and intertextuality of the American and German rap style may have something to do with the influence of Protestantism, which in conjunction with the augmented functional differentiation of society and the individualization of the subject during the period of Romanticism introduces a new definition of man as a self-organized creature. The duality of "good" and "bad" is now incorporated so that concepts such as "self-love," "self-awareness," and "self-guidance" emerge as evidence for the replacement of the fundamental relationship between man and God to the relationship from man to himself.[32] As Weber points out, by means of this discovery of the "inner self,"[33] the conditions for the development of capitalism are prepared by the introduction of self-discipline as the basic component of competition. One begins to compare one's own advantages and virtues with those of other people.[34] Thus, in the German rap lyrics we can observe that the MCs tend to accentuate their singularity, revealing a strong centering of self. However, the Brazilian rapper tends to understand himself as a representative of a certain social and ethnic class and therefore acts with reference to the

---

30 Monika Sokol, "Verbal Duelling: Ein universeller Sprachspieltypus und seine Metamorphosen im US-amerikanischen, französischen und deutschen Rap," in *Rap: More Than Words*. Ed. Eva Kimminich (Frankfurt am Main: Peter Lang, 2004), 117.
31 Daniel Köhler, "Berlin: Rap-Hauptstadt Deutschlands?" *Juice* 11 (2003): 64.
32 Niklas Luhmann, *Gesellschaftsstruktur und Semantik. Studien zur* Wissenssoziologie der modernen Gesellschaft. Band 3 (Frankfurt am Main: Suhrkamp, 1989), 179.
33 Max Weber, *Die protestantische Ethik I. Eine Aufsatzsammlung* (Gütersloh: Gütersloher Verlagshaus Gerd Mohn, 1991).
34 Compare the relationship between literalization, Protestantism, and individualism in German culture on one hand and the relationship between oralization, Catholicism, and collectivism in Brazilian culture on the other. Ulrike Schröder, *Brasilianische und deutsche Wirklichkeiten. Eine vergleichende Fallstudie zu kommunikativ erzeugten Sinnwelten* (Wiesbaden: Deutscher Universitäts-Verlag, 2003).

hearer. Therefore, it is not surprising that political rap is very rare in German culture. As Landsberg holds, today politics and social criticism do not sell in Germany anymore.[35]

By contrast, in Brazil the most successful rap style is that of political and social protest, which originates in São Paulo. Here, the main topic resides in everyday ghetto life. However, unlike in the fatalistic and glorifying descriptions of the American gangsta rap, the overriding aim is related to the intention to make the hearer aware of social inequalities. Consequently, other speech acts and communicative functions are underscored in comparison to the German lyrics. Whereas in the latter the poetic and metacommunicative functions were most salient, in the former the referential and especially the directive functions with speech acts such as "commenting," "reporting," "condemning," "appealing," and "alerting" are more pervasive.[36] The dominant style is an imperative and pedagogic one that strives to address the hearer directly, whereby the phatic function of communication is also stressed.

In this context hip-hop is often conceived as a medium of education by which the real history of the black Brazilian peoples should be transmitted. Rap becomes a "second school"[37] because "the school tells part of history and we tell the real one."[38] Correspondingly, the war metaphor appears in cohesion with the idea of hip-hop as a medium of "mental revolution": "The 'target' is the *conscience* and the 'weapon' the *word*."[39] This declared goal might be connected to the previously discussed fact that most of the target audience has little contact with the products of written culture.[40] As Ong concludes, whereas "writing separates the knower from the known and thus sets up the conditions for 'objectiv-

---

[35] Torsten Landsberg, "Slow Down. Der langsame Abstieg des relevanten Hip Hop," *MIK'x News. Das Deutschsprachige Magazin für Vibrationen* 35.1 (2005): 7.
[36] Concerning the communicative functions, compare Hymes ("Functions of Speech: An Evolutionary Approach," in *Anthropology and Education*. Ed. Frederick C. Gruber [Philadelphia: University of Pennsylvania Press, 1961], 5–83), who himself builds on the classification of Roman Jakobson ("Linguistik und Poetik," in *Literaturwissenschaft und Linguistik. Ergebnisse und Perspektiven*. Ed. Jens Ihwe [Frankfurt am Main: Athenäum, 1971], 142–178).
[37] *Segunda escola.*
[38] Mano Brown, "Em entrevista," *Pode Crê* 13 (February–March 1993): 13.
[39] Glória Diógenes, *Cartografias da cultura e da violência: gangues, galeras e o movimento hip-hop* (São Paulo: Annablume, 1998), 142.
[40] According to a survey of the institute Indicador Nacional de Alfabetismo Funcional (2005), only 26 percent of Brazilians are able to read and write fluently (see http://www.ipm.org.br/ipmb_pagina.php?mpg=4.02.07.00.00&ver=por), 9 July 2013. For an update, see http://www.ipm.org.br/ipmb_pagina.php?mpg=4.02.01.00.00&ver=por.

ity,' in the sense of personal disengagement or distancing,"[41] oral cultures are strongly dependent on their immediate social context and therefore less distant and more personally engaged. This is reflected in the persuasive style of Brazilian rap as opposed to the self-referential tendencies of the German one, also present in the prophetic and messianic subgenres, where we often encounter blends of war and apocalypse. There are also many groups belonging to the so-called Rap Gospel Nacional, whose rappers participate in one of the numerous evangelical churches and who understand themselves as spokesmen for God and tellers of their personal life story. This usually includes a typical conversion from being a drug dealer, alcoholic, playboy, or criminal to a self-aware person who found the right path through religion.

Conclusions

The study presented has portrayed how one conceptual metaphor, the MC's "Life Is War" metaphor, acts in a significant way on the construction of rap lyrics in German and Brazilian culture on a very generic level. It not only varies in its culture-specific mappings but is also greatly dependent on the discourse context. This by itself is embedded in a greater historical cultural background, which bears disparate modes of reterritorialization to the original culture arising out of the ghettos of New York. Consequently, a deeper analysis was needed to explore this conceptual metaphor with its intrinsic cultural variation concerning the scope of the source and the specific mapping parts involved. Starting from an analysis of the correspondences, the mapping of this conceptual metaphor include in each case, in the course of the interpretation of the data, the revelation that distinct elements have been picked up from the original U.S. context. The encountering of globally circulating cultural forms and regional target cultures does not result simply in unidirectional adoption and assimilation but rather in recontextualization. This in turn hinges on the respective necessities of the target so that we in effect can use the term *glocalization* to talk about this phenomenon. Additionally, the findings demonstrate the necessity of making some general modifications to the conceptual metaphor approach, namely, the relativization of the postulation of the universality of certain conceptual metaphors. It can thus be shown that it would be insufficient to account for the use of metaphors in particular discourse contexts because mappings seem to

---

41 Walter J. Ong, *Orality and Literacy. The Technologizing of the Word* (London: Routledge, 2004), 45.

change together with the particular communicative situations in which they apply according to different cultural contexts and frames.

References

Abrahams, Roger D. "Playing the Dozens." *Journal of American Folklore* 75 (1962): 209–220.

Al-Zahrani, Abdulsalam. "Darwin's Metaphors Revisited: Conceptual Metaphors, Conceptual Blends, and Idealized Cognitive Models in the Theory of Evolution." *Metaphor and Symbol* 23.1 (2008): 50–82.

Bennett, Andy. "Hip-Hop am Main, Rappin' on the Tyne: Hip-Hop Culture as a Local Construct in Two European Cities," in *That's the Joint!: The Hip-Hop Studies Reader*. Ed. Murray Forman and Mark Anthony Neal (New York: Routledge, 2004), 177–200.

Boers, Frank, and Murielle Demecheleer. "A Few Metaphorical Models in (Western) Economic Discourse," in *Discourse and Perspectives in Cognitive Linguistics*. Ed. Wolf-Andreas Liebert (Amsterdam: John Benjamins, 1997), 115–129.

Brown, Mano. "Em entrevista." *Pode Crê* 13 (February–March 1993).

Cameron, Lynne. "Confrontation or Complementarity? Metaphor in Language Use and Cognitive Metaphor Theory." *Annual Review of Cognitive Linguistics* 5 (2007): 107–135.

Deleuze, Gilles, and Félix Guattari. *A Thousand Plateaus: Capitalism and Schizophrenia* (London: Continuum, 1987).

Diógenes, Glória. *Cartografias da cultura e da violência: gangues, galeras e o movimento hip-hop* (São Paulo: Annablume, 1998).

Dufresne, David. *Rap Revolution. Geschichte, Gruppen, Bewegung* (Zürich: Atlantis Musikbuch-Verlag, 1997).

Hawkeye, Falk aka. "Das letzte Wort: Unterschichten-Rap." *Juice* 8 (2005): 162.

Herschmann, Micael. *O Funk e o Hip-Hop invadem a cena* (Rio de Janeiro: Editora UFRJ, 2005).

Hymes, Dell. "Functions of Speech: An Evolutionary Approach," in *Anthropology and Education*. Ed. Frederick C. Gruber (Philadelphia: University of Pennsylvania Press, 1961), 5–83.

Jakobson, Roman. "Linguistik und Poetik," in *Literaturwissenschaft und Linguistik. Ergebnisse und Perspektiven*. Ed. Jens Ihwe (Frankfurt am Main: Athenäum, 1971), 142–178.

Johnson, Mark. *The Body in the Mind: The Bodily Basis of Meaning, Imagination, and Reason* (Chicago: University of Chicago Press, 1987).

Klein, Gabriele, and Malte Friedrich. *Is This Real? Die Kultur des Hip Hop* (Frankfurt am Main: Suhrkamp, 2003).

Kochman, Thomas. "Rapping in the Black Ghetto." *Trans-Action* 2 (1969): 26–34.

Köhler, Daniel. "Berlin: Rap-Hauptstadt Deutschlands?" *Juice* 11 (2003): 63–66.

Koller, Veronika. *Metaphor and Gender in Business Media Discourse: A Critical Cognitive Study* (Basingstoke, England: Palgrave Macmillan, 2004).

Kövecses, Zoltán. *Language, Mind, and Culture. A Practical Introduction* (Oxford, England: Oxford University Press, 2006).

Kövecses, Zoltán. *Metaphor in Culture. Universality and Variation* (Cambridge, England: Cambridge University Press, 2005).

Köves, Nikoletta. "Hungarian and American Dreamworks of Life" (Term paper, Eötvös Loránd University, 2002).
Lakoff, George. "The Contemporary Theory of Metaphor," in *Metaphor and Thought*. Ed. Andrew Ortony (Cambridge, England: Cambridge University Press, 1995), 202–251.
Lakoff, George. *Women, Fire and Dangerous Things: What Categories Reveal About the Mind* (Chicago: University of Chicago Press, 1987).
Lakoff, George, and Mark Johnson. *Metaphors We Live By* (Chicago: University of Chicago Press, 1980).
Lakoff, George, and Mark Johnson. *Philosophy in the Flesh. The Embodied Mind and Its Challenge to Western Thought* (New York: Basic Books, 1999).
Landsberg, Torsten. "Slow Down. Der langsame Abstieg des relevanten Hip Hop." *MIK'x News. Das Deutschsprachige Magazin für Vibrationen* 35.1 (2005): 6–9.
López Maestre, Maria Dolores. "War in the News: Fight in Cognitive Stylistics Research." *Resla* 14 (2000–2001): 217–243.
Luhmann, Niklas. *Gesellschaftsstruktur und Semantik. Studien zur* Wissenssoziologie der modernen Gesellschaft. Band 3 (Frankfurt am Main: Suhrkamp, 1989).
Lull, James. *Media, Communication, Culture. A Global Approach* (Cambridge, England: Polity, 1995).
Ong, Walter J. *Orality and Literacy. The Technologizing of the Word* (London: Routledge, 2004).
Robertson, Roland. *Globalization. Social Theory and Global Culture* (London: Savage Publications, 1992).
Schröder, Ulrike. *Brasilianische und deutsche Wirklichkeiten. Eine vergleichende Fallstudie zu kommunikativ erzeugten Sinnwelten* (Wiesbaden: Deutscher Universitäts-Verlag, 2003).
Schröder, Ulrike. "Tendenzen gegenläufiger Reterritorialisierungen in brasilianischen und deutschen Rap-Texten." *Lusorama* 71–72 (2007): 217–243.
Sokol, Monika. "Verbal Duelling: Ein universeller Sprachspieltypus und seine Metamorphosen im US-amerikanischen, französischen und deutschen Rap," in *Rap: More Than Words*. Ed. Eva Kimminich (Frankfurt am Main: Peter Lang, 2004), 113–160.
Steen, Gerard J. *Finding Metaphor in Grammar and Usage* (Amsterdam: John Benjamins, 2007).
Steen, Gerard J. "Identifying Metaphor in Language: A Cognitive Approach." *Style* 36.3 (2002): 386–407.
Toop, David. *Rap Attack 2. African Rap To Global Hip Hop* (London: Serpent's Tail, 1991).
Weber, Max. *Die protestantische Ethik I. Eine Aufsatzsammlung* (Gütersloh: Gütersloher Verlagshaus Gerd Mohn, 1991).

Wolfgang Fuhrmann
Transnational Film History? Um Cinema Teuto-Brasileiro[*]

Cultural hybridity and national cinema do not get along well. Whereas the first emphasizes the mixing, interaction, and exchange of cultures, the latter tries to avoid any influences that could blur the concept of a national cultural unity. National film historiographies often focus on domestic film productions and exclude the enormous quantity of foreign productions that also characterize a national film industry. However, the exclusive focus on domestic productions is problematic in itself. The international success of many European cinemas, as is the case with the "Newer German Cinema," is often based on the success of directors and actors with an international background.[1] In this respect German cinema's international reputation of the last twenty years rests in large parts on its cultural hybridity.

Film studies' recent interest in questions of transnational cinema can be understood as a reaction to the obvious hybrid character of modern film cultures.[2] It acknowledges the significant changes in world order that have taken place in the recent past and the new cultural constellations and intercultural encounters that have resulted from it. However, as Peter Burke has shown, cultural hybridity is not a recent phenomenon at all but has been characterizing all cultures for ages.[3] In other words, there is no reason to limit the scope of studies of transnational cinemas in recent decades; rather, there should be a widened focus for a historical perspective.[4] The following anecdote from Colombia in the early 1920s illustrates such a historical perspective and shows the complex character of a cinema culture that can hardly be reduced to an identifiable national subject.

---

[*] This chapter is a revised translation of "Deutsche Kultur- und Spielfilme im Brasilien der 1930er Jahre Eine transnationale Perspektive," in *Film – Kino – Zuschauer: Filmrezeption/Film – Cinema – Spectator: Film Reception*. Ed. Irmbert Schenk, Margrit Tröhler, and Yvonne Zimmermann (Marburg: Schüren, 2010), 399–418.
[1] The term "Newer German Cinema" was first used by U.S. film scholar Jennifer Kapczynski, "Newer German Cinema: From Nostalgia to Nowhere," *The Germanic Review* 82.1 (2007): 3.
[2] See the launching of the new cinema journal *Transnational Cinemas* in 2010: http://www.tandfonline.com/action/journalInformation?show=aimsScope&journalCode=RTRC20#.VOMdy691vA 29 July 2014.
[3] Peter Burke, *Cultural Hybridity* (Cambridge, England: Polity, 2009).
[4] See Randall Halle, *German Film After Germany. Toward a Transnational Aesthetic* (Urbana: University of Illinois Press, 2008), 5.

In May 1923 a certain Pablo Zumpe, secretary of trade at the German embassy in Colombia, informed the Colombian Ministry of Foreign Affairs about a scandal in the Colombian cinemas. The reason for Zumpe's outrage was the exhibition of D. W. Griffith's propaganda film *Hearts of the World* (USA 1918), which was causing fierce protests among German immigrants living in Colombia. Concerned about maintaining a good mood in German communities and good political and economic relations with Germany, the Colombian government advised all the federal states to prohibit the screening of anti-German films.[5]

Whose history is being told in this anecdote? The incident stands at the intersection of U.S. distribution, national Colombian film, and German-Colombian migration history. No matter from which perspective one investigates this historical event, one can never fully grasp all aspects of it. The anecdote is emblematic for countries whose film cultures are historically framed by a small domestic film industry, domination by foreign productions, and a large percentage of immigrant viewers. The anecdote is the point of departure for the following investigating of a hybrid cinema culture in Brazil, the biggest immigration country on the South American continent.

In "The Limiting Imagination of National Cinema" Andrew Higson critically reconsiders his canonical article "The Concept of National Cinema."[6] Starting from Benedict Anderson's approach of an imagined community, Higson questions the usefulness of the concept of national cinema, which is, as he argues, a helpful taxonomic labeling device but "always to some degree tautologous, fetishising the national rather than merely describing it."[7] In many cases the analysis of a national cinema leads to a limitation on films that present the nation as a demarcated geopolitical space with a homogeneous community, closed off to other identities. A concept of national cinema obscures "the degree of cultural diversity, exchange and interpenetration that is so much cinematic activity."[8]

What remains unsaid in approaches to national cinema are the dynamics of modern societies in which political, cultural, and economic developments and identity formation do not stop at a nation's border. Borders are not only bounda-

---

[5] Archivo General de la Nación Colombia, Ministerio de Gobierno, Sección Primera, Rollo 226, Tomos 892–893, Folio 5–13.

[6] Andrew Higson, "The Concept of National Cinema," *Screen* 30.4 (1989): 36–46; "The Limiting Imagination of National Cinema," in *Cinema and Nation*. Ed. Mette Hjort and Scott MacKenzie (London: Routledge, 2000), 63–74.

[7] Andrew Higson, "The Limiting Imagination of National Cinema," in *Cinema and Nation*. Ed. Mette Hjort and Scott MacKenzie (London: Routledge, 2000), 64.

[8] Andrew Higson, "The Limiting Imagination of National Cinema," in *Cinema and Nation*. Ed. Mette Hjort and Scott MacKenzie (London: Routledge, 2000), 64.

ries of the state but, as Higson remarks, also passageways that allow migration and exchange. In other words, speaking and thinking *transnationally* means considering cultural and economic formations, cultural cross-breeding, and interpenetration that are per se hybrid and impure.[9] In this sense transnational phenomena can be studied in all areas of film: the coproductions or the effect of migrating filmmakers on the production side; censorship, dubbing, subtitling, and marketing issues in the sphere of distribution; and the ways audiences receive films in their specific cultural context.[10] In addition to the reception of films in a new cultural context, one must add the specific exhibition context for foreign films, an aspect that is not mentioned by Higson but is particularly important for the analysis of German films in Brazil.

In his book on the reception of Weimar cinema in South Africa, Michael Eckardt has shown that transnational film history as reception, impact, or effective history (*Wirkungsgeschichte*) can be particularly rich in countries whose production was too small to cover the national market.[11] The same goes for film relations between countries that are linked by a common migration history. The number of German immigrants in South America was different from country to country and even from region to region (German immigrants chose the south of Brazil, the northeast of Argentina, or the south of Chile), but the example from Colombia shows that immigrants could be active historical agents with a great influence on the film culture in their new *Heimat*.

Brazil has been one of the most important destinations of German immigrants since the eighteenth century. It has been estimated that in the 1930s the number of immigrants of German origin in Brazil was around a million (approximately 80,000–100,000 for imperial Germans).[12] German immigrants settled mainly in the south of Brazil, in states such as Santa Catarina and Rio Grande de Sul, where they were up to 20 percent of the population.[13] Until the

---

9 Andrew Higson, "The Limiting Imagination of National Cinema," in *Cinema and Nation*. Ed. Mette Hjort and Scott MacKenzie (London: Routledge, 2000), 67.
10 Andrew Higson, "The Limiting Imagination of National Cinema," in *Cinema and Nation*. Ed. Mette Hjort and Scott MacKenzie (London: Routledge, 2000), 68.
11 Michael Eckardt, *Zwischenspiele der Filmgeschichte. Zur Rezeption des Kinos der Weimarer Republik in Südafrika 1928–1933* (Berlin: Trafo, 2008).
12 Luiz Nazario, "Nazi Film Politics in Brazil, 1933–1942," in *Cinema and the Swastika. The International Expansion of the Third Reich*. Ed. Roel Van de Winkel and David Welch (New York: Palgrave MacMillan, 2007), 85. The term *Reichsdeutsche* (imperial Germans) refers to German citizenship, *Volksdeutsche* (ethnic Germans) refers to German origin but with a different citizenship.
13 Flaviano Bugatti Isolan, *Das páginas à tela: cinema alemão e imprensa na década de 1930* (Santa Cruz do Sul: EDUNISC, 2006), 38. German names of Brazilian cities such as Blumenau,

1930s German immigrants had a perfect infrastructure in the form of more than a thousand schools, countless associations, and different German-speaking newspapers. In addition, German Brazilians benefited from the good economic and political relations between Brazil and Germany. In April 1938 a decree of the Brazilian government prohibited foreigners from taking part in political activities.[14] German schools were closed or converted into Brazilian schools, and formerly German companies received Brazilian management. With Brazil's entry into World War II in 1942, an assembly ban was passed for German immigrants, and the government prohibited the use of the German language.

South America, particularly countries such as Brazil, Argentina, and Chile, was not only an important destination for German immigrants but also an important export market for the German film industry. Articles and news from South America in early German film journals often reported about the success of German-born cinema owners and the German film trade in Brazil.[15] Studying the minutes of the Universum Film AG (UFA) board of directors also shows that the company was continuously observing the South American market.[16] Since the world economy crisis in 1929, South America had become an important sales market for U.S. film companies, and its biggest European competitor, the German UFA did not change with the outbreak of World War II: South America never was a battlefield in the war, and Brazil entered it at a very late stage.[17]

The multifaceted history of German immigration in Brazil has attracted little attention in German film historical research.[18] This is all the more surprising because until today Brazil is inspiring the exoticist desires of some German direc-

---

Pomerode, Schroeder, or Teutonia remind one of the influence of German immigration. The city of Blumenau, for example, holds the second largest Oktoberfest in the world.

14 Jürgen Müller, *Nationalsozialismus in Lateinamerika. Die Auslandsorganisation der NSDAP in Argentinien, Brasilien, Chile und Mexiko, 1931–1945* (Stuttgart: Hans-Dieter Heinz, 1997), 305.
15 Representative is an ad of the Rombauer Company from Rio de Janeiro, in which the company promotes its cinemas with a high-quality program exclusively of German films. *Lichtbild-Bühne* 11 (1922): 61.
16 Lisa Shaw and Stephanie Dennison, eds., *Brazilian National Cinema* (London: Routledge, 2007); Michael Chanan, "Cinema in Latin America," in *The Oxford History of World Cinema*. Ed. Geoffrey Nowell-Smith (Oxford, England: Oxford University Press, 1996), 427–435.
17 Hollywood productions clearly dominated the Brazilian market, but European film industries managed to gain some market share. Flaviano Bugatti Isolan, *Das páginas à tela: cinema alemão e imprensa na década de 1930* (Santa Cruz do Sul: EDUNISC, 2006), 34.
18 Wolfgang Fuhrmann, "Fortschritt, Modernität und neue Lebenswege. Brasilienbilder im westdeutschen Kino der 1950er Jahre," in *Kulturdialog Brasilien-Deutschland. Design, Film, Literatur, Medien*. Ed. Geane Alzamora, Renira Rampazzo Gambarato, and Simone Malaguti (Berlin: Tranvía, 2008), 61–75.

tors and characterizes the image of Brazil on the German screens.[19] Studies on the history and aesthetics of the German *Kulturfilm* (culture film) in the 1920 and 1930s or on the history of the UFA, the biggest and most prestigious German film company in its time, have shown the significance of the cultural film as a central and distinguished genre of the nonfictional film form and the efficiency of a film enterprise that became Hollywood's most serious competitor on the world market.[20] However, film and cinema have not been well discussed in relation to the South American market. Focusing on the distribution and reception of German films in the early 1930s in Brazil means understanding German films not primarily as the extension of German fascistic propaganda abroad but as films that were subjected to the dynamics of an active and sometimes very peculiar Teuto-Brazilian film culture.

The Cultural Film Service

The Brazilian film audience was not unfamiliar with the *Kulturfilm* genre: In January 1927, Hanns Walter Kornblum's feature-length nonfiction film *Wunder der Schöpfung/Our Heavenly Bodies* (D 1925) was shown in Brazilian cinemas.[21] A special distribution of the documentary film in the form of instructional and educational films in the German-speaking regions seems to have begun only in the late 1920s. A possible but still provisional starting point could have been Edgar Beyfuss's visit to Brazil in August 1925. At the time Beyfuss was a script editor in the UFA documentary department and presumably on a promotion tour for German cultural film in Brazil. One of his stops during his trip was Olinda in São Paulo, the biggest German school in the city. His lecture explained to the German-Brazilian audience the significance of the film medium, and the screening

---

19 *Brasilianischer Volkstanz* (Elge, D 1910), *Die Tante aus Brasilien* (Karlchen-Film GmbH Berlin, D 1921), *Das Frauenhaus von Rio/Plüsch und Plümowski* (Hans Steinhoff, D 1927), *Donogoo Tonka* (Reinhold Schünzel, D 1935–1936), *Kautschuk* (Eduard von Borsody, D 1938), *Stern von Rio* (Karl Anton, D 1939–1940), *Stern von Rio* (Kurt Neumann, BRD 1955–1956), *Mannequins für Rio* (Kurt Neumann, BRD 1954), *Stefanie in Rio* (Kurt Bernhardt, D 1960), *Mord in Rio* (Horst Hächler, D 1963), *Streets of Rio* (Alexander Pickl, D/BRA 2005–2006), *Schroeder liegt in Brasilien* (Zé do Rock, D/BRA 2008).
20 On the history of the German *Kulturfilm* see all three volumes of *Geschichte des dokumentarischen Films in Deutschland:* Uli Jung and Martin Loiperdinger, eds., *Kaiserreich. 1895–1918* (Stuttgart: Reclam, 2005); Klaus Kreimeier, Antje Ehmann, and Jeanpaul Goergen, eds., *Weimarer Republik. 1918–1933* (Stuttgart: Reclam, 2005); and Peter Zimmermann and Kay Hoffman, eds., *Drittes Reich. 1933–1945* (Stuttgart: Reclam, 2005).
21 *Deutsche Rio Zeitung*, 27 January 1927.

of film gave the viewers the opportunity to look behind the scenes of the German cultural film production.²² During the years that followed, the German schools – particularly the Olinda school – strengthened their film activities. The new interest in film was not influenced just by the political changes in Germany but by a private film network in Brazil as well.

Very soon after Hitler's takeover, the German Ministry of Propaganda started its international collaboration with the foreign organizations of the National Socialist German Workers' Party (NSDAP), the so-called *Auslandsorganisationen* (AOs). A Brazilian foreign organization already existed in Rio de Janeiro since 1931 and had about 40,000 members.²³ In the years that followed the German government expanded its support and planned the export of German films.

Parallel to the NSDAP's efforts but independent from it, two German-Brazilian film initiatives began supplying German immigrant regions with film shows. Before Hitler's takeover, the Association of German Teachers in São Paulo (Deutscher Lehrerverein São Paulo) purchased a film projector in 1930 to increase the number of film screenings in the metropolitan area. In 1932 in São Leopoldo, in the state of Rio Grande de Sul, a Dr. Kosche founded the German Brazilian Cultural Film Service (Deutschbrasilianische Kulturfilmdienst [DKD]), which from 1934 on was administered by the National Association of German Brazilian Teachers (Landesverband Deutsch-Brasilianischer Lehrer.²⁴ The Film Service received support from the overseas branch of the German Reich Railway (Deutsche Reichsbahn) in Brazil and from companies such as Zeiss, Agfa, and Siemens.²⁵

The Film Service rapidly expanded in the country, soon opening its first branch in São Paulo, and very quickly connected with other regional, district, and city branches and finally reached up to Bahia in the northeast of Brazil. The film programs that were shown were exclusively silent films in 16-mm or the very rare 24-mm format.²⁶ Films could be rented at cost. The idea of the

---

22 "Diario G. A. Hoch 1924–1926" (São Paulo: Arquivo do Instituto Martius-Staden [henceforth AIMST]).
23 Luiz Nazario, "Nazi Film Politics in Brazil, 1933–1942," in *Cinema and the Swastika. The International Expansion of the Third Reich*. Ed. Roel Van de Winkel and David Welch (New York: Palgrave MacMillan, 2007), 87.
24 *Allgemeine Lehrerzeitung für Rio Grande do Sul* 5 (May 1934): 13. The idea of distributing cultural films in South America probably did not start in Brazil but in Chile. "Correspondência Deutscher Lehrerverein São Paulo 1930, 'Verein Deutscher Lehrer in Chile, 1. Rundschreiben, Ende März 1930'" (São Paulo: AIMST).
25 Olga Rodrigues de Moraes von Simson, "Imagem e memória," in *O Fotográfico*, 2nd ed. Ed. Etienne Samain (São Paulo: Editora Hucitec, 2005), 21–34.
26 *Bericht Deutsche Schule São Paulo 1933* (1934), 75.

Film Service was to reach the entire German-speaking population in Brazil and to show them "lifelike pictures of German scenery, historic places and sites of German labor" and "to bring the great national festivities to life."[27] As a "living link with the *Stammesheimat*" the films were intended to maintain German folklore and strengthen the German schooling system in Brazil.[28] In turn, films that were produced by the Film Service were intended to show the audience in Germany "Germanhood in Brazil."[29] Film screenings by the Deutscher Lehrerverein or the Film Service were extremely popular and successful. The number of requests and correspondences between 1931 and 1938 show that German associations and clubs not only asked for film shows but also supplied the organizations with information and requests for further acquisition of films.[30] In the first year of its activity the Film Service organized 121 screenings, 85 of them in the metropolitan area of São Paulo and 36 in the interior of the state of São Paulo.[31] The district office in Santa Catarina reported about 3,000 viewers per screening.

Yet films that were shown in the German schools or German-speaking regions were not exclusively about or produced in Germany. Likewise, the audience was not exclusively German or of German origin. A screening at the Olinda School in São Paulo in May 1934, for example, started with the animation film *Wupp lernt das Gruseln* (Wupp learns to be scared; Hermann Diehl, D 1932), followed by *Mit dem Condorflugzeug von Natal bis Santos* (With the Condor Airplane from Natal to Santos) and *Der schöne Rhein. II. Teil* (The Beautiful Rhine, Part II). The animation films were hardly suitable to strengthen Germanhood in Brazil, but their function was first of all to present an entertaining film show for a broad audience.

In analogy to Thais Blank's thesis that films about German immigrants in Brazil that were shown in the German *Wochenschau* (weekly review) in Germany

---

27 Bericht Deutsche Schule São Paulo 1933 (1934), 74.
28 Bericht Deutsche Schule São Paulo 1936, 88.
29 Bericht Deutsche Schule São Paulo 1936, 88. An exact list of films that were produced by the DKD could not be found. Titles that are mentioned in the correspondences are *Rio Grandenser Giftschlangen, Die grosse Parade in Porto Alegre vor Flores da Cunha am 24.10.1933, Das grosse Gauturnfest in Ijuhy, Quer durch Santa Catharina oder Bertioga [Reise nach den Iguassufällen], [Die Eroberung des Urwaldes (Deutsche Siedlung in Südbrasilien)]*, and *[Brasil Grandiosa]*. Titles in brackets refer to films that probably were donated by German Brazilians to the DKD.
30 "Correspondência Landesverband Deutsch-Brasilianischer Lehrer 1933, '22 April 1933'" (São Paulo: AIMST).
31 GIV f 7: "Instituto Hans Staden 1925–1941. Hans Staden-Verein São Paulo, Rundschreiben 4/35, o.A." (São Paulo: AIMST).

strengthened the bond of a fascist imagined community,[32] one could argue that cultural films from Germany exhibited in Brazil had a similar function: The films gave the German-speaking community in Brazil a feeling of belonging, still being part of a German, fascist community. For example, a subtitle such as "From Koblenz to Rotterdam" in *The Beautiful Rhine* could demonstrate that German landscapes reach beyond the national borders. Likewise, viewers could interpret the flight in a Condor airplane along the Brazilian coast as a masterpiece of German technology that aeronautically measured or surveyed the new *Heimat*.[33]

However, considering the heterogeneity of the film audience and the specific program structure of the film shows, it is very difficult to argue for a clear reception of the films.[34] It seems more plausible to speak in terms of Stuart Hall's encoding/decoding model: German films in Brazil offered the chance for a negotiated or even oppositional reading.[35] A more nuanced discussion of the reception of German films reveals that the relationship between the NSDAP's AOs and the German-Brazilian population was not without tension. The majority of the German population was still speaking German and was practicing German art and tradition, but it showed little interest in fascist ideology.[36] Only a small part supported Hitler and considered it their right to speak and stand up against "Teuto-Brazilians" who did not follow the Nazi ideology.[37]

---

32 Thais Blank, "O Papel dos Cinejornais Alemaes sobre o brasil na 'Comuindade Imaginada' Nazista," paper presented at the XXXI Congresso Brasileiro de Ciências da Comunicação, Natal, RN 2–6 September 2008, http://www.intercom.org.br/papers/nacionais/2008/resumos/R3-1708-1.pdf, 29 July 2014.

33 The Condor originated from the association between the Colombian Sociedad Colombo Alemana de Transporte Aéreo (SCADTA) and the German Aero Lloyd in 1924.

34 The films that Blank discusses are *Ilha de Marajó* (The Marajó Island) and *Colonos Alemães no Brasil* (German Colonies in Brazil). The latter seems to be identical to *Auf Grosser Fahrt. Ein Film von Kriegsmarine und Auslandsdeutschen* (Hans-Hein von Adlerstein, D 1936), http://www.filmarchives-online.eu/viewDetailForm?FilmworkID=dca453179b5df647038de54ffb3240ff&con content_tab=deu, 29 July 2014.

35 Stuart Hall, "Encoding, Decoding," in *The Cultural Studies Reader*, 2nd ed. Ed. Simon During (London: Routledge, 1999), 507–517.

36 Luiz Nazario, "Nazi Film Politics in Brazil, 1933–1942," in *Cinema and the Swastika. The International Expansion of the Third Reich*. Ed. Roel Van de Winkel and David Welch (New York: Palgrave MacMillan, 2007), 86.

37 Luiz Nazario, "Nazi Film Politics in Brazil, 1933–1942," in *Cinema and the Swastika. The International Expansion of the Third Reich*. Ed. Roel Van de Winkel and David Welch (New York: Palgrave Macmillan, 2007), 86; René Geertz, *O fascismo no sul do Brasil* (Porto Alegre: Editora Mercado Aberto Ltd., 1987), 82.

Some groups considered the activities of the AOs insensitive and dangerous for the reputation of Brazilians of German origin in Brazil.[38] In November 1931 the minutes of the board of directors of the associations of German clubs reported on the board's growing concern about the NSDAP's influence on the German community.[39] Furthermore, studying reports and correspondences about film shows in the cities and on the countryside discloses that the audience was anything but purely German or of German origin. Germans made up only the smallest part of the Olinda students. The school had mainly Teuto-Brazilian students, and one quarter were Brazilians or students of other nationalities.[40] Without the attendance of the Portuguese-speaking, that is the Brazilian population, film screenings in the countryside often became an incalculable risk.

In June 1931 a screening in Cosmópolis in the interior state of São Paulo had to be relocated to the local cinema because the electricity was out at the first exhibition venue. Only because of the Brazilian audience who came to see the film show did the evening not become a financial disaster for the organizers. A report about the evening remarked:

> Though the stories of the films were easy to comprehend, it is interesting that especially the Brazilians lamented that the texts were just edited in German and not in Portuguese. Without any doubt we could be even more successful, if we considered this request in future.[41]

Similarly "Brazilian" was a screening in Congonhas do Campo in Minas Gerais in 1938, where only 10–15 out of 200 viewers were of German origin.[42] That some organizers were even including the Brazilian population in their planning of a film program is apparent from a peculiar combination of German and Brazilian film titles for a screening in March 1935 in São Caetano in Minas Gerais. German titles such as *Von Ammergau zum Staffelsee* (From Ammergau to Lake Staffel),

---

38 Jürgen Müller, *Nationalsozialismus in Lateinamerika. Die Auslandsorganisation der NSDAP in Argentinien, Brasilien, Chile und Mexiko, 1931–1945* (Stuttgart: Hans-Dieter Heinz, 1997), 43 and 296.
39 "Correspondência Deutscher Lehrerverein, São Paulo 1931, 'Bericht aus der Vorstandssitzung des Verbandes Deutscher Vereine, 9 November 1931'" (São Paulo: AIMST).
40 Of 426 students in 1923, 259 were German-Brazilian, 79 German, and 88 Brazilian or other nationality. At the 60th anniversary in 1938 the school had 947 students, of whom 126 were German, 520 German-Brazilian, 249 Brazilian, and 52 other nationalities (Joachim Tiemann, "Deutsche Schulen in Brasilien im Rahmen des brasilianischen Bildungssystems," http://www.topicos.net/fileadmin/pdf/Tiemann.pdf (2008), 29 July 2014, 4).
41 GIV f. Nr. 25/Schubert-Chor, "Bericht des Deutschen Lehrervereins-São Paulo über die Filmvorführungen am 22 May 1931" (São Paulo: AIMST).
42 "Correspondência Landesverband Deutsch-Brasilianischer Lehrer, '22 April 1938'" (São Paulo: AIMST).

Die Ostsee, 5. und 6. Teil (The Baltic Sea, Part 5 and 6), and *Sport im Schnee* (Snow Sports) were shown together with the films *Os 3 Cavalheiros* (The Three Gentlemen) and *Koko e o Cacique* (Koko and the Chief).[43] Significant in this programming structure is not just the side-by-side presentation of German and Brazilian titles but the division of *Kulturfilm* and animation films: The German titles refer to the genre of the *Kulturfilm*, the Brazilian titles to animation films. The programming structure of this film show can be regarded as an alternative to the complaint of the Brazilian audience in Cosmópolis. Although it is not known in what language the film evening was presented or introduced, or whether intertitles of the first three German films were translated into Portuguese, the animation films did not require any explanatory text or introduction. They simply were what they wanted to be: amusing entertainment for a broad audience, regardless of the audience's origin, German or Brazilian.

While the content of a program was one chance for public entertainment, the screening in itself was an entertaining event. The problem of missing or unstable electricity at some venues made film screenings in the interior of Brazil masterpieces in improvisation. In contrast to film shows in the cities, film screenings in interior Brazil often were the first screenings ever for the local public of remote, small villages.[44] One report about such a first screening retells cinema's founding myth, in which the moving images of an arriving train made viewers run out of the cinema or hide under their seats. However, in the German-Brazilian version it was not the arrival of a train but the arrival of a military truck that scared the audience.[45] The anecdote refers to the ideological content of the film that speculates on the viewers' fascist-patriotic or reverent admiration, but it also refers to the projection of a film as an attraction in itself, which was experienced by viewers "insecure between fear and admiration."[46] Film screenings were a viewing experience of the fantastic and a novelty in themselves. Films about the Day of Potsdam, the day the German Reichstag started its work after the Nazis came into power, the First of May, or a sports meet in Stuttgart offered a range of possible reception contexts: from political propaganda, to visual attraction, or the aesthetic pleasure of watching a nonfictional event, something Tom Gun-

---

[43] GIV f. Nr. 25/Schubert-Chor, "13 March 1935" (São Paulo: AIMST).
[44] *Bericht Deutsche Schule 1933* (1934), 76.
[45] *Bericht Deutsche Schule 1933* (1934), 76. There is no proof for the legendary panic at the first film screening by the Lumière brothers in Paris. According to Martin Loiperdinger, the "panic" rather refers to the new experience of reality, in this case a fantastic experience of reality. Martin Loiperdinger, "Lumières *Ankunft des Zuges*. Gründungsmythos eines neuen Mediums" *Kintop* 5 (1996): 49.
[46] *Bericht Deutsche Schule 1933* (1934), 76.

ning calls the "view aesthetic." Foreign films introduced exotic elements in the indigenous culture and thereby contributed to the diversity of a nation's film repertoire.[47] But regarding the sparse entertainment that existed in remote regions in Brazil, it was not just the films that made a contribution to the local culture but the exhibition of the films in form of a never-before-seen event as well.

The specific "view aesthetic" in actualities and travelogues that Tom Gunning defines as films in which the "subject filmed either pre-existed the act of filming or would have taken place even if the camera had not been there" adds a particularly important reception context.[48] In the specific context of views of German sites in films that the audience was watching with "tearful eyes" and with a "melancholic memory of the old Heimat," the films turned viewers into virtual time travelers, watching images not from the present but from a bygone time, as if looking at a photo album.[49] Against the background of the specific time experience while watching films from Germany, the film screening at the Olinda school in May 1934 offers an interesting alternative: The view from a plane flying into Brazilian territory, crossing 3,000 kilometers along the Brazilian coast, from the northeast (Natal) to São Paulo (Santos) in *Mit dem Condorflugzeug von Natal bis Santos* and 400 kilometers from Koblenz to Rotterdam in *Der schöne Rhein. II. Teil* certainly corroborates the *Volk ohne Raum* (people without space) ideology. Considering the critical stance of many German-Brazilians toward NSDAP ideology, however, the German-Brazilian viewers also could come to the conclusion that Brazil and Germany stood for different periods in life: huge Brazil as the aspiration for a new and better life and small Germany for the outdated memory.

For Brazilian viewers the programing of the two films could have had a different effect: They could enjoy the film for its demonstration of Brazil's enormous size compared with the small European country. The shot from an airplane associated Brazil with modernity and technology, whereas the view of the Rhine, probably taken from a ship, referred to a traditional, old transportation system. Studying the program structures of the film demonstrates that the shows were not standardized but varied according to the specific local needs and inquiring

---

47 Andrew Higson, "The Limiting Imagination of National Cinema," in *Cinema and Nation*. Ed. Mette Hjort and Scott MacKenzie (London: Routledge, 2000), 69.
48 Tom Gunning, "Before Documentary: Early Nonfiction Films and the 'View' Aesthetic," in *Uncharted Territory: Essays on Early Nonfiction Film*. Ed. Daan Hertogs and Nico de Klerk (Amsterdam: Stichting Nederlands Filmmuseum, 1997), 14.
49 Tom Gunning, "Before Documentary: Early Nonfiction Films and the 'View' Aesthetic," in *Uncharted Territory: Essays on Early Nonfiction Film*. Ed. Daan Hertogs and Nico de Klerk (Amsterdam: Stichting Nederlands Filmmuseum, 1997), 14.

institutions. It is too limited to understand film shows exclusively as extensions of National Socialist film propaganda. Brazilian viewers could consider the shows as interesting contributions to local cultural life, but German-Brazilian viewers could react differently: Cultural films strengthened the bond of an imagined community but not necessarily that of a German or German fascist community. Thinking of a heterogeneous audience, it could also strengthen the bond of an imagined Brazilian community that was composed of Brazilians and Teuto-Brazilians.

Feature films in Brazil

Reviews of German feature films that were released in Brazil show that German productions were first of all considered as a welcoming change and challenge to the dominant Hollywood cinema. Only later did the films become associated with fascist propaganda.[50] In contrast to the privately organized network for the distribution of cultural films discussed earlier, feature films were distributed on the commercial market. Films were distributed by different companies, but for the Brazilian audience every film was an U-F-A film, *um-filme-alemão*.[51] German feature films were popular because of their high technical standard. Reviews praised the mise-en-scène of light, music, and camera work. *Metropolis* (Fritz Lang, D 1925–1926), *Faust* (Friedrich Wilhelm Murnau, D 1925–1926), *Varieté* (Ewald A. Dupont, D 1925), and *Walzertraum/The Waltz Dream* (Ludwig Berger, D 1925) were applauded as "wonder[s] of modern cinematography" and "brilliant work[s] of art."[52] Reviews were full of superlatives. Hans Steinhoff's *Der alte und der junge König/The Making of a King* (D 1934–1935) was the "most terrific film ever, that Germany has produced," and some months later it was *Mazurka* (Willi Forst, D 1935), that was the best film ever made in Germany.[53]

Some cinema owners used the UFA's quality label in a particular way: In April 1935 the UFA office in Berlin received a letter from a certain Eugenio de

---

50 See Luiz Nazario, "Nazi Film Politics in Brazil, 1933–1942," in *Cinema and the Swastika. The International Expansion of the Third Reich*. Ed. Roel Van de Winkel and David Welch (New York: Palgrave MacMillan, 2007), 88–90.
51 Bundesarchiv Berlin (BArch) R 109/5379, fol. 536. Report of the Brazilian UFA representative Ugo Sorrentino.
52 Flaviano Bugatti Isolan, *Das páginas à tela: cinema alemão e imprensa na década de 1930* (Santa Cruz do Sul: EDUNISC, 2006), 89.
53 Flaviano Bugatti Isolan, *Das páginas à tela: cinema alemão e imprensa na década de 1930* (Santa Cruz do Sul: EDUNISC, 2006), 90.

Felix, who introduced himself as "German in mind and Austrian in emotion," who was living in Brazil. De Felix was outraged about recent film programs in Brazil and drew the UFA's attention to a scandalous situation in the Brazilian cinemas.[54] De Felix reported about cinemas in São Paulo and Rio de Janeiro that showed German films of the category "Only for men" from 2 p.m. until midnight every day:

> About the films that are shown, they all are silent films and intercut at all possible and impossible moments with pure pornographic scenes, to give the audience the impression that the films were full-blown productions. What is particularly interesting: Almost all films are old UFA films with well-known artists such as Willi Fritsch, Lilian Harvey, Werner Kraus, Werner Fuetterer, Gustav Fröhlich, Ivan Petrovitch, etc.[55]

De Felix had investigated the production of the films and reported that the cinema owner bought the films from the Brazilian distributor Urania and intercut them with pornographic scenes. It is not known how the UFA reacted to the incident or how it answered De Felix, but the anecdote indicates a particular mode of cultural appropriation.

In his analysis of the reception of German cinema in the Brazilian press in the south of Brazil, historian Flaviano Bugatti Isolan argues that the popularity of German films was also due to Weimar Republic's liberal image in Brazil. It stood in sharp contrast to Hollywood cinema, which had to follow the Hays Code after 1930.[56] German films often transgressed this code and were dealing with issues such as prostitution, abortion, and sexual taboos appreciated by the Brazilian audience. The liberal image changed with the Nazi regime's coming into power, but, surprisingly, reviews started to mention and applaud the educational character of the films, which were now standing for a new Germany that continued to produce films of high artistic quality.[57] The "UFA Pornos" stand in sharp contrast to the paradigmatic shift in the morality discourse of German cinema. However, it is possible that the cinema owners who were showing the porn movies were speculating not just about quick success among the men in Rio de

---

54 BArch R 109 I/5379, fol. 398–399.
55 BArch R 109 I/5379, fol. 398–399. de Felix mentions the following UFA productions: *Almas Perdidas/Die Carmen von St. Pauli* (Erich Waschneck, D 1928), *Inferno das Virgen/Die Hoelle der Jungfrauen* (Robert Dinesen, D 1927), *Embriaguez da Mociedade/Jugendrausch* (Georg Asagaroff, D 1926–1927), and *Caste Suzana/Die keusche Susanne* (Richard Eichberg, D 1926).
56 Flaviano Bugatti Isolan, *Das páginas à tela: cinema alemão e imprensa na década de 1930* (Santa Cruz do Sul: EDUNISC, 2006), 91.
57 Flaviano Bugatti Isolan, *Das páginas à tela: cinema alemão e imprensa na década de 1930* (Santa Cruz do Sul: EDUNISC, 2006), 93–95.

Janeiro and São Paulo but also about UFA's reputation for producing films of high quality and German cinema's image of producing films that were once famous for their transgressive moments that represented Weimar cinema in Brazil. Maybe viewers noticed the compilation technique of the films, but maybe they could not figure out the agents behind it. From this perspective the "UFA Pornos" may be understood either as another liberal product of the German film industry or as a smart appropriation and parody or spoof of the new decent German cinema.

In contrast to Brazilian reviews that praised the new UFA productions for their high production values, the UFA headquarters in Berlin was not too euphoric about the performance of their films at the Brazilian box office. The UFA was concerned about new marketing strategies for the South American market. According to the minutes of the UFA's board of directors, the Brazilian market was especially hard to assess.

For example, the UFA was quite sure that *Das Hofkonzert/The Court Concert* (Detlef Sierck, D 1936) would be as successful in Brazil as in other Monopol areas, but that proved not to be the case; it was unsuccessful.[58] Films such as *Schlussakkord/The Final Chord* (Detlef Sierck, D 1936) and *Der Bettelstudent/ The Beggar Student* (Georg Jacoby, 1936) were just moderately successful.[59] One solution to this dilemma was to raise UFA's visibility in the South American market, for example, through their own UFA cinemas.[60] This way, the UFA could face the growing competition from Hollywood in Brazil and accommodate the demand of the German-speaking population for German-language films. In 1933 the *Deutscher Morgen*, mouthpiece of the NSDAP in São Paulo, complained about the exhibition of French-language versions of German films in the city.[61] In the same year the local branch of the NSDAP addressed the UFA and asked for the exhibition of German-language films.[62]

The UFA explained that German-language films would make money only in the very first days after their release, when Germans and German-Brazilians were attending the cinemas. In contrast to the German-language film, the French version of Ludwig Berger's *Walzerkrieg/The Battle of the Waltzes* (D 1933) did well at the box office.[63] Therefore, cinema owners had no other choice but to program

---

58 BArch R 109 I/1032b, p. 295.
59 BArch R 109 I/1032b, p. 295.
60 In March 1935 the board also discussed the opening of additional UFA cinemas in cities such as London or New York. BArch R 109 I/1030a.
61 *Deutscher Morgen* 41 (13 October 1933): 7.
62 GIV f. Nr. 25/Schubert-Chor, "12 June 1934" (São Paulo: AIMS).
63 GIV f. Nr. 25/Schubert-Chor, "12 June 1934" (São Paulo: AIMS).

German-language films together with Hollywood productions. Under the condition that the German-speaking population would make sure that UFA films made enough profit, the UFA promised the NSDAP São Paulo to show exclusively German-language films from then on.[64]

But much more troubling to the UFA than complaints by the German-speaking population was Hollywood's market control in Brazil (about 85.9 percent at the end of World War II).[65] In the mid-1930s the UFA decided to expand its efforts on the Brazilian market by running their own premiere theater.[66] Responsible for leasing the new cinema was the UFA's Brazilian distributor, Sorrentino, who also got permission to use the official name "UFA Palácio."[67]

On 13 November 1936 the UFA celebrated the inauguration of its first South American Palácio, a name that was taken from the German name *Kino-Palast*. The UFA Palácio had about 3,119 seats and was located at the prestigious Avenida São Joao in the heart of the city of São Paulo.[68] The Palácio was a masterpiece of modern cinema architecture and equipped with the latest film projection technology. The architect of the new cinema was Rino Levi, one of the most famous architects of Brazilian modernity.[69] For the very first time in Brazilian cinema architecture, Levi developed a new acoustic and illumination system.[70] Brazilian and German representatives celebrated the inauguration of the UFA cinema, and Berthold von Theobald, deputy member of the board of directors and head of UFA's foreign department, flew to Brazil on a Zeppelin that circled above the new UFA Palácio on opening day. The German-language press praised

---

64 GIV f. Nr. 25/Schubert-Chor, "12 June 1934" (São Paulo: AIMS).
65 Kristin Thompson, *Exporting Entertainment. America in the World Film Market 1907–1934* (London: BFI Publishing, 1985), 134.
66 Already in 1926 the cinema Colyseo Paulista in São Paulo advertised with the UFA logo. It is not known whether this was authorized by the UFA. "Colyseo Paulista (São Paulo-SP)," http://salasdecinemadesp2.blogspot.com/search/label/Colyseo%20Paulista, 29 July 2014.
In June 1928 the UFA board decided to renovate the Lyrico Theater in Rio de Janeiro. With this the UFA intended to secure its market position in Latin America. However, the project probably never was realized. BArch-R 109 I/1028b, Vorstand, Nr. 334, 12 June 1928.
67 BArch R 109 I/1031a.
68 "UFA-Palácio (São Paulo-SP)," http://salasdecinemadesp2.blogspot.com/2008/06/ufa-palace-so-paulo-sp.html, 29 July 2014.
69 Paula Freire Santoro, "A relacão das salas de cinema com o urbanismo moderno na construçao de uma centralidade metropolitana: A cinelandia paulistana," http://www.anpur.org.br/revista/rbeur/index.php/anais/article/view/3465/3395, 29 July 2014.
70 Paula Freire Santoro, "A relacão das salas de cinema com o urbanismo moderno na construçao de uma centralidade metropolitana: A cinelandia paulistana," http://www.anpur.org.br/revista/rbeur/index.php/anais/article/view/3465/3395, 29 July 2014.

the new cinema as a monument of German-Brazilian friendship and cultural exchange that stood for mutual understanding between nations.[71]

The UFA Palácio quickly became one of the best exhibition venues in the city. From then on, the UFA was no longer exclusively associated with artistic films but with a unique film theater that was clearly also Brazilian in its architectural design. The reaction of the neighboring cinemas did not take long. A study of the first three months of the UFA Palácio in the *Deutsche Zeitung* shows that the new cinema interfered with competition for the German-speaking and Portuguese-speaking audiences in São Paulo. Ads of new German films always appeared with the German original title und the Brazilian Portuguese distribution title.

A first competitor appeared at the end of November 1936. The Pedro II had shown German films before and did not seem to make way for the new Palácio. The last week before Christmas, the Broadway was the third cinema to show a German film: *Ave Maria* (Johannes Riemann, D 1936), starring Italian tenor Benjamin Gigli. The day before Christmas it was the UFA Palácio with *Liebeslied* (Fritz P. Buch, Herbert B. Fredersdorf, D 1935), the Pedro II with *Kleine Mutti/Little Mother* (Henry Koster, AU 1935), the Broadway with *Ave Maria*, and, finally, the Rosario with *Der Postillon von Lonjumeau/The Postman from Lonjumeau* (Carl Lamač, A/CH 1935).

A more detailed study of the UFA Palácios remains to be done, but the success of the cinema encouraged the UFA to invest even more in Brazil. In April 1938, von Theobald visited Rio de Janeiro to promote the establishment of a UFA chain in Brazil, the UFA Palácios do Brasil Limitada.[72] There is no doubt that with this new chain the UFA was interested in more than just the German-speaking population. The location of the São Paulo UFA Palácio in the center of the city shows that the UFA aimed to address all citizens.

Conclusion

One major counterargument in the discourse of national cinema is the danger of cultural imperialism through foreign films and culture.[73] However, the example

---

71 *Deutsche Zeitung* 4 November 1936.
72 BArch R 109 I/2909, no foliation.
73 Ian Jarvie, "National Cinema. A Theoretical Assessment," in *Cinema and Nation*. Ed. Mette Hjort and Scott MacKenzie (London, Routledge, 2005), 78; Higson, Andrew. "The Limiting Imagination of National Cinema," in *Cinema and Nation*. Ed. Mette Hjort and Scott MacKenzie (London: Routledge, 2000), 69.

of the distribution of German cultural films and feature films in Brazil shows that Brazilian film and cinema culture never was in danger, neither in the cities nor in the rural regions. On the contrary, foreign German films contributed to the diversity of the national film repertoire. The anecdote of the intercut, hybrid "UFA Pornos" is an example of a very particular kind of cultural appropriation. The cinema owner's strategy to produce "new" UFA films can be regarded as an expression of Brazilian ambivalence toward foreign productions, as described by Randall Johnson and Robert Stam. Through parody of foreign films, "Brazilian filmmakers could make fun of foreign films and laugh at their own inability to emulate their glossy production values but also capitalize and indirectly capitalize on their success."[74] One can dispute how far the intercut UFA porn movies were intended as a parody of a morally decent Nazi cinema, but they certainly guaranteed a rich source of income for cinema owners and demonstrate how something exotic or foreign was integrated in a new "familiar" reception context.

This brief overview of the distribution and exhibition of German films in Brazil shows that the analysis of national film history from a transnational perspective does not just open new ways of approaching film history, but it stresses once more that film was an international, circulating medium to the core from its beginning. In February 2011 the U.S. film journal *Variety* reported that German-Brazilian coproductions were on the rise, "with filmmakers on both sides of the Atlantic eager to tell stories that explore intercultural themes while tapping domestic sources of soft money." *KulturConfusão* seems to me more promising than ever.[75]

References

Allgemeine Lehrerzeitung für Rio Grande do Sul 5 (May 1934): 13.
Archivo General de la Nación Colombia, Ministerio de Gobierno, Sección Primera, Rollo 226, Tomos 892–893, Folio 5–13.
Bericht Deutsche Schule São Paulo 1933 (1934).
Bericht Deutsche Schule São Paulo 1936.
Blank, Thais. "O Papel dos Cinejornais Alemães sobre o Brasil na 'Comunidade Imaginada' Nazista." Paper presented at the XXXI Congresso Brasileiro de Ciências da Comunicação, Natal, RN, 2–6 September 2008, 1–13. http://www.intercom.org.br/papers/nacionais/2008/resumos/R3-1708-1.pdf. 29 July 2014.

---

[74] Randal Johnson and Robert Stam, ed., *Brazilian Cinema* (New York: Columbia University Press, 1995), 23.
[75] Ed Meza. "Germany, Brazil Back 'Bach,' 'Beach,'" *Variety*, 15 February 2011, http://www.variety.com/article/VR1118032299, 11 July 2013.

Bundesarchiv (BArch). BArch-R 109 I/1028b; BArch R 109 I/1030a; BArch R 109 I/1031a; BArch R 109 I/1032b, fol. 295; BArch R 109 I/2909; R 109/5379, fol. 536; BArch R 109 I/5379, fol. 398–399.
Burke, Peter. Cultural Hybridity (Cambridge, England: Polity, 2009).
Chanan, Michael. "Cinema in Latin America," in The Oxford History of World Cinema. Ed. Geoffrey Nowell-Smith (Oxford, England: Oxford University Press, 1996), 427–435.
"Colyseo Paulista (São Paulo-SP)." http://salasdecinemadesp2.blogspot.ch/2014/04/colyseo-paulista-sao-paulo-sp.html. 29 July 2014.
"Correspondência Deutscher Lehrerverein, São Paulo 1930, 'Verein Deutscher Lehrer in Chile, 1. Rundschreiben, Ende März 1930'" (São Paulo: Arquivo do Instituto Martius-Staden [AIMST]).
"Correspondência Deutscher Lehrerverein, São Paulo 1931, 'Bericht aus der Vorstandssitzung des Verbandes Deutscher Vereine, 9 November 1931'" (São Paulo: Arquivo do Instituto Martius-Staden [AIMST]).
"Correspondência Landesverband Deutsch-Brasilianischer Lehrer, '22 April 1933,' '22 April 1938'" (São Paulo: Arquivo do Instituto Martius-Staden [AIMST]).
Deutsche Rio Zeitung, 27 January 1927.
Deutsche Zeitung, 4 November 1936.
Deutscher Morgen 41 (13 October 1933): 7.
"Diario G. A. Hoch 1924–1926" (São Paulo: Arquivo do Instituto Martius-Staden [AIMST]).
Eckardt, Michael. Zwischenspiele der Filmgeschichte. Zur Rezeption des Kinos der Weimarer Republik in Südafrika 1928–1933 (Berlin: Trafo, 2008).
Freire Santoro, Paula. "A relação das salas de cinema como o urbanismo moderna na construção de uma centralidade metropolitana. A cinelândia paulistana." Paper presented at the XI Encontro Nacional da Associação Nacional de Pós-Graduação e Pesquisa em Planejamento Urbano e Regional (ANPUR), Salvador, 23–25 May 2005, Bahia, Brasil. http://www.anpur.org.br/revista/rbeur/index.php/anais/article/view/3465/3395. 29 July 2014.
Fuhrmann, Wolfgang. "Fortschritt, Modernität und neue Lebenswege. Brasilienbilder im westdeutschen Kino der 1950er Jahre," in Kulturdialog Brasilien-Deutschland. Design, Film, Literatur, Medien. Ed. Geane Alzamora, Renira Rampazzo Gambarato, and Simone Malaguti (Berlin: Tranvía, 2008), 61–75.
Geertz, René. O fascismo no sul do Brasil (Porto Alegre: Editora Mercado Aberto Ltd., 1987).
GIV f. 7: "Instituto Hans Staden 1925–1941. Hans Staden-Verein São Paulo, Rundschreiben 4/35, o.A." (São Paulo: Arquivo do Instituto Martius-Staden [AIMST]).
GIV f. Nr. 25/Schubert-Chor, "Bericht des Deutschen Lehrervereins-São Paulo über die Filmvorführungen am 22 May 1931, '12 June 1934,' '13 March 1935'" (São Paulo: Arquivo do Instituto Martius-Staden [AIMST]).
Gunning, Tom. "Before Documentary: Early Nonfiction Films and the 'View' Aesthetic," in Uncharted Territory: Essays on Early Nonfiction Film. Ed. Daan Hertogs and Nico de Klerk (Amsterdam: Stichting Nederlands Filmmuseum, 1997), 9–24.
Hall, Stuart. "Encoding, Decoding," in The Cultural Studies Reader, 2nd ed. Ed. Simon During (London: Routledge, 1999), 507–517.
Halle, Randall. German Film After Germany. Toward a Transnational Aesthetic (Urbana: University of Illinois Press, 2008).
Higson, Andrew. "The Concept of National Cinema." Screen 30.4 (1989): 36–46.

Higson, Andrew. "The Limiting Imagination of National Cinema," in Cinema and Nation. Ed. Mette Hjort and Scott MacKenzie (London: Routledge, 2000), 63–74.

Isolan, Flaviano Bugatti. Das páginas à tela: cinema alemão e imprensa na década de 1930 (Santa Cruz do Sul: EDUNISC, 2006).

Jarvie, Ian. "National Cinema. A Theoretical Assessment," in Cinema and Nation. Ed. Mette Hjort and Scott MacKenzie (London: Routledge, 2005), 75–87.

Johnson, Randal, and Robert Stam, eds. Brazilian Cinema (New York: Columbia University Press, 1995).

Jung, Uli, and Martin Loiperdinger, eds. Geschichte des dokumentarischen Films in Deutschland. Band 1: *Kaiserreich. 1895–1918* (Stuttgart: Reclam, 2005).

Kapczynski, Jennifer. "Newer German Cinema: From Nostalgia to Nowhere." The Germanic Review 82.1 (2007): 3–6.

Kreimeier, Klaus, Antje Ehmann, and Jeanpaul Goergen, eds. Geschichte des dokumentarischen Films in Deutschland. Band 2: Weimarer Republik. 1918–1933 (Stuttgart: Reclam, 2005).

Lichtbild-Bühne 11 (1922): 61.

Loiperdinger, Martin. "Lumières Ankunft des Zuges. Gründungsmythos eines neuen Mediums." Kintop 5 (1996): 36–70.

Meza, Ed. "Germany, Brazil Back 'Bach,' 'Beach.'" Variety, 15 February 2011. http://www.variety.com/article/VR1118032299. 29 July 2014.

Müller, Jürgen. Nationalsozialismus in Lateinamerika. Die Auslandsorganisation der NSDAP in Argentinien, Brasilien, Chile und Mexiko, 1931–1945 (Stuttgart: Hans-Dieter Heinz, 1997).

Nazario, Luiz. "Nazi Film Politics in Brazil, 1933–1942," in Cinema and the Swastika. The International Expansion of the Third Reich. Ed. Roel Van de Winkel and David Welch (New York: Palgrave MacMillan, 2007), 85–98.

Rodrigues de Moraes von Simson, Olga. "Imagem e memória," in O Fotográfico, 2nd ed. Ed. Etienne Samain (São Paulo: Editora Hucitec, 2005), 21–34.

Salas de Cinema de São Paulo (Blog). http://salasdecinemadesp.blogspot.ch. 29 July 2014.

Shaw, Lisa, and Stephanie Dennison, eds. Brazilian National Cinema (London: Routledge, 2007).

Thompson, Kristin. *Exporting Entertainment. America in the World Film Market 1907–1934* (London: BFI Publishing, 1985).

Tiemann, Joachim. "Deutsche Schulen in Brasilien im Rahmen des brasilianischen Bildungssystems." http://www.topicos.net/fileadmin/pdf/Tiemann.pdf (2008). 29 July 2014.

"UFA-Palácio (São Paulo-SP)." http://salasdecinemadesp2.blogspot.com/2008/06/ufa-palace-so-paulo-sp.html. 29 July 2014.

Zimmermann, Peter, and Kay Hoffman, eds. Geschichte des dokumentarischen Films in Deutschland. Band 3: *Drittes Reich 1933–1945* (Stuttgart: Reclam, 2005).

Literary Fusions and Interstitial Spaces

Horst Nitschack*
Tropical Subjectivity and the European Tradition of *Bildung: Macunaíma, a Hero Without a Character,* by Mário de Andrade

The history of the creation of new nation-states since the eighteenth century is in many ways linked and entangled with the stories that are told in those states; they reflect and comment on that history, stimulate the imagination, and provide symbolic references. They permit and encourage readers to identify with newly developing or still-to-be-founded national communities or warn them against errors and potential failures. In this way, stories contribute to the development of imaginary national communities. Readers are encouraged to compare their own lives and experiences with those of the heroes found in novels and to imbue them with meanings that go beyond their own immediate experiences and tie them into the nation as a whole.

The medium of storytelling that was created for this purpose is the novel. This is as true for Latin American countries as it was for European nations in the nineteenth century, and is just as true for a country such as Germany, which is tightly bound up with the cultural traditions of Europe, as for a tropical country such as Brazil, which gained its final independence from Portuguese colonialism in 1822.[1] The first important manifestations of independent novelistic storytelling in Brazil during the Romantic period were the novels of José de Alencar. Although they are full of the spirit of the tropics and celebrate indigenous Indian heroes, in their basic structure they remain tied to European cultural patterns.

The act of cultural liberation in Brazil occurred with *modernismo*, as the Brazilian and Portuguese avant-garde of the 1920s was called. From this point on, Brazilian culture proclaimed its independence from Europe; in painting, music, and literature its role would henceforth be that of an "export nation," no longer a dependent "import nation," as one of the most important exponents of Brazilian Modernism, Oswald de Andrade, provocatively declared in his man-

---
* This article was written as part of a research project, Fondecyt no. 1120116: "Rebeldes, malandros, delincuentes y locos: resistencias, transgresiones y expectativas utópicas en la literatura brasileña del siglo XX." Translated by Kenneth Kronenberg.
1 Doris Sommer, *Foundational Fictions: The National Romances of Latin America* (Berkeley: University of California Press, 1991); and Benedict Anderson, *Imagined Communities* (London: Verso, 1994 [1983]).

ifesto "Pau Brasil" (1924). A few years later, in 1928, he published his much more widely known manifesto, which has lent its name to a theory of culture: the "Anthropophagy Manifesto."[2] Anthropophagy in the metaphorical sense means "ingesting" the best of one's opponent, without fear of contact, without fear of losing one's own identity. In fact, it proceeds with the conviction that one's own identity is actually strengthened by incorporation of the other. Mário de Andrade was a contemporary of Oswald de Andrade and a comrade-in-arms. The same year in which Oswald published the "Anthropophagy Manifesto," Mário de Andrade published a novel titled *Macunaíma, a Hero Without a Character,* which all of his avant-garde acquaintances, especially Oswald de Andrade, celebrated as the great anthropophagic novel of Brazilian literature and which is still one of the most important novels in the Brazilian canon.[3]

By examining the rich meshwork of connections between this novel and German cultural traditions, my intention is to point out complex processes of reevaluation and reinterpretation in this novel in the back-and-forth between cultures and also to show that despite all the differences in terms of provenance and life circumstances between this tropical hero without character and the classical hero of the quintessential German Bildungsroman, Wilhelm Meister, we will find more similarities than we might presume.[4]

The history of the momentous cultural contacts between the world of Macunaíma and that of Wilhelm Meister begins in the middle of the sixteenth century, approximately 50 years after the European discovery of Brazil, in 1500. That was when German mercenary Hans von Staden took off for those far-distant parts. On his second foray into Brazil he was captured by the Tupinambá tribe, miraculously escaped their cannibalistic rituals, and returned to his native haunts to tell the tale in a bestseller titled *Warhaftige Historia und beschreibung eyner Landtschafft der wilden nacketen grimmigen Menschenfresser Leuthen in der Newenwelt America gelegen* (The True Story and Description of a Landscape of Wild, Naked, and Fierce Cannibals, Located in the New World of America).[5]

---

2 Cultural anthropophagy, cf. Carlos Jáuregui, *Canibalia. Canibalismo, calibanismo, antropofagia cultural y consumo en América Latina* (Frankfurt: Vervuert, 2008); or Anette Keck, Inka Kording, and Anja Prochaska, eds., *Verschlungene Grenzen. Anthropophagie in Literatur und Kulturwissenschaften. Literatur und Anthropologie,* Vol. 2 (Tübingen: Narr, 1999).
3 Mário de Andrade, *Macunaíma: o herói sem nenhum caráter.* Ed. Telê Porto Ancona Lopez (Paris: ALLCA XX; México, D.F.: Fondo de Cultura Económica, 1996 [1928]).
4 The German word *Bildung* refers to a very specific Romantic educational tradition, the point of which was the cultivation and transformation of the individual and the essential harmony between intellect and emotion. Bildungsromane are novels in which this process is exemplified.
5 This bestseller, written by Hans von Staden (born circa 1525; date of death unknown) had an enormous effect in the sixteenth century. The first edition appeared in 1557, and new editions

This "testimonial text" is an early indication of how the European powers attempted to take possession of this part of the world. Not only did they subject the *Newenwelt* to their hegemonic claims, they simultaneously larded it with their own projections, fantasies, and interpretations. In addition to the technologies of civilization, they exported their myths, fabulous mythical creatures, and horror fantasies across the Atlantic, from one-eyed giants to man-killing Amazons and human-eaters. From the very beginning, the New World was ambivalently perceived, and even today this ambivalence has not been fundamentally shaken in that it continues to be both a space of hope and a space of terror. In the sixteenth century it was the site of El Dorado and of Hell; in the twentieth century it became known for both political utopias and military dictatorships and terrorism.

These discourses provoke various reactions in Latin America. The "Anthropophagy Manifesto" is surely one of the most polemical in that it uses rhetorical jujitsu to turn an unspeakable accusation into a source of self-affirmation and strength. Almost 400 years after Staden's accusation of cannibalism, which was to be repeated over and over, and which Europeans used to pillory the supposed lack of culture and morality of the tropics, Oswald de Andrade's manifesto proclaimed its platform in its very title. The projections of European conquerors and travelers, intent on seeing a cannibal in every Indian, are challenged head on and polemically made the basis of a cultural strategy that proclaimed the future superiority of the tropical cultures over those of the European interlopers, its given substance. It is not a matter of finding their own culture by isolation and looking inward but rather nourishing it on the model of the ancestors of their opponents. It is self-definition, anthropophagy by the co-optation or ingestion of other cultures. And so the most famous sentence of the manifesto, which propounds its platform in condensed form, is, "Tupi or not Tupi, that is the question."[6] By this pun, Hamlet's existential question is provocatively restated as "To be or not to be a cannibal, that is the question here." And in this restatement, the sentence not only proclaims anthropophagy as a cultural strategy, it also practices it by transforming ironically one of the most iconic sentences in

---

continued to be published in the sixteenth century in pirated editions. It was also translated into French. Hans von Staden, *Warhaftige Historia und beschreibung eyner Landtschafft der wilden nacketen grimmigen Menschenfresser Leuthen in der Newenwelt America gelegen*. Critical edition, Franz Obermeier. Translated into modern German by Joachim Tiemann. Translated into Portuguese by Guiomar Carvalho Franco [Reprint of the 1557 Marburg edition] (Kiel: Westensee Verlag, 2007).

6 Oswald de Andrade, "O manifesto antropófago," in *A utopia antropófaga* (São Paulo: Editora Globo, 1990), 47. In English in the original.

world literature – cannibalizing it – thereby stripping it of its existential content. In this form it becomes the vehicle of a uniquely Brazilian claim, the claim of a peripheral, colonized culture to recognition. It becomes a metaphor of liberation while using the potential of world literature for its own purposes as a carnival-like masquerade. This act of ironic distortion conceals within it the claim of self-identity, which, however, does not hesitate to incorporate elements of another culture, the colonizing culture, for the purposes of decolonization. By turning the dominant European cultures ridiculously on their head, anthropophagy is declared a universal principle, and the argument is thus made that these practices are much more reflective of real societal processes and dynamics. This confirms the superiority of Brazilian cultural practices because – according to their conviction – it cancels or nullifies their suppression by and sublimation to industrialized cultures, especially to those of the European nations. In terms of theory, Oswald de Andrade referenced Freud's *Totem and Taboo*.[7] This anticipated Freud's speculations about cannibalism in *Civilization and Its Discontents*, which he published in 1930, two years after the manifesto: the ritual ingestion (internalization) of the murdered father by his sons, the suppression of which, according to Freud, is the root cause of discontent in culture.

Upon publication, Oswald de Andrade celebrated *Macunaíma* as a successful example of cultural anthropophagy. However, if it was that at all, the novel represented a very different sort of (cultural) anthropophagy than the kind envisioned by Oswald de Andrade. Mário de Andrade emphasized this difference expressly in a letter to well-known critic Tristão de Athayde (Alceu Amoroso Lima).[8] His novel, he stated, was neither a call to nor an example of the "anthropophagic" co-optation of advanced European culture, science, and technology, as Oswald de Andrade's manifesto had proclaimed, referencing Freud, Lévy-Bruhl, William James, and Voronoff.[9] If anything, Mário de Andrade's was more a second-degree anthropophagy. His "anthropophagic desire" refers to the ethnological studies of Theodor Koch-Grünberg's *Vom Roraima zum Orinoco* (From the Roraima to the Orinoco) (Berlin, 1917, Stuttgart 1924) with their descriptions of

---

[7] The "Anthropophagy Manifesto" explicitly refers to Freud's *Totem and Taboo* (1913), and Freud is repeatedly referenced.
[8] Mário de Andrade to Manuel Bandeira about his stance toward anthropophagy, in Mário de Andrade, "Correspondência," in *Macunáima: o herói sem nenhum caráter*. Ed. Telê Porto Ancona Lopez (Paris: ALLCA XX; México, D.F.: Fondo de Cultura Económica, 1996 [1928]), 497.
[9] The "Anthropophagy Manifesto" was surely the first manifesto in which television was mentioned. The first attempts to transmit images were made in early 1928, in Berlin.

the myths of the indigenous peoples of the Amazon.[10] Mário de Andrade back-translated parts of the myths from German and incorporated them in his novel.[11] The back-translation itself has not survived, however. The myths of the Arekuna and Taulipang that Koch-Grünberg recorded with such meticulous precision on his arduous and dangerous expedition through uncharted territories were transformed in his hands into a sort of picaresque Bildungsroman-com-ethnological satire. It is a book that, according to the author, he wrote over the course of six vacation days while lying in a hammock.[12] This seems plausible inasmuch as he took only a few days to write a first draft of his rhapsodic novel from the material he obtained from reading Koch-Grünberg, although he seldom mentioned its origin. But then he spent all of 1927 giving friends chapters of his manuscript to read and requesting additional material from others. It was not until the beginning of 1928 that the text was sent to the printer, at almost the same time as the *Anthropophagy Manifesto*. And as previously mentioned, in his letter to Athayde, the author rejected Oswald de Andrade's enthusiastic reception of *Macunaíma* as an anthropophagic novel.

To return to my main point, this novel occupies a place in the history of Brazilian literature similar to that of the classic bildungsroman *Wilhelm Meister* in German literary history. Both novels are accorded a privileged status in their respective literary canons. Each is the history of a young man. Each follows him from birth, chronicling his journey (odyssey) across his country, where he is confronted with various realities. Both heroes must surmount a variety of tests, and they experience disappointments and sufferings. But whereas Wilhelm marries Natalie at the end, Macunaíma is mutilated in a bloody battle with the siren Uiara, after which he ascends into the heavens as a star. But that is only one of the numerous significant differences, which should not lead us to overlook the very similar situations that confront both fictional characters: the possibilities and impossibilities facing a hero in the modern world, more precisely in the nation and culture that he must come to terms with and accept as his own as he goes about finding his place in the nation and culture. This is the basic trope of all Bildungsromane, and it is also the story of Macunaíma. If Goethe's *Wilhelm*

---

10 Koch-Grünberg was one of the first ethnologists to use the then advanced technologies of phonograph recordings and film in his work.
11 Theodor Koch-Grünberg, *Vom Roroima zum Orinoco. Ergebnisse einer Reise in Nordbrasilien und Venezuela in den Jahren 1911–1913*, Vol. 1 (Berlin: Dietrich Reimer, 1917); Theodor Koch-Grünberg, *Vom Roroima zum Orinoco*, Vol. 2 (Stuttgart: Strecker und Schröder, 1924).
12 Mário de Andrade, "Correspondência," in *Macunaíma: o herói sem nenhum caráter*. Ed. Telê Porto Ancona Lopez (Paris: ALLCA XX; México, D.F.: Fondo de Cultura Económica, 1996 [1928]), 497.

Meister was the first successful German Bildungsroman, the same may be said of Mário de Andrade's *Macunaíma* and his transformation in the tropical world of Brazil: Both meet the challenge of creating an independent national literature.¹³

Formally, comparing *Wilhelm Meister* and *Macunaíma* may be further justified by recalling the role accorded each of these figures, not only in the novels themselves but also in the imaginary of the traditions of *Bildung* in Germany and Brazil, respectively. At first glance, however, there seems to be very little left over from this migration of the German *Wilhelm Meister*. This should come as no surprise if we consider the fundamentally different conditions under which subjectivity becomes possible in the world of the tropics.¹⁴

In Goethe's novel *Wahlverwandtschaften* (Elective Affinities), Ottilie voices the opinion that the tropical world might be a problematic place for someone from the north when she comments on her desire to "hear Humboldt" on the subject: "You cannot walk among palm-trees with impunity, and your sentiments must surely alter in a land where elephants and tigers are at home."¹⁵ Ottilie interprets as punishment this change of attitude, which at the same time means a change in values and judgments. Another later and very different traveler, Ernst Jünger, was no less drastic in his description of the dangers that the tropical world holds for Western travelers and their sense of subjectivity:

> While gliding [through the mouth of the Amazon delta], I tried to imagine the existence one might lead between the arms and islets of this enormous delta, whether one settled as a hunter or a fisher or as a gardener or simply as an observer of the torrent and its overabundance of life. However, one could not do so for long; the growth is too immense to withstand it over time. One would burn from the pure oxygen of it, one's fate an early death with spiritual and physical devastation, a fate similar to that of Rimbaud.¹⁶

In his *Reise in die Aequinoctial-Gegenden des neuen Continents* (Travels in the Equinoctial Regions of the New Continent), Alexander von Humboldt (1769 – 1859), the most important European "traveler" to the American tropics, described

---

13 Friedrich Schlegel on Goethe's *Wilhelm Meister Apprenticeship:* "The French Revolution, Fichte's Doctrine of Science, and Goethe's *Meister* are the greatest tendencies of the Age," Athenäum, Fragment 216: KFSA 2, 198 (No. 216). Friedrich Schlegel, *Kritische Friedrich Schlegel Ausgabe* (KFSA), Vol. 2. (Paderborn: Schöningh Verlag, 1967).
14 A German-language film adaptation of *Wilhelm Meister* was made in the 1970s. Its protagonist was only distantly similar to the original, although he also traveled through Germany. Wim Wenders, *Falsche Bewegung*, with a script by Peter Handke.
15 Johann Wolfgang Goethe, *Elective Affinities*. Trans. R. J. Hollingdale (Hammondsworth, UK: Penguin, 1971), 215.
16 Ernst Jünger, *Atlantische Fahrt* (Tübingen: Otto Reichl Verlag, 1949), 17. Unless otherwise specified, all translations by Kenneth Kronenberg.

in detail the measures taken to protect himself from the dissolution brought about by tropical entropy.[17] This he accomplished by incessant measurement of that world, the attempt to record without gaps the phenomena he encountered, and to inscribe them precisely in terms of the strict coordinates of objective science. Humboldt's travelogue provides impressive evidence that the conquest of foreign lands and the subjugation of nature are impossible without consistently applied self-control and the subjugation of one's own nature. Radical self-control is the price the subject pays for ruling the world. The conviction that the world may be measured, along with the conviction that only what can be measured is of any importance, was a *sine qua non* for the countless researchers who spread across the world from Europe in the eighteenth century, first to subjugate rocks, plants, and animals – and then human beings as well – to the principles of order developed and elaborated by European scholars in European academies.

This scientific colonization was consistent with colonization of the economic and political kind, and was often its precursor. The rationalism, instrumentalism of action, and obsession with efficiency so characteristic of northern industrial countries were viewed with skepticism by Latin Americans, intellectuals and artists, including Brazilians. And this skepticism, it should be noted, was not rare in Europe either. The discovery of exotic worlds by European artists around the turn of the twentieth century (e.g., by Gauguin, and somewhat later Carl Einstein) was not merely a flight from civilization but also a response to the ceaseless and disruptive process of modernization.[18] In Brazil, this corresponded to the discovery of their "own" Indian worlds (whose cultures are only now being slowly recognized after years of expropriation and exploitation of their lands), although this has not necessarily been characterized by a radical critique of modernization but by ambivalence.

World War I and its consequences have been interpreted by many Latin American intellectuals as the beginning of the "Decline of the West," and Spengler's work of that name is often referenced in this context, although contrary to the actual argumentation.[19] It did not engender some kind of radical hostility to

---

[17] Alexander von Humboldt, *Reise in die Aequinoctial-Gegenden des neuen Continents*. Ed. Hermann Hauff (Stuttgart: Cotta, 1859–1860).
[18] Carl Einstein, *Negerplastik* (Leipzig: Verlag der Weißen Bücher (Kurt Wolff), 1915).
[19] Oswald Spengler, *The Decline of the West*, 2 vols., trans, Charles F. Atkinson (New York: Alfred A. Knopf, 1926 [1928]). In the preface to the first edition of Vol. 1, Spengler wrote, "The title, which had been decided upon in 1912, expresses quite literally the intention of the book, which was to describe, in the light of the decline of the Classical age, one world-historical phase of several centuries upon which we ourselves are now entering" (Vol. 1, p. xv).

technology but rather the desire for a utopian fusion of technology and "primitive" cultures.[20] Oswald de Andrade later called for a future synthesis, the "naturally technologized man," the *homem natural tecnizado*.[21] This would allow him once more to take up his idea of the "technologized barbarian," *o bárbaro tecnizado*,[22] which he had already mentioned in his *Anthropophagy Manifesto*, where he cited the traveler and philosopher Hermann Keyserling – a misunderstanding and mistake, it turns out, but one that Latin American intellectuals had already made with regard to Spengler.[23]

Mário de Andrade's *Macunaíma* may be an avant-garde adaptation of Indian myths by way of its translation into German, as is its back-translation into Brazilian Portuguese.[24] But more than that, the novel is itself a sarcastic confrontation with a critique of Western reason and morality that seeks to invoke the "good savage," as the artists and intellectuals of Brazilian *modernismo* did.[25] As he wrote, Mário de Andrade "suffered" along with his hero, but this does not mean, as critics have sometimes claimed, that he identified with Macunaíma's amorality. In all things, Macunaíma focused purely on his own advantage and his sexual pleasure; when expedient, he lied to his brothers and even killed his mother, though not on purpose.

Here we see repeated in a completely new way the disillusionment of the bildungsroman, especially the German one but also the French.[26] In the European tradition, the model of *Bildung* proved contradictory from the very beginning. The ideal subject into which the individual is asked to transform himself through the process of *Bildung*, the flowering that was expected of him by society, simply could not be achieved under the historical, social, and political circumstances that pertained at the time. The individual was thrown into a paradoxical situation. On one hand, society demanded that he make himself into a responsible citizen, while that society made this ideal unachievable. So from the very beginning the bildungsroman was a disillusionment novel, a novel in which its pro-

---

20 Oswald de Andrade, *A utopia antropofágica* (São Paulo: Editora Globo, 1990).
21 Oswald de Andrade, "A Crise da Filosofia messiânica," in *A utopia antropofágica* (São Paulo: Editora Globo, 1990), 103.
22 Oswald de Andrade, *A utopia antropofágica* (São Paulo: Editora Globo, 1990), 48.
23 Hermann Keyserling, *The Travel Diary of a Philosopher* (New York: Harcourt Brace, 1925).
24 The descriptions of the myths are found in Vol. 2, which was published in Stuttgart in 1924. Vol. 1 is the description of the voyage, published in 1917 in Berlin.
25 Horst Nitschack, "O mito do índio no modernismo brasileiro e nas vanguardas hispano-americanas," in *As Américas do Sul: o Brasil no contexto latino-americano. Beihefte zur Iberoromania* Vol. 17. Walter Bruno Berg et al. (Tübingen: Max Niemeyer, 2001), 108–118.
26 We see this in Stendhal's *The Red and the Black*, Balzac's *Lost Illusions*, and Flaubert's *Sentimental Education* as well.

tagonist learned that these ideals could not be achieved in everyday life, or at most in his internal life, and that only by abnegation and renunciation.[27] Where the protagonist was not prepared for renunciation and did not understand the necessity of subjecting himself to the law, failure threatened, as it did in the case of Stendhal's Lucien. The conclusion of *Wilhelm Meister* may be somewhat more conciliatory – in the end he marries Natalie – but then he immediately sets out for Italy with his son Felix, a child from his first love, Marianne. At the same time, the conclusion is marked by Mignon's death and the harpist's suicide.

Macunaíma's end is also an enormous failure. He fails as a hero, one who materialized from the depths of the Amazonian rainforest, and as a satirical critic of a rationality and abstract logic that was foreign to him he undertook his adventurous odyssey across Brazil all the way to São Paulo, a city endowed with all the latest technologies. The favorite utterance of this hero without a character, "Que preguiça," "What laziness," which runs like a leitmotif through the novel, represents the finger-pointing judgment of the Protestant work ethic of the industrialized societies. At the same time, however, it is also a critique of a romanticized image of the indigenous Indians and the much-praised primitive world as it has repeatedly been celebrated in Brazilian literature from Romanticism to Modernism. There is nothing of Oswald de Andrade's *homem natural tecnizado* in Macunaíma. Mário de Andrade may have borrowed individual episodes from Koch-Grünberg, but how this mythical material was shaped and elaborated and how the novel was structured was unquestionably the achievement of the author.[28] As with all such mythical stories, it begins with the hero's conception, birth, and childhood, the exceptional nature of which was the first sign that he was destined to be just that. However, his satirizing of the idealization of Indian culture begins here as well, an idealization that characterizes Brazilian Indianist Romanticism as a whole, which took the northern idealizations of, say, a François-René de Chateaubriand (*Atala* and *René*) or a James Fenimore Cooper (*The Last of the Mohicans*) and refashioned them into the noble Brazilian Indian. We see this tendency in Gonçalves de Magalhães, José de Alencar, and Gonçalves Dias as well, though expressed in very different ways.

---

27 "The type of personality and the structure of the plot are determined by the necessary condition that a reconciliation between interiority and reality, although problematic, is nevertheless possible; that it has to be sought in hard struggles and dangerous adventures, yet is ultimately possible to achieve." Georg Lukács, *The Theory of the Novel* (Cambridge: MIT Press, 1971), 132.
28 Manoel Cavalcanti Proença's *Roteiro de Macunaíma* (Rio de Janeiro: Editora Civilização Brasileira, 1973 [1950]) contains a detailed study of the episodes Andrade incorporated.

At the outset, Macunaíma is given an essentially worthless stone, the Muiraquitã, from Ci, the mother of the rainforest. This stone is stolen from him, and the hero crisscrosses Brazil searching for it. Although he manages to recover his Muiraquitã, he loses it again during a passionate love affair with the siren Uiara. In her passion, Uiara bites off Macunaíma's right leg. And so the hero loses his life and ascends to the heavens, where he takes his place as a star in the constellation Ursa Major.

As a "hero without a character," Macunaíma is completely amoral, egoistic, and lazy; in him Mário de Andrade united all the negative traits he identified in his compatriots, without providing countervailing ones to leaven the whole.[29] Mário de Andrade was fascinated by Macunaíma's negativity, by his mythical world and its irrationality. Its mixture of dream and reality, compulsive sexuality, willingness to use the most varied forms of force, and its lack of responsibility – these behaviors cannot be taken as a critique of modernity.

Even though a number of critics have emphasized the positive aspects of the subversive or contrahegemonic potential of Macunaíma's *malandragem,* this interpretation is contradicted by Mário de Andrade's own comments about his hero.[30] In his correspondence, he plainly distinguished between his poetic work – this "rhapsodic" novel being a success in his view – and Macunaíma's amorality, which he always viewed as problematic. At the beginning, he saw in him primarily comical traits and a satire of Brazilian conditions; by the 1940s, however, he expressed reservations about his own text. The *malandragem* of his hero, his lack of moral mooring, his challenging of all rules, which later critics would view as positive qualities, came to have negative connotations for the author. In a letter to the young author Fernando Sabino dated 1942, the year in which he frequently struggled around his characterization of his hero, we find the following passage:

> So if [the text] was written in a state of complete obsession (I wrote the entire first manuscript in six days), from which I did not suffer because I was working in an elevated state of creativity – from which I was unable to perceive this elevated state consciously because I

---

[29] Letter to Manuel Bandeira dated 7 November 1927: "do qual eu procurava tirar todos os valores nacionais" ("from whom I attempted to take all national values"). Mário de Andrade, "Correspondência," in *Macunaíma: o herói sem nenhum caráter.* Ed. Telê Porto Ancona Lopez (Paris: ALLCA XX; México, D.F.: Fondo de Cultura Económica, 1996 [1928]), 495.

[30] The *malandro,* whose (mis)-deeds are called *malandragem,* is a Brazilian version of the picaresque. It is characterized by small, usually amiable transgressions of the law, which often make the absurdities and injustice of the law clear. Those who are harmed by a *malandro* usually have only themselves to blame, and readers rarely side with them. Their sympathy and understanding are always reserved for the *malandro.*

was completely under its thrall since it clouded all analytic consciousness – I may nonetheless assure you that Macunaíma was terribly painful for me. Even in the highly anecdotal moments, the funny passages, I never ceased to suffer for my hero, suffer from his lack of any disposition to morality (which mirrored that of Brazilians, whom he embodied satirically), to condemn the things he did against my will.[31]

And in a letter to the poet Henriqueta Lisboa, he complained about the immorality (*imoralidade*) of this hero[32] and his amorality (*desmoralidade*). Nonetheless, he insisted that the immorality he depicted was the result of an artistic process, "and if I presented it to the public, then I did so because I felt it was very necessary [i.e., the helplessness in the face of his immorality]. The novel is a satire, a critique, and in the end the hero is made aware of this [by the novel itself] and punished by causing him to live as a useless light among the stars because he is incapable of leading a productive life."[33]

But his most definitive self-criticism is contained in a letter to Álvaro Lins:

> But the truth is, I failed. If the entire book is a satire, a rejection of conformity with what Brazilians are, as I feel and observe it, the enjoyable aspect takes priority. It is true, I failed. Because I am not satisfied ascribing faults to the Brazilians; the fault must lie within myself because I was the one who wrote the book. Look at the preface to this little book in which they celebrated me! For these idiots, as for the modernists of my generation, *Macunaíma* is the lyrical projection of the Brazilian feeling, he is the virginal and unknown Brazilian soul! There is nothing virginal about him! Unknown? My foot. Virgin? My God! He is rather more like a Nazi devil. I failed.[34]

As Mário de Andrade lamented, the critical dimension of his book was recognized by only a few, not even by those who pondered it. Because they were either "those for whom Brazil is the greatest and who didn't want to perceive the satire

---

[31] Mário de Andrade, "Correspondência," in *Macunaíma: o herói sem nenhum caráter*. Ed. Telê Porto Ancona Lopez (Paris: ALLCA XX; México, D.F.: Fondo de Cultura Económica, 1996 [1928]), 514.

[32] Mário de Andrade, "Correspondência," in *Macunaíma: o herói sem nenhum caráter*. Ed. Telê Porto Ancona Lopez (Paris: ALLCA XX; México, D.F.: Fondo de Cultura Económica, 1996 [1928]), 515.

[33] Mário de Andrade, "Correspondência," in *Macunaíma: o herói sem nenhum caráter*. Ed. Telê Porto Ancona Lopez (Paris: ALLCA XX; México, D.F.: Fondo de Cultura Económica, 1996 [1928]), 515.

[34] Mário de Andrade, "Correspondência," in *Macunaíma: o herói sem nenhum caráter*. Ed. Telê Porto Ancona Lopez (Paris: ALLCA XX; México, D.F.: Fondo de Cultura Económica, 1996 [1928]), 515.

and were very satisfied continuing in their lives, or those who merely read in the book a conscious confirmation of their – national – amorality."[35]

According to these passages from Mário de Andrade's correspondence, *Macunaíma* satirized an intellectual stance in which amorality and irrationality were a suitable counterreaction to the modernization of the country by a foreign rationality and performance ethic. What is remarkable about Mário de Andrade's stance is that he accepted neither a Brazilian reality that subjugated itself to an instrumental modernization process nor a critique that celebrated the mystical and irrational. For him, the various cultural and technological practices that Brazil adopted from the northern industrialized nation were no solution. Nor was Oswald's utopian vision of the "technologized barbarian." Nor was the celebration of mythical irrationality, violence, and sexual desire as exemplified by Macunaíma. As in all literary texts, including this one, the reader should not confuse the amorality/immorality of the hero with the convictions of the author. Mário de Andrade himself made clear that the rhapsody was not immoral but that he "uses immorality, not mine but that of my hero, *as well*, in order to characterize the moral inadequacies of Brazilians."[36]

Macunaíma is driven across Brazil, but his search for the lost stone is not like the search for the redeeming power of the Holy Grail. His odyssey does not end in Ithaca, even though he returns to the Amazonian jungle at the end, where he again loses his stone and ascends, mutilated, to Ursa Major. What is comical about his adventure elicits more the laughter of despair than of liberation in both the hero and the reader. His compulsive sexual obsession is more self-destructive enjoyment than precursor to the mutual enjoyment possible in a successful love relationship. Macunaíma is still on the search, a desperate search despite the laughter, for the path that might lead to a future Brazilian culture. There is nothing fortunate about being a "hero without a character"; it is a disaster. Mário de Andrade wrote *Macunaíma* out of a deep sense of longing for a genuine, authentic Brazilian culture, a culture in which the regional contradictions, historical inequalities, and social structures of the country, which make solidarity and the recognition of the Other impossible, are surmounted. If at the end we once again compare *Macunaíma* and *Wilhelm Meister*, *Macunaíma* is surely the more radical and disillusioned book, despite all historical and cul-

---

[35] Mário de Andrade, "Correspondência," in *Macunaíma: o herói sem nenhum caráter*. Ed. Telê Porto Ancona Lopez (Paris: ALLCA XX; México, D.F.: Fondo de Cultura Económica, 1996 [1928]), 514.

[36] Mário de Andrade, "Correspondência," in *Macunaíma: o herói sem nenhum caráter*. Ed. Telê Porto Ancona Lopez (Paris: ALLCA XX; México, D.F.: Fondo de Cultura Económica, 1996 [1928]), 515.

tural differences between the Germany of the end of the eighteenth century and the Brazil of the beginning of the twentieth. Macunaíma knows nothing about the confidence in the power of the idea of *Bildung* that results from the deep congruence between the anthropological disposition of humanity and the contents of *Bildung*. For Goethe, these contents were "inherited" from Antiquity by way of Italy and needed only to be newly "acquired" by each generation, but they also came to the fore in European modernity itself, especially in Shakespeare with his existential question "To be or not to be," which contrasts deeply with the "Tupi or not tupi" of Oswald de Andrade.

Georg Lukács' much-quoted formulation about the Bildungsroman hero, "The voyage is completed: the way begins," does not apply to Macunaíma.[37] His voyage ended without his finding a way. Especially when read against the backdrop of the comments made by the author himself, his end is much more like that in Hyperion's penultimate letter, which Hölderlin wrote in dedication to his hero's despair at being forced once more to live "among the Germans."[38] The German and the Brazilian cultural elites, which were separated by more than a hundred years and were responses to very different cultural contexts, stand before the very same dilemma: the desire to create a national culture while recognizing the impossibility of this project because the ideal and the real are irreconcilable. Mário de Andrade appears to feel the fact that the creation of a national culture is necessary but can be created only in an international context, in much the same way as Goethe did in his time. In the end, Wilhelm Meister makes his way to Italy; likewise, Mário de Andrade hopes that his *Macunaíma* might benefit from translation into another language. And so we read in a letter to Manuel Bandeira dated 12 December 1930, in which he comments on his first attempts at translating his rhapsody into English:

> Perhaps *Macunaíma* will gain in English because, to tell the truth, it seems to me that the satire is not directed merely at Brazilians, some of whose characteristic aspects it illustrates while their good sides are systematically hidden; what is true is that it always appeared to me to be a more universal satire about contemporary man, especially when seen from the perspective of this aimless indecisiveness, these moral principles that are only formulated at the moment they are applied, as I sense and observe in people today.[39]

---

37 Georg Lukács, *The Theory of the Novel* (Cambridge: MIT Press, 1971), 73.
38 Friedrich Hölderlin, *Hyperion*. Ed. Michael Knaupp (Stuttgart: Reclam, 1997 [1797 and 1799]).
39 Mário de Andrade, "Correspondência," in *Macunaíma: o herói sem nenhum caráter*. Ed. Telê Porto Ancona Lopez (Paris: ALLCA XX; México, D.F.: Fondo de Cultura Económica, 1996 [1928]), 509–510.

What we have in *Macunaíma* is very much a critique of modernity that, with its radical process of modernization, becomes – to cite Lukács again – a cause of "transcendental homelessness."[40] Here, Mário de Andrade's *Macunaíma* again touches on the observations of Koch-Grünberg, who observed and felt the destructive power of Western civilization and the consequences of modernization in the most remote settlements along the Amazon. Wherever it occurs, it causes intermixings and hybridizations that destroy local forms of life and traditions, and in their place it introduces novelties that are completely foreign to those who alternate between playing around with them, becoming habituated to them, and falling into despair. Actually appropriating this novelty, actually "acquiring" that which globalization "bequeaths," to paraphrase Goethe, is the key challenge. The "process of digestion" advanced by (cultural) anthropophagy is not a natural one but requires a high degree of cultural work. This is what Oswald de Andrade left out and Mário de Andrade overplays when he mythologizes the writing of his novel. However, it is very much the topic in his hero's tragic desperation to find a path. The playful adoption of elements from other cultures leads to a comical patchwork that must seem to the outside observer as a derelict carnivalistic staging, even if he is, like Theodor Koch-Grünberg, a fundamentally sympathetic and interested professional ethnologist.

> The dancing began on September 7 in the usual manner. Pitá's costume deserves description. He did wonders with the few things that I gave him. An infantry sidearm hangs from the officer's sash that girds his loins. His wife sewed proud-looking sapper's epaulets on his gray denim jacket. He's wearing a bicycling cap on his head. He sewed the trademark, which had been on the lining, to the front of the cap, and so the inscription "Tip-top" is emblazoned atop his eternally smiling and cunning face![41]

With the admiration by a certain strain of cultural theory for bricolage, the fragmentary, and the hybrid, it pays to ask whether this is not only a transitional phase, whose creativity is to be lauded, because it embodies the desire for new forms of order that seek to compensate for the disintegration induced by contact with modernization processes by returning to the archaic. In this sense, Macunaíma's amorality is as archaic as the rituals observed in the new tribal groups in the suburbs. Except that Mário de Andrade was much more critical of this return to mythical archaism than Oswald de Andrade. For Mário de

---

40 Georg Lukács, *The Theory of the Novel* (Cambridge: MIT Press, 1971), 61.
41 Theodor Koch-Grünberg, *Vom Roroima zum Orinoco. Ergebnisse einer Reise in Nordbrasilien und Venezuela in den Jahren 1911–1913*, Vol. 1 (Berlin: Dietrich Reimer, 1917), 80.

Andrade, the cannibalism engaged in by the giant Piaimã in *Macunaíma* was a part of the satire.

Reading *Macunaíma* as a (failed) Bildungsroman, and discerning an elective affinity between Wilhelm Meister and the "hero without a character," is not to imply that the Brazilian text is in any way dependent on the German classic, even though, as we have seen, there are many references to European and especially to German culture. What it does mean, however, is that historical challenges such as the formation of a national state or the search for a subjective morality, which encourage the individual to become a responsible "citizen," are comparable even if very different responses will emerge. In contrast to Wilhelm Meister, there is no ideal of *Bildung* in Mário de Andrade, nor the hope that such an ideal will be achieved by the hero as he makes his way in life. In this respect, *Macunaíma* is much closer to a picaresque novel than to a bildungsroman. No matter how many metamorphoses the hero undergoes, he remains a "hero without a character." But even in the case of the paradigmatic bildungsroman *Wilhelm Meister*, contemporary critics were already commenting on the failure of the ideal of *Bildung*. The renowned critic Friedrich Nicolai wrote of "poor Meister," "who learned little during his apprenticeship other than to allow himself to react to every creature he happened upon."[42]

The fundamental ambiguity of the ideal of *Bildung*, a societal ideal, the achievement of which is made impossible, something that all bildungsromans attested, is repeated in the postcolonial tropical world but with a twist. And the fundamental reason is certainly not, as Ernst Jünger observed earlier, the "spiritual and physical devastation" wreaked by the tropical world. The reason is the deep cultural anchoring of this idea of *Bildung* in the northern Protestant world. There is nothing wrong with this anchoring per se; the problem arises when universalist claims are made that betray a certain blindness to the conditions under which the idea developed. Such universalist claims run the danger of turning the ideal of *Bildung* into an asset of the imperialist ideology and project, as Fernández Vázques argues.[43] *Macunaíma* was most certainly immune to such an abso-

---

[42] Friedrich Nicolai, "Vertraute Briefe von Adelheid B** an ihre Freundin Julie S**," in *Kritik ist überall, zumal in Deutschland, nötig. Satiren und Schriften zur Literatur*. Ed. Wolfgang Albrecht (Leipzig/Weimar 1987), 44–180. In Hendrik Birus, "Grösste Tendenz des Zeitalters. Oder Ein Candide, gegen die Poesie gerichtet? Friedrich Schlegels und Novalis' Kritik des *Wilhelm Meister*." http://www.goethezeitportal.de/db/wiss/goethe/meisterslehrjahre_birus.pdf. 16 July 2013.

[43] José Santiago Fernández Vázques, *La novela de formación. Una aproximación a la ideología colonial europea desde la óptica del Bildungsroman clásico* (Alcalá de Henares, Spain: Universidad de Alcalá, 2002); and *Reescrituras postcoloniales del Bildungsroman*, chapter 4, "El Bildungsroman postcolonial: reescribiendo la tradición" (Madrid: Ed. Verbum, 2003), 115–121.

lutist ideal of *Bildung*. However, Mário de Andrade entered into a pact with the bildungsroman as a result of his (at least initial) faith in the poetic and the power of the aesthetic, a pact that he himself was probably not aware of. As pointed out earlier, he was satisfied with the poetic realization of his hero. Just as the bildungsroman was convinced of the transformative educational and cultural impact of aesthetics and art, so was Mário de Andrade convinced of the "enlightening" potential of his *Macunaíma* – enlightenment through laughter, through the laughter of the reading public at the amorality of the hero, which allows readers to perceive their own weaknesses and pacts with amorality.

Mário de Andrade wrote his despairing letter to Álvaro Lins at the height of the "Estado Novo" (1937–1945), a Brazilian version of the New Deal advocated by the government of Getúlio Vargas, which despite its military and economic alliance with the United States had decidedly fascist overtones. Mário de Andrade must have realized that he had not succeeded in developing an aesthetic in his novel that might have contributed to resistance to this fascistic turn. In fact, the wrong people were applauding him. But even so, he shared a hope or an illusion with the bildungsroman, which was equally convinced not only that he would retell the story of the hero's *Bildung*, whether resigned or failed, but that this retelling might have an "educational" or enlightening effect on the reader.

Viewing Macunaíma as Wilhelm Meister's younger brother, and claiming an elective affinity between the two, is not a reference to a common past – in that they were too different. Rather, it unites them in a common desire for a future national culture in which the subjectivity of its citizens may develop and which promotes their well-being. The barriers to this project are much more difficult to overcome under Brazilian conditions than they were in the world of Wilhelm Meister. This is why Mário de Andrade seemed so despairing in his correspondence. For Wilhelm, family happiness and the prospect of finding a place for himself in this society was paid for with Mignon's death and the harpist's suicide. For Macunaíma, a more peaceful and happy world seems to be conceivable only as a star.

References

Anderson, Benedict. *Imagined Communities* (London: Verso, 1994 [1983]).
Andrade, Mário de. "Correspondência," in *Macunaíma: o herói sem nenhum caráter*. Ed. Telê Porto Ancona Lopez (Paris: ALLCA XX; México, D.F.: Fondo de Cultura Económica, 1996 [1928]).
Andrade, Mário de. *Macunaíma: o herói sem nenhum caráter*. Ed. Telê Porto Ancona Lopez (Paris: ALLCA XX; México, D.F.: Fondo de Cultura Económica, 1996 [1928]).

Andrade, Oswald de. "A Crise da Filosofia messiânica," in *A utopia antropofágica* (São Paulo: Editora Globo, 1990), 101–159.
Andrade, Oswald de. *O Manifesto antropófago*, in *A utopia antropofágica* (São Paulo: Editora Globo, 1990 [1928]), 47–55.
Andrade, Oswald de. "Pau Brasil," in *A utopia antropofágica* (São Paulo: Editora Globo, 1990 [1924]), 41–45.
Andrade, Oswald de. *A utopia antropofágica* (São Paulo: Editora Globo, 1990).
Cavalcanti Proença, Manoel. *Roteiro de Macunaíma* (Rio de Janeiro: Editora Civilização Brasileira, 1973 [1950]).
Einstein, Carl. *Negerplastik* (Leipzig: Verlag der Weißen Bücher (Kurt Wolff), 1915).
Fernández Vázques, José Santiago. *La novela de formación. Una aproximación a la ideología colonial europea desde la óptica del Bildungsroman clásico* (Alcalá de Henares, Spain: Universidad de Alcalá, 2002).
Fernández Vázques, José Santiago. *Reescrituras postcoloniales del Bildungsroman* (Madrid: Ed. Verbum, 2003).
Goethe, Johann Wolfgang. *Elective Affinities*. Trans. R. J. Hollingdale (Hammondsworth, UK: Penguin, 1971).
Goethe, Johann Wolfgang. *Wilhelm Meister's Apprenticeship*. The Harvard Classics Shelf of Fiction (New York: P.F. Collier & Son, 1917).
Hölderlin, Friedrich. *Hyperion*. Ed. Michael Knaupp (Stuttgart: Reclam, 1997 [1797 and 1799]).
Humboldt, Alexander von. *Reise in die Aequinoctial-Gegenden des neuen Continents*. Ed. Hermann Hauff (Stuttgart: Cotta, 1859–1860).
Jáuregui, Carlos A. *Canibalia. Canibalismo, calibanismo, antropofagia cultural y consumo en América Latina* (Frankfurt: Vervuert, 2008).
Jünger, Ernst. *Atlantische Fahrt* (Tübingen: Otto Reichl Verlag, 1949).
Keck, Anette, Inka Kording, and Anja Prochaska, eds. *Verschlungene Grenzen Anthropophagie in Literatur und Kulturwissenschaften*. Literatur und Anthropologie, vol. 2 (Tübingen: Narr, 1999).
Keyserling, Hermann. *The Travel Diary of a Philosopher*, 2 vols. (New York: Harcourt Brace, 1925).
Koch-Grünberg, Theodor. *Vom Roraima zum Orinoco. Ergebnisse einer Reise in Nordbrasilien und Venezuela in den Jahren 1911–1913*, Vol. 1 (Berlin: Dietrich Reimer, 1917).
Koch-Grünberg, Theodor. *Vom Roroima zum Orinoco*, Vol. 2 (Stuttgart: Strecker und Schröder, 1924).
Lukács, Georg. *The Theory of the Novel* (Cambridge: MIT Press, 1971).
Nicolai, Friedrich. "Vertraute Briefe von Adelheid B** an ihre Freundin Julie S**," in *Kritik ist überall, zumal in Deutschland, nötig. Satiren und Schriften zur Literatur*. Ed. Wolfgang Albrecht (Leipzig/Weimar 1987), 44–180. In Hendrik Birus, "Grösste Tendenz des Zeitalters. Oder ein Candide, gegen die Poesie gerichtet? Friedrich Schlegels und Novalis' Kritik des *Wilhelm Meister*." http://www.goethezeitportal.de/db/wiss/goethe/meisterslehrjahre_birus.pdf. 16 July 2013.
Nitschack, Horst. "O mito do índio no modernismo brasileiro e nas vanguardas hispanoamericanas," in *As Américas do Sul: o Brasil no contexto Latino-Americano. Beihefte zur Iberoromania*, Vol. 17. Ed. Walter Bruno Berg (Tübingen: Max Niemeyer, 2001), 108–118.

Rocha, João Cézar de Castro and Jorge Ruffinelli. *Anthropophagy Today? Nuevo Texto Crítico*, no. 23/24 (Stanford, CA: Stanford University, January–December 1999).

Schlegel, Friedrich. *Kritische Friedrich Schlegel Ausgabe* (KFSA), Vol. 2. (Paderborn: Schöningh Verlag, 1967).

Sommer, Doris. *Foundational Fictions: The National Romances of Latin America* (Berkeley: University of California Press, 1991).

Spengler, Oswald. *The Decline of the West*, 2 vols. Trans. Charles F. Atkinson (New York: Alfred A. Knopf, 1926 [1928]).

Staden, Hans von. *Warhaftige Historia und beschreibung eyner Landtschafft der wilden nacketen grimmigen Menschenfresser Leuthen in der Newenwelt America gelegen.* Critical edition, Franz Obermeier. Translated into modern German by Joachim Tiemann. Translated into Portuguese by Guiomar Carvalho Franco [Reprint of the 1557 Marburg edition] (Kiel: Westensee Verlag, 2007).

Marlen Eckl
"Everywhere Paradise Is Lost": The Brazilian National Myth in the Works of Refugees of Nazism

The vision of paradise and the promise of a great future: fundamental elements of the Brazilian national myth

Describing Brazilian nature has had a long tradition; since the European discovery of the country, no one who has ever set foot on Brazilian soil has missed the chance to express admiration for its natural wonders. Allusions to the Garden of Eden are already to be found in the first account of the official Portuguese expedition to Brazil, in the letter of Pero Vaz de Caminha, some consider to be Brazil's birth certificate.[1] Similar to Christopher Columbus, Amerigo Vespucci believed that terrestrial paradise, if it really exists in some part of the world, certainly would not be far from those regions.[2] In that sense,

> America and later Brazil [...] [were not] actually discovered, but rather *found*. They had already existed before, they existed in the minds of the seamen and the missionaries. [...] The old texts [...] had already described to the smallest detail paradise on earth. [...] High mountains form the boundary of the Garden of Eden. [...] The vegetation is luxuriant, flora and fauna are stunning and exotic, a deep sea, a sky of purest indigo and unknown stars, a temperate climate [...] an eternal spring and eternal cosmic renewal. That's how the seamen and missionaries described America and Brazil.[3]

The national myth created in these early texts has not only decisively formed the Brazilian imagination and the self-image of the country but also, because of the reception of these first accounts, influenced the European idea of Brazil. Intrinsically linked to the myth of the terrestrial Garden of Eden found in Brazil is the myth of the promise of a great future. "God's generosity regarding the country

---
[1] Eduardo Bueno, *Brasil: Terra à vista! A aventura ilustrada do descobrimento* (Porto Alegre: L&PM Editores, 2003), 107–108.
[2] Robert Wallisch, ed. *Der Mundo Novus des Amerigo Vespucci. Text, Übersetzung und Kommentar* (Vienna: Verlag der Österreichischen Akademie der Wissenschaften, 2002), 24–25.
[3] Marilena Chauí, "Politische Kultur und Kulturpolitik," in *Brasilien. Land der Zukunft?* Ed. Rafael Sevilla and Darcy Ribeiro (Unkel am Rhein/Bad Honnef: Edition Länderseminare Horlemann Verlag, 1995), 195–196. Unless another source is provided, all translations in this chapter are mine.

was so great that, besides the gift of a natural paradise, he also promised historic paradise. The greatness of nature was the promise of a future big and powerful empire."[4] Yet, in contrast to the vision of having found paradise, related to Brazil from the very beginning, the nimbus that was to be the country of great promise arose only later. "The discovery of gold only occurs in 1562 and this causes a revival of the myth of Eldorado, now on Brazilian territory."[5] Being part of the national myth and cornerstone of national identity, faith in Brazil's future and greatness (especially in the figurative sense) passed down through the centuries.

In the first half of the nineteenth century, Europeans started to deal with Brazil in a more scientific way. Many German and Austrian naturalists, such as Carl Friedrich Philipp von Martius, Johann Baptist Ritter von Spix, and Georg Heinrich von Langsdorff, set out on expeditions to Brazil.[6] Although the task of the scholars was to study the Brazilian fauna and flora objectively, and they did not hide the difficult travel circumstances and illness in their letters and accounts, they felt like they were in the Garden of Eden. Thus, it is not surprising that because of the limitations of language, the scientists referred to the visions of terrestrial paradise in Brazil coined by its discoverers in order to describe the country's natural environment.

In Brazil itself, the paradisiacal motif found its way into literature in these years. Furthermore, nature became a decisive element during the separation from the motherland and in the search for Brazil's own national artistic and literary identity.[7] Poet Antônio Gonçalves Dias praised Brazilian nature in dithyrambic verse and in so doing created a poem that became an integral part of the national literary canon. From exile in Coimbra – that is how he felt about his stay in Portugal – he sang of the beauty of his beloved homeland in his "song of exile," "Canção do exílio":

> My homeland has many palm trees
> and the thrush song fills its air;

---

[4] José Murilo de Carvalho, "O Brasil e seus nomes," *Revista de História da Biblioteca Nacional* 15.2 (December 2006): 20.
[5] Celeste H. M. Ribeiro de Sousa, *Retratos do Brasil. Hetero-imagens literárias alemãs* (São Paulo: Editora Arte & Cultura, 1996), 47–48.
[6] Cf. Gerd Kohlhepp, "Das Bild Brasiliens im Lichte deutscher Forschungsreisender des 19. und der ersten Hälfte des 20. Jahrhunderts," *Martius-Staden-Jahrbuch* 53 (2006): 213–238; Christa Riedl-Dorn, "Die Erforschung Brasiliens durch Österreicher im 19. Jahrhundert," in *Brasilien. Von Österreich zur Neuen Welt*. Ed. Tayfun Belgin (Krems: Kunsthalle Krems, 2007), 9–17.
[7] Valéria Piccoli, "Das Nationalgefühl und andere Aspekte in der brasilianischen Kunst des 19. Jahrhunderts," in *Brasilien. Von Österreich zur Neuen Welt*. Ed. Tayfun Belgin (Krems: Kunsthalle Krems, 2007), 23–28.

> no bird here can sing as well
> as the birds sing over there.
> We have fields more full of flowers
> and a starrier sky above,
> we have woods more full of life
> and a life more full of love.[8]

In the course of the celebrations of the 400th anniversary of Brazil's discovery, Afonso Celso wrote his book on *Porque me ufano do meu país* (Why I Am Proud of My Country). Brazil has to thank him for a very special term for patriotism: *ufanismo*. Celso praised the singularity and superiority of Brazilian nature and people: "From so many promises of greatness, only a grandiose conclusion can be deduced. Let us trust in ourselves. Let us believe in the future. Above all let us trust in God. [...] God won't abandon us. If he endowed Brazil in that especially generous way, it is because he reserved higher destinies for it."[9] The national bestseller thus anchored the national myth in the Brazilian collective consciousness.

The interpretation of the meaning of the national flag also shows the outstanding importance of nature because, for Brazilians, the colors green and yellow represent nature more than they are symbols of the Braganza and Habsburg dynasties: "It is the garden Brazil, paradise Brazil."[10] The Brazilian national anthem (1922) contains a stanza from the "Canção do exílio," and nature is lauded in the following words:

> Brazil, an intense dream, a vivid ray
> of love and hope descends to earth
> if in thy lovely, smiling and clear skies
> the image of the (Southern) Cross shines resplendently.
> A giant by thine own nature,
> thou art a beautiful, strong and intrepid colossus.[11]

---

8 Antônio Gonçalves Dias, *Poesia e Prosa completas. Primeiros cantos*. Ed. Alexei Bueno (Rio de Janeiro: Editora Nova Aguilar, 1998), 105. For the English translation see http://www.poemhunter.com/poem/the-song-of-exile/, 13 July 2013.
9 Celso in Marilena Chauí, *Brasil. Mito fundador e sociedade autoritária* (São Paulo: Editora Fundação Perseu Abramo, 2000), 55.
10 Marilena Chauí, *Brasil. Mito fundador e sociedade autoritária* (São Paulo: Editora Fundação Perseu Abramo, 2000), 62. Regarding the history and origin of the Brazilian flag, see Ingrid Schwamborn, "Der fünfte Stern im Kreuz des Südens: Die brasilianische Fahne und ihre 'interstellare' Geschichte," *Martius Staden Jahrbuch* 54 (2007): 277–300..
11 For the English translation see http://www.southamerica.cl/Brazil/National_Anthem.htm.

The myth of a promising future has also found its way into the anthem: "Thy future mirrors thy greatness." Yet at same time, a slow turning away from emphasizing paradisiacal nature to openly naming the negative national characteristics began in these years. In this context, Paulo Prado's essay *Retrato do Brasil. Ensaio sobre a tristeza brasileira* (Portrait of Brazil. Essay About the Brazilian Sadness) articulates this idea, taking up the concept of Brazil as terrestrial Garden of Eden but only to give the reader an idea about the fatal consequences of a paradisiacal environment on people. Thus, it is

> a tragic concept of "terrestrial paradise." [...] Paulo Prado deconstructed the Edenism of Afonso Celso with one or two sentences. [...] Both in one sentence – "a sad nation lives in a radiant land" – as in the other – "they lived sadly in a radiant land" – Prado's dissatisfaction inexorably becomes apparent.[12]

For lack of an alternative, the only perspective for Prado was to have modest confidence about the time to come. Instead of prophesying a grand destiny, he merely expressed a restrained faith in the future, "which cannot be worse than the past."[13]

In contrast to Prado, the Europeans who got to know Brazil as simple travelers or in another function at the beginning of the twentieth century were convinced of the promising future of the country. After the long isolation caused by World War I and its aftermath, German publicists and authors prepared to travel through foreign countries (often professionally for a media group or a publishing house) and to publish their experiential accounts. The fact that in these travel books journalism mingled with fiction was no disadvantage to their popularity. Quite to the contrary, the poetic function was "by no means ornamental adornment or a disruptive element, but rather an essential part of the Western travel literature in its modern form."[14] Even though this kind of literature is naturally focused on distant countries, it did not remain unaffected by the social tensions

---

[12] Cláudio Lúcio de Carvalho Diniz, "Tristeza Tupiniquim: a melancolia brasileira no Retrato do Brasil de Paulo Prado," Lecture at I. Memorial do Instituto de Ciências Humanas e Sociais (9–12 November 2004), http://www.ichs.ufop.br/memorial/trab/h9_4.pdf. In this context also cf. Paulo Prado, *Retrato do Brasil. Ensaio sobre a tristeza brasileira*. Ed. Carlos Augusto Calil (São Paulo: Companhia das Letras, 2001), 53, 183.
[13] Paulo Prado, *Retrato do Brasil. Ensaio sobre a tristeza brasileira*. Ed. Carlos Augusto Calil (São Paulo: Companhia das Letras, 2001), 212.
[14] Ottmar Ette, "Est-ce que l'on sait où l'on va? Dimensionen, Orte und Bewegungsmuster des Reiseberichts," in *Die Wiederentdeckung Lateinamerikas. Die Erfahrung des Subkontinents in Reiseberichten des 19. Jahrhunderts*. Ed. Walther L. Bernecker and Gertrut Krömer, eds. (Frankfurt am Main: Vervuert Verlag, 1997), 41.

and political unrest of the Weimar Republic. It rather reflected the political camps that existed at that time. "The social involved internationalism [...] responded to the elite or reactionary exoticism."[15]

Several of the authors not only wrote down their travel experiences of the journeys through Brazil in travel accounts but also used them as material for novels, as Heinrich Eduard Jacob did. Some did not miss the opportunity to draw the reader's attention to Brazil's promising future in the title of their books. The precursor to Stefan Zweig's classic *Brazil: Land of the Future* was a book of the same title written in 1912 by Heinrich Schüler, consul and founder of the first German Latin American Institute, which was republished in revised editions until 1924. Another precursor was *Land der Zukunft. Reise in Brasilien* (Land of Future. Journey Through Brazil), written by publicist Hermann Ullmann in 1937.[16] At that time Hitler had already seized power. At the will of the Nazis, the "Aryan master race" should dominate over Europe and gain world dominance with the aid of an expansive policy of conquest and extermination. Someone who did not fit in this world view for racial or political reasons had no other choice but to flee, as the writers under discussion here did. Their works were mostly banned and their careers cut short since they were forced to leave Germany because of their Jewish origin or political convictions.

The writers who sought refuge in Brazil did not know[17] that they had come into a country in a process of nation building at that time. After the Revolution of

---

15 Hans Christoph Buch, *Die Nähe und die Ferne. Bausteine zu einer Poetik des kolonialen Blicks* (Frankfurt am Main: Suhrkamp Verlag, 1991), 127.
16 Cf. Heinrich Schüler, *Brasilien. Ein Land der Zukunft*, 5th ed. (Stuttgart/Berlin: Deutsche Verlagsanstalt, 1921); Hermann Ullmann, *Land der Zukunft. Reise in Brasilien* (Jena: Eugen Diederichs Verlag, 1937).
17 Between 1933 and 1945 Brazil received 16,000 to 19,000 German-speaking, mostly Jewish refugees and became the second most important country of refuge in South America after Argentina. The majority of them found a new home there. In Brazil, strongly influenced by French culture, the émigré intellectuals and writers became important mediators, making Brazilian society familiar to the German culture, particularly German literature. In return, their publications gave a closer insight into this tropical country for the European audience. See Marlen Eckl, "Das geistige Band zwischen der Alten und Neuen Welt: Publizisten, Schriftsteller, Übersetzer und Theaterschaffende als Kulturvermittler," in *"...Mehr vorwärts als rückwärts schauen..." Das deutschsprachige Exil in Brasilien 1933–1945. / "...Olhando mais para frente do que para trás..." O exílio de língua alemã no Brasil 1933–1945*. Ed. Sylvia Asmus and Marlen Eckl (Berlin: Hentrich & Hentrich Verlag, 2013), 10–33; "'Europa im Urwald': Ulrich Bechers Auseinandersetzung mit dem Nationalsozialismus und dem Exil in Brasilien in den Theaterstücken *Samba* und *Makumba*," *Zwischenwelt. Zeitschrift für Kultur und Literatur des Exils und Widerstands* 27.3 (November 2010): 28–33; "Goethe in den Tropen: Kulturvermittlung im brasilianischen Exil," *Études Germaniques* 63.4 (October–December 2008): 773–789.

1930 and even more after the coup d'état in 1937 that established the Estado Novo (New State) under the dictatorial regime of Getúlio Vargas, Brazil was deeply engaged in a debate on *brasilidade* (Brazilianism) and bethought itself of national values and myths.

Brazilian national identity was promoted by the so-called *campanha de nacionalização* (nationalization campaign) in order to ensure a better "integration" of immigrant minorities, such as the Italian, Japanese, German, or Jewish communities, into Brazilian mainstream culture. As part of this campaign the use of foreign languages in education and religious services and in the publication of newspapers was prohibited, and immigrant organizations had to "nationalize" their names and elect native-born Brazilians to their boards of directors.

Ideologically, the construction of a Brazilian nation was based on two aspects: "first with the help of the restoration of Brazilian history, and second, with the help of the identification and upgrading of the collective memory of our nation based on our culture and our traditions."[18] The 1930s and 1940s became two of the most prolific periods for the reinterpretation of the country's history, and Brazil was "rediscovered."[19] As in the case of the real discovery, this "rediscovery" was accompanied by the creation of myths that decisively influenced the self-image and public image of the country and has been linked to Brazil ever since. So it was a matter of course that the image of the Garden of Eden and the land of the future became one of the most important elements of the policy of the Vargas regime.

It is also not surprising that it was part of the "marketing ploy" of the regime that wanted to present Brazil not only as a promising country with great economic potential but also as a holiday paradise, especially for the United States. One of the most famous manifestations of this promotion of the "true" image of Brazil was Ary Barroso's samba "Aquarela do Brasil" (Watercolor of Brazil), composed in 1939. After the Vargas regime entered into the war on the side of the Allies in August 1942, the relationship between Brazil and the United States deepened in a number of ways. Featured in the Walt Disney movie *Saludos Amigos* under the title *Brazil*, Barroso's hymn became a hit in the United States and the first Brazilian song to be played more than a million times on American

---

18 Ângela Maria de Castro Gomes, "O redescobrimento do Brasil," in *Estado Novo. Ideologia e poder*. Ed. Ângela Maria de Castro Gomes et al. (Rio de Janeiro: Jorge Zahar Editor, 1982), 144–145.
19 Cf. Renato Moscateli, "Um redescobrimento historiográfico do Brasil," *Revista de História Regional* 5.1 (Summer 2000), http://www.revistas2.uepg.br/index.php/rhr/article/viewFile/2100/1581, 9 February 2015.

radio.[20] In his song, Barroso seizes on the country's image of terrestrial paradise and God's home on earth: "Oh, Brazil of my love / Land of Our Lord / [...] Oh, Brazil, green that makes / The world amazed [...] / Oh, hear these murmuring fountains / Where I slake my thirst / And where the moonlight comes to play."[21]

Although not all were written in the same period, the representations of Brazil in German-language texts by Frank Arnau, Ulrich Becher, Marte Brill, Vilém Flusser, Wolfgang Hoffmann-Harnisch, Heinrich Eduard Jacob, Richard Katz, Hugo Simon, and Stefan Zweig were all certainly influenced by the climate of Brazilian self-reflection in those years and by the authors' experiences as refugees from Nazism in Brazil. Consequently, the main focus of this chapter is on these questions: How and to what extent did the authors use elements of the Brazilian national myth of terrestrial paradise and the land of the future? What function do they have in these texts, considering the fact that the authors fled the Nazis for Brazil and came from a different cultural tradition? And what may be the reasons that lie behind the refusal of some authors to draw on Brazilian traditional images?

"Brazil has the effect of a drug. [...] It captivates mind and soul."[22] The depiction of Brazilian nature

This sentence is quoted from *Brasilien. Bildnis eines tropischen Großreiches* (Brazil: Image of a Tropical Empire), written by Wolfgang Hoffmann-Harnisch, who fled the Nazis for Brazil in 1938 and returned to Germany in 1951.[23] It describes the full range of the impact of Brazilian nature on its observer. As if under the influence of drugs, one can either be "inebriated" by it or, rather, feel like being transferred into a nightmare, as the multifaceted depictions of nature of the émigré writers impressively show. The most prominent refugee from Nazism

---

20 Cecília Prada, "Ary do Brasil," *Revista Problemas Brasileiros* 357 (May–June 2003). http://www.sescsp.org.br/sesc/revistas_sesc/pb/artigo.cfm?Edicao_Id=153&breadcrumb=1&Artigo_ID=2239&IDCategoria=2292&reftype=1.
21 Daniella Thompson and Ricardo Paoletti, "Aquarela do Brasil," n.d. http://daniellathompson.com/ary/aquarela.html.
22 Wolfgang Hoffmann-Harnisch, *Brasilien. Bildnis eines tropischen Großreiches* (Hamburg: Hanseatische Verlagsanstalt, 1938), 458.
23 Regarding the Brazilian exile of Hoffmann-Harnisch and his way of depicting the country of refuge, see Marlen Eckl, *"Das Paradies ist überall verloren," Das Brasilienbild von Flüchtlingen des Nationalsozialismus* (Frankfurt am Main: Vervuert Verlag, 2010), 248–256, 270–273, 318–326, 388–397, 429–434. Izabela Maria Furtado Kestler, *Die Exilliteratur und das Exil der deutschsprachigen Schriftsteller und Publizisten* (Bern, Switzerland: Peter Lang Verlag, 1992), 89–92.

in Brazil, Stefan Zweig, was particularly fascinated by the natural beauty there. In his hymn of praise for Brazil, written in 1941, he showed his brilliance with a stylistically polished depiction of a terrestrial Garden of Eden. The long-lasting impact of the first encounter with an exotic, tropical natural setting had already emerged during his first visit to Brazil in 1936 in his diary entries of that time. "Marvelous primordial nature. [...] Deeply moved you enjoy this unimaginable beauty and you don't want to go. [...] Everything shines in a magic light, under Brazilian palms you experience the gentlest summer party."[24] Indeed, the interaction of nature and city in Rio de Janeiro cast a spell on Zweig. By including entire paragraphs of his texts from his first visit of the country, the Austrian writer was able to preserve for his readers the magic of the first encounter with what he evidently considered to be a fascinating and exotic landscape. The following excerpt illustrates the kind of description of the tropical environment Zweig never ceased to praise:

> Before me here was [...] one of the most magnificent landscapes in the world. [...] I was overwhelmed by a rush of joy and beauty. [...] The first impression of this country is one of bewildering abundance. Everything is violent – the sun, the light, the colours. The glare of the sun is stronger here; the greens are deep and full; the earth tight-packed and red. No painter could mix on his palette more glowing, dazzling, or more brilliant colours. [...] Nature is always in a state of climax. [...] The sea is free for bathing, beauty free for all eyes. [...] There is something soft and relaxing in the air. [...] Here one is constantly absorbing pleasure through the eye; a mysterious comfort radiates from this landscape as from anything beautiful and exceptional on this earth. With its myriad stars and lights at night, by day its dazzling, hot, and explosive colours, its scented sultriness and its tropical outbursts [...] the longer one knows it, the more difficult it becomes to describe it.[25]

In these paragraphs Zweig used repetitive superlatives not only as an expression of the overwhelming emotions caused by the sight of this literally breathtaking landscape but also consciously as a stylistic device.

> The writer works especially with the help of a method oscillating between two extremes in the quantitative category by, on the one hand, equating exotic phenomena with European

---

24 Stefan Zweig, *Tagebücher*. Ed. Knut Beck (Frankfurt am Main: S. Fischer Verlag, 1984), 401, 405 (Diary entries, 21.08.1936, 23.08.1936).
25 Stefan Zweig, *Brasilien. Ein Land der Zukunft* (Frankfurt am Main: S. Fischer Verlag, 1990), 10–11, 94, 191. For the English translation cf. Stefan Zweig, *Brazil. Land of the Future* (London: Zweig Press, 2008), 3, 82, 170.

issues (and respectively vice versa). On the other hand he introduces exotic phenomena of equal quality as superlatives of their European counterpart and by that defines the exotic.²⁶

Using Europe as a point of reference, Zweig stands in the tradition of the discoverers who thought to have found in Brazil in the visions of paradise they had already had in their minds. Apart from Zweig's hymn of praise, the enthusiastic description of Brazilian flora and fauna of his old acquaintance from Berlin, banker and patron of the arts Hugo Simon, is exceptional among the émigré writers. Simon succeeded in finding refuge in Brazil in 1941 with the help of forged documents and a venturesome flight, and even so he was temporarily threatened with expulsion. Hence, contrary to Zweig, he soon experienced the dangerous and seamy sides of this apparently paradisiacal country. Nevertheless, he strongly held on to the myth of the terrestrial paradise Brazil – "wonderland," as Simon used to call it²⁷ – perhaps more so than any of the other émigré writers analyzed here.

The country's natural environment plays an important part in his novel *Seidenraupen*, written in Brazilian exile, because it represents the source of the longing of the protagonist Hubert/Hugo (Simon changed the name of the character in the middle of the novel). He thinks that only in Brazil will he be able to realize his childhood dream of raising silkworms. In the novel, botanist Dr. Heinrich Niels acts as mediator between Germany and Brazil, as it is he who acquaints Hubert/Hugo with Brazil and its nature from an early age. By including this figure, Simon showed reverence to the explorers and naturalists of the nineteenth century. The multiple mentions of Alexander von Humboldt and his travel chronicle *Personal Narrative of Travels to the Equinoctial Regions of America Dur-*

---

26 Klaus Zelewitz, "Stefan Zweig: Exotismus versus (?) Europhilie," in *Die letzte Partie. Stefan Zweigs Leben und Werk in Brasilien (1932–1942)*. Ed. Ingrid Schwamborn (Bielefeld: Aisthesis Verlag, 1999), 156.
27 Hugo Simon, *Seidenraupen*. Unpublished manuscript, n.d. Collection Hugo Simon (Deutsche Nationalbibliothek. Deutsches Exilarchiv 1933–1945. Frankfurt am Main, E 2005/63), 528. Simon was not the only one who gave Brazil this name. Already in 1912 Schüler described Brazil as a wonderland for its fauna and flora (Heinrich Schüler, *Brasilien. Ein Land der Zukunft*, 5th ed. [Stuttgart/Berlin: Deutsche Verlagsanstalt, 1921], 178). *Wunderland Brasilien* (Wonderland Brazil) was also the title of the edition of Hoffmann-Harnisch's Brazil book printed under license of the book club Deutsche Hausbücherei in 1938, in the awareness that this title would remind the readers of the idea of paradise. Wolfgang Hoffmann-Harnisch, *Brasilien. Bildnis eines tropischen Großreiches* (Hamburg: Hanseatische Verlagsanstalt, 1938).

ing the Years 1799–1804[28] and the fact that Dr. Niels goes butterfly hunting, collects plant samples in Brazil, and, after his return to Germany, donates these objects to the Museum of Natural History in Berlin give evidence of the author's admiration of the former scholars. The letters sent to Hubert/Hugo's family from Brazil reveal the enthusiasm of Dr. Niels and his wife, traveling through Brazil, for the Garden of Eden they encounter there:

> Most of all, Heinrich [Niels] is fond of the great diversity of the vegetation [...] and he doesn't miss any opportunity to undertake his studies in the famous botanical garden. [...] He longs to go to the interior of the country where virgin forest still exists. [...] Here a fairy tale has become reality. [...] Our love grew ever stronger for this, the most beautiful creation of the tropical plant world, for this huge living textbook.[29]

It is not surprising that, later, Hubert/Hugo wants to convince his friend Robert that, in case of war, Brazil would be a better country of exile than France.

> You don't think that Brazil will stand on the sidelines when the entire civilized world rises up against Germany, do you? [...] Imagine a beautiful coffee plantation in the state of São Paulo or Minas Gerais. [...] There are bromeliads and orchids. [...] And besides the always ripe bananas there are the most diverse fruits, the majority of which we don't even know by name. [...] One fruit is called Mamão. [...] Another is called Jaboticaba. [...] It goes without saying that there are pineapples, oranges, lemons. [...] You can eat fresh vegetables all year. [...] In addition, flowers constantly blossom in all colors. Many of the flowers and trees pour out a delightful fragrance and colorful butterflies and hummingbirds flutter around them.[30]

Because of the passionate plea for Brazil and such an unspoiled and enthusiastic description of the flora and fauna in the tradition of paradise found in Brazil, Simon constitutes an exception.

Similar to Simon, very soon after her comparatively early arrival in Brazil in 1933, Marte Brill was confronted with the other side of this supposed paradise. Sensitized by her own difficult situation, being forced to rebuild her life in this alleged Garden of Eden, Sylvia, the protagonist of her autobiographical *roman à clef Der Schmelztiegel* (The Crucible), views Brazil with a sharpened look. She becomes aware that in this paradise, nature has also cruelly placed

---

[28] Cf. Hugo Simon, *Seidenraupen*. Unpublished manuscript, n.d. Collection Hugo Simon (Deutsche Nationalbibliothek. Deutsches Exilarchiv 1933–1945. Frankfurt am Main, E 2005/63), 27, 1046 a + b.

[29] Hugo Simon, *Seidenraupen*. Unpublished manuscript, n.d. Collection Hugo Simon (Deutsche Nationalbibliothek. Deutsches Exilarchiv 1933–1945. Frankfurt am Main, E 2005/63), 31, 36.

[30] Hugo Simon, *Seidenraupen*. Unpublished manuscript, n.d. Collection Hugo Simon (Deutsche Nationalbibliothek. Deutsches Exilarchiv 1933–1945. Frankfurt am Main, E 2005/63), 527–528.

danger and outer beauty next to each other.[31] In the daily struggle for survival, Sylvia, like Brill, finds that the challenges of life can be met only with significant efforts:

> In the interior region of this enormous continent called Brazil, people work, slave away, white, brown, ebony-colored people struggle. [...] They are exposed to the venom of snakes, the bite of dangerous insects, threatened by leprosy and fever. They fertilize the soil with sweat and blood. The land was rich in goods, immeasurably, lavishly rich. Nature had generously, blindly poured out its gifts over the piece of earth, more than people could ever strive to recover.[32]

Furthermore, she becomes aware of the depressing effect of the Edenic beauty of the landscape. Only someone free of sorrow is able to enjoy it without worry. But as a refugee she knows not only of the fear for the future but also of an irretrievable loss: "The stars shimmer differently, and the crescent of the moon is different; [...] The sky is deep, clear as a bell, hyacinth in color. It is not the sky of your childhood."[33] Brill is the only one of the émigré writers who posed the question as to whether the paradise Brazil is really paradise or whether the beloved homeland, now that it is lost, it becomes the real paradise. Like her protagonist Sylvia, the more Brill felt at home in Brazil, the more her economic situation improved, the more the negative sides of paradise take a back seat, the more she is receptive to its splendor, exoticism, and richness:

> The beautifully sweeping arc of a bridge curved over the pond, dark as the night; at its shore a broad pinnate agave held an enormous fairytale-like blossom in the blue air at the end of its bolt-upright, strong stem. [...] The eye took a bath in all shades of light to deep green. [...] There was an aromatic smell of soil, of thyme and jasmine.[34]

When Brazil finally became a new home for her, she had no doubts about the Garden of Eden that offers all people need for life: "Sylvia was fascinated by the magnificent vastness and the deep self-sufficiency of this country. Far away beyond the horizon there was the end of the world. [...] But life continued to grow. Everything prospered, everything what these people needed, everything that they could form with their hands."[35]

---

31 Cf. Marte Brill, *Der Schmelztiegel* (Frankfurt am Main: Büchergilde Gutenberg, 2002), 156.
32 Marte Brill, *Der Schmelztiegel* (Frankfurt am Main: Büchergilde Gutenberg, 2002), 141–142.
33 Marte Brill, *Der Schmelztiegel* (Frankfurt am Main: Büchergilde Gutenberg, 2002), 120.
34 Marte Brill, *Der Schmelztiegel* (Frankfurt am Main: Büchergilde Gutenberg, 2002), 277, 301, 303.
35 Marte Brill, *Der Schmelztiegel* (Frankfurt am Main: Büchergilde Gutenberg, 2002), 325.

In contrast, examining the depiction of nature in the works of Frank Arnau it is evident that the description of flora and fauna has lost its importance with the passage of time. In his book about Brazil, *Der verchromte Urwald* (Chromed Virgin Forest), written in the 1950s after his return to Europe, the portrayal of Brazilian flora and fauna and the myth of terrestrial paradise, inextricably linked with it, play only a minor part. Arnau mentions the country's nature only in very few contexts; depictions of the landscape are completely missing. Right at the beginning of the book, the author lets the readers know that in spite of his deep and almost sentimental love for this amazing country, he is capable of seeing and describing things realistically.[36] In his opinion, promoting the myth of terrestrial paradise is not necessary. Accordingly, his treatment of the diversity of species, the abundance of natural resources and gems is objective. He studies these aspects mainly under the auspices of export and economical points of view. Moreover, he specifies the existing deficiencies:

> In many places extremely precious metals were [...] found. [...] Brazil is a real Garden of Eden, whose marvelous huge forests [...] are, however, exploited relentlessly. [...] The magnificent gems and semi-precious stones [...] are also frequently subject to the mischief of exploitation. [...] The abundance is unimaginable. The poverty, too. [...] The latent political and economic crises never end. But Brazil is so rich that even the most systematic mismanagement is not able to hamper the breathtaking development. Yet, a question arises: why this country preferred by God in such a unique manner is so far away from real balance, true social contentment and domestic political order.[37]

Writing some of his books about Brazil in the 1950s and 1960s, Richard Katz, like Arnau, had a retrospective view on the country of exile he closely felt connected to, even after his return to Europe for health reasons. Much like Zweig, the journalist knew Brazil as a travel writer before seeking refuge there in the 1940s. He first visited the country on his world trip in the 1930s. His first impression of Brazil remained deeply imbedded in his memory and was an important influence in his decision to choose Brazil as his country of exile.[38] Nonetheless, when he arrived in Rio de Janeiro in 1941 after various failed escape attempts, he too, like Brill, soon realized that "everywhere paradise is lost."

---

36 Cf. Frank Arnau, *Der verchromte Urwald. Licht und Schatten über Brasilien* (Frankfurt am Main: Umschau Verlag, 1956), 7–8.
37 Frank Arnau, *Der verchromte Urwald. Licht und Schatten über Brasilien* (Frankfurt am Main: Umschau Verlag, 1956), 10–11.
38 Cf. Marlen Eckl, "Hugo Simon: Vom Kunst liebenden Bankier in Berlin zum Seidenraupen züchtenden Autor im brasilianischen *Interior*," *Martius-Staden-Jahrbuch* 57 (2010): 133.

> Despite sunny glitter and a shiny blue sea,
> Despite white clothes people slave away
> Here, too, with longing and with physical pain,
> Almost like us – this I know today.[39]

However, the following description of the gardens on the island of Paquetá, situated in Guanabara Bay near Rio de Janeiro, proves that he had not become totally "indifferent"[40] to the seemingly paradisiacal flora and fauna.

> The gardens of Paquetá are not big but luxurious. [...] The *Euphorbia* blazes in loud scarlet. [...] Outdoors [...] it is the loudest red that nature yields, by far redder that the reddest of roses. [...] Nowhere in the South Sea [...] have I seen so beautiful hibiscus flowers than on this island in the Gulf of Rio de Janeiro.[41]

Nevertheless, such a depiction characterized by delight is an exception in Katz's narrative of Brazilian nature. Precisely because the author was very attached to Brazil, he did not want to present it as a "wonderland." Instead, he tried to direct attention toward neglected regions such as the *sertão*, situated in the northeast of Brazil. His image of the drought that often plagues this region reminds the readers more of hell than of a blooming paradise: "The sun burns like a white-hot stove. Steppe becomes desert. The elderly die. Then the children die. [...] From a distance raising dust shows the way on which the Cearenses [...] trek to the coast – raising dust which is followed by flocks of black vultures in the blue sky."[42] Likewise he sensitized the readers to the destruction of the coastal rainforest called the Mata Atlântica, more precisely, the virgin forest that contributed so much to the creation of the myth of the terrestrial paradise of Brazil because it once lined the entire coast of the country. This was the first impression that the discoverers gained of Brazil from the sea. The malicious obliteration did not escape the eyes of the nature lover Katz: "The hilly ground is [...] sparsely green. [...] Rarely a high tree, only a few single windswept palms. And all that had once been virgin forest! [...] Now the country anxiously notices

---

39 Richard Katz, *Begegnungen in Rio* (Erlenbach-Zürich: Eugen Rentsch Verlag, 1951), 7.
40 Richard Katz, *Mein Inselbuch. Erste Erlebnisse in Brasilien* (Zürich: Schweizer Druck- und Verlagshaus, 1950), 116.
41 Richard Katz, *Mein Inselbuch. Erste Erlebnisse in Brasilien* (Zürich: Schweizer Druck- und Verlagshaus, 1950), 96, 98.
42 Richard Katz, *Auf dem Amazonas* (Zürich: Schweizer Druck- und Verlagshaus, 1961), 115.

the decreasing abundance of its forests. [...] But trees mean money. [...] Ordinances cannot fight against it."[43]

Today, only 1 percent of the original Mata Atlântica is left, which partially belongs to the UNESCO World Heritage Centre. In view of the ongoing overexploitation of Amazonia for economic reasons, Katz's charge has not lost its relevance today. By including the sunny and seamy sides in equal measure, the travel writer tried to draw as realistic a picture of Brazil as possible. That said, he never left room for doubt about the uniqueness of this country: "From the moist virgin forest of the Amazonas Basin [...] to the blooming apple trees in the cool meadows of Santa Catarina: *one* country! If there is one country in the world which really could be 'self-sufficient' [...], it is Brazil, which [...] possesses all natural resources, absolutely all of them."[44]

Whereas Katz has already specified death as an element of the alleged paradisiacal Brazilian nature in his depiction of the *sertão*, Heinrich Eduard Jacob and Ulrich Becher's works put even more emphasis on this aspect. Although Jacob did not find refuge in Brazil, but rather in the United States in 1939, his portrayal of Brazilian nature will be analyzed here. He knew the country too, because in March and April 1932 he traveled through it for research for his internationally successful nonfiction book *Coffee: The Epic of a Commodity*.[45] His memories of Brazil were so long-lasting that he later repeatedly chose the country as a setting for his literary works. The imprint of the first encounter is recognizable in the following enthusiastic passage of the novella "Aracy und das Fieber" (Aracy and the Fever), published in a collection of novellas titled *Treibhaus Südamerika* (Greenhouse South America) in 1934:

> Great sweet Brazil! He [i. e. Paul, the protagonist of the novella] had breathed its fragrance, the divine poison of these wild mixtures – and desire took hold of his heart again. [...] How did he suddenly love everyone and everything he had encountered there! Oh, hold tight to everything – before it disappears over the horizon forever.[46]

In the same book Jacob stressed the simultaneity of life and death in Brazilian nature: "Afraid, of what? Of death? Of life? Life! Life! Rampant Life! Bacillus,

---

[43] Richard Katz, *Seltsame Fahrten in Brasilien* (Erlenbach-Zürich: Eugen Rentsch Verlag, 1947), 21.
[44] Richard Katz, *Mein Inselbuch. Erste Erlebnisse in Brasilien* (Zürich: Schweizer Druck- und Verlagshaus, 1950), 228.
[45] Heinrich Eduard Jacob, *Coffee. The Epic of a Commodity* (Short Hills, NJ: Burford Books, 1998).
[46] Heinrich Eduard Jacob, *Treibhaus Südamerika. Novellen* (Zürich: Bibliothek Zeitgenössischer Werke, 1934), 304.

plant, animal and human being took away each other's space. There was no death! Constantly new life grew and was mixed into the tropical nature."⁴⁷ In Brazil he observed that

> miraculous are the cities of this vibrant tropical world in which money, diseases, ambition, love, religious needs, superstition assume more mammoth-like forms compared to the ones in our latitudes. I believe I have discovered this principle of the tropical growth in things that are generally human. My novellas deal with this rampant life and this dangerous splendor of life.⁴⁸

Hence, in his immigrant novel *Estrangeiro* (Foreigner), the alleged paradise Brazil turns into hell for his Hungarian protagonist, Elemer Hegedüs. Given the resentments toward foreigners and their political and economic influence in parts of Brazilian society, he feels vindicated in his mistrust and sense of superiority toward the Brazilian people. He is confronted with a ruthless struggle for survival, which Jacob allegorized in his description of Brazilian virgin forest:

> Virgin forest was the war of all against all; hell. [...] The battle of plants against each other happened silently, vehemently and grimly. [...] Not only did the aliens eat the alien. The more related the species even were, the more they killed each other. [...] Although every son ate his father here [...], unless the father had already crushed the son to death by his excessive shadow. [...] Here everything lived on corpses [...] since even the dead were not dead. By crumbling they formed new cell cultures and symbiosis; they mated, split, arose, left the Hades and lived once again! A congealed laughter went through it all, unimaginably high spirits.⁴⁹

Consequently, the picture of nature drawn by the author queried the idea of terrestrial paradise grounded in the national myth. The result is that the protagonist Hegedüs does not find a future for himself in Brazil.

Even more frankly than Jacob or Katz, Ulrich Becher, who came to Brazil as member of the "group Görgen" in 1941,⁵⁰ alluded to death as an omnipresent el-

---

47 Heinrich Eduard Jacob, *Treibhaus Südamerika. Novellen* (Zürich: Bibliothek Zeitgenössischer Werke, 1934), 305.
48 Heinrich Eduard Jacob quoted in Jens-Erik Hohmann, *Unvergänglich Vergängliches. Das literarische Werk Heinrich Eduard Jacobs* (Lübeck: Der andere Verlag 2006), 181.
49 Heinrich Eduard Jacob, *Estrangeiro. Einwanderungsschicksal in Brasilien* (Reinbeck bei Hamburg: Rowohlt Taschenbuch Verlag, 1988), 171–173.
50 The "group Görgen" was a group of 48 refugees, including 3 children, that was headed and organized by Hermann Mathias Görgen. Thirty-eight of them were considered Jews according to the Nuremberg Laws. Besides Ulrich Becher and his wife, Dana (daughter of the famous Austrian Alexander Roda Roda), Georg Wassermann (the second eldest son of Jakob Wassermann), Walter Kreiser, an aviation engineer and journalist who was sentenced together with Carl von Ossietzky,

ement of the seemingly paradisiacal landscape in his portrayals of the country's nature. He purposely challenged the myth of paradise by describing nature with the help of paradise-like images but using adjectives the readers would not necessarily link to a Garden of Eden. Thus, the break with traditions was all the more impressive, as these excerpts from his verse romance *Brasilianischer Romanzero* (Brazilian Romanzero) of 1950 illustrate:

> Many yellow rivers flowed through the land without end.
> Whenever the rain came, they were full of ichorous yellow.
> Limp hortensiae and stone-dead rats
> And orange-colored dog cadaver floated on top.
> [...]
> And while the fast coming night refreshed our heights
> With coldness, brought to the pathless wildness to our feet
> Inky blackness, filled the zenith like glossy
> Tracing paper, perforated by planetary stars,
> Uneasy images, from the steaming closeness
> That the plain blew escaped a fervent salute,
> A brownishly fluttering lunar creature screaming if catastrophe,
> Not related to the guileless dreamer at distant noon.
> [...]
> Completely outside, in the jungle,
> [...]
> Where the macaw dressed in a tailcoat of a fairy-tale prince
> loudly proclaims "Macaw!,"
> From the jungle-night smithy
> Woodpecker's volcanic smiting on the anvil booms
> Cobras, 16 feet in size,
> Silently falling asleep, encircle rabbits,
> Crocodiles, swimming on their backs in the river's water,
> Swollen lemon-bellies.[51]

These verses bring not only death and destruction, always present in nature, to light but also Becher's way of stylistically mirroring nature's abundance by use of an exuberant vocabulary. "Urwaldbarock" (Virgin forest Baroque)[52] is how he himself named the language he created: "Becher uses countless images, drastic or fantastic word inventions, exotic local color, and agglomeration to capture in

---

and Johannes Hoffmann, the first minister president of the Saarland after the war, were part of the group that managed to flee to Brazil in 1941. The group undertook to establish a company in the interior. Although the firm was never successful, all the members of the "group Görgen" survived Nazi persecution in this way.

51 Ulrich Becher, *Brasilianischer Romanzero* (Zürich: Werner Classen Verlag, 1950), 7, 13, 38.
52 Ulrich Becher, *Brasilianischer Romanzero* (Zürich: Werner Classen Verlag, 1950), 68.

words the Latin American experience, the strange and dangerous beauty of the landscape."[53] In his stage play *Samba*, the author went one step further than Katz and Jacob, who confined themselves to allusions to hell in their works. Becher depicted the Brazilian landscape in a concrete way:

> Dante's hell, without Virgil [...] *forests* of pale blue wild hortensiae – puddles covered by green mucous algae [...] which whinge and shout, virtually explosions of grieving cries. [...] Ghostly flames flicker – orchids. Then, in an opening the black souls of the inmates of hell fly past by my nose. At least fifty vultures! Then there is rustling in the bush – suddenly three thick black heads roll across the path. [...] Black pigs. [...] Then the bushes end and it gets completely quiet, no damned anymore. [...] The black chimney of a pinnacle looms into nowhere to the top and bottom [...] like a stanchion of hell.[54]

Hence, Brazilian nature emerges very ambivalently in Becher's works. On one hand, it seduces people with the help of its magic, almost divine abundance and beauty. On the other hand, in its primitiveness, it reveals its brutality and deadens the mind und senses of men, leading to death in the worst case.[55]

However, none of the émigrés mentioned here broke as radically with the myth of the blooming, lush, and overflowing Garden of Eden as did Vilém Flusser. In his study of the country of refuge, *Brasilien oder die Suche nach dem neuen Menschen* (Brazil or the Search for the New Man), published in 1994, the philosopher, who fled the Nazi-occupied Czechoslovakia for Brazil in 1940, deliberately referred to pertinent texts of the myth of terrestrial paradise in order to uncover their ideological function:

> The Brazilian bourgeois claims to love his landscape, doesn't he? [...] "My homeland has many palm-trees and the thrush-song fills its air." Or even the national anthem [i.e., verses of the "Canção do exílio"]: "We have fields more full of flowers." [...] This statement is true for local inhabitants, precisely because there are no fields and flowers here. Hence, when they do exist they constitute an exception and are a hallmark of the landscape. [...] For the love of palm trees and nightingales, for the fields with their flowers and for the splendor of the Brazilian "cradle" is nothing else than literature, a belated descendant of French romanticism [...] nothing else than a part of that bourgeois ideology.[56]

---

53 Nancy Anne McClure Zeller, *Ulrich Becher. A Computer-Assisted Case Study of the Reception of an Exile* (Bern, Switzerland: Peter Lang, 1983), 58–59.
54 Ulrich Becher, *Spiele der Zeit 1. Samba, Feuerwasser, Die Kleinen und die Großen* (Hamburg: Rowohlt Verlag, 1957), 79.
55 Celeste H. M. Ribeiro de Sousa, *Do cá e do lá. Introdução à imagologia* (São Paulo: Associação Editorial Humanitas/FAPESP, 2004), 241.
56 Vilém Flusser, *Brasilien oder die Suche nach dem neuen Menschen. Für eine Phänomenologie der Unterentwicklung* (Mannheim: Bollmann Verlag, 1994), 46, 48, 51–52.

Considering the experience immigrants generally had with Brazilian nature, Flusser not only indirectly reflected on his own experiences but also took up metaphors that decisively influenced the formation of the national myth and are intrinsically linked to the foreigners' idea of Brazil.

> The first aesthetic impression the immigrant receives of Brazilian nature may be summarized as follows: It promises a lot without delivering much at all, [...] because the immigrant approaches it with a number of prejudices connected with the collective term "tropics." [...] "Tropics" mean paradise for the European, namely in the sense of innocence and the absence of the sweat of the brow caused by labour as well as of the place of original sin, i.e. of sexual enjoyment. At first, Brazilian beaches validate this paradisiacal character. [...] But a while later the [...] immigrant experiences the well deserved disappointment. It arises out of the enormous boredom (one which is, so to speak, paradisiacal as well), a result of incredibly inarticulate Brazilian nature.[57]

He repeated these observations in his philosophical autobiography *Bodenlos* (Groundless), launched in 1999, enforcing his opinion:

> Nature appears as an old woman. [...] For those who come from Europe, the senile and archaic appearance is the characteristic quality of Brazilian nature. Its geological forms are old and exhausted [...] and its biological forms are ancient. [...] But in this regard we had the usual European notions of a tropical paradise. [...] But Brazil's grandness is not grand, but rather a huge collection of countless trifles [...] and that in an endless repetition. Not grandeur, but boredom. [...] It defeats you by gentle monotony, not by brutal, wild attacks. In such nature you cannot live, since you can only get lost in it, and never find yourself.[58]

"You have been given a future as hardly any other nation."[59] – Thematizing the future potential of Brazil

The question of the "land of the future" always accompanies the implicit question of what kind of future is meant.[60] Affected by their traumatic experiences

---

57 Vilém Flusser, *Brasilien oder die Suche nach dem neuen Menschen. Für eine Phänomenologie der Unterentwicklung* (Mannheim: Bollmann Verlag, 1994), 48–49.
58 Vilém Flusser, *Bodenlos. Eine philosophische Autobiographie* (Frankfurt am Main: Fischer Taschenbuch Verlag, 1999), 71–72.
59 Cf. Stefan Zweig, "Dank an Brasilien," in *Zeit und Welt. Gesammelte Aufsätze und Vorträge 1904–1940* (Stockholm: Bermann-Fischer Verlag, 1946), 156.
60 At a symposium on the occasion of the 65th anniversary of Stefan Zweig's *Brazil. Land of the Future*, Bolívar Lamounier called Brazil "land of various futures." Cf. Bolívar Lamounier, "Brasil, país de varios futuros." Lecture at the special Forum "Brasil, um país do futuro? Projeto de Bra-

and escape, the refugees, particularly the Jewish ones, did not give Brazil's natural resources and the resultant economic power special emphasis. On grounds of the highly cordial, hospitable, and allegedly harmonic multiracial society and the apparent inexistence of the so-called racial issue or *Rassenfrage,* they deemed Brazilian society to be the society of the future. However, this aspect is closely linked with the question of Brazil's supposedly existing racial democracy. An in-depth elucidation of this sensitive issue would go beyond the scope of this chapter; therefore, the focus of the analysis is only on the elements that go beyond the special social composition of the country and that made Brazil the "land of the future" in the opinion of the émigré writers.

Like few other émigré writers, Zweig made Brazil's promising future the leitmotif of his portrait of the country by turning his classic epithet "land of the future" into a national metaphor. Brazil became globally known as such. Already in 1936, during his first visit to Brazil, the Austrian writer was fascinated by the country: "Whoever experiences today's Brazil is looking into the future."[61] In light of the *Anschluss* of Austria in 1938 and the irretrievable loss of his homeland, the writer needed to cling to Brazil as a glimmer of hope. He thought he had found a new home there. At the same time, he was inspired by the wish to resolve the refugee problem caused by Nazi persecution. Believing he had discovered this possibility in the extensive unsettled territory, he had boundless enthusiasm:

> A world huge enough to hold three hundred, four hundred, five hundred million people, with immeasurable wealth beneath the fertile virgin earth, only a thousandth part of which has been exploited. [...] Men for Brazil! Men at all costs! [...] The cure for the Old World and, at the same time, for this New World would be thorough, patient and wisely carried out transfusion of blood and capital.[62]

In the context of the despair about Europe's seemingly unstoppable destruction, Zweig was inclined to stylize the supposedly uninhabited regions as a vital strength and the promising future of the country as a sensual experience:

---

sil: opções de país e opções de desenvolvimento" (2006). www.forumnacional.org.br/trf_arq.php?cod=EP01630.
61 Stefan Zweig, "Kleine Reise nach Brasilien," in *Länder, Städte, Landschaften.* Ed. Knut Beck (Frankfurt am Main: Fischer Taschenbuch Verlag, 1992), 158.
62 Stefan Zweig, *Brasilien. Ein Land der Zukunft* (Frankfurt am Main: S. Fischer Verlag, 1990), 11, 136, 146. For the English translation cf. Stefan Zweig, *Brazil. Land of the Future* (London: Zweig Press, 2008), 3, 121, 130.

> Space [...] is also spiritual strength. It enlarges the outlook and it enlarges the soul; it gives to the man who inhabits it, whom it embraces, the courage and the confidence to venture forward. Where there is space, there is not only time, but also the future. And in Brazil one can feel the strong rustling of its wings.[63]

Whereas Zweig's faith in the great future of Brazil proved too weak at the end to help him to overcome the pain of loss, other émigré writers gained new courage to face life from the confidence in a promising future of their exile country. This is especially true for Brill and her novel *Der Schmelztiegel*. More than any other of the works in question, her text is driven by an acceptance of life and the unbroken faith in the future for herself in Brazil, which in some paragraphs seems almost defiant. This attitude is also reflected in her language. Phrases such as "Life goes on" or "Life must be conquered anew day by day" as well as "heavy with future" or "Land of the future! A blessed land" [64] run like a thread trough the entire novel and provide an undismayed and confident purport. In the opinion of the journalist, and beyond the social aspects, Brazil's future potential can especially be explained by the youth of South America. She was sure that this "sparkling new continent" would prove to be more intelligent than Europe regarding the Pan American politics and would "learn from the Old World's mistakes."[65] Besides this precious chance, Brill witnessed the stirring dynamics of this **continuously** growing world inherent to this continent in São Paulo every day: "Old houses were demolished, new ones were built. [...] Life went on. Everything was unfinished, everything was in progress."[66] The more the author felt at home in Brazil, the steadier her faith in the promising future of the country of exile: "I believe in a new rising world."[67]

Simon presented a similarly imperturbable conviction of the future potential of the country. Because he died prematurely, he was not able to write the last chapter of his novel about his years in Brazilian exile. In contrast to Brill's work, then, there are only some hints about the promising future in his text. For him, Brazil became the "land of the future," if only because a return to Ger-

---

[63] Stefan Zweig, *Brasilien. Ein Land der Zukunft* (Frankfurt am Main: S. Fischer Verlag, 1990), 149–150. For the English translation cf. Stefan Zweig, *Brazil. Land of the Future* (London: Zweig Press, 2008), 133.
[64] Marte Brill, *Der Schmelztiegel* (Frankfurt am Main: Büchergilde Gutenberg, 2002), 283, 311, 241, 223.
[65] Brill, in Marlen Eckl, *"Das Paradies ist überall verloren." Das Brasilienbild von Flüchtlingen des Nationalsozialismus* (Frankfurt am Main: Vervuert Verlag, 2010), 263.
[66] Marte Brill, *Der Schmelztiegel* (Frankfurt am Main: Büchergilde Gutenberg, 2002), 162.
[67] Marte Brill quoted in Marlen Eckl, *"Das Paradies ist überall verloren." Das Brasilienbild von Flüchtlingen des Nationalsozialismus* (Frankfurt am Main: Vervuert Verlag, 2010), 264.

many was out of the question. In this sense, Hubert/Hugo's best friend, Robert, who to some extent assumed the role of his alter ego, declares, "If ever war breaks out, I want to live neither in a victorious nor in a defeated Germany."[68] Therefore, Brazil appears as a "land of the future" with extraordinary opportunities. Like so many others, Simon saw the future potential primarily in Brazil's huge unsettled territories and the freedom allegedly granted for immigrants: "I think of a country like Brazil, one could live there. Brazil is large, it is empty. It needs people who are willing to establish a new life, and such people are provided with personal freedom there."[69]

Jacob, who received his first impression of Brazil from a Zeppelin, also marveled at the size of the country and the sparse population. In his opinion, both aspects were closely linked to Brazil's promising future: "Enormous land underneath our airship. Flat as a board, and eighteen times bigger than Germany. But only half as many inhabitants. Land of a future, Brazil!"[70] From above he perceived the size of the country:

> Brazil. There it is. A border lying in the noon-sun! A long shore! The horizon, at first sight blue, becomes green. [...] It looks like in the legend of Columbus: Green, green, a shield of infinite green with a white hemline (ten thousand kilometers of breakers!) moves along the blue hunch of the sea.[71]

In this context Flusser, comparable to Simon and Jacob, called Brazil a "no man's land" in which immigrants could experience an unprejudiced reception.

> I submerged myself in the enthusiasm for establishing a new humane homeland free of prejudice. [...] Brazil was an existential "no man's land," when the waves of immigrants began in the nineteenth century. It was nobody's home. Thus, the war cry of the patriots who wanted to have a home: "Este país tem dono" [This country has an owner]. [...] Hence, immigrants were not received as nasty foreigners, but without prejudice as homeless comrades in distress. [...] The unprejudiced atmosphere differed so strongly from the

---

68 Hugo Simon, *Seidenraupen*. Unpublished manuscript, n.d. Collection Hugo Simon (Deutsche Nationalbibliothek. Deutsches Exilarchiv 1933–1945. Frankfurt am Main, E 2005/63), 520–521.
69 Hugo Simon, *Seidenraupen*. Unpublished manuscript, n.d. Collection Hugo Simon (Deutsche Nationalbibliothek. Deutsches Exilarchiv 1933–1945. Frankfurt am Main, E 2005/63), 526.
70 Heinrich Eduard Jacob, *Mit dem Zeppelin nach Pernambuco* (Berlin: Katzengraben-Presse, 1992), 36. Jacob's modification of the much-quoted epithet "land of the future" is interesting. The author knew Schüler's work of the same title. There was a copy of the book in his personal library. Cf. Hans Jörgen Gerlach, letter to author, 14 July 2008. However, Jacob named Brazil "land of *a* future."
71 Heinrich Eduard Jacob, *Mit dem Zeppelin nach Pernambuco* (Berlin: Katzengraben-Presse, 1992), 35–36.

> European atmosphere of the homelands the immigrants were expelled from. [...] Moreover, in this no man's land you were pioneer in every field you wanted to work in.[72]

But beyond the huge unsettled territories, Flusser also noticed the great future potential whose realization, in his opinion, had already begun.

> Brazil is preparing to become a "power," namely not only in a geopolitical, but also in Nietzschean sense, that is to say, of "will." [...] Even if the achieved reality still partly bears signs of outmoded elements, [...] the tendency of what is coming is palpable. [...] New forms and new contents [...] are the expression of a new experience of reality. The tired West is creatively conserved by them and elevated to a new force. In this sense Brazil's present is already the future of the West.[73]

However, the philosopher was also absolutely aware that, in a promising country, forward-looking projects are not all crowned with success. Regarding the prestige project of building a new capital called Brasília, and the more intensive development of the interior of the country with the existing resources, Flusser, who knew of the outcome and the unfulfilled hopes, was skeptical in 1970 in "Die Stadt welcher Zukunft?" (The city of which future?). He considered Brasília

> an example for the fact that the man does not know what he wants or, which is the same, that he wants contradicting things at the same time. In this sense [...] Brasília is a model for the entire of humanity [...] since it is a phenomenon that arose from the crisis and reflects it.[74]

Arnau's judgment about the Brasília project was as critical as Flusser's. The publicist was also acquainted with the mishaps caused by hastily carrying out the project and by the failed aim of developing the Brazilian hinterlands at that time. However, Arnau acknowledged the importance of this project. For that reason he dedicated a whole chapter to Brasília, titled "Ein Land bekommt eine neue Hauptstadt" (A country gets a new capital) in the fifth revised edition of his Brazil book. There he explained his point of view:

---

[72] Vilém Flusser, *Bodenlos. Eine philosophische Autobiographie* (Frankfurt am Main: Fischer Taschenbuch Verlag, 1999), 256–257. In the same way, Swiss poet Blaise Cendrars called Brazil a "land that belongs to nobody." Cf. Blaise Cendrars, *Trop c'est trop* (Paris: Edition Denoël, 1957), 61.
[73] Vilém Flusser, *Brasilien oder die Suche nach dem neuen Menschen. Für eine Phänomenologie der Unterentwicklung* (Mannheim: Bollmann Verlag, 1994), 268–269.
[74] Vilém Flusser, *Brasilien oder die Suche nach dem neuen Menschen. Für eine Phänomenologie der Unterentwicklung* (Mannheim: Bollmann Verlag, 1994), 275–276.

The idea is completely right. It was only carried out in senseless hurry, with insufficient means and lacking preparation. [...] The name of this man, Juscelino Kubitschek, will forever be linked with the dream of Brasília and the beginning of its reality. And as well as with the national economic catastrophe. [...] Today Brasília exists: an already presentable, smaller-sized city. [...] But the real power rests are still in Rio de Janeiro. [...] It will take years, decades before a true and deep-rooted integration of the new capital Brasília can take place.[75]

All the same, Arnau made it quite clear that "Brazil is [...] a gigantic economic area whose natural resources and whose increase of inhabitants and economic power offer the greatest future prospects imaginable."[76] He explained "that Brazil must be counted as one of the richest countries in the world. [...] It is almost in realm of fantasy what prosperity Brazil will achieve once it manages to establish healthy and well-balanced circumstances structures with the help of a clear, purposeful, *economically determined* production policy."[77] The journalist emphasized the abundance of natural resources in Brazil's promising future and in the depiction of its natural habitat. This fact can be ascribed to his job as economic advisor for German-speaking industrialists and tradespeople who aimed to start businesses in Brazil after World War II. Although he indirectly took part in the Brazil's rising economy and earned a good salary, Arnau felt that his future did not lie there forever. As Flusser believed, Brazil was only to be a country of refuge and was not to become a "land of the future" for him.

This is also true for Becher. The verse in his *Brasilianischer Romanzero*, "In the country I was a wanderer, never one who rested,"[78] reflects his own experiences in this country of exile, although he also perceived the future potential of Brazil. But he interpreted it in his own special way and expressed it in the same text: "In the memory of the Romanzero-writer, these 'huge flowers,' which in all their true magical splendor and beauty may appear unreal, degenerate, almost morbid to the European, are metaphors for the *colossal, not fully formed* country where the cock crows before midnight."[79]

---

75 Frank Arnau, *Der verchromte Urwald. Licht und Schatten über Brasilien*. 5th ed. (Gütersloh: Bertelsmann Verlag, n.d.), 281.
76 Frank Arnau, *Der verchromte Urwald. Licht und Schatten über Brasilien* (Frankfurt am Main: Umschau Verlag, 1956), 303.
77 Frank Arnau, *Der verchromte Urwald. Licht und Schatten über Brasilien* (Frankfurt am Main: Umschau Verlag, 1956), 179.
78 Ulrich Becher, *Brasilianischer Romanzero* (Zürich: Werner Classen Verlag, 1950), 7.
79 Ulrich Becher, *Brasilianischer Romanzero* (Zürich: Werner Classen Verlag, 1950), 108 (emphasis added).

However, in his play *Samba*, the figure of the refugee from Nazism, Leo Parisius, did not understand the quality of "not fully formed" as future potential but rather as a backwardness that needs to be overcome: "PARISIUS: [...] People here, I see that a first sight. But they are not any. They have not come down from the trees yet. Apes and sloths. Also the whites. [...] I do not intend to settle down here. I was washed up on this shore by war. I will let myself dry in the sun a little bit, and then I will get out of here immediately. [...] Better to die than to vegetate."[80]

Aviation engineer Walter Kreiser, who had been accused of betraying military secrets together with Carl von Ossietzky in the famous Weltbühne trial,[81] provided the model for the character of Leo Parisius. In contrast to Becher Kreiser, he managed to establish a new existence in Brazil and found a new home there. Even though there was not any future for Becher in South America and he eventually returned to Europe via the United States, the years spent in Brazilian exile strongly influenced his literary work, and they stayed in his memory throughout his life. Hence the verse of his *Brazilian Romanzero*, "I still dream of the country each night, each day. Never have known such an unforgettable one,"[82] is not pure fiction. Becher's wife, Dana Roda Becher, the daughter of writer Alexander Roda Roda, confirmed in an interview in 1988, "Looking back, I can say that the years in Brazil were the happiest in our lives."[83] Nonetheless, Becher made clear that foreigners would never be able to understand fully the country in all its cultural, social, and public aspects, and so its promising future could only be guessed at. Thus, he named Brazil "never-know-me-fully [...] country always faraway."[84]

Although Katz completely agreed with Becher on this last viewpoint, he was less ambivalent in his description of the future potential inherent in his country of exile. Like Brill, Katz saw a promising future not just for Brazil but for the whole of South America. During his first visit of this continent in the 1930s he

---

80 Ulrich Becher, *Spiele der Zeit 1. Samba, Feuerwasser, Die Kleinen und die Großen* (Hamburg: Rowohlt Verlag, 1957), 17.
81 In 1929 Carl von Ossietzky published an article on the secret rearmament, written by Walter Kreiser under the pseudonym Heinz Jäger in the famous magazine *Die Weltbühne*, whose editor was Ossietzky. This led to the so-called Weltbühne trial, in which he and Kreiser were accused of revealing military secrets and sentenced to 18 months of imprisonment. Whereas Kreiser managed to flee the Nazis to Brazil, Ossietzky died in 1938 as a result of tuberculosis and the aftereffects of the abuse he suffered in concentration camps after he had been arrested in 1933.
82 Ulrich Becher, *Brasilianischer Romanzero* (Zürich: Werner Classen Verlag, 1950), 52.
83 Roda Becher in Izabela Maria Furtado Kestler, *Die Exilliteratur und das Exil der deutschsprachigen Schriftsteller und Publizisten* (Bern, Switzerland: Peter Lang Verlag, 1992), 51.
84 Ulrich Becher, *Brasilianischer Romanzero* (Zürich: Werner Classen Verlag, 1950), 34.

had already observed, "South America is an interesting continent because its fulfillment still is to come in the future. [...] A continent in childhood [...] a continent rich in possibilities."[85] Although Katz echoed Simon, Brill, Jacob, and Zweig by making out the future potential of the country in its youth and size, he did not share their unanimous indestructible optimism in this regard. Quite on the contrary, he presented the negative facts in such a ruthless way that the promising future of the unsettled country was completely pushed to the background. As a victim of National Socialist racial policy, Katz discussed this aspect mainly in connection with the Nazi ideology of *Lebensraum* (living space) and *Blut und Boden* (Blood and Soil). Contradicting Zweig, Katz maintained,

> Such a size is not advantageous. The ones who talk of "Lebensraum" should keep in mind that space does not only mean life. [...] The Lebensraum fanatic should not rejoice too early: "There is a lack of people in Brazil! *We* will provide them!" He should rather try to settle in the hinterland himself, in the swamps of the Amazonas, for instance, or on the plains of Northeast. But he does not want to do this at all. *He* wants to remain in the healthy cities. [...] While I am writing this, Hitler is standing in front of the gates of Moscow, asking for Lebensraum, and when this book will be published, Hitler – I hope – will have experienced firsthand that open space does not necessarily mean life.[86]

Katz intended to rob his readers of their illusions about the politics of *Lebensraum*, as the numerous examples in his books illustrate. It is not surprising then that he completely dismissed Brazil's size as a component of its future potential and emphasized the role of the Brazilian people: "If the achievements already obtained are measured by its still young history, one can predict this huge country a promising future. Because of its *people,* not because of its 'Lebensraum.'"[87] From the beginning, Katz was willing to make Brazil the "land of his own future." And even though he was forced to return to Europe for health reasons in the 1950s, his bond with the country was no less intimate.

The literary works examined here thus represent a broad range of images of Brazil conveyed by a group of German-speaking émigré writers who have received little attention thus far. This chapter, then, is an attempt at a modest contribution to making these images, their authors, and a more differentiated notion

---

85 Richard Katz, *Begegnungen in Rio* (Erlenbach-Zürich: Eugen Rentsch Verlag, 1951), 6.
86 Richard Katz, *Mein Inselbuch. Erste Erlebnisse in Brasilien* (Zürich: Schweizer Druck- und Verlagshaus, 1950), 228–229.
87 Richard Katz, *Mein Inselbuch. Erste Erlebnisse in Brasilien* (Zürich: Schweizer Druck- und Verlagshaus, 1950), 230.

of the country better known, hopefully extending beyond Stefan Zweig and his classic work.

References

Arnau, Frank. Der verchromte Urwald. Licht und Schatten über Brasilien (Frankfurt am Main: Umschau Verlag, 1956).
Arnau, Frank. Der verchromte Urwald. Licht und Schatten über Brasilien. 5th ed. (Gütersloh: Bertelsmann Verlag, n.d.).
Becher, Ulrich. Brasilianischer Romanzero (Zürich: Werner Classen Verlag, 1950).
Becher, Ulrich. Spiele der Zeit 1. Samba, Feuerwasser, Die Kleinen und die Großen (Hamburg: Rowohlt Verlag, 1957).
Brill, Marte. Der Schmelztiegel (Frankfurt am Main: Büchergilde Gutenberg, 2002).
Buch, Hans Christoph. Die Nähe und die Ferne. Bausteine zu einer Poetik des kolonialen Blicks (Frankfurt am Main: Suhrkamp Verlag, 1991).
Bueno, Eduardo. Brasil: Terra à vista! A aventura ilustrada do descobrimento (Porto Alegre: L&PM Editores, 2003).
Carvalho, José Murilo de. "O Brasil e seus nomes." Revista de História da Biblioteca Nacional 15.2 (December 2006): 14–22.
Cendrars, Blaise. Trop c'est trop (Paris: Edition Denoël, 1957).
Chauí, Marilena. Brasil. Mito fundador e sociedade autoritária (São Paulo: Editora Fundação Perseu Abramo, 2000).
Chauí, Marilena. "Politische Kultur und Kulturpolitik," in Brasilien. Land der Zukunft? Ed. Rafael Sevilla and Darcy Ribeiro (Unkel am Rhein/Bad Honnef: Edition Länderseminare Horlemann Verlag, 1995), 187–201.
Dias, Antônio Gonçalves. Poesia e Prosa completas. Primeiros cantos. Ed. Alexei Bueno (Rio de Janeiro: Editora Nova Aguilar, 1998).
Diniz, Cláudio Lúcio de Carvalho. "Tristeza Tupiniquim: a melancolia brasileira no Retrato do Brasil de Paulo Prado," Lecture at I. Memorial do Instituto de Ciências Humanas e Sociais (9–12 November 2004). http://www.ichs.ufop.br/memorial/trab/h9_4.pdf.
Eckl, Marlen. "Das geistige Band zwischen der Alten und Neuen Welt: Publizisten, Schriftsteller, Übersetzer und Theaterschaffende als Kulturvermittler," in "...Mehr vorwärts als rückwärts schauen..." Das deutschsprachige Exil in Brasilien 1933–1945. / "...Olhando mais para frente do que para trás..." O exílio de língua alemã no Brasil 1933–1945. Ed. Sylvia Asmus and Marlen Eckl (Berlin: Hentrich & Hentrich Verlag, 2013), 10–33.
Eckl, Marlen. "Das Paradies ist überall verloren." Das Brasilienbild von Flüchtlingen des Nationalsozialismus (Frankfurt am Main: Vervuert Verlag, 2010).
Eckl, Marlen. "'Europa im Urwald': Ulrich Bechers Auseinandersetzung mit dem Nationalsozialismus und dem Exil in Brasilien in den Theaterstücken Samba und Makumba." Zwischenwelt. Zeitschrift für Kultur und Literatur des Exils und Widerstands 27.3 (November 2010): 28–33.
Eckl, Marlen. "Goethe in den Tropen: Kulturvermittlung im brasilianischen Exil." Études Germaniques 63.4 (October–December 2008): 773–789.

Eckl, Marlen. "Hugo Simon: Vom Kunst liebenden Bankier in Berlin zum Seidenraupen züchtenden Autor im brasilianischen Interior." Martius-Staden-Jahrbuch 57 (2010), 113–137.
Ette, Ottmar. "Est-ce que l'on sait où l'on va? Dimensionen, Orte und Bewegungsmuster des Reiseberichts," in Die Wiederentdeckung Lateinamerikas. Die Erfahrung des Subkontinents in Reiseberichten des 19. Jahrhunderts Ed. Walther L. Bernecker and Gertrut Krömer, eds. (Frankfurt am Main: Vervuert Verlag, 1997), 29–75.
Flusser, Vilém. Bodenlos. Eine philosophische Autobiographie (Frankfurt am Main: Fischer Taschenbuch Verlag, 1999).
Flusser, Vilém. Brasilien oder die Suche nach dem neuen Menschen. Für eine Phänomenologie der Unterentwicklung (Mannheim: Bollmann Verlag, 1994).
Gomes, Ângela Maria de Castro. "O redescobrimento do Brasil," in Estado Novo. Ideologia e poder. Ed. Ângela Maria de Castro Gomes et al. (Rio de Janeiro: Jorge Zahar Editor, 1982), 109–150.
Hoffmann-Harnisch, Wolfgang. Brasilien. Bildnis eines tropischen Großreiches (Hamburg: Hanseatische Verlagsanstalt, 1938).
Hohmann, Jens-Erik. Unvergänglich Vergängliches. Das literarische Werk Heinrich Eduard Jacobs (Lübeck: Der andere Verlag 2006).
Jacob, Heinrich Eduard. Coffee. The Epic of a Commodity (Short Hills, NJ: Burford Books, 1998).
Jacob, Heinrich Eduard. Estrangeiro. Einwanderungsschicksal in Brasilien (Reinbeck bei Hamburg: Rowohlt Taschenbuch Verlag, 1988).
Jacob, Heinrich Eduard. Mit dem Zeppelin nach Pernambuco (Berlin: Katzengraben-Presse, 1992).
Jacob, Heinrich Eduard. Treibhaus Südamerika. Novellen (Zürich: Bibliothek Zeitgenössischer Werke, 1934).
Katz, Richard. Auf dem Amazonas (Zürich: Schweizer Druck- und Verlagshaus, 1961).
Katz, Richard. Begegnungen in Rio (Erlenbach-Zürich: Eugen Rentsch Verlag, 1951).
Katz, Richard. Mein Inselbuch. Erste Erlebnisse in Brasilien (Zürich: Schweizer Druck- und Verlagshaus, 1950).
Katz, Richard. Seltsame Fahrten in Brasilien (Erlenbach-Zürich: Eugen Rentsch Verlag, 1947).
Kestler, Izabela Maria Furtado. Die Exilliteratur und das Exil der deutschsprachigen Schriftsteller und Publizisten (Bern, Switzerland: Peter Lang Verlag, 1992).
Kohlhepp, Gerd. "Das Bild Brasiliens im Lichte deutscher Forschungsreisender des 19. und der ersten Hälfte des 20. Jahrhunderts." Martius-Staden-Jahrbuch 53 (2006): 213–238.
Lamounier, Bolívar. "Brasil, país de varios futuros." Lecture at the special Forum "Brasil, um país do futuro? Projeto de Brasil: opções de país e opções de desenvolvimento" (2006). www.forumnacional.org.br/trf_arq.php?cod=EP01630.
Moscateli, Renato. "Um redescobrimento historiográfico do Brasil." Revista de História Regional 5.1 (Summer 2000). http://www.revistas2.uepg.br/index.php/rhr/article/view File/2100/1581. 9 February 2015.
Piccoli, Valéria. "Das Nationalgefühl und andere Aspekte in der brasilianischen Kunst des 19. Jahrhunderts," in Brasilien. Von Österreich zur Neuen Welt. Ed. Tayfun Belgin (Krems: Kunsthalle Krems, 2007), 23–28.

Prada, Cecília. "Ary do Brasil." Revista Problemas Brasileiros 357 (May–June 2003). http://www.sescsp.org.br/sesc/revistas_sesc/pb/artigo.cfm?Edicao_Id=153&breadcrumb=1&Artigo_ID=2239&IDCategoria=2292&reftype=1.

Prado, Paulo. Retrato do Brasil. Ensaio sobre a tristeza brasileira. Ed. Carlos Augusto Calil (São Paulo: Companhia das Letras, 2001).

Riedl-Dorn, Christa. "Die Erforschung Brasiliens durch Österreicher im 19. Jahrhundert," in Brasilien. Von Österreich zur Neuen Welt. Ed. Tayfun Belgin (Krems: Kunsthalle Krems, 2007), 9–17.

Schüler, Heinrich. Brasilien. Ein Land der Zukunft, 5th ed. (Stuttgart/Berlin: Deutsche Verlagsanstalt, 1921).

Schwamborn, Ingrid. "Der fünfte Stern im Kreuz des Südens: Die brasilianische Fahne und ihre 'interstellare' Geschichte." Martius Staden Jahrbuch 54 (2007): 277–300.

Simon, Hugo. Seidenraupen. Unpublished manuscript, n.d. Collection Hugo Simon (Deutsche Nationalbibliothek. Deutsches Exilarchiv 1933–1945. Frankfurt am Main, E 2005/63).

Sousa, Celeste H. M. Ribeiro de. Do cá e do lá. Introdução à imagologia (São Paulo: Associação Editorial Humanitas/FAPESP, 2004).

Sousa, Celeste H. M. Ribeiro de. Retratos do Brasil. Hetero-imagens literárias alemãs (São Paulo: Editora Arte & Cultura, 1996).

Thompson, Daniella, and Ricardo Paoletti. "Aquarela do Brasil," n.d. http://daniellathompson.com/ary/aquarela.html.

Ullmann, Hermann. Land der Zukunft. Reise in Brasilien (Jena: Eugen Diederichs Verlag, 1937).

Wallisch, Robert, ed. Der Mundo Novus des Amerigo Vespucci. Text, Übersetzung und Kommentar (Vienna: Verlag der Österreichischen Akademie der Wissenschaften, 2002).

Zelewitz, Klaus. "Stefan Zweig: Exotismus versus (?) Europhilie," in Die letzte Partie. Stefan Zweigs Leben und Werk in Brasilien (1932–1942). Ed. Ingrid Schwamborn (Bielefeld: Aisthesis Verlag, 1999), 145–157.

Zeller, Nancy Anne McClure. Ulrich Becher. A Computer-Assisted Case Study of the Reception of an Exile (Bern, Switzerland: Peter Lang, 1983).

Zweig, Stefan. Brasilien. Ein Land der Zukunft (Frankfurt am Main: S. Fischer Verlag, 1990).

Zweig, Stefan. Brazil. Land of the Future (London: Zweig Press, 2008).

Zweig, Stefan. "Dank an Brasilien," in Zeit und Welt. Gesammelte Aufsätze und Vorträge 1904–1940 (Stockholm: Bermann-Fischer Verlag, 1946), 151–158.

Zweig, Stefan. "Kleine Reise nach Brasilien," in Länder, Städte, Landschaften. Ed. Knut Beck (Frankfurt am Main: Fischer Taschenbuch Verlag, 1992), 153–184.

Zweig, Stefan. Tagebücher. Ed. Knut Beck (Frankfurt am Main: S. Fischer Verlag, 1984).

Christopher Larkosh
Submarine: Germany Resurfacing in the Contemporary Brazilian Novel

The truth is that sexuality is everywhere; the way a bureaucrat fondles his records, a judge administers justice, a businessman causes money to circulate; the way the bourgeoisie fucks the proletariat; and so on. And there is no need to resort to metaphors, any more than the libido to go by way of metamorphoses. Hitler got the fascists sexually aroused. Flags, nations, armies, banks get a lot of people aroused. A revolutionary machine is nothing if it does not acquire at least as much force as these coercive machines have for producing breaks and mobilizing flows.[1]
– Deleuze and Guattari, *Anti-Oedipus*, 1983

The hard lesson of Virtual Sex is not that we no longer have "real sex," intense contact with another person's body, simply a simulation engendered by substanceless images that bombard us from the screen. Rather, it is the much more uncomfortable discovery that there never was "real sex": sex was always-already a game sustained by some masturbatory fantasmatic scenario. The common notion of masturbation is that of "sexual intercourse with an imagined partner": I do it to myself, while I imagine it doing it with or to another. Lacan's "there is no sexual relationship" can be read as an inversion of this common notion: what if "real sex" is nothing but masturbation with a real partner? What if, even when I am doing it with a real partner, what ultimately sustains my enjoyment is not the partner as such, but the secret fantasies I invest in it?[2]
– Slavoj Žižek, *Did Somebody Say Totalitarianism?*, 2001

Sexualizing the emergent and virtual dual state

Imagine, if you will, a fictional dual state, one with a hyphenated name, like that of so many others in history: in this case, Germany-Brazil. One might well be tempted to claim right from the outset, much as Lacan once characterized sexual relationships and as reiterated in the more recent work of Slovenian theorist Slavoj Žižek, that "there is no relationship" between these two states beyond an imaginary one, either one in the other or both in one's self, if not others[3] In whatever way one might dare to invoke them together, this national dyad – for all that

---

[1] Gilles Deleuze, and Félix Guattari, *Anti-Oedipus* (Minneapolis: University of Minnesota Press, 1983), 293.
[2] Slavoj Žižek, *Did Somebody Say Totalitarianism? Five Interventions in the (Mis)use of a Notion* (New York: Verso, 2001), 252.
[3] Slavoj Žižek, *The Ticklish Subject: The Absent Centre of Political Ontology* (New York: Verso, 1999), 94, 344.

it suggests and convenes thematically and culturally both in relation to itself and one another – continues to reappear, and it is in the ways it reemerges that one might conclude that this two-state fiction already holds the seeds of its own undoing.

At the same time, these histories are and remain irreconcilably different and incommensurable to one another, and all the same, each forms a separate yet overlapping territorialized composite of cultural norms or sets of ideas in transnational movement, continually attracting and superimposing themselves culturally, ideologically, and linguistically not only on the space assigned to them on a landscape, seascape, or visual or literary mapping but also inexorably onto one another if not onto others. In the end, even the most doctrinaire Lacanian would have to concede that this "no relationship" remains a kind of relationship, however tentative, random, long-distance, or "on-hold" the connection may be.

Perhaps more importantly, whether we like it or not, such a (non-)relationship also means that each side continues to tell stories about themselves and others, as well as about those apparently uninvolved, either on one side or the other or even somewhere in between, who write, read, or continue to speculate about "what is really going on." This is also true in the case of Germany-Brazil: never completely separate and, by the same token, all too understandably never completely together. And yet this is still all a fantasy to a great extent: one of always incomplete togetherness, of culturally confused identities and communities, symbolized and reinterpreted through yet another national or transnational dream state capable of existing only at the limits of conscious visual image and language (and as Deleuze and Guattari remind us, any national story cannot be considered anything near complete without a sexual chapter). So who is really speaking when Germany and Brazil speak together, whether to one another or just to themselves, with a presumed goal of a common story?

There are countless textual spaces, to say nothing of the places they create, where these recurrent questions might play themselves out, with the mass media and Internet only intensifying this virtual transnational imaginary; the Brazilian novel, especially as it enters the new millennium, shows no signs of becoming the exception. Although choosing such examples may always be arbitrary, there are two that nonetheless stand out for me from any number of recent instances.

The first example is from a recent work by one of Brazil's most popular writers, Luis Fernando Verissimo's novel from 2000 titled *Borges e os orangotangos eternos* (Borges and the Eternal Orangutans). In this latter-day reworking of the fantastic literary world of Argentine writer Jorge Luis Borges, Germany also resurfaces, albeit in the context of a concurrent relationship between Brazil and yet another country, in this case its South American neighbor and primary transnational economic and political partner, Argentina. The novel tells the story of Vogelstein, a translator and English teacher from the Jewish neighborhood of Bonfim in the southern Brazilian city of Porto Alegre who, perhaps like any truly Borgean character, lives in a small apartment filled with his books he shares with his Aunt Raquel. Vogelstein once translated Borges's work but could not resist altering the source text, making changes to the plot that ended up as comparable to adding an animal tail to a human being. Vogelstein was brought up by this maternal aunt; his mother, Miriam, stayed behind in Nazi Germany to die in a concentration camp after being handed over to the Gestapo by her mysterious "protector"; the novel hinges not on uncovering the identity of this figure but rather, as in most post-Borgean literary narratives, on the web of literary references that continue to emanate from this pivotal event.

Vogelstein is called to Buenos Aires for an academic conference on Edgar Allan Poe. The star of the conference is German scholar Joachim Rotkopf, now living in Mexico and occupied with academic projects, often preoccupied with the relationship between Europe and the Americas:

> [Rotkopf] did not understand that modern lament that the conquest of America had been a cultural rape. The conquest had never taken place, the primitives had won, and their indolent and fatalistic culture still dominated the continent. They only allowed white people to think that that they ruled in order to expose them to constant frustration and ridicule. Only routed Europeans, like him, belonged in America, where his resignation passed itself off as assimilation.[4]

Centuries of genocide and enslavement notwithstanding, one might still suspend judgment about Rotkopf's naiveté, especially if his denial of any possibility of lingering European cultural hegemony in the Americas is understood as a seemingly innocuous, yet ultimately no less noxious, form of the totalitarian ideology from which it emanates. After all, it is one easily reconciled with the ideologies of the New World in which so many Europeans, and no small number of "former Nazis" among them, found refuge after World War II.

There will still be room for a measure of retribution, after all: When Rotkopf is murdered in his hotel room, Vogelstein and Borges, here as a reinvented literary character, team up to solve this literary murder mystery. For the reader of the novel with even a basic knowledge of German, however, the mystery is already over almost before the novel even begins, as the last name of this character, Rot-

---

4 Luis Fernando Verissimo, *Borges e os orangotangos eternos* (São Paulo: Companhia das Letras, 2000), 23–24 (my translation).

kopf, or "redhead," corresponds to the description of the man in the photo that his Aunt Raquel has preserved of this shadowy protector: "his red hair, his skin so very white, his all-too-innocent heart."[5] Could it be said that the novel hinges on Brazilian readers' ignorance of the German language, to say nothing of today's Germany, to keep the mystery alive, or perhaps that the murder mystery is secondary to a host of other literary concerns, most importantly the enduring place of the literary in the interpretation of life and its multiple meanings between cultures?

Moreover, while trying to solve Rotkopf's murder, Vogelstein argues that a painter had once tied himself to the mast of a boat to see the true colors of a storm on the open sea and that, in much the same way, stabbing a real person might help someone writing about murder to improve the style and substance of his story. Verissimo's character Borges responds, "I don't think I can kill anyone, apart from my characters. And I would not feel well at sea. At sea one can't have libraries. The sea replaces the library." Vogelstein counters that "Jules Verne's Captain Nemo had both the sea and a library," but Borges naturally has the last word: "But as one should know, no literary talent."[6] Ultimately, through his rereading and rewriting of classic short stories by Borges, most notably "La muerte y la brújula" (Death and the Compass), "Deutsches Requiem," and "Emma Zunz," Verissimo reestablishes that the idea of books occupying other spaces other than land-based territories claimed by nations is not a new one. The library has been submarine for some time now, occupying the murky, subconscious spaces beneath the surface of the earth's oceans and thus already part of the mystery.

The second example may well be minor in comparison, yet it is no less evocative of the way Germany continues to resurface in the contemporary Brazilian novel: not as a contemporary presence, much less an isolated occurrence, but all too often as a spectral, historical one, as if from a former life. I am referring to the 2001 novel by Luiz Ruffato, *Eles eram muitos cavalos*, which chronicles the apparently disconnected details of a single day in the global megalopolis of São Paulo, 9 May 2000: anonymous monologues from evangelical preachers, drug dealers, or a man who finds unexpected success looking for sex online; apparently random conversations between business associates and a couple whose apartment block is broken into by a violent criminal presence; a series of angry voice messages left on a woman's answering machine by her lover's

---

[5] Luis Fernando Verissimo, *Borges e os orangotangos eternos* (São Paulo: Companhia das Letras, 2000), 17 (my translation).
[6] Luis Fernando Verissimo, *Borges e os orangotangos eternos* (São Paulo: Companhia das Letras, 2000), 86 (my translation).

wife; the odd newspaper clipping of job openings, personal ads, and listings for female, male, and transsexual sex workers; and a letter from a mother living in a rural area to her son, who has migrated for good to this city.[7]

Although the traces of Germany resurfacing in this space are few in comparison in this broad overview of twenty-first-century Brazilian urban life, they still appear, and in the same all-too-predictable corner: on a bookcase stocked with titles that appear to have little or nothing to do with one another, which includes everything from the great works of world literature such as the *Bhagavad Gita* and Stendhal's *Le Rouge et le Noir,* canonical twentieth-century Brazilian novels by Graciliano Ramos and Jorge Amado, and even the classic Brazilian children's stories by Monteiro Lobato, all interspersed with the inevitable international bestseller by Paulo Coelho or the perhaps equally unavoidable self-help books from the United States. Nonetheless, one can hardly ignore in this diverse context of literary production that ends up on a single bookcase that the list begins with Joachim Fest's biography *Hitler* and is complemented by others on related topics: Sven Hassel's *Gestapo, Himmler* by Alan Wykes, *It Happened in Warsaw* by Helen McInnis, two additional World War II–related titles by Frederick Forsyth, *Churchill Lord of War* by Ronald Lewin, and Gerald Green's *Holocaust.* Yet a look down the list reveals other German voices, such as the exiled Stefan Zweig's *Brasil, país do futuro,* along with Hermann Hesse's *Voyage to the Orient;* as one can see, the list goes on. The works on any bookshelf through which one might choose to reexamine this imaginary relationship thus begins to border on the limitless, with the references to both states, however unintentionally, invoking a ever-widening series of other countries and points of passage on any number of continents, and the unavoidable return to national drama, punctuated by equally ineluctable escape routes. Here both narrative directions coexist alongside each other, interspersed among yet others. The challenge becomes one of selectivity, choosing the works that best suit the hybrid narrative that unfolds before us.

On the utility of life and work: a brief introduction to João Gilberto Noll

Imagining Germany-Brazil also leads, perhaps unavoidably, to the work of contemporary Brazilian author João Gilberto Noll. As I attempt to venture an even cursory introduction, however, I cannot but wonder how useful any introductory

---

7 Luiz Ruffato, *Eles eram muitos cavalos* (Rio de Janeiro: Record, 2001).

description of an author and his work can be, especially when it involves such complex and challenging fictions as those of Noll. After all, even a fleeting glance at any of his novels or short stories will reveal that his literary world is populated by a series of anonymous protagonists and other transient characters, whose shadowy personal narratives and overlapping trajectories seem all too often to blur the lines between realistic narrative fiction, fantasy, and autobiography, no matter how residual these divergent traces and trajectories may be. The irresolvable mystery surrounding these characters – as well as the ongoing drama of being, becoming, concealing, and revealing – is grounded precisely in this tenuous and ambivalent relationship to naming, identity, and personal history. So even if many of the protagonists in Noll's work still appear to share at least some biographical overlap with the author himself, are we ever really close enough to Noll himself to consider his own biography unequivocally pertinent to textual interpretation?

It is no wonder, then, that some might shy away from writing this kind of introduction. Although some might consider it simplistic to view these narrators or protagonists as fictional stand-ins for Noll himself (or anyone else, for that matter), especially after more than four decades of poststructuralist literary critique that separated life and work by privileging the "death of the author" (a theory that, like the author, may nonetheless be as much at risk of dying and reincarnating as any hypothetical author), it would still be equally ingenuous to imagine these texts as entirely separate from the personal, lived experience that unavoidably permeates them. Moreover, the pervasive sensation of indistinct identity – of being set adrift between fiction, fact, and fantasy – might also provoke not only a reconsideration of but perhaps an outright crisis in a reader's own sense of identity as he or she enters and moves through these texts. How close any reader can truly come, then, to an understanding of Noll's work through a biographical or bibliographical overview ultimately depends on the continually alternating interpretations that result from retracing these blurred and ever-shifting lines, ones that may well depart from some biographical detail, yet as part of an ever-evolving fiction still thwart the attempt of becoming familiar with this or any author through his own work, much less by way of a presumably introductory "life-and-work" sketch such as this. That said, not all readers share the same concerns as literary theorists or cultural critics, nor do they need to, and perhaps for this reason alone no author, even the most reclusive, secretive, or even fictional among them, can ever completely escape the seemingly insatiable demand for biographical detail that persists, however fictional it may appear, and in spite of any critical turns to the contrary.

In the case of Noll's early years, then, one might begin by offering the following: Of mixed German, Portuguese, and indigenous background, he was born in

1946 in Porto Alegre, the capital city of the southern Brazilian state of Rio Grande do Sul, one with a distinctive regional culture of cattle herding and traditional folklore. Its inhabitants are known as *gaúchos*, much like the traditional rural populations of neighboring Argentina and Uruguay, although in Rio Grande do Sul this popular designation now extends to everyone from the state, regardless of their ethnic background or whether they live in the city or the countryside. Noll spent his early years studying at the Catholic Colégio de São Pedro, developing what, by all accounts, would become a lifelong appreciation for music while learning to play the piano. The early years of military dictatorship coincided with his growing political interest in Marxism, one shared by so many writers in his generation. In 1967 he began his studies in literature at the Federal University of Rio Grande do Sul, later interrupted when he moved to Rio de Janeiro to begin work as a journalist for the newspapers *Última Hora* and *Folha da Manhã;* this activity was also punctuated by a short hiatus working as a copy editor at the São Paulo publishing house Editora Nacional. Two of his earliest short stories appeared in an anthology of *gaúcho* writers titled *Roda de Fogo: 12 gaúchos contam* (Ring of Fire: 12 Gaúcho Writers), published in Porto Alegre in 1970.

On the basis of this biographical information, one might ask, Can Noll still be read as a *gaúcho* writer at this point? Certainly, though by no means exclusively: Although references to his home city and state are frequent enough over the course of his work, the occasional use of regional vocabulary or details of local geography are certainly not the sole defining characteristic of his work, especially when considered against the ever-expanding map of places, both within and beyond Brazil, that mark his recognition in the national and international literary arena over the course of a lifelong literary career. His partial German ethnic background is one possible lens for interpretation of his work, yet by no means the only one, or even the primary one. One might ask the same of his sexual identity, one that might be considered primarily gay-identified from his lived experiences yet one that transcends easy characterization, especially when juxtaposed with the broad landscape of sexual fantasy that characterizes his literary work.

Noll's formal literary debut on the national scene came when his first collection of short stories, *O cego e a dançarina* (The Blind Man and the Dancer), appeared in 1980, to critical acclaim. One of the best-known stories from this collection, "Alguma coisa urgentemente" (Something Urgent), tells the story of a boy who is sent off to boarding school when his father is imprisoned during the years of the Brazilian military dictatorship (1964–1985). When the father is later released, the two move to a friend's apartment in Rio. The story deals not only with the boy's loss of his father to illness but also, as the title suggests, with his own growing awareness of an urgent need to do something to survive on his own, whether through prostituting himself to an older man or seeking help from the few others with whom he comes in contact: a hot dog vendor or a friend from school who comes to check up on him in the squalid apartment in Copacabana that he lives in while his father lies dying in the other room. It is this sense of utter hopelessness, one often inseparable from the narrator's precarious existence, that consistently reappears in Noll's work: a story that cannot be told, *in any language,* yet somehow must be told all the same.

Noll's first novel, *A fúria do corpo* (The Body's Fury, 1981), sets the stage for this kind of narrative impact: A nameless protagonist recounts his relationship with his ex-wife, known here by the pseudonym Afrodite, whose lives alternate between their own sexual encounters, sex work with others, run-ins with the police, and the continuing flow of popular culture, from the music of Roberto Carlos to Carnival in Rio. His next novel, *Bandoleiros* (Bandits, 1985), takes place between Porto Alegre and memories of a trip to the city of Boston in the United States. The main character is an author set adrift after his last novel, despite having received a measure of critical acclaim, did not achieve the status of a bestseller. On his visit to the States, he appears obsessed with finding something noteworthy to write about – whether through a sexual encounter with a green-eyed redhead named Jill or a recollection of Argentine writer Ernesto Sábato's visit to the city years before – that might capture the attention of a Brazilian audience, yet he finds little or nothing of importance that might inspire him. His U.S. counterpart in the novel, a man named Steve, is medicated to such an extent by psychologists during college that he suffers from partial amnesia and is now at the point of physical and mental collapse. Aside from these fleeting missed encounters between characters, the novel also describes the development by the protagonist's wife, Ada, of a new form of social order called Minimal Societies, small isolated communities in which people are able to experience sexual liberation and other forms of escape from social norms and projects of national ideology: "[Ada] no longer saw in nationality an evaluating criterion of any human content. Nations, without exception, were doomed. What was left was entry into Minimal Societies."[8] Nonetheless, it ultimately appears increasingly doubtful whether such utopian projects can ever be realized in any lasting way, whether in this particular novel or elsewhere in his work. In Noll's subsequent novel, *Rastros de verão* (Traces of Summer, 1986), the narrator recounts his experiences of a brief sexual encounter with a younger man over the last days of Carnival in Porto Alegre, underscoring the polymorphous approach to

---

[8] João Gilberto Noll, *Romances e contos reunidos*. Intro. David Treece (São Paulo: Companhia das Letras, 1997), 239 (my translation).

human sexuality, one that may well remain the most recurrent characteristic of his work.

Two of his two best-known novels have been translated into English by the British academic David Treece for publication in the United Kingdom: *Hotel Atlantico* (1989) is the story of a one-time soap opera actor who takes off from Rio for the South of Brazil after a murder in his Copacabana hotel leaves him psychologically shaken. On the bus he encounters another North American character, a Canadian archeologist by the name of Susan Fleming, who commits suicide out of grief over the death of her seven-year-old daughter. After an attempt on his life and an accident in which one of his legs is amputated, he ends up in a hospital, only to be brought by his nurse to die on a beach outside Porto Alegre. The protagonist of his subsequent novel, *Harmada* (1993) is also an actor, this time living in a homeless shelter, who eventually attempts to restart his career with his adopted daughter, Cris, in an obscure model city named Harmada. At the end of the novel, a mute boy who appears in their apartment leads him to the founder and namesake of the city, but it is left unclear whether this final encounter with Pedro Harmada can provide any answers to the lingering existential questions that the narrative poses. One possible interpretation might be, as U.S.-based Brazilian literary critic Idelber Avelar has suggested, is one of Brazil in the aftermath of military dictatorship: a posttraumatic country, one as adrift morally and existentially as Noll's protagonists are.[9] Indeed, the argument can still be made that it is precisely the often self-imposed silence characteristic of such posttraumatic memory that may make it difficult, if not impossible, to elicit an outright denunciation of the state and its often dysfunctional institutions in any definitive and identifiable way, hence the often elliptical nature of Noll's narrative style, in which the silences do the most important task of recounting.

Nonetheless, such silences have proven legible to many, especially as Noll's work has received a considerable amount of curiosity and attention from literary critics and academics in recent years, both in Brazil and internationally, to such a great extent that this academic is no longer completely foreign to a body of work that has begun to venture into and continue its narration at the very heart of English-speaking academia. It is here that one can recognize a crucial thematic turn in Noll's work, away from characters on the edges of Brazilian society and toward those within the international university, its prestigious research centers, and international grant foundations. Noll's time spent as a visiting professor of Brazilian literature both at Berkeley and in London have left a

---

[9] Idelber Avelar, *The Untimely Present: Postdictatorial Latin American Fiction and the Task of Mourning* (Durham, NC: Duke University Press, 1999), 209.

noticeable imprint on his more recent fiction, especially in the novels *Berkeley em Bellagio* (2002) and *Lorde* (2004), about the academic, aesthetic, and, yes, always sexual adventures of a visiting professor in Europe.

In his most recent work, these two spaces, both the familiar streets and common places of his native Porto Alegre and an ever-expanding world on the margins between the lived, dreamed, and imaginary, continue to be fused in the collection short stories *A Máquina de ser* (The Being Machine, 2006) and in his most recent novel, *Acenos e afagos* (2008), in which, as one shall see, a newfound vein of humor and absurdity permeates his recurrent thematic preoccupations between the representations of sex and an underlying critique of the body politic.

After all, what emerges in Noll's work as much more pervasive than the question of personal identity is a recurrent preoccupation with the human body itself: whether in relation to other bodies, through sexual contact or other forms of sensorial perception; its fluids, secretions, and functions; its open wounds and scars and sites of amputation; and in its inevitable contamination, disease, death, and decay. Although Treece may have good reason to propose that Noll's recurrent narration of sexual activity, at "the borders of the sexually thinkable," may represent "the fluctuation of sexual identity as expression of the multiple and heterogeneous possibilities of being,"[10] it might also be that such sexual activity actually supersedes, if not completely negates, any desire for fixed identity, as an exercise not only in being but also in nonbeing, as an acting out of the fantasy of effaced identity that is predicated by the alternation of sexual naming and namelessness. Although these multifarious representations of corporeal experience, especially when set against the unwillingness to privilege identity through naming the self, may disorient or even provoke a sense of shock or disgust in many readers, those uncomfortable with such representations might also want to ask themselves the more difficult questions: Why might these depictions of being-in-body have the power to set off such intense emotional reactions? What sensorial dimensions of our own bodily experience must each of us suppress or ignore on a daily basis to maintain our selective and separate sense of identity? However unwanted or invasive such realizations may be, they nonetheless draw the reader into an almost unavoidable and uncommon sense of intimacy with the text and its alternative understandings of corporeal reality, one that eventually comes to take its place at the center of the experience of reading the work of another.

---

10 João Gilberto Noll, *Romances e contos reunidos*. Intro. David Treece (São Paulo: Companhia das Letras, 1997), 13 (my translation).

Confined spaces, con-fused identities: Noll's *Acenos e afagos*

At the center of this discussion of the irrepressible reemergence of Germany in the Brazilian novel, I place Noll's 2008 work *Acenos e afagos* (Gestures and Caresses) for precisely its peculiar way of reinventing this in-between place, not only for imagining it in manifestly sexual terms but for leading it inexorably into an oneiric realm of dreams and unmitigated psychic fantasy. Here as elsewhere in his work, Noll makes three separate mentions of his narrator's German-Brazilian origins at the beginning of the novel. It is the part of cultural identity partially obscured and buried in the past yet still inscribed in the author's last name, one that calls forth what lies beneath its surface to transit its conscious spaces, and in so doing, provokes what can only be called *KulturConfusão* at its most intense and extreme.

Entering the novel, it becomes clear from the outset that there will be no breaks, neither for chapters nor for paragraphs; the textual submersion into this literary world comes with no greater pause of blank space on the page than that between the words themselves, as if one were under water, holding one's breath, or breathing white air bubbles out through a oxygen tube from a tank on the surface. The story that emerges is one of a protagonist who lives a life in love with another man, known only as "O Engenheiro" (the Engineer), in spite of each of them having a wife and a son along the way and an interminable series of other sexual partners. Although this romantic relationship does not appear to ever be consummated in any definitive way (which thereby makes it the romantic relationship par excellence), the narrative of their invariably postponed "love story" is accompanied by an almost continual barrage of sexual episodes with others, not only other men but also women, not only compatriots but also foreigners and complete strangers. After all, over the course of the novel the main character not only embarks on a submarine and territorial sexual odyssey but also challenges the very dimensions of this assumed identity through a series of other transformations: becoming a woman, bearing a child, passing between the states of the living and the dead and back again, his love for another creating a revolution not in the world around him but a "sex change" in his own body. Once again, we confront the question of whom we are having sex with when we are observing a fantasy, whether our own or that of others, and the answer cannot be easily rendered, as the fantasy inevitably begins to transit the libido of the observer and that of the participant.

That may well be the true cultural confusion of "homosexuality": not that of the homosexual who conforms to societal norms and expectations and acts "straight," nor the one who assumes an exclusively oppositional, "queer" identity, all the while assuming to varying degrees normativizing constructions of marriage and monogamy, but rather those who continue to disrespect either of these conformist or dualistic distinctions by continually passing back and forth and in between sexual identities, roles, and positions. That is the primary implication of this unrelenting sexual activity that emanates both from a territorialized Brazil continually under siege by a never precisely identified enemy and from the arrival of a German submarine off the Brazilian coast or docked in Porto Alegre. Nonetheless, it is impossible to imagine this reemergence of Nazi weaponry in contemporary Brazil as an isolated occurrence; when is the specter of fascism not a constantly recurrent possibility, offshore and underwater, always about to resurface? After all, where we cannot see it but can only imagine it, is that not when it is most undeniably there? This submarine reemerges as an ambiguous signifier, both as one from the Nazi era (as exemplified in black-and-white propaganda films and other residual media messages from that all-too-irrepressible period of German cultural history) and simultaneously as one that transfers the signs and symbols of a differently politicized liberal-democratic LGBT/queer present. The point of this, one that continually resurfaces in this novel, may well be to confuse the message and complicate and multiply its possible sexual and political interpretations:

> A German submarine had been wrecked on the coast of Angola. It had got caught on the debris of another shipwreck. This insolent invention of already rotted-out iron was in fact a German scrapheap from World War II. Inside it there lived a kind of international disorienting force, always at sea, without ever staying for long in any port. They used to allow a month-long break in the port of Hamburg. Now, not even that. Like Christ, they said they had come *to confuse* [my emphasis]. The crew was made up predominantly of Germans. What united them was an aristocratic taste for the arts of sodomy. Some observers thought it possible that the shipwreck had been planned by the German intelligence service.[11]

Those who have read Noll before are no doubt prepared for this: the detailed descriptions of a wide compendium of sexual acts held together by an often tenuous narrative thread seemingly made up of every conceivable bodily fluid, one that always seems to linger on the edge between memory, dreams, and fantasy, as if taking place not only below the surface of the ocean but in the darkened spaces of cinemas and the films they show, other obscured spaces such as saunas or bars, or the demimonde of the *entendidos* (literally, "those who understand," a slang term used for homosexuals in Brazil before the arrival of the

---

11 João Gilberto Noll, *Romances e contos reunidos*. Intro. David Treece (São Paulo: Companhia das Letras, 1997), 51–52 (my translation).

more international term *gay* with the rise of the liberation movement in the 1970s).

In any case, to lose sight of the other messages legible in the novel by focusing only on the sexual would be to miss much of its political message, perhaps most importantly a trenchant critique of ethnic and national identity as articulated through literature. It is no coincidence that between sexual episodes the main character is repeatedly solicited to donate to "the Brazilian cause" in the face of an obscure foreign threat facing the nation. Although the recurrent descriptions of sexual activity may do much to distract from other elements, they cannot completely conceal the complex discussion of the limits of national discourse and cultural community by drawing the narrative through the points of dislocation and confusion that may be unimaginable were it not for the interference of a sexualized narrative. Sex here is by no means submerged but actually the surface narrative that covers and points to a series of even more subliminal political discussions going on below.

In Noll's work this often takes the form not only of disorientation, or a mere breakdown of national border ideologies, but a sexualized "elsewhere," one that some psychoanalytic theorists such as Žižek in the recent slew of books, most notably in *The Ticklish Subject*, continue to classify as "perversion," even if in quotes and an often affirmative connotation, as if only for lack of a better word, and one that others might just name simply their normal, everyday state of things. Žižek makes much of the fact that "queer demands" appear to want it both ways, to be considered both "normal" and still separate from normative constructions of sexual identity.[12] Thus, this recurrent sexual (dis)orientation, as it appears and reappears in the novel, should neither completely comfort nor disturb us necessarily, unless it does both at the same time. After all, confusion, be it cultural or sexual, may simply be what is happening all the time, even when it appears nothing at all is taking place.

This is the creativity of a sexuality without limits, a sexualized transnational landscape and seascape connecting everything, all bodies of all kinds, creating thereby a vertiginous kind of community, one implicated with another through sexual contact and confusion of bodily fluids, with transformation of all bodies the ultimate and inevitable outcome thereof. In Noll's literary imagination, man thus becomes woman (and even gives birth as a mother), his predominantly "homo-" imaginary turns hetero, hermaphrodite, bisexual, and back again, and the protagonist continues to explore spaces both above and below the sur-

---

[12] Slavoj Žižek, *The Ticklish Subject: The Absent Centre of Political Ontology* (New York: Verso, 1999), 270–271.

face of consciousness, if not life and death itself, in a sexualized body without limits: "My body as a whole was a sexual organ."[13]

It is not long into the novel, though, that one notices a perhaps disquieting odor: Some bodily fluid is flowing through this text, be it blood, semen, urine, or feces, all of which bind us in a form of inescapable corporeal community. Following the thought of German theorist Klaus Theweleit, who has probably explored this connection between the male body and the subconscious meanings of these fluids more exhaustively than any other, one might even imagine a nation that takes the colors of these bodily substances – red and black, white or gold – as its identifying banner,[14] to say nothing of the simultaneous suppression and strategic deployment of homosexual activity as part of the Nazi body politic.[15] Noll is similarly committed to engaging long term these experiences of sight and smell as part of a reminder of the never completely suppressible embodied experience that accompanies the act of reading. It is not only bodies and their odors but the words on the page, the sense functions that they set off, if not the lingering ideologies that accompany these fluids and smells that have set these human bodies into motion and contact. It is precisely the redeployment, if only in this literary world, that makes the bodily stench most perceptible to the senses. One need only imagine it in words to smell it, as it has always been there, it is a part of all of us, both within and on us while reading, as a form of embodied knowledge of the inescapable daily functions that punctuate our reading and writing, ones that we repress all too often in order to imagine community with other, even though it is this stench that is at the very core of our shared sense of community, our meta-individual human bodily function. Or perhaps it is ideology itself that gives off an odor here, as a representation of the never completely repressible awareness of bodily function, so often displaced or concealed by ideology in order to imagine a social commonality with others.

And what if dying and being buried with one's lover is part of the sexual romantic fantasy, as it is in *Acenos e afagos?* In the death of the narrative voice, literature becomes "con-fused" with the soil in which one's body is buried, along with other dead bodies, organic material, even cosmic dust. Ironically enough, this is precisely the moment in which this character appears to achieve his greatest plenitude: "All of a sudden, I coagulated. And before I could no longer formulate anything, I realized that now, at last [...] I would start living."[16] But

---

13 Noll, 195 (my translation). (2008).
14 Klaus Theweleit, *Männerphantasien* (Munich: Piper Verlag, 2000), II, 279–288.
15 Klaus Theweleit, *Männerphantasien* (Munich: Piper Verlag, 2000), I, 61–66; II, 302–323.
16 João Gilberto Noll, *Acenos e afagos* (São Paulo: Record, 2008), 206 (my translation).

live how? Simply as a partially dissolved idea, in residual and decomposed organic form? Or in the flesh, still in living circulation in between other bodies, if not countries?

"Wir können noch tiefer": submersion, subversion, resurfacing

It is in the darkened space of the cinema so often transited in Noll's novel, with its illuminated screen and obscure rows of participant spectators, that the notion of a tangibly functioning "dream state" achieves a recurrent spatial model. For Noll it is the space not only of viewing a limitless series of images to feed this imaginary but also of action, of cruising its dark corridors and pungent facilities. For this reason alone, I too find it difficult to resist transnational comparisons with other similar sites where such spaces are examined and represented, first with the red underwater glow of the emergency lights in Wolfgang Petersen's 1981 film *Das Boot*.[17] Many will recall how postwar West German musical icon Herbert Grönemeyer plays a Navy war reporter on a Nazi U-boat: the all-male underwater environment, with uniformed men in this confined space, often bathed in red or blue lights or alternately cloaked in darkness, one that can hardly avoid a queer reading in its resemblance to a Berlin or Munich leather bar of the period. This similarity, which might even be considered unintentional were it not for the thinly veiled yet constant homoerotic innuendo, whether between sailors flexing their muscles and lifting barbells or even in an underwater drag show between the sailors' bunks, to say nothing of the French chanteuse in the red dress who performs in the initial scene of drunken debauchery before their departure. Each successive image underscores the almost complete absence of women in the rest of the film, with scene after suspenseful underwater scene of men drunk and drowning on the prospect of military heroism, whereas women are present only in photographs, letters home, or the ultimately obscured memories of those they must leave behind by entering this underwater confinement. Add to this the imagery of the sailors greasing up the missiles that that will penetrate and destroy the female, "lady" warships on the surface ("in die Dame stecken"), from a space below marked explicitly as being without anyone's mother or any female: "keines Mutter, kein Weib."

---

17 Wolfgang Petersen (dir.), *Das Boot*. Starring Herbert Grönemeyer and Jürgen Prochnow. (Bavaria Film/PSI International, 1981).

But as the Captain Lieutenant, or "Kaleun," played by Jürgen Prochnow, utters repeatedly at key points in the narrative, "Tiefer. Wir können noch tiefer" ("Deeper. We can go even deeper"). Nowhere is more cinematic attention given to the male body, the selfsame fluids and stench so accentuated in Noll's novel, and nowhere a clearer dramatic reiteration of the tropes of *Damm und Fluß* (dam and flow) developed theoretically in Theweleit's theoretical work on masculinity under totalitarianism than in the visual images and dialogue of *Das Boot*, to say nothing of its unrelenting quest for realism in the directorial approach, to show, as the English language trailer stresses, "what war is all about": the "descent into madness" that is the all-male world of wartime heroism.

In stark contrast, compare this overarching goal of realism in the similarly eerie mix of artificial golden light and white pages of text that punctuate the dark interiors of Rainer Werner Fassbinder's 1982 film *Querelle*, a adaptation of Jean Genet's 1947 novel about a sailor in the French seaport of Brest, this consciously aestheticized rendering of his spiral into the depths of love, sex, and murder.[18] Foremost in the rendering of this artificiality is the use of a narrator's voice, one that speaks in English and might well be imagined as that of both Genet and Fassbinder simultaneously. This disembodied voice introduces the main characters, develops the plot, reveals explicitly the character's motivations, and even directs the viewer's attention to certain details of the story, with narrative lines such as "We'd like you to perceive." The film's message could hardly be more blunt in its will to direct not only the scene but the viewer's perception of it; as in *Das Boot*, yet another French chanteuse appears in *Querelle*, this time not to sing a conventionally sentimental French chanson but instead one with the words "Each man kills the thing he loves." In spite of this difference in artistic approach, one might still ask, Is this explicitly homoerotic film truly any more or any less "queer" than *Das Boot*? Perhaps it is only more insistent on limiting the range of possible interpretations – at least on the surface – in its depictions of male–male sexual activity.

Ultimately, the political landscape and sexual imagery of either film would not be out of place if juxtaposed against that of Noll's *Acenos e afagos*. In much the same way, the studied excess in the representation of both political ideology and sexual acts as artifice might have much the same numbing effect as that of a popular culture so preoccupied with the mass transmission of sexual images to the extent that Walter Benjamin in his essay could hardly have imagined, whether through DVD players, the Internet, or smart phones, to the point

---

[18] Rainer Werner Fassbinder (dir.). *Querelle*. Starring Brad Davis, Franco Nero and Jeanne Moreau (Planet Film/Albatros Produktion/Gaumont, 1982).

where any representation of sex, cinematic, literary, or otherwise, devolves into a kind of absurdist and futile repetition. Ultimately, little has changed in Benjamin's analysis of the fascist media regime in "The Artwork in the Age of Technological Reproducibility": "Fascism tries to organize the newly established proletarian masses without disturbing the property relations that the masses struggle to eliminate."[19] In the meantime, moreover, the web of media-generated sexual simulation has become irreversibly transcontinental, with the sexual relationship clearly not only in the submarine cables but also in outer-space satellites, now extending clearly not only between Germany and Brazil but to any number of users in different global cultures. Each dual relationship is now unavoidably multiple and repeating, and just as Deleuze and Guattari on one hand and Žižek on the other take care to remind us – that sexuality is omnipresent whereas the sexual relationship is increasingly stubborn in its elusiveness – what was once long distance is still inexorably closing in on us.

Nevertheless, even the most definitive entry into a new ideological era cannot entirely abate the continual flow of history repeating itself, however far away that may appear. Additional cinematic examples from outside the Brazil–Germany dyad might also serve as illustrations: In the late 1970s, an author by the name of Ira Levin published a bestseller titled *The Boys from Brazil*, a novel that spawned two film versions. In the first, from 1978, Doctor Mengele, the concentration camp doctor responsible for the most horrific experiments on twins, was still alive and living in Brazil. He had cloned Adolf Hitler and had put the 94 boys resulting from this experiment up for adoption throughout the Western world, even attempting to replicate circumstances that might trigger the same psychological conditions that were the product of his environment. For those of us who saw this film as adolescents when it was first released, it was frightening, for the possibility not only that Nazism could repeat itself but that the return of Nazism could happen in any country, and in any generation including our own, that any of us might also be "Boys from Brazil," acting out the global hegemonic fantasies of a dictator both dead and monstrously still alive in others, if not ourselves, alongside a host of other fantasies, be they sexual, political, or both.

In the strangest case of fact following fiction, it was revealed only a few years after the original film version was released that Mengele and his family had been living in Brazil all along, in a small coastal town in the state of São Paulo called Bertioga. And even stranger facts continued to emerge: a Nazi

---

19 Walter Benjamin, "Die Kunstwerk im Zeitalter der technischen Reproduzierbarkeit," in *Illuminationen* (Frankfurt am Main: Suhrkamp, 1977), 167 (my translation).

graveyard from the 1920s found in the Amazonian rainforest,[20] and yes, even the newly discovered wreckage of a Nazi U-boat off the coast of the southern Brazilian state of Santa Catarina in July 2011. The limits of Nazi Germany have always been more indeterminate and shifting than those on any map, obeying neither the limits of coastline nor the ocean's surface, and its symbols and ideological residue will continue to reappear far from its points of origin.

A final thought on the lures of totalitarianism (and the necessity for self-implication)

Of course, all this in no way implies that the juxtaposition of successive examples that speak to the rise and reemergence of totalitarian imagery in admittedly divergent contemporary literatures and cultures make them in any way "the same." In fact, teasing out such distinctions may by the very point of this kind of cultural critique. In fact, if there were any one unavoidable body of work that might warn us about making such facile equivalencies between cultures and systems in the context of a discussion of totalitarianism, it would probably be that of Hannah Arendt. As she points out in *The Origins of Totalitarianism*, "Totalitarian rulers rely on the compulsion with which we can compel ourselves, for the limited mobilization of people which even they still need; this inner compulsion is the tyranny of logicality against which nothing stands but the great capacity of men to start something new."[21] Interestingly enough, coupled to Arendt's prescient discussion of logicality's complicity in the rise of totalitarian systems is the role of loneliness and uprootedness as the "common ground for terror."[22]

With this all-too-common (yet never shared) experience of loneliness and uprootedness in mind in the face of totalitarian logicality, it might actually be of some importance to mention – as self-implication is quite often the most honest means of approaching questions of totalitarian dictatorship – that I am from neither Germany nor Brazil but a small island in the North Atlantic. It was here, in the summer of 1974 to be exact, that a Hollywood director named Steven Spielberg decided to make a multimillion-dollar film, *Jaws*, about a monstrous shark that emerged from the depths of the ocean to prey on the inhabitants of a small coastal town; in fact, many of its fictional victims were played by the same peo-

---

20 Alan Hall, "The First Boys from Brazil: Nazi Graveyard Discovered Deep in Amazonian Rainforest." *The Mail Online*, 24 October 2008. http://www.dailymail.co.uk. 21 August 2014.
21 Hannah Arendt, *The Origins of Totalitarianism* (New York: Harcourt, 1994), 473.
22 Hannah Arendt, *The Origins of Totalitarianism* (New York: Harcourt, 1994), 473.

ple with whom I grew up, went to elementary school, or performed in community theater productions. Although I was not part of the film's cast, I did once sneak into the yard where the props were stored, to climb inside the severed head of the shark retooled as a mechanical prop and stare out through the mouth, either as its devoured victim or perhaps even as a fantasmatic stand-in, disguised and hidden inside a Hollywood mechanical device, to resemble and act out the role of the shark, with "little me" playing the part of the underwater menace to my own community.

In his discussion of Frederic Jameson's reading of *Jaws* in his book *Enjoy Your Symptom!*, Žižek brought me back to consider the wide range of "multiple realities" of this film,[23] the one that is, whether I like it or not, symbolically inextricable from my own childhood. As he suggests, the underwater monster victimizing the inhabitants and vacationers could be consumer capitalism, he argues, or perhaps "the Third World" exacting its revenge on a prosperous U.S. town (funny he should say that, now that my island just so happens to have one of the highest percentages of Brazilian migrant workers in relation to the general population of anywhere outside Brazil). Although part of me is naturally tempted to maintain the illusion that at times "a shark is just a shark," I must admit – deep down? – that this underwater menace to a fictional town with the ironic name of Amity is just as much a stunt double to any number of "real" threats to my own home, among them any number of perceived political institutions that might be imaged to linger right offshore, waiting for just the moment to surface. The possibilities are multiple, as are the modes of interpreting "reality," in much the same way that Foucault underscores the possible contexts of this discussion in an obscure, buried endnote in his work *Discipline and Punish:* "I shall choose examples from military, medical, educational and industrial institutions. Other examples might have been taken from colonization, slavery and child rearing."[24] Yes, the monster that we consume and that consumes us is no doubt a product of the ultimate phase of multinational corporate consumerism, perhaps best embodied and promoted through the Hollywood mass media and entertainment industry. Moreover, as the mutual feeding frenzy of mass consumption – as well as one of being consumed by the system of consumption – continues into the present day, we can no longer so easily ignore that a constantly remilitarizing imperialist war machine and securitized police and surveillance

---

[23] Slavoj Žižek, *Enjoy Your Symptom! Jacques Lacan in Hollywood and Out*, 2nd ed. (New York: Routledge, 2001), 133–134.
[24] Michel Foucault, *Discipline and Punish: The Birth of the Prison.* [1975]. Trans. Alan Sheridan (New York: Vintage Books, 1995), 314.

state has also always been one of the imminent dangers lurking just below the surface.

Or perhaps the shark is also yet another embodied and mechanical form of submarine, whether "queer," "Nazi," or both: no longer of enemy German sailors who continue to haunt the social imaginary, much less of newly arrived Brazilian migrants, or any other presumably foreign contingent among us, but simply a stage prop this time, either with that curious nine-year-old boy I once was or any one of the rest of us inside. No matter in which ideologically tinged form it may resurface, this severed head of a mechanical underwater monster still can barely mask the lingering vulnerability, within any one of us, to the lures of totalitarian thought and attendant ideological manipulation.

References

Arendt, Hannah. *The Origins of Totalitarianism* (New York: Harcourt, 1994).
Avelar, Idelber. *The Untimely Present: Postdictatorial Latin American Fiction and the Task of Mourning* (Durham, NC: Duke University Press, 1999).
Benjamin, Walter. "Die Kunstwerk im Zeitalter der technischen Reproduzierbarkeit," in *Illuminationen* (Frankfurt am Main: Suhrkamp, 1977), 136–169.
Deleuze, Gilles, and Félix Guattari. *Anti-Oedipus* (Minneapolis: University of Minnesota Press, 1983).
Fassbinder, Rainer Werner (dir.). *Querelle*. Starring Brad Davis, Franco Nero and Jeanne Moreau (Planet Film/Albatros Produktion/Gaumont, 1982).
Foucault, Michel. *Discipline and Punish: The Birth of the Prison*. [1975]. Trans. Alan Sheridan (New York: Vintage Books, 1995).
Hall, Alan. "The First Boys from Brazil: Nazi Graveyard Discovered Deep in Amazonian Rainforest." *The Mail Online* 24 October 2008. http://www.dailymail.co.uk. 21 August 2014.
Noll, João Gilberto. *Acenos e afagos* (São Paulo: Record, 2008).
Noll, João Gilberto. *Romances e contos reunidos*. Intro. David Treece (São Paulo: Companhia das Letras, 1997).
Petersen, Wolfgang (dir.). *Das Boot*. Starring Herbert Grönemeyer and Jürgen Prochnow. (Bavaria Film/PSI International, 1981).
Ruffato, Luiz. *Eles eram muitos cavalos* (Rio de Janeiro: Record, 2001).
Theweleit, Klaus. *Männerphantasien* I and II [1977, 1978]. (Munich: Piper Verlag, 2000).
Verissimo, Luis Fernando. *Borges e os orangotangos eternos* (São Paulo: Companhia das Letras, 2000).
Žižek, Slavoj. *Did Somebody Say Totalitarianism? Five Interventions in the (Mis)use of a Notion* (New York: Verso, 2001).
Žižek, Slavoj. *Enjoy Your Symptom! Jacques Lacan in Hollywood and Out*, 2nd ed. (New York: Routledge, 2001).
Žižek, Slavoj. *The Ticklish Subject: The Absent Centre of Political Ontology* (New York: Verso, 1999).

Edith Wolfe
"Exiled from the World": German Expressionism, Brazilian Modernism, and the Interstitial Primitivism of Lasar Segall

In 1928 German-trained artist Lasar Segall opened his first exhibition of painting produced in Brazil. In the four years since his immigration from Germany, Segall had gained notoriety among an active Brazilian avant-garde struggling to define a distinctly national modern aesthetic. Segall's exhibition, mounted in Rio de Janeiro's tony Copacabana Palace, generated no little debate relative to both nationalist and modernist concerns. Responses to the artist's stylized renderings of Brazilian landscapes and local types ranged from pride at the artist's nationalist insight to indignity at his distortion of the local reality. Thus, whereas one critic attributed an artistic "conquest" to the artist's cultural assimilation, declaring, "Segall [. . .] was born and raised here; he was naturalized Brazilian,"[1] another protested that the work "offended his patriotism."[2] If supporters applauded his authenticity, detractors derided his foreign gaze, condemning his work, as did one critic, for issuing a "savage aspect" and invoking "an Africanism repugnant to [Brazilian] tastes."[3]

The ambivalence regarding Segall's position in Brazilian art and society dogged the artist throughout his career and continues to punctuate the literature on his life and painting. Like the commentary from the 1920s, scholars and art historians have regarded him alternately as a German primitivist fascinated with Brazilian exoticism or as a Brazilian nationalist whose own "melancholy" Jewish origins and perceived proximity to the "primitive" allowed him intimate access to Brazil's racial particularism. Historical perspective seems to exacerbate rather than relieve these tensions, as Segall becomes a deeply contradictory representative of a colonialist discourse of the non-European Other *and* of Brazilian modernism's anticolonial response, which laid claim to the "primitive" as a function of national patrimony.

How do we explain such radically divergent accounts of the artist? My research suggests that such critical ambiguity originates in Segall's role as the

---
[1] Guilherme de Almeida, "Lasar Segall: A exposição em São Paulo, um novo realismo," *O Jornal* (11 July 1928): 30. All translations by the author unless otherwise noted.
[2] The author describes the exhibition as "a conquest that can only make us feel proud and noble," "Vandalismo moribundo?" *Diário Nacional* (18 December 1928).
[3] Victor Néstor, "A exposição Lasar Segall," *O Globo* (30 July 1928).

"outsider within." Although his work used many of the formal and thematic tendencies characteristic of each movement, Segall never subscribed to the cultural politics of either. He played a pivotal role in the direction of both Dresden expressionism and São Paulo modernism yet was estranged by their political contexts and deeply opposed the underlying nationalist currents of each and of post-World War I modernism in general. This chapter argues that Segall's position at once outside and inside Brazilian modernism *and* German Expressionism facilitated a critique of certain aesthetic and ideological assumptions issued from within the movements themselves.

Far from the allusions to national belonging constructed in Brazilian modernism and equally removed from the assimilative universalist discourse characteristic of European avant-garde primitivism, Segall constructed a universalizing alterity, conflating the Jew, the immigrant, and the Afro-Brazilian in a shared experience of diaspora and displacement. I propose that the counternarrative of primitivism and modernity articulated in Segall's painting reveals unexpected similarities in purpose and practice between German colonialist and Brazilian postcolonial aesthetics. On one hand, his redeployment of primitivist and nationalist iconography as markers of exclusion rather than inclusion reveals the ethnocentric Othering characteristic of *both* German Expressionism and Brazilian modernism. On the other hand, the struggles by Segall's contemporaries to position him relative to the ideological underpinnings of each movement lays bare the ethnic exclusion and racial hierarchy obscured within the universalist claims of both modernist projects.

Segall's position as a foreigner, an immigrant, and a Jew in Germany and Brazil reinforced a sense of alterity that deeply marks his work in both countries. Born in Vilnius in 1891, Segall left for Germany at the age of 15 to study at Berlin's prestigious Royal Prussian College of Fine Arts. He abandoned the academy in solidarity with the secessionist revolt of the early 1910s, relocating to Dresden to continue his studies. Upon his encounter with the art and writing of expressionist pioneers Wassily Kandinsky and Franz Marc, Segall abandoned naturalism and became a founding member of the expressionist collaborative, the secessionist Gruppe 1919. By 1923, however, financial hardship and rising xenophobia prompted him to emigrate to São Paulo, where several siblings were already residing. There he was quickly conscripted into the service of Brazilian modernism, joining an iconoclastic first-generation avant-garde, including poets Mário de Andrade and Oswald de Andrade, painter Tarsila do Amaral, and journalists Manuel Bandeira, Geraldo Ferraz, and Sergio Milliet. Through all of Segall's social and physical migrations, he pursued a single aesthetic project, merely altering his iconography relative to the novelties of a new environment. As this chapter suggests, the failure of critics to reconcile Segall's distinct objectives with the dominant artistic contexts in which he worked has created the ambivalence surrounding the significance of his art and activity in the 1920s.

Border thinking, German primitivism, and the cult of the *Ostjude*

Art historians have speculated that in moving to Brazil, Segall entered a long tradition of artists "going away," moving to the margins of Western "civilization" in search of alternatives to the decadence of modern society.[4] Segall first traveled to Brazil in 1913, the same year that The Bridge (Die Brücke) artists Max Pechstein and Emil Nolde toured the German colonies in the South Seas; and his work in the 1910s displayed a harsh angularity and asymmetry formally linking him to this more senior generation. In Dresden, Segall collaborated with Nolde and others, most notably in a group exhibition organized by the Folkwang Museum around 1921 that juxtaposed Expressionist painting with Pechstein's collection of tribal sculpture (Figure 1).[5] Yet the formal affinities that invited mutual participation are deceptive in that they cloud critical philosophical differences that separated Segall's younger generation from the movement's founders. Foremost among these were primitivism's nationalist underpinnings, which Segall's work emphatically refused.

Despite their radical affront to conservative social and artistic values, the Brücke's fundamental ideals were, as Jill Lloyd has observed, "marked by the imperialist consciousness of their times."[6] Not only did propaganda aimed at fostering German patriotism accompany the ethnographic exhibitions that inspired their work, but on a much more insidious level modernist imaginings of the colonial Other contributed to a normative understanding of German identity by polarizing "us" and "them." Even seemingly innocuous works such as the

---

[4] Gill Perry labeled the phenomenon in his essay, "Primitivism," in *Primitivism, Cubism, Abstraction: The Early Twentieth Century*, ed. Charles Harrison (New Haven, CT: Yale University Press, in association with the Open University, 1993). On Segall's work as representative of a "typical" European gaze see Frederico Morais, *Lasar Segall e o Rio de Janeiro* (Rio de Janeiro: Museu de Arte Moderna do Rio de Janeiro, 1991); and Stephanie D'Alessandro, "The Absorption of Spectacular, Unedited Things: Brazil in the Work of Lasar Segall," in *Still More Distant Journeys: The Artistic Emigrations of Lasar Segall*, ed. Stephanie D'Alessandro and Reinhold Heller (Chicago: David and Alfred Smart Museum of Art, University of Chicago, 1997), 110–160.

[5] The Folkwang Museum owned the painting *Widows*, which was included in the Nazi "Entarte Kunst" (Degenerate Art) exhibition in Munich in 1937 and subsequently destroyed.

[6] Jill Lloyd, *German Expressionism: Primitivism and Modernity* (New Haven, CT: Yale University Press, 1991), 193.

Figure 1. Expressionists and Exotics Gallery, Folkwang Museum, Hagen (now Karl Ernst Osthaus-Museum), displaying paintings by Emil Nolde and Lasar Segall with ancestral portraits from New Guinea, c. 1915. Foto Marburg / Art Resource, New York.

"ethnographic" still lifes Nolde included in the *Folkwang* exhibition were not ideologically neutral. Inspired by decorated human skulls in a shop window in colonial New Guinea, these violently rendered portraits challenged traditional notions of beauty by thrusting the grotesque into the staid realm of the still life. The desired effect relied on familiar tropes of "primitive" difference that presumed an unsophisticated tribal mentality and cultural order, thus reinforcing precisely the associations of barbarism, superstition, and irrationalism used to justify European imperialism.[7]

Although Segall shared Die Brücke's fascination with non-Western culture and "primitive" aesthetics, he represented German Expressionism's younger

---

[7] Lloyd discusses the attitudes express by Nolde, who accompanied an official expedition to German New Guinea and whose imagery simultaneously evoked the fear of the "savages" and "cannibals" who had slaughtered Catholic missionaries in military battles and articulated a critique of the colonialist enterprise. His gaze thus departs significantly from Pechstein in Palau and others who "turned a blind eye to changes wrought by imperial rule." Lloyd, *German Expressionism: Primitivism and Modernity* (New Haven, CT: Yale University Press, 1991), 213–234.

"Second Generation" artists, more concerned with rising German nativism and the consequences of World War I than with the cultural politics of a waning imperial power. Visits to the ethnographic collections, colonial exhibitions, and exotic carnivals (Figure 2) informed his aesthetic handling, as did the Africanizing imagery of Pablo Picasso and genuine African sculpture displayed in the Folkwang Museum and elsewhere.[8] Yet, rather than the diametrically constructed assertions of cultural and ethnic difference characteristic of German primitivism's colonialist aesthetics, Segall's imagery fostered a broadly humanist affirmation of sameness consistent with Gruppe 1919's central mission.[9] The collective, which included Otto Dix, Otto Lange, Conrad Felixmuller, and Ludwig Meidner, had been conceived as a "brotherhood of an unadulterated humanity," mobilizing around a shared "disdain [for] the insanity of border posts, chauvinism, nationalism."[10] Violent, angular distortions and masklike faces charge the themes of dispossession Segall elaborated during his time with the group. A tone of brutality and dehumanization suffuses his imagery of widows, abandoned children, and displaced Jews as exemplified by *The Eternal Wanderers* (1919; Figure 3). At the same time, however, the allegory of wandering adds conceptual thrust to the Africanizing forms, suggesting a shared history of persecution, displacement, and diaspora that defied the oppositional nationalism of pre-

---

[8] Under the directorship of Karl Ernst Osthaus since 1912, the Folkwang Museum, which Segall frequented, treated non-Western objects not as ethnographic curiosities but as equivalent to Western art. He undoubtedly visited the 1914 exhibition Picasso und "Negerplastik" at the Emil Richter Gallery in Dresden, and his personal library included Carl Einstein's immensely popular 1915 publication *Negerplastic* (Black Sculpture; Munich: K. Wolff, 1920)). Indicative of Osthaus's curatorial mission see Ernst Fuhrmann, *Afrika: Sakralkulte Vorgeschichte der Hieroglyphen*, vol. VI, *Schriften-Reihe, Kulturen der Erde: Material zur Kultur und Kunst Geschichte Aller Völker* (Dresden: Folkwangverlag, 1922).
[9] This is not to oversimplify the ideological variations within Expressionist Primitivism, in which artists displayed a wide variety of attitudes toward both colonialism and the direction of national politics and society, but which Lloyd has persuasively demonstrated was charged with a tension internal to modernity between "forward and backward looking tendencies" (Jill Lloyd, *German Expressionism: Primitivism and Modernity* (New Haven, CT: Yale University Press, 1991, vii). Nevertheless, imperialist ideologies were so deeply hegemonic that even in the critique of colonialism it was virtually impossible to transcend a dominant racialist discourse that positioned the non-Western "primitive" as the antithesis of "civilization," defined through a series of well-established binaries.
[10] From Herbert Kühn, "Expressionismus und Sozialismus," *Neue Blätter für Kunst und Dichtung* 2:1 (May 1919): 29, translated in Reinhold Heller, "'His Sole Subject Is Suffering Humanity': Lasar Segall in Germany, 1906–1923," in *Still More Distant Journeys: The Artistic Emigrations of Lasar Segall*, ed. Stephanie D'Alessandro and Reinhold Heller (Chicago: David and Alfred Smart Museum of Art, University of Chicago, 1997), 72.

war expressionism. In their stateless and subaltern position, these eternal wanderers embodied a spiritual profundity and universalism that repudiated the materialism of partisan and national politics.

Figure 2. Peters, Dresden photographer. Lasar Segall and colleagues from the Dresden Academy of Fine Arts during a carnival parade, 1912. Black and white photograph. 12.3 × 17.2 cm. Arquivo Fotográfico Lasar Segall – Museu Lasar Segall, São Paulo/IBRAM/MinC-Brasil.

Segall's art and writings suggest an intersubjectivity between the artist and the Other that further distinguished his vision from the essentializing colonial gaze. Deeply influenced by contemporary theorists who valorized the essential humanism of non-Classical art, Segall added the Jewish artist to the more common inventory of blacks, Asians, Byzantine and Egyptian artists, children, and the mentally ill.[11] Reasoning that the Jew "still lives in accordance with the

---

[11] Segall agreed with figures popular among the Expressionists such as Aloïs Riegl and Wilhelm Worringer that the emotional and spiritual primacy of the "primitive" mentality and a corresponding aesthetic indifference to external phenomenon produced a more universal expression. For more specific discussion of the influence of such theorists on German art of the time, see Jill Lloyd, *German Expressionism: Primitivism and Modernity* (New Haven, CT: Yale Uni-

Figure 3. Lasar Segall, *Eternal Wanderers*, 1919. Oil on canvas, 138 × 184 cm. Acervo do Museu Lasar Segall – IBRAM/MinC-Brasil.

depth of his racial instinct," thus "more from the inside out than from outside in," he attributed "a problematic relationship with nature and the depiction of nature" to the Jewish artist.[12] Segall's 1919 self-portrait (Figure 4) evokes this position as the "kindred primitive." Adopting a particularly violent gesture, Segall turns the objectifying gaze inward, portraying himself through the formal language of primitivism. Applying the paint crudely with a the angular strokes of a pallet knife, he depicts the shallow, concave space of the eyes, the hollow irises set into asymmetrical sockets, and the deep striations on the forehead and cheekbones to conflate the individual appearance of the subject with the anon-

---

versity Press, 1991), especially pp. 51–57; and Joseph Masheck, "Raw Art: 'Primitive' Authenticity and German Expressionism," *RES* 4 (1982).

12 Lasar Segall, untitled manuscript, Arquivo Lasar Segall, Museu Lasar Segall, São Paulo, Instituto do Patrimônio Histórico e Artístico Nacional, Ministério da Cultura do Brasil. The connection between the Jewish and "primitive" artist is established by Segall's parallel construction of Asian, African, and Byzantine art in Lasar Segall, "Sobre Arte," in *Lasar Segall: Textos, depoimentos e exposições* (São Paulo: Museu Lasar Segall, 1993).

ymous visage of a mask. The image is provocatively ambiguous; whether the motif represents the mask as having the capacity to reveal man's inner nature, or the contrary, to conceal, is unresolved, and presumably unresolvable. Rather than romanticizing his exotic position, the image suggests a marginality over which Segall had no control, and indeed, a necessary alterity.

Figure 4. Lasar Segall, *Self-Portrait II*, 1919. Oil on canvas, 68 × 58.5 cm. Acervo do Museu Lasar Segall – IBRAM/MinC-Brasil.

A German cult of the Eastern Jew (*Ostjude*) gaining popularity at the time gave substance to Segall's identification as the Jewish "primitive." The postwar occupation of Lithuania and Poland, and the migration of thousands of Central European refugees into Western Europe after the war, had introduced a caricature of the Eastern Jew into the German popular imagination.[13] Resonating with the similar romanticization of native peoples, the Eastern Jew represented an unbroken sense of community and essential cultural integrity that war-ravaged Europe had regrettably forfeited.[14] Segall's peers praised his work in the rhetoric of the mystical and mysterious East. "Sounds of the Orient!" one critic exclaimed after visiting a 1920 exhibition, "The pre-rational soul is allowed to resound among us from its depths."[15] His dealer, Paul Ferdinand Schmidt, proclaimed his art "more eastern, darker, more mystically toned than anyone else's [...] [because] he feels within himself the melancholy, thousands of years old, of the Eastern Jew."[16]

If the position as the venerated Eastern Jew fostered Segall's greatest inclusion within the international avant-garde, it also presumed his exclusion, shedding light on his self-portrayal through bombastic tropes of the savage.[17] Rather

---

13 Steven E. Aschheim, *Brothers and Strangers: The East European Jew in German and German Jewish Consciousness, 1800–1923* (Madison: University of Wisconsin Press, 1982). Claudia Valladão de Mattos discusses Segall's relation to the *Ostjude* at length in *Lasar Segall, expressionismo e judaísmo: o período alemão de 1906–1923* (São Paulo: Editora Perspectiva, 2000).

14 Segall's notion that a Jewish world view was antithetical to artistic naturalism and bourgeois materialism resonated with the rhetoric of the *Ostjude*. Perceived as an embodiment of traditional social orders and religious practices, they were considered the antithesis of modernization, timeless and spiritually whole. Such idealistic impressions coexisted with the xenophobic bigotry by the mass migrations. Steven E. Aschheim, *Brothers and Strangers: The East European Jew in German and German Jewish Consciousness, 1800–1923* (Madison: University of Wisconsin Press, 1982). 186–209. See also Shulamit Volkov, "The Dynamics of Dissimilation: Ostjuden and German Jews," in *The Jewish Response to German Culture: From the Enlightenment to the Second World War*, ed. Jehuda Reinharz and Walter Schatzberg (Hanover, NH: University Press of New England, 1991).

15 Rosa Schapire, "Über den Maler Lasar Segall," *Kündung: Eine Zeitschrift für Kunst* 2 (February 1921), translated in Heller, "'His Sole Subject Is Suffering Humanity': Lasar Segall in Germany, 1906–1923," in *Still More Distant Journeys: The Artistic Emigrations of Lasar Segall*. Ed. Stephanie D'Alessandro and Reinhold Heller (Chicago: David and Alfred Smart Museum of Art, 1997), 98–99.

16 From Schmidt's introduction to Segall's portfolio, Bubu, translated in Heller, "'His Sole Subject Is Suffering Humanity': Lasar Segall in Germany, 1906–1923," in *Still More Distant Journeys: The Artistic Emigrations of Lasar Segall*. Ed. Stephanie D'Alessandro and Reinhold Heller (Chicago: David and Alfred Smart Museum of Art, 1997), 103.

17 Segall struggled with the tension between these two roles. His focus on Jewish themes was generally vague and universalist, never succumbing to the folkloric themes and mysticism of

than a source of collective ease, Jewish symbols were critical elements in the constructions of a universalizing alterity, which included the artist himself. In this capacity, Segall's work emanates from what cultural theorist Walter Mignolo calls a "border," that is, one of the "epistemic and territorial *frontiers*" that produce a hybrid or double positionality. This position, according to Mignolo, causes one "to think from both traditions and, at the same time, from neither of them," facilitating a critique in two directions.[18] Not entirely conforming to mainstream currents of German art, nor fully outside key practices and philosophies, Segall's work occupied an interstitial space of modernism. His imagery transcended dominant tropes of the Other, contravening the romantic mysticism associated with an imagined *shtetl* culture and the raw exoticism on the non-Western savage.[19] To the contrary, Segall's imagery invokes a broadly universalist "primitive" identity that subverts such narrow particularities.

Segall recognized the capacity for a type of border painting in his own territorial origins and displacements. Born into the Russian-occupied region that is modern-day Lithuania, he attributed an ability "to transcend the limits imposed by tradition" to the "intermediate geographic position" of his youth.[20] In Germany he was treated with suspicion during World War I and was briefly interned as an enemy combatant. Ironically, at nearly the same time the avant-garde revered him as the venerated Other, owing largely to the quasicolonial position his

---

Marc Chagall, with whom he was often compared, or the German-Jewish avant-garde; indeed, he distanced himself from the latter in opposition to the movement's Zionist position. Likewise, in 1922 he declined an invitation by Polish modernist Jankel Adler inviting him to exhibit in the Russian-Jewish section of "Erste Internationale Kunstausstellung" (First International Art Exhibition), opting instead to enter with the Dresden Secessionists, listing his residence as Dresden and his nationality as Russian. Segall had participated in a Russian exhibition in Hannover the prior year, further indication of his trepidation about a specifically Jewish designation. Addler's invitation is discussed in Mattos, *Lasar Segall, expressionismo e judaísmo: o período alemão de 1906–1923* (São Paulo: Editora Perspectiva, 2000), 171. Segall's participation is documented in Gabriele Horn, "Segall und Deutschland," in *Lasar Segall, 1891–1957: Malerei, Zeichnungen, Druckgrafik, Skulptur* (Berlin: Staatliche Kunsthalle Berlin, 1990), 33–36.

18 Walter Mignolo, "Border Thinking and the Colonial Difference," in *Local Histories/Global Designs: Coloniality, Subaltern Knowledges, and Border Thinking* (Princeton, NJ: Princeton University Press, 2000), 67.

19 Claudia Valladão de Mattos discusses Segall's departure from modernists associated with Germany's Jewish Renaissance, particularly the folkloric mysticism of Marc Chagall, in *Lasar Segall: Expressionism e Judaísmo* (São Paulo: Editora Perspectiva, 2000), 140–157. For a discussion of Segall's relation to German primitivism, see Edith A. G. Wolfe, *Melancholy Encounter: Lasar Segall and the Brazilian Avant-Garde* (PhD diss., University of Texas at Austin, 2005), 67–86.

20 Lasar Segall, "O Expressionismo," in *Lasar Segall: Textos, depoimentos e exposições* (São Paulo: Museu Lasar Segall, 1993), 41.

homeland assumed during the German occupation. Segall's art of the period suggests as much identification with the colonial Other as with the German artists who imagined this Other. Heightening the cogency of his interstitial gaze, Segall ultimately lost all national identity. After the war, like many Poles and Russians he was stripped of statehood and citizenship as victorious forces remapped Central Europe. Thus, Segall arrived in Brazil in January 1924 a true universal citizen, carrying no passport nor carrying return passage.[21]

Brazilian modernism and the self as other

Segall's sense of isolation increased in the early 1920s with the accelerating political imperatives of German modernism. Zehder, who envisioned the Gruppe 1919 as "storm troopers of Expressionism," had left the group disgusted by their political apathy, followed by Felixmuller, who lamented his failure to conscript Segall and Dix, inveighing that "Segall [...] was a Jew and a Pole, a foreigner – for that reason he could belong to no German party. Dix [said] – leave me alone with your stupid politics. I'd rather go to a brothel."[22] Felixmuller's recriminations divulge the substance of Segall's growing unease in Germany. If his inability to participate in partisan politics explained his disregard for the increasingly ideological forms of German art, he derived little more comfort from the sardonic and Dadaesque social critiques that occupied Dix. Segall remained an idealist and a romantic, doggedly pursuing first-generation ideals of spiritual humanism as they waned in relevance to his German cohort.[23] He longed to escape political distractions. In his memoirs he recalled,

> After all accounts, there was only fatigue [...] of the interior tension of the post-war years [...] of the sterile and interminable discussions and artistic struggles that had little to do with art anymore, degenerating, for the most part, to politics of art, commerce and speculation

---

21 Segall traveled on Nansen Papers. Named after the high commissioner for refugees for the League of Nations, Dr. Fridtjof Nansen, these travel documents were initially awarded to Russians fleeing the Bolshevik Revolution and eventually distributed to many refugee communities between the wars. Segall's documents are in the Arquivo Lasar Segall, São Paulo.
22 Joan Weinstein, *The End of Expressionism: Art and the November Revolution in Germany, 1918–1919* (Chicago: University of Chicago Press, 1990), 158.
23 Moreover, as a foreigner he was undoubtedly anxious about the increasing government repression against his overtly critical colleagues, a risk he was ill disposed to take.

of art, programs, theories, etc. [...] I longed for a change of physical and spiritual climate. It was then that the idea to move to Brazil began to dominate my thoughts.[24]

He began to contemplate a move to Brazil, where he would fully immerse himself in his incomplete universalist project.

Here it is instructive to return to the notion of the artist "going away." The search for a "primitive" culture, uncorrupted by "civilization," most famously personified by Gauguin in Tahiti, inevitably left the sanguine artist disillusioned, confronted with the global realities of contact and colonialism that allowed the West to imagine the Other in the first place.[25] In the case of Segall, the terms were inverted, yet the end would be the same. On one hand, were he engaged in this type of going away, as some scholars have suggested, he would never have gone to São Paulo, which at the time was one of the fastest-growing cities in the Americas, if not the world. On the other hand, however, Segall's fantasy of a Brazil free of the politics of nationalism, where art and ideology occupied separate realms, could not have been further from artistic and political reality.

Upon his arrival in São Paulo, Segall was swept into a mounting cultural revolution, deeply imbricated with local and national politics. In 1922 many of the artists and intellectuals who would become his inner circle had organized the Week of Modern Art (*Semana de Arte Moderna*). A three-day spectacle of avant-garde art, music, and literature, the deliberately iconoclastic event targeted academic artificiality and the Eurocentrism associated with the Republican ruling class. Participants derided the sentimental, salon-style images of noble Indian maidens and classicizing European nudes produced in the National School of Fine Arts (*Escola Nacional de Belas Artes*) as *passadista* and *retardário*[26]; they charged that such imagery stigmatized Brazil as parochial and dependent on Europe.[27] The modernists demanded cultural autonomy, declaring their mission "to

---

24 Lasar Segall, "Minhas recordações," in *Lasar Segall: Textos, depoimentos e exposições* (São Paulo: Museu Lasar Segall, 1993), 25.
25 On the relation between primitivism in modern art and imperialism, see Susan Hiller, ed., *The Myth of Primitivism: Perspectives on Art* (London: Routledge, 1991); Sally Price, *Primitive Art in Civilized Places* (Chicago: University of Chicago Press, 2002); and Tim Barringer and Tom Flynn, eds., *Colonialism and the Object: Empire, Material Culture, and the Museum* (London: Routledge, 1998).
26 *Passadista* is an invented term ridiculing academicians as antithetical to *modernista*, or "modernist," and *retardário* is the figurative equivalent of "retrograde" but literally is "retarded."
27 Although complaints were aimed largely at the literary old guard and the Parnassianism that ruled the Academia Brasileira de Letras (Brazilian Academy of Letters), the event launched an

Brazilianize the Brazilian."[28] Urging nativist introspection, they implored, "Forget the marble of the Acropolis and the towers of the Gothic cathedrals. We are the sons of the hills and the forests. Stop thinking of Europe. Think of America."[29]

The rhetoric of the Week of Modern Art resonated with increasing opposition to Brazil's Old Republic (1888–1930) and a growing power struggle between heavily industrialized São Paulo and the capitol in Rio de Janeiro. Despite São Paulo's economic influence, the bourgeoisie remained excluded from a corrupt national political system controlled by the landed oligarchy. Moreover, critics derided liberal efforts to modernize Brazil in the image of Europe for having increased rather than decreased inequality and precluded national conciliation. Intellectuals and professionals – in law schools, medical schools, and the emerging social sciences – began to reexamine the particularities of Brazil's colonial and Afro-Brazilian history in search of autochthonous solutions to the problems of the nation. Segall's presence served the movement's call for artistic renovation and its underlying political purposes. Not only did his decision to locate to São Paulo (and not Rio de Janeiro) validate a sense of regional superiority, but also his very move to Brazil represented a reversal of the hierarchical influence between metropolis and colony associated with Republican neocolonialism. Whereas the academy sent Brazilian artists to Europe to assimilate the trappings of Western "civilization," Segall had come to São Paulo of his own volition, attracted not by the lure of the "primitive" but by the promises of modernity.[30]

By 1926 Segall had divorced his German wife, married into an elite Brazilian family, and adopted Brazilian citizenship, a transformation depicted in the lan-

---

implicit assault against the artistic equivalent in the Escola Nacional. See Aracy A. Amaral, *Artes plásticas na Semana de 22* (São Paulo: Editora 34, 1998).
28 Cited in David T. Haberly, *Three Sad Races: Racial Identity and National Consciousness in Brazilian Literature* (Cambridge, England: Cambridge University Press, 1983), 128.
29 From a lecture titled "A pintura e a escultura moderna do Brasil," quoted in E. Bradford Burns, *A History of Brazil* (New York: Columbia University Press, 1993), 327–328.
30 One of the modernists' principal objections to academic pedagogy was the National Academy's continued practice of awarding the Premio da Viagem ao Exterior (Travel Abroad Prize) to outstanding students each term to study in France with the last remaining salon-style practitioners and not with modern painters. Paulistas (who issued their own travel prize) condemned this policy as perpetuating the academy's anachronistic profile. Therefore, it was significant that Segall's attraction to Brazil was not inspired by the promise of imagined primitive splendor that had captivated foreign and national artists alike; rather, his presence was the result of the high levels of modernity offered by metropolitan São Paulo (and most definitively not the capital). This is confirmed in much of the language of the press surrounding Segall's arrival. See Edith A. G. Wolfe, *Melancholy Encounter: Lasar Segall and the Brazilian Avant-Garde* (PhD diss., University of Texas at Austin, 2005), 129–134.

guage of modernist nationalism in his self-portrait, *Encounter* (1924; Figure 5). Darkening his skin, painting his lips in a deep salmon, and giving himself a dense head of tight curls, Segall appears to have recast himself as the modernist archetype, as the Brazilian mulatto. The mixed-race Afro-Brazilian was a critical countersymbol in the modernist struggle against the Eurocentric dictates of the academy and Republican hegemony. Deeply concerned with the demographic "consequences" of abolition in 1888, liberal statesmen sought to reverse determinist predictions of racial degeneration by soliciting European immigration to "whiten" the nation. Academic norms reinforced oligarchic fantasies of a Hellenized Brazil, institutionalizing the superior moral and physical beauty of European stock and the unparalleled artistic achievement of the Greeks to the absolute exclusion of peoples of African descent.[31]

Modernism parodied the racial anxieties of elite society by embracing often pejorative tropes of blackness, projecting them outward as positive assertions of cultural nationalism. Tarsila do Amaral unveiled a disfigured and voluptuous African nude in 1923 that flew in the face of the conservative values and misgivings. Far from the submissive, reclining, alabaster nudes that dominated the national salons, *The Negresse* (1923; Figure 6) sits upright, solid, defiant, and fecund, a counterhegemonic archetype of ethnonational identity. The image bespeaks Amaral's intimate relation with the Parisian avant-garde. Many of the most influential figures in the development of Paulista modernism took lengthy sojourns in Paris, participating actively in Surrealist circles captivated by both *art nègre* and Brazilian culture.[32] Like their European peers, Brazilians sketched in the Trocadeiro Museum, frequented the Russian Ballet, and attended world expositions that exhibited art, antiquities, and people from colonial territories, yet unlike the French, the Brazilians did not encounter the "Other" in these sanctified spaces of non-Western difference but discovered an equally imagined and essentialized "Self." The same year that Tarsila painted *The Negresse*, Oswald de

---

[31] The dearth of academic representations of Afro-Brazilian themes is apparent in their absence from the numerous recent publications that attempt to survey Brazilian representations of blackness, including Carlos Eugênio Marcondes de Moura, *A travessia da Calunga Grande: três séculos de imagens sobre o negro no Brasil, 1637–1899* (São Paulo: EDUSP, 2000); *Negro de corpo e alma*, Vol. 12 in *Mostra do redescobrimento* (São Paulo: Fundação Bienal de São Paulo: Associação Brasil 500 Anos Artes Visuais, 2000); and Emanoel Araujo, *A mão afro-brasileira: significado da contribuição artística e histórica* (São Paulo: Tenenge, 1998). Although there is a rich tradition of *costumbrista* paintings of rural genre themes that feature blacks and slaves, "elite" production is limited to portraiture, generally self-commissioned by members of the black elite.

[32] The group included Swiss poet Blaise Cendrars, composer Darius Milhaud, poet Jean Cocteau, painters Fernand Lèger and Andre Lhote, and sculptor Constantin Brancusi.

Figure 5. Lasar Segall, *Encounter*, 1924. Oil on canvas, 66 × 54 cm. Acervo do Museu Lasar Segall – IBRAM/MinC-Brasil.

Andrade announced to a rapt audience at the Sorbonne that in Brazil, "Black is a realist element," proclaiming, "Nothing is more modern than the Indian chant and the African drum."[33]

Although the Brazilians exhibited a level of comfort with their role as Europe's Other that Segall did not, negotiating primitivist stereotypes of difference with Brazil's industrial realities elicited a hybrid aesthetic that, at least superficially, aligned the two bodies of imagery. In a precocious engagement with the postcolonial condition, Brazilian artists and writers of the 1920s celebrated cultural impurity, exploring the rich contradictions produced by the meteoric pace of development in the country. Their Brazilian "reality" reflected neither the pure difference imagined in the non-Western "primitive," nor the pure sameness desired by the Eurocentric liberal Republic, but rather inhabited the often paradoxical spaces in between.[34] Mario de Andrade, who once declared himself a "Tupi playing a lute,"[35] narrated the antics of his anti-hero Macunaíma in an error-laden vernacular that rejected the pure Portuguese mandated by the National Academy.[36] The composite personification of Brazil's European, Indian, and Af-

---

[33] Oswald de Andrade, "O esforço intelectual do Brasil contemporâneo," in *Brasil: primeiro tempo modernista 1917/29, documentação*, ed. Marta Rossetti Batista, Telê Porto Ancona Lopez, and Yone Soares de Lima (São Paulo: Instituto de Estudos Brasileiros, 1972), 210. Andrade's lecture enjoyed wide and immediate circulation, published within months in France in the *Revue d l'Amerique Latine* and in Brazil in the *Revista do Brasil*.

[34] Nicolau Sevcenko discusses the ironic coexistence of the modern and the premodern, citing the sale of "Bélikens," small talismans, to raise money for a monument to positivist intellectual Olavo Bilac, and medical students funding a pioneering radiotherapy institute by selling images of Saci, a trickster from local mythology. Nicolau Sevcenko, *Orfeu extático na metrópole: São Paulo, sociedade e cultura nos frementes anos 20* (São Paulo: Companhia das Letras, 1992), 225–227. A fascination with such contradictions informs contemporary press accounts of the city and the modernist movement. See for instance Francisco de Assis Chateaubriand, "Como São Paulo está cultivando a arte moderna," in *Brasil: Primeiro tempo modernista 1917/29, documentação*, ed. Marta Rossetti Batista, Telê Porto Ancona Lopez, and Yone Soares de Lima (São Paulo: Instituto de Estudos Brasileiros, USP, 1972), 118–19. This resonates with Néstor García Canclini's theorization of Latin America's "multitemporal heterogeneity," the product of the failure of modernization to entirely subsume premodern social and cultural orders, thus fostering a nonhierarchical relation of high, low, and popular culture in avant-garde art and literature. *Culturas híbridas: Estrategias para entrar y salir de la modernidad* (Mexico City: Grijalbo, 1989).

[35] Mário de Andrade, *Hallucinated city = Paulicea desvairada*, trans. Jack E. Tomlins (Nashville, TN: Vanderbilt University Press, 1968).

[36] In a letter to Tarsila do Amaral, dated 1 December 1924, Mario de Andrade defended his errors, explaining, "They are correct in Brazilian, my current language." In Aracy Amaral, ed., *Correspondência Mário de Andrade & Tarsila do Amaral* (São Paulo: EDUSP, 1999), 89. On Andrade's cultivation of errors and the national imaginary, see Esther Gabara's fascinating analysis of the

Figure 6. Tarsila do Amaral, *The Negresse,* 1923. Oil on canvas, 100 × 81.3 cm. Museu de Arte Contemporânea da Universidade de São Paulo (MAC/USP), São Paulo.

---

poet's photography in *Errant Modernism: The Ethos of Photography in Mexico and Brazil* (Durham, NC: Duke University Press, 2008).

rican ethnicities, Andrade's motley protagonist traverses asphalt boulevards that meet mud roads and mingle with "primeval dust." Oswald de Andrade's Brazilwood (*Pau Brasil*) program for national literary reform published the same year similarly called for the rejection of Portuguese "archaisms" and an embrace of "the millionaire contribution of all mistakes."[37] His fragmented bricolage of the Brazilian character collapses a panorama of seeming opposites; "Wagner yields to the samba schools," "Black women" visit "the Jockey Club," and Brazil's "credulous race" practices "geometry, algebra and chemistry," emphasizing a "dual heritage" that subsumes a legacy of (neo)colonial disadvantage within rich metaphors of postcolonial advantage.

Tarsila do Amaral cultivated an analogous visual vernacular resulting in pictures that in many ways approximated those of Segall. Undertaking her own anti-academic "erring," Amaral rejected one-point perspective and adopted the simplified forms of naive painting and the garish colors of the popular landscape to represent rural and industrial landscapes as indistinguishable elements of Brazil's hybrid modernity.[38] Works such as *Favela Hill* (Figure 7) resonated with Oswald's "dual heritage," evoking uncertain artistic bloodlines from the calculated geometries and machine aesthetic of French Purism or the spontaneity of local visual culture. Moreover, the culturally heterogeneous favelas – destination of generations of rural migrants and thus elaborated as enclaves of Afro-Brazilian culture and tradition in an urban context – epitomized modernism's porous and pluralistic ideal of *brasilidade* (Brazilianness).

Favela culture and São Paulo's urban Afro-Brazilians, likewise, fascinated Segall. In 1923 he described the city in terms of a "dualism" he found "unbelievably arousing," writing,

> The most wonderful thing here, apart from the primitiveness of the surroundings, is to observe the expanse and progress in the city. Nowhere else are so many buildings being built as in São Paulo. Skyscrapers, whole neighborhoods, whole avenues emerge and among them Mulattos, Negroes move in their phlegmatic rhythms.[39]

---

[37] Oswald de Andrade, *Brazilwood Manifesto*, in *Art in Latin America: The Modern Era, 1820–1980*, ed. Dawn Ades (New Haven, CT: Yale University Press, 1989), 310.

[38] Amaral described her process of liberation from her academic training, which occurred on a trip to Minas Gerais, explaining, "I found in Minas the colors that I loved as a child. I was taught later that they were ugly and common. I obeyed the monotonous routine of refined tastes. [...] But later I retaliated against this oppression, passing it on to my canvases: pure, pure blue, pink violations, live yellow, singing green, all in more or less strong gradations." Cited in Aracy Amaral, *Tarsila: Sua obra e seu tempo* (São Paulo: Tenenge, 1986), 121–122.

[39] Unpublished correspondence from Lasar Segall to "Herr Brattskoven," 8 July 1927, Arquivo Lasar Segall.

Figure 7. Tarsila do Amaral, *Favela Hill*, 1924. Oil on canvas, 64.5 × 76 cm. Coleção Hecilda e Sérgio Fadel, Río de Janeiro.

Encounter invokes a parallel urban heterogeneity, challenging European stereotypes and seeming to reinforce modernist discourse. The modern skyscraper dwarfs the tropical foliage, and the non-European man dons the cosmopolitan suit and tie. Indeed, non-Western culture trumps nature, depicted as male, urban, and contemporary. Yet despite the correspondence of symbols and iconography, Segall's self-portrait must be read as a declaration of alterity internal to his allegiance to his new homeland. The sobriety of the odd encounter, in which the couple grasp hands yet stare absently past one another, suggests an existential alienation despite social interaction, while the litany of conjoined opposites (black–white, male–female, self–other) at once contests and reinscribes difference.

Segall's palette and imagery so closely approximated Brazilian modernism that critics championed his "Brazilianization." At the same time, his melancholy portraits contravened the celebratory tone of modernism's reformist nationalism, giving even his most ardent supporters pause. Commending "authentically" Brazilian motifs, consistent with the nationalist vocabulary such as "the banana plantation and the black man," critics lauded "Lasar, Brazilian style."[40] "Naturalized Brazilian, everything that emerges from his paintbrush is also naturalized."[41] His melancholy, on the other hand, originated elsewhere, attributed to an innate and foreign ethnic predisposition at odds with his perceived Brazilianization. "Like all his Russian compatriots, he has a natural intuition toward tragedy, innate to their fatigued nationalities, characteristic of their millenary suffering,"[42] went one account, while another identified in his paintings "the stoicism of the children of Israel."[43]

The thinly veiled reference to Segall's Jewishness and the ambivalence toward his position in Brazilian art and society betrays the large corpus of images of immigrants and Jews included in the exhibition yet consistently excluded from reviews. In Brazil, Segall continued to portray people uprooted by the rapid social and economic transformations occurring globally, returning to themes prefigured by his work in Germany in images such as *Eternal Wanderers*. In the analogous works *Black Mother Among Houses* (1930; Figure 8) and *Mother and Children Among Sky Scrapers* (c. 1929; Figure 9), for instance, Segall casts the Afro-Brazilian and European (Jewish) immigrant as indistinguishable actors in an existential drama of urbanization and migration. In *Black Mother Among Houses* the colorful, aleatory houses of the favela consume a plaintive Afro-Brazilian mother. With a wide-eyed infant on her back, she is besieged on all sides by the encroaching urban environment. In a virtual mirror image, *Mother and Children Among Sky Scrapers*, Segall replaces the Afro-Brazilian with the European immigrant and the colorful human favela with the drab monochrome of the industrial metropolis. Also with children in tow, the transplanted matriarch wanders disoriented through the dense wilderness of skyscrapers that threatens to asphyxiate its human occupants.

Both the social urgency and the inclusion of symbols outside the Brazilian vocabulary threatened the coherence of modernism's construction of an inclusive nationalism. Indeed, black rural migrants from the country's drought-ridden interior and European immigrants navigated Brazil's industrial terra incognita side by side, lending an explicitly sociopolitical dimension to Segall's spiritual universalism. Although critics went to great lengths to identify national themes in Segall's work, designating images of Afro-Brazilians and lush tropical landscapes as the "clearest and most legitimate documents of Brasilidade," themes

---

40 Zagus [pseud. Geraldo Ferraz] Ferraz, "Notas de arte," *Diário de Noite* (16 January 1928).
41 "Uma exposição de Segall no Rio de Janeiro," *O Jornal* (30 May 1928).
42 "Vida artística: exposição de pintura," *Folha da Manhã* (26 December 1927).
43 "A inquietação contempôrania," *Diario de Noite* (29 October 1926).

Figure 8. Lasar Segall, *Black Mother Among Houses*, 1930. Watercolor on paper, 38 × 51 cm. Acervo do Museu Lasar Segall – IBRAM/MinC-Brasil.

outside this paradigm forced critics to qualify their position.[44] Even critic Geraldo Ferraz later tempered Segall's assimilation with a measured disclaimer: "He has identified in part with the country where he lives," adding, "One hears in his cries a Slav with *caboclo* accents."[45] Segall is the Slav who speaks *like* the cabo-

---

44 "Uma exposição de Segall no Rio de Janeiro," *O Jornal* (30 May 1928).
45 Zagus [pseud. Geraldo Ferraz] Ferraz, "Notas de arte," *Diário de Noite* (16 January 1928). "Caboclo" is a reference to the mixed-race backwoods people of the Brazilian interior, celebrated in contemporaneous naturalist literature as representative of Brazilian authenticity. Even his close friend and admirer poet Mário de Andrade ultimately broke ties with Segall on the basis of an ethnic incompatibility attributed to Segall's Jewishness. In a 1942 correspondence he explained his frustrations with Segall, writing, "He does not hold any hope of friendship for me. [...] I am unable to like the 'man' Lasar Segall, although I recognize that some of his defects possibly derive more from his race than from him individually. Beyond any doubt, race is not what bothers me, but that he has acquired many of his unpleasant ways of being from the injustices and persecution that they have suffered for two thousand years." Letter dated July 7, 1942, reproduced in Annateresa Fabris, ed., *Portinari, amico mio: cartas de Mário de Andrade a Candido Portinari* (Campinas: Mercado de Letras, 1995), 101–105.

Figure 9. Lasar Segall, *Mother and Children Among Sky Scrapers*, c. 1929. Drypoint etching on paper, 21 × 24 cm. Acervo do Museu Lasar Segall – IBRAM/MinC-Brasil.

clo but is not the caboclo himself. While the association with the caboclo, the archetypical symbol of Paulista autonomy and Brazil's mixed-race authenticity, positions Segall's assimilation within nationalist paradigms that identify ethnic and cultural hybridity as the essential character of *brasilidade*, his Slavic retention precludes full entry into the nation. To be Brazilianized is to be emphatically *not* Brazilian.[46]

---

46 Referring to the inconsistencies of colonial mimesis in the Indian subcontinent, Homi Bhabha, "Of Mimicry and Man: The Ambivalence of Colonial Discourse," *October* 28 (1984): 128, concludes, "To be Anglicized is to be emphatically not English." Similarly, Mary Louise Pratt, *Imperial Eyes: Travel Writing and Transculturation* (New York: Routledge, 1992), 175, explores the distinction between "European" and "Europeanizing" in her discussion of Creole reinventions of America through art and literature aimed at earning legitimacy in Europe. The ambivalent, partial inclusion of Segall as "Brazilianized," in contrast to Brazilian, demonstrates the contingency of national identity declared and measured relative to a constantly changing Other.

The ambivalence with which critics regarded Segall reveals certain ideological underpinnings at odds with modernist allusions to a more authentic and inclusive Brazilian nationalism. On one hand, the nativist currents, particularly efforts to formalize a Brazilian vernacular, reflect a perceived threat to national culture posed by the tens of thousands of immigrants arriving in São Paulo annually. The call for patriotism and the "Brazilianization of Brazilians" voiced at the Week of Modern Art went hand in hand with the anti-immigrant rallying cry, "Brazil for Brazilians."[47] Despite Jews being one of the most assimilated ethnic groups, in nativist rhetoric they were one of the most emphatic markers of non-national alterity, retaining language, religion, and customs perceived as different from the national norm.[48] Even the well-established Jewish Brazilian family into which Segall married was described in some papers as a "foreign family" that was merely "residing in São Paulo."[49] Thus the images of Jews and Jewry disturbed Segall's otherwise "nationalist" oeuvre to reveal the ethnic exclusion within modernist paradigms of Brazilian hybridity and cultural pluralism.

Beyond this thematic variance, Segall's location of Afro-Brazilians in a distinct sociopolitical moment underscored, through contrast, Brazilian artists' treatment of the mulatto as a political symbol but not a political subject. The ideological struggles that underpinned Paulista modernism had little to do with the conditions of Afro-Brazilians. Indeed, as Randall Johnston has discussed, in its explicit illiberalism modernism was fundamentally antidemocratic. The modernist fascination with popular culture and autochthonous traditions served solely as an inspiration for aesthetic renewal within elite artistic and literary production and in no way implied "a redistribution of economic or even symbolic goods."[50] This hedonistic phase of nationalist modernism ended with

---

47 A 1920 São Paulo presidential campaign warned, "Assimilate or be assimilated!" declaring, "Brazilians are in danger of reverting [...] from land owners to *colonos* [wage agricultural laborers] working for foreigners, who will take over! The nationalist reaction will, therefore, necessarily be a cultural reaction through national supremacy." Quoted in Sevcenko, *Orfeu extático na metrópole: São Paulo, sociedade e cultural nos frementes anos 20* (São Paulo: Companhia das Letras, 1992), 245–246.
48 Jeffrey Lesser, *Welcoming the Undesirables: Brazil and the Jewish Question* (Berkeley: University of California Press, 1995).
49 Manoel Bandeira, "A exposição de Lasar Segall," *A Provincia* (19 August 1928).
50 "Consonant with nationalist currents of authoritarian thought generally including its emphasis on the need for dominance of enlightened elites," modernism conformed to a political and judicial ideology that pursued "institutional modernization through nationalist authoritarianism." An enlightened elite took it upon themselves to reorganize culture and society and lead by example. Randal Johnson, "The Dynamics of the Brazilian Literary Field, 1930–1945," *Luso-Brazilian Review* 31.2 (1994): 8–10.

the Great Depression and the Revolution of 1930 that replaced the Old Republic with a populist, authoritarian state. Oswald de Andrade denounced his bourgeois past and embraced Marxism, and Tarsila do Amaral adopted social realist currents after a visit to the Soviet Union, all transformations anticipated in the work of Segall yet ones that Segall himself would repudiate as threatening art's autonomy.

Modernism's hybrid aesthetic of the 1920s challenged the dominant social and artistic order while asserting non-European cultural autonomy; nevertheless, much of its rhetoric merely collapsed the colonialist binaries that structured difference, without undermining such tropes or the racialist ideologies that underlay them. Thus, although the originality and primacy of Brazilian modernism's postcolonial aesthetic warrant recognition, Segall's counterexample reveals the limits of modernist enunciation. Modernist art and literature objectified a national Other, redefining the Afro-Brazilian and Amer-Indian in terms of an urban, anti-Republican, and ultimately cosmopolitan cultural politics. That is, they appropriated symbols of Brazil's subaltern populations to represent their own political disenfranchisement and to redress Brazil's legacies of inequality with Europe. However, despite their construction of a collective Brazilian Self defined as Europe's Other, constructions of this Brazilian Other provided little subjectivity to those represented, assimilating difference into a broad imaginary of national hybridity. Segall's border identity facilitated a transcendence of such programmatic parameters, scarcely perceptible in his representation of Brazil yet emphatically evident in the ambivalence surrounding the artist and his work relative to nationalist paradigms.

Diaspora, displacement, and Segall's counterculture of modernity

Yet I want to stress that the critique posed by Segall's work goes beyond the mere production of contrasting symbols of a Brazilian reality. That is, it is not just *that* he paints images of Jews, but what his images of Jews (and blacks) – his universalizing construction of alterity – represent, which I contend poses a broader critique of modernity and challenges the universalist claims of the avant-garde modernist project writ large. Far from a condemnation of modernity akin to those embodied in the utopian alterimage of the "primitive," Segall's work emanates from a "counter-culture of modernity," presenting often dystopian accounts of the "dark side" of the Enlightenment project and modern progress.⁵¹ Images such as *Black Mother Among Houses* and *Mother and Children Among Sky Scrapers* do not portray those uncorrupted by Western culture or those assimilated into the fabric of a pluralistic modern nation but rather those thoroughly modern subjects excluded from the universal promises of modernity and the comforts of belonging.

Examined as a whole, Segall's production during his first years in Brazil constructs a critical counternarrative to both the universalizing imaginaries of European "primitivism" and Brazilian mythologies of national belonging, identifying diaspora and the shared realities of migration, exile, and displacement as the defining experience of the modern condition. Ships and sailors represent not only the physical motion across space, the fanlike dispersal of Europeans and Africans into the New World, but also ties and communications between the old country and the new, as these ships crisscross the oceans, moving across *and back*, transporting peoples, traditions, and ideas between nations and across borders.⁵² For Segall, ships were a truly cosmopolitan space, where place and nation functioned relative to imagination.

On his first ocean voyage to Amsterdam in 1912, Segall had marveled at the spectacle of multinationalism:

> I visited ports. For the first time in my life I saw the sea and I saw ships. I saw how men of all nationalities boarded these ships and continued for distant and unknown lands, impelled by the destiny of the "stuff of the other" [*algo de outro*]. I was also attracted to these remote lands; my destiny also impelled me toward them.⁵³

Fulfilling what he perceived as his own migratory predestination, intrigued by the "stuff of the other," Segall sailed to Brazil, accumulating the essential visual vocabulary for his diasporic universe. "I was en route for four weeks," he recalled, "between the sky and the ocean, surrounded by humanity, by 'emigrants,'

---

51 Gilroy's interpretation of various forms of black expression not as premodern or nonmodern cultural attributes but as thoroughly modern, ethically constituted critiques of the shortcomings of modernity anticipates Mignolo's similar critique of coloniality. *The Black Atlantic: Modernity and Double-Consciousness* (Cambridge, MA: Harvard University Press, 1995).

52 In his theorization a diasporic counterculture of modernity, Gilroy discusses the central organizing symbol of the ship, representing the "micro-systems of linguistic and political hybridity" that characterize the diasporic experience. Gilroy, *The Black Atlantic: Modernity and Double-Consciousness* (Cambridge, MA: Harvard University Press, 1995), 13–17.

53 Segall, "Minhas recordações," in *Lasar Segall: textos, depoimentos, exposições* (São Paulo: Museu Lasar Segall, Biblioteca Jenny K. Segall, Fundação Nacional Pró-Memória, 1985), 14.

human beings with longing and nostalgia, with hope and disappointment."⁵⁴ Countless sketches and paintings of immigrants and immigrant ships invoke this experience, such as *Emigrants* (1929; Figure 10), which conveys a metaphysical desolation and the general anxiety of modernity through the diminutive scale of the huddled, wearied travelers, consumed by the enormous mechanics of the inhuman ship. The sense of social and spiritual dispossession and the intense apprehension of an unknown destination echoes *Black Mother Among Houses* and *Mother and Children Among Sky Scrapers*, locating such maritime imagery within a broader pictorial program.

It is less the immigrant per se than the repeated inclusion of black sailors manning the decks of the immigrant ship that represent Segall's most cogent metaphors of modern rootlessness and wandering. In *Sailors and Immigrants on the Deck* (c. 1929; Figure 11), the prominently positioned black sailor guides bearded and shrouded passengers toward Brazilian shores. The figure of the sailor personifies the idea of circulation; he lives his life on the seas, himself a vessel of travel and knowledge. Moreover, in the symbolic context of flight and exile, the black sailor invokes an association between the slave ship and the immigrant ship that engages both the origins of modernity and its unspoken consequences.⁵⁵ Segall's rendering of the trans-Atlantic voyage unites the black, the immigrant, and the Jew in a shared identity based in "routes" rather than "roots."⁵⁶ They are a link between the old and the new, between families and communities separated by exile. And for refugees, as for slaves, ships also represented the hope for return, either real or redemptive, a notion that facilitates "border thinking" and troubles traditional limiting concepts of nationalism.

Segall ultimately abstracts his representations of ships into the simple peaked form of the vessel's bow, rising like a Gothic arch above the sea. His employment of this schematic form to a variety of situations reinforces the metaphoric connotations of the ship as the universal brotherhood of man produced by the shared experience of diaspora. Therefore, the boat in his 1939 magnum opus *Immigrant Ship* (Figure 12) crowded with a dense multitude of humanity, mirrors the form of the slave ship in an illustration for Jorge de Lima's *Black Poems* (*Poemas negros*, 1947; Figure 13). Both images evoke the turmoil and an-

---

54 Segall, "Minhas recordações," in *Lasar Segall: textos, depoimentos, exposições* (São Paulo: Museu Lasar Segall, Biblioteca Jenny K. Segall, Fundação Nacional Pró-Memória, 1985), 14.
55 Gilroy, *The Black Atlantic: Modernity and Double-Consciousness* (Cambridge, MA: Harvard University Press, 1995), 13–17.
56 Gilroy, *The Black Atlantic: Modernity and Double-Consciousness* (Cambridge, MA: Harvard University Press, 1995), 13–17.

guish of displacement. They depict a new community of the disinherited, united by the holds of the transatlantic vessel.

Figure 12. Lasar Segall, *Immigrant Ship*, 1939–1941. Oil with sand on canvas, 230 × 275 cm. Acervo do Museu Lasar Segall – IBRAM/MinC-Brasil.

Segall reproduced this same arched form in numerous drawings of favelas, a gesture that reaffirmed the immutable alterity shared by the Jew and the black. Like the immigrant ship and the slave ship, the favela is rendered within the iconic and symbolic peak, here outlining the rising hill, rather than the boat's forward-pointing bow. Images like *Favela* (1930; Figure 14) depict the crowded, disordered, and impoverished rural landscape of the favela rising between the posh, modern apartment buildings of Rio's elite beachside neighborhoods of Ipanema and Copacabana. Virtually void of any human presence and rendered with ruler straight lines, the high-rise dwellings represent the controlled rationality of modernity and the estranging effect of dictating normative social and cultural identities. Yet in Brazil, according to Segall, modernity includes its Other, a dualism symbolized by the cacophony of robust humanity, which the artist encloses

Figure 13. Lasar Segall illustration for Jorge de Lima's *Poemas negras* (Rio de Janeiro: Editora O Construtor, 1947).

within the silent frame of progress. Like both his slave ship and his immigrant ship, the arched area is crowded with humanity, estranged by the pictorial delimitations yet thriving within them. In the case of the favela dwellers, however, their social and cultural dispossession and their duality are signaled not by their isolation on the sea but rather by their insulation within dominant, urban culture.

Figure 14. Lasar Segall, *Favela*, 1930. Drypoint etching on paper, 17.5 × 13.5 cm. Acervo do Museu Lasar Segall – IBRAM/MinC-Brasil.

Segall's interpretation of such a popular Brazilian literary and artistic subject as the favela positioned him within modernist currents. Yet it is from this position within that Segall's work issued its most profound critique. Whereas Brazilian modernism championed the favela as "the single defining thing that Brazil possesses in terms of art,"[57] depicting pristine yet hybrid spaces of national culture, Segall's renderings betray such utopian allusions to a racial democracy with dystopian realities of poverty and dispossession – not limited to Afro-Brazilians or Brazil but intrinsic to a universal modern condition. Segall's repetition of the shiplike arched form became an index of the ambivalent position of the immi-

---

57 Clemente, José, "O Brasil e o morro da Mangueira," Revista do Brasil, no. 6 (30 November 1926): 29–30.

grant and black to the nation and of the nation toward them, challenging fixed notions of identity and undermining claims of universal citizenship. Much later, with the production of his magnum opus *Immigrant Ship* in 1939 that likewise adopts this form, Segall elaborated on the philosophical motivation for his work. Invoking broad themes of exile and alterity that apply to all diasporic cultures, he recalled the story of an imaginary ship that

> sailed the seas without direction, a ship crammed full of men belonging to a certain race. Nobody wanted them. They were exiled from the world. [...] Long before the ship's start on its phantasmagorical voyage to the forbidden ports of this world, this state of spirit had already existed; it is powerfully reflected in the work to which I am dedicated.[58]

Segall's pictorial entrenchment of difference, through allusions to the shared marginality of the Jew and the black, pursued an alternative expression of humanism that acknowledged alterity within a broader universalism. Rather than allusions to the utopian fulfillment of the universal promises of the Enlightenment – be it in Brazilian modernism's new inclusive nationalism or the messianic humanism of prewar Expressionism – his particular brand of modernism voiced a dystopian mirror image that revealed the tensions and contradictions internal to modernity.

Conclusion

Positioned firmly within modernity and speaking via the language of avant-garde modernism, Segall nevertheless possessed a critical distance facilitated by his interstitial gaze that allowed him to subtly interrogate both projects from within. Perhaps Segall's representation of Brazil was the product of his "going away." He clearly idealized Brazil, although not as a tropical paradise but as a social manifestation of the universalism he struggled to capture in his art. Unlike his German predecessors, he neither sought nor encountered natives in an "original state" of nature, safely outside the dialectics of historical change. Closer to his Brazilian cohort, his representations of Brazil did not offer a timeless, ahistorical counterimage to the industrial world but rather suggested an alternative understanding of modernity that included the Other. But even here Segall departs from Brazilian aesthetics in his empathetic interrogation of this still imagined Other. For Segall the historical reality of diaspora and alterity – rather than the romantic ideal of national belonging – represented the defining experience of the mod-

---

58 Quoted in Jurandir Calcido, "Segall: A arte pura e o homem do povo," *Dietrizes* 48 (1943).

ern age. His work above all dramatizes the contact and clash of disparate worlds that resulted from forced migrations and the vagaries of modern capitalism – the other "universals" at the core of modern "civilization."

My argument that Segall's critique issues from his interstitial gaze does not preclude the border thinking and critical potential of Brazilian artists and intellectuals at the time. Indeed, Brazilian modernism emanated from a tripartite gaze that shifted frenetically from Europe to the Republican elite to a national Other and deftly navigated tropes of Brazilian difference through parody and adaptation. As I have argued, the ambiguities internal to Brazilian constructions of race and nation strongly affected the Brazilian reception of Segall's version of the national reality. Responses shifted schizophrenically between exaltation of his empathetic identification with local types and doubts about the absolute difference of the artist himself. The encounter between Segall and Brazilian modernism is rich in revisionist potential for a deeper understanding of avant-garde primitivism and international modernism. Both bodies of imagery negotiate stereotypes of non-Western peoples while posing a conscious self-identification through blackness as Europe's Other. Moreover, both engaged primitivism – through thematic references and the formal distortions and simplifications associated with popular and tribal art – to signify a collective sense of alterity. Yet the counternarratives expressed in these intersecting primitivizing gestures tell vastly different stories, reflecting the authors' and the cultures' distinct experiences with the "West." The introduction of these competing versions of modernity and identity into the dominant narrative of the international avant-garde strip the "primitive" of the ahistoric and monolithic appearance constructed in Western art and reveal an Other that is negotiated, nonessential, and heterogeneous.

References

Almeida, Guilherme de. "Lasar Segall: A exposição em São Paulo, um novo realismo." O Jornal (11 July 1928): 30.
Amaral, Aracy A. *Artes plásticas na Semana de 22* (São Paulo: Editora 34, 1998).
Amaral, Aracy A. (ed.). *Correspondência Mário de Andrade & Tarsila do Amaral* (São Paulo: EDUSP, 1999).
Amaral, Aracy A. *Tarsila, sua obra e seu tempo* (São Paulo: Tenenge, 1986).
Andrade, Mário de. *Hallucinated City = Paulicea desvairada*. Trans. Jack E. Tomlins (Nashville, TN: Vanderbilt University Press, 1968).
Andrade, Oswald de. *Brazilwood Manifesto*, in *Art in Latin America: The Modern Era, 1820–1980*. Ed. Dawn Ades (New Haven, CT: Yale University Press, 1989), 310–312.

Andrade, Oswald de. "O esforço intelectual do Brasil contemporâneo," in *Brasil: primeiro tempo modernista 1917/29, documentção*. Ed. Marta Rossetti Batista, Telê Porto Ancona Lopez, and Yone Soares de Lima (São Paulo: Instituto de Estudos Brasileiros, 1972).

Araujo, Emanoel. *A mão afro-brasileira: significado da contribuição artística e histórica* (São Paulo: Tenenge, 1998).

Aschheim, Steven E. *Brothers and Strangers: The East European Jew in German and German Jewish Consciousness, 1800–1923* (Madison: University of Wisconsin Press, 1982).

Bandeira, Manoel. "A exposição de Lasar Segall." A Provincia (19 August 1928).

Barringer, Tim, and Tom Flynn (eds.). *Colonialism and the Object: Empire, Material Culture and the Museum* (London: Routledge, 2012).

Bhabha, Homi. "Of Mimicry and Man: The Ambivalence of Colonial Discourse." *October* 28 (1984): 125.

Burns, E. Bradford. *A History of Brazil* (New York: Columbia University Press, 1993).

Calcido, Jurandir. "Segall: A arte pura e o homem do povo." *Dietrizes* 48 (1943).

Canclini, Néstor García. *Culturas híbridas: Estrategias para entrar y salir de la modernidad* (Mexico City: Grihalbo, 1989).

Chateaubriand, Francisco de Assis. "Como São Paulo está cultivando a arte moderna," in *Brasil: Primeiro tempo modernista 1917/29, documentação*. ed. Marta Rossetti Batista, Telê Porto Ancona Lopez, and Yone Soares de Lima (São Paulo: Instituto de Estudos Brasileiros, USP, 1972), 118–119.

D'Alessandro, Stephanie. "The Absorption of Spectacular, Unedited Things: Brazil in the Work of Lasar Segall," in *Still More Distant Journeys: The Artistic Emigrations of Lasar Segall*. Ed. Stephanie D'Alessandro and Reinhold Heller (Chicago: David and Alfred Smart Museum of Art, 1997), 110–160.

Einstein, Carl. *Negerplastik* (Munich: K. Wolff, 1920).

Fabris, Annateresa (ed.). *Portinari, amico mio: cartas de Mário de Andrade a Cândido Portinari* (Campinas: Mercado de Letras, 1995).

Ferraz, Zagus. "Notas de arte." *Diário de Noite* (16 January 1928).

Fuhrmann, Ernst. *Afrika: Sakralkulte Vorgeschichte der hieroglyphen* (Dresden: Folkwangverlag, 1922).

Gabara, Esther. *Errant Modernism: The Ethos of Photography in Mexico and Brazil* (Durham, NC: Duke University Press, 2008).

Gilroy, Paul. *The Black Atlantic: Modernity and Double Consciousness* (Cambridge, MA: Harvard University Press, 1995).

Haberly, David T. *Three Sad Races: Racial Identity and National Consciousness in Brazilian Literature* (Cambridge, England: Cambridge University Press, 1983).

Heller, Reinhold. "'His Sole Subject Is Suffering Humanity': Lasar Segall in Germany, 1906–1923," in *Still More Distant Journeys: The Artistic Emigrations of Lasar Segall*. Ed. Stephanie D'Alessandro and Reinhold Heller (Chicago: David and Alfred Smart Museum of Art, 1997), 26–106.

Hiller, Susan (ed.). *The Myth of Primitivism: Perspectives on Art* (London: Routledge, 1991).

Horn, Gabriele. "Segall und Deutschland," in *Lasar Segall, 1891–1957: Malerei, Zeichnungen, Druckgrafik, Skulptur* (Berlin: Staatliche Kunsthalle, 1990), 19–45.

"A inquietação contempôrania." *Diario de Noite* (29 October 1926).

Johnson, Randal. "The Dynamics of the Brazilian Literary Field, 1930–1945." *Luso-Brazilian Review* 31.2 (December 1994): 5–22.

Lesser, Jeffrey. *Welcoming the Undesirables: Brazil and the Jewish Question* (Berkeley: University of California Press, 1995).
Lloyd, Jill. *German Expressionism: Primitivism and Modernity* (New Haven, CT: Yale University Press, 1991).
Masheck, Joseph. "Raw Art: 'Primitive' Authenticity and German Expressionism." *RES* 4 (1982).
Mattos, Cláudia Valladão de. *Lasar Segall, expressionismo e judaísmo: o período alemão de 1906–1923* (São Paulo: Editora Perspectiva, 2000).
Mignolo, Walter. *Local Histories/Global Designs: Coloniality, Subaltern Knowledges, and Border Thinking* (Princeton, NJ: Princeton University Press, 2000).
Morais, Frederico. *Lasar Segall e o Rio de Janeiro* (Rio de Janeiro: Museu de Arte Moderna do Rio de Janeiro, 1991).
Mostra do redescobrimento: Negro de corpo e alma. Vol. 12. 14 vols. (São Paulo: Fundação Bienal de São Paulo: Associação Brasil 500 Anos Artes Visuais, 2000).
Moura, Carlos Eugênio Marcondes de. *A travessia da Calunga Grande: três séculos de imagens sobre o negro no Brasil, 1637–1899* (São Paulo: EDUSP, 2000).
Néstor, Victor. "A exposição Lasar Segall." *O Globo* (30 July 1928).
Perry, Gillian. "Primitivism," in *Primitivism, Cubism, Abstraction: The Early Twentieth Century.* Ed. Charles Harrison, Francis Frascina, and Gillian Perry (New Haven, CT: Yale University Press, in association with the Open University, 1993), 3–85.
Pratt, Mary Louise. *Imperial Eyes: Travel Writing and Transculturation* (New York: Routledge, 1992).
Price, Sally. *Primitive Art in Civilized Places* (Chicago: University of Chicago Press, 2002).
Segall, Lasar. "Minhas recordações," in *Lasar Segall: textos, depoimentos, exposições* (São Paulo: Museu Lasar Segall, Biblioteca Jenny K. Segall, Fundação Nacional Pró-Memória, 1985), 9–29.
Segall, Lasar. "O expressionismo," in *Lasar Segall: textos, depoimentos, exposições* (São Paulo: Museu Lasar Segall, Biblioteca Jenny K. Segall, Fundação Nacional Pró-Memória, 1985), 39–42.
Segall, Lasar. "Sobre Arte," in *Lasar Segall: textos, depoimentos, exposições* (São Paulo: Museu Lasar Segall, Biblioteca Jenny K. Segall, Fundação Nacional Pró-Memória, 1985), 31–36.
Sevcenko, Nicolau. *Orfeu extático na metrópole: São Paulo, sociedade e cultural nos frementes anos 20* (São Paulo: Companhia das Letras, 1992).
"Uma exposição de Segall no Rio de Janeiro." *O Jornal* (30 May 1928).
"Vandalismo moribundo?" *Diário Nacional* (18 December 1928).
"Vida artística: exposição de pintura." *Folha da Manhã* (26 December 1927).
Volkov, Shulamit. "The Dynamics of Dissimilation: Ostjuden and German Jews," in *The Jewish Response to German Culture: From the Enlightenment to the Second World War.* Ed. Jehuda Reinharz and Walter Schatzberg (Hanover, NH: University Press of New England, 1991), 195–241.
Weinstein, Joan. *The End of Expressionism: Art and the November Revolution in Germany, 1918–19* (Chicago: University of Chicago Press, 1990).
Wolfe, Edith Angelica Gibson. *Melancholy Encounter: Lasar Segall and Brazilian Modernism, 1924–1933* (PhD diss., University of Texas at Austin, 2005).

Rainer Guldin
Between São Paulo and Stuttgart: Multilingualism, Translation, and Interculturality in Haroldo de Campos's and Vilém Flusser's Work

> There are no border-lines. Two phenomena that could be separated by a line do not exist. [...] Let us hope that the drawing of borders will finally be blurred. [...] There are no white and black people, no pure cultures and no pure disciplines.[1]
> – Vilém Flusser, *Zwiegespräche*, 1996

> The changes in the way we experience the world today, correspond to the fact that in our poems, ideograms, visible-texts, constellations these configurations behave quite effortlessly in a polyglot way.[2]
> – Eugen Gomringer, "Die konkrete poesie als übernationale sprache," 1988

In this chapter, I focus on a significant moment of the intense and prolific contact between the Noigandres Group around Haroldo de Campos and Décio Pignatari and the Stuttgart School of Max Bense and Reinhard Döhl. In this multifaceted and multilingual milieu, texts were exchanged and translated from Portuguese into German and vice versa. Bense traveled several times to São Paulo and De Campos to Stuttgart. Attempts at intercultural exchange on all levels including literature, architecture, and the arts were undertaken. In this specific context, Czech-Brazilian bicontinental philosopher and writer Vilém Flusser translated the third and fourth fragments of Haroldo de Campos's multilingual poem *Galáxias* from Portuguese into German. In March 1966, the translation was published in Stuttgart by Max Bense and Elisabeth Walther-Bense as text 25 of the series *rot*, with a short introduction by De Campos himself.

De Campos's third fragment considers, above all, the process of multilingual writing and the status of the plurilingual text, that is, the relationship of the different (writing) languages to each other. In his view, languages are not separated by clear-cut borders but meet, overlap, and merge with each other on different levels. To express this particular point of view he makes use of a very apt metaphor: the protean, ever-moving sea. De Campos's fragment tells the story of a sea crossing without mentioning departure or arrival. In his text, there are no coastlines to speak of but only the open-ended trip across the water. Both Flusser and

---

[1] Vilém Flusser, *Zwiegespräche. Interviews 1967–1991* (Göttingen: European Photography, 1996), 97.
[2] Eugen Gomringer, "die konkrete poesie als übernationale sprache," in *zur sache der konkreten poesie I*. Ed. Eugen Gomringer (Sankt Gallen: Erker, 1988), 51.

De Campos view translation processes as (re)creative acts. Furthermore, this specific translational move takes place in a multilingual context, which in turn is embedded in a complex, multilayered mesh of intertextual allusions: constellations within constellations.

I first concentrate briefly on some aspects of the intricate transatlantic net of personal relationships that made this translation possible. I then have a closer look at Flusser's translation of the third fragment of De Campos's *Galáxias* – the only literary translation Flusser ever produced – and focus on Haroldo de Campos's and Vilém Flusser's translation theories and the way they influenced their collaboration. Furthermore, I point to the possible relevance of De Campos's experimental text, Flusser's congenial recreation, and their common innovative practice of translation – especially in view of the prevailing paradigm of equivalence, asking for absolute faithfulness to the original – for a possible reevaluation of intercultural exchanges. In fact, the suggestions contained in their literary and linguistic approach might be used as an interpretive model for intercultural relationships.

Transatlantic constellations: cooperation across cultures

Haroldo De Campos and Max Bense got to know each other personally in July 1959, while De Campos was on a trip through Europe. Max Bense had already met Décio Pignatari at Eugen Gomringer's in 1955. Gomringer had awakened Bense's interest in 1953 with the publication of his *Konstellationen* (Constellations). Two years later Bense published in the second issue of the newly founded magazine *Augenblick* Gomringer's manifesto of Concrete Poetry: *vom Vers zur Konstellation* (from verse to constellation).[3]

The constellation metaphor with its cosmic implications stands for an open-ended, shifting, netlike structure. It is not only a very apt comment on the dynamic network of personal collaborations and friendships linking the different artists and writers across continents and languages for more than three decades – and a very fitting metaphor for intercultural exchanges – but also a recurrent image in both Flusser's and de Campos's work. Gomringer envisaged Concrete Poetry as a transnational polyglot language. In the universe of Concrete Poetry, texts do not follow a strict linear order from left to right and top to bottom but

---

[3] Eugen Gomringer, "vom vers zur konstellation. zweck und form einer neuen dichtung," in *eugen gomringer worte sind schatten, die konstellationen 1951–1968*. Ed. Eugen Gomringer (Reinbeck bei Hamburg: Rowohlt 1969), 277–288, and "die konkrete poesie als übernationale sprache," in *zur sache der konkreten poesie I*. Ed. Eugen Gomringer (Sankt Gallen: erker, 1988), 9–11.

are multilingual word constellations on the white surface of the page. De Campos's *Galáxias* is no exception to this rule.

In a letter of 5 March 1989 written to Hans-Joachim Lenger, Flusser comments on the term *constellation* and some of its implications for his own work:

> Language, politics and Jews: this constellation (in Antiquity one would have said "con-sideration" instead) is a downright challenge for people like me. Perhaps you know that I write everything in five languages [...] and that I do not make any difference between translation and reflection (that is, "con-sideration").[4]

Flusser plays here with the presence of a similar concept within the word in con*sidera*tion – *sidera* from the Latin *sidus*, "orb or celestial body" – and the word con*stella*tion – from Latin *stella*, "star" – using them subsequently as metaphors for translation and reflection. To translate and to think imply the creation of a flexible three-dimensional stellar configuration analogous to the structure of a crystal in which a set of concepts and languages creatively interact with each other. This specific conception can also be found in Flusser's philosophical essays: From the linear structure of the single lines emerge netlike clusters of concepts. Below the monolingual surface of the finished texts, multilingual meanings carried over from the plural processes of self-translation still reverberate.[5]

An intense series of two-way transatlantic exchanges followed the first encounters in the late 1950s. In February 1961, Bense held a series of lectures on his aesthetic theory, meeting different Brazilian artists and writers. Bense organized a series of exhibitions of works by Brazilian artists in the 1960s and 1970s. In February 1962, text 7 of the series *rot*, dedicated exclusively to the Noigandres-Group, was published. De Campos, in turn, translated works by Bense and published reviews of Bense's texts in Brazilian newspapers.

Within the transcontinental constellation of Concrete Poetry, the work of Mira Schendel, to whom Flusser dedicated an essay in his autobiography *Bodenlos*,[6] played an important role. In January 1967 Max Bense organized in the Studiengallerie der Technischen Hochschule of Stuttgart a first exhibition of her drawings. In February 1975, a second followed. In his essay *Indagações sobre a origem da língua*, published on 29 April 1967, Flusser explores the ambivalent

---

[4] Vilém Flusser, *Jude sein. Essays, Briefe, Fiktionen* (Mannheim: Bollmann Verlag, 1995), 136 (my translation).
[5] Rainer Guldin, "Translation, Self-Translation, Retranslation: Exploring Vilém Flusser's Multilingual Writing Practice," in *Das Spiel mit der Übersetzung. Figuren der Mehrsprachigkeit im Werk Vilém Flussers*. Ed. Rainer Guldin (Tübingen: Francke, 2004).
[6] Vilém Flusser, *Bodenlos. Eine philosophische Autobiographie* (Düsseldorf und Bensheim: Bollmann Verlag, 1992), 197–206.

nature of Schendel's graphic work, ingeniously suspended halfway between picture and text, the same way Concrete Poetry was. Breaking away from the line structure and the verse as a rhythmic and formal unit, Concrete Poetry aimed at a redefinition of the page as a graphic space. In Schendel's work, there is a similar dialectics to be discovered, a violent tension toward articulation,

> an explosive intention. [...] If I could capture the moment of the explosion, that fugitive moment, in which I am not language yet but not inarticulated any more, [...] this critical moment between the chaotic other and the subject that is structured by symbols, I would have captured the origin of language. [...] There is a turmoil of lines, dots, curves and figures that desperately ask for permission to leave the limbo of virtuality to be admitted to the refulgent reign of reality: language.[7]

Haroldo de Campos and Vilém Flusser got to know each other in the early 1960s. Because of personal and aesthetic disagreements, however, this did not lead to any further collaboration or lasting friendship. It was Haroldo de Campos himself who suggested Flusser and Rosenfeld as translators of his first fragments from *Galáxias*. Because Bense already knew Flusser from some publications, he accepted De Campos's proposal.

Translating multilingual texts

In his autobiography *Bodenlos*, Flusser dedicated a chapter to his short-lived and unfortunate friendship with Haroldo de Campos and his attempt to translate two fragments of *Galáxias*, focusing on the main reasons for their intellectual and aesthetic differences. In Haroldo de Campos's work, argues Flusser, everything revolves around the unresolved dialectics of intent and chance, ultimately thwarted by the impossibility of harmonizing political stance and creative activity. For Flusser, any form of politically committed art, as De Campos envisaged it, was out of the question. To illustrate this difference in detail I would like to quote a lengthy passage from Flusser's essay, offering a starting point both for the workings of De Campos's multilingual writing practice and for Flusser's own translating strategies. When De Campos

> was invited by Max Bense to publish a part of his *Galaxies* in the book series *rot*, published in Stuttgart, he asked me to translate two paragraphs of this work into German. This project made it possible for me to delve into his work and to actively perform within its borders.

---

[7] Vilém Flusser, "Indagações sobre a origem da língua," in *O Estado de São Paulo. Suplemento Literário*, São Paulo, 29 April 1967 (my translation).

Through this, however, the conflict dominating Campos's poetic endeavor became my own concern and thus fully apparent. *Galaxies* consists of a series of variations of a few topics defined by specifically selected words such as *book* or *journey*. These words are modified on three levels: As sounds, they are made to resonate in different ways, as visible forms they are transformed by anagrammatic play, and as significant units of meaning, they are transmuted into a fan of possible connotations. In this way, a grammatically unstructured discourse, an uninterrupted stream of words from different languages and neologisms, is generated, suggestive of the free play of association and stream of consciousness but with a difference: Strict observance of the initially set topic is mandatory. *Galaxies* is composed of circular streams of words, with each of them returning to its original meaning. In this way, the whole text becomes a circular system around which other discourses revolve like satellites. (Hence the title *Galaxies*.) In a certain way, these discourses revolve within the universe of the Portuguese language acting as a foundation, but they keep piercing through this foundation, expanding into other languages and beyond all languages. It could be described as a pulsation during which some new "star-words" condense in certain places, while in others Portuguese words evaporate to become cosmic dust-clouds. The problem does not become apparent when new thematic words are chosen. This is the result of a deliberate choice based on chance. The contradiction between intention and chance, between *dé* and *hasard*, is the very point of departure of the whole work. In this sense, Campos is responding to Mallarmé, and this is not problematic in itself. But then something happens: The word suggested as a subject matter generates a spontaneous stream of variations on all levels, moving in unpredictable directions and developing intensities that threaten to get out of hand. Instead of surrendering to this stream, Campos deliberately intervenes to realign it, with his own political convictions pushing it on from there. The result for the reader is a feeling of unease. If Campos wants to convey an intentional message, the spontaneous flow of variation is not the proper method, and if he attempts a concrete experiment with the Portuguese language, his deliberate interferences distort the results. You cannot eat the cake and have it at the same time. While I was undertaking the translation of two circular discourses of *Galaxies*, this negative dialectics became painfully manifest. One chose a German equivalent for one of Campos's thematic Portuguese terms, and a spontaneous stream of variations arose. This stream was so powerful that it became immediately clear that it had to be curbed. By doing this one realized that "curbing" did not imply changing direction or pushing on but restraining. One had to deal with intuition economically. [...] As I was doing this, the passages where Campos had interfered with the stream became noticeable. The result was the opposite of what Campos had intended. The ideological message looked contrived and therefore sounded phony. The repeated jolts Campos imparted to the stream gave an impression of weakness, not strength. But this had an impact on one's own spontaneity during the process of translation.[8]

In this passage Flusser is referring to Stéphane Mallarmé's poem *Un coup de dés*, which influenced not only Concrete Poetry but also the later conception of the hypertext, with its deliberate use of blank space and careful placement of single

---

8 Vilém Flusser, *Bodenlos. Eine philosophische Autobiographie* (Düsseldorf und Bensheim: Bollmann Verlag, 1992), 151–152 (my translation).

words or word strings on the white surface of the page, allowing multiple nonlinear readings of the text. As we shall see, Mallarmé is also an important reference figure indirectly evoked by De Campos in the third fragment. According to Flusser, three major aspects have played a role in De Campos's associative multilingual writing strategy: sound variation, anagrammatical reordering of letters, and creation of secondary meanings. These three aspects, along with the problem signaled by Flusser, would have to be taken into account in comparing the original Portuguese version with its German counterpart.

Galaxies is a book without beginning or end, consisting of 50 single pages without numbering. On each page one stable component has been placed, a word or a concept, around which other more ephemeral and unstable linguistic elements are freely floating. De Campos calls these interchangeable key terms running throughout the text "semantic vertebrae." The linear structure has been consistently and successfully disarranged and the page turned into an open field on which distinct elements are called to interact like points, lines, and geometric figures on a canvas, the way they do in Mira Schendel's paintings. The jagged right margins enhance the idea that each page represents a constellation of its own. The complete absence of punctuation marks and capital letters creates an endless phrase revolving around itself, a flux of signs flowing uninterruptedly across the page, as a galactic expansion. Each page, by itself, is an autonomous body, interchangeable with any other page. The image of ever-expanding galaxies has both visual and musical connotations. De Campos works with neologisms, citations, multilingual puns, and heterogeneous juxtapositions and makes frequent use of different languages, very often at the outset of a new page. This is also the case for the third fragment translated by Flusser, which I would like to examine more closely. German, Latin, Greek, Italian, English, French, and Spanish words or sentences are interspersed in the text, sometimes to set a specific geographic or cultural context or to gesture toward a metalinguistic dimension. This creates an all-encompassing web of quotations, including a variety of linguistic registers ranging from everyday language to citations from classical literature. This multilingual metalanguage abolishes all borders between languages and within languages themselves.

Flusser stresses Haroldo de Campos's attempt at combining information theory and ideogrammatic writing, as well as his interest in the study of oriental languages and the work of Marshall McLuhan, whom he met in the United States in 1967.[9] In the same text Flusser also argues that De Campos broke up the Gu-

---

9 Vilém Flusser, *Bodenlos. Eine philosophische Autobiographie* (Düsseldorf und Bensheim: Bollmann Verlag, 1992), 156.

tenberg Galaxy – the play on words is intentional here – by introducing nonlinearity in his writing, using oriental ideograms as a model. De Campos was inspired by the presence of the numerous Japanese immigrants in Brazil and the work of Ezra Pound and Ernest Fenollosa, whose influence on the poet are well documented.[10]

Text 25 of the editorial series *rot* contains four fragments from Haroldo de Campos's *Galáxias*. Anatol Rosenfeld translated the first and the sixteenth fragments, which Campos completed on 18 November 1963 and on 3 March 1965, respectively. Flusser translated the third and the fourth, finished on 19 November 1963 and on 24 July 1964. The four fragments were the first parts of *Galáxias* to be actually translated. Apart from the fact that these parts were already finished at the time, there must have been other reasons for them being chosen for translation. These reasons can no longer be reconstructed at this point but only guessed at.

In an afterword to the first edition of the complete text of *Galáxias,* written in May 1983, nearly 20 years after the completion of the first fragment, Haroldo de Campos mentioned that some fragments had been translated in the past: "Fragments of *Galáxias* were translated (I prefer to call it 'transcreated') in German, French, Spanish, and English, nearly always with a revision by the author."[11] This means that De Campos must have at least examined, if not reviewed and edited, Flusser's translation. Of central importance in this context is also De Campos's use of the concept of *transcriação,* implying re-creation of a poem from the phonetic, morphologic, and semantic conditions of the target language. Did Flusser succeed in transposing the triple creative principle of De Campos's aesthetics into German? And how did he manage to solve the enormous semantic and phonetic difficulties that a translation of such a complex writing strategy entails?

I chose to concentrate on the third fragment, – "multitudinous seas," – because its themes, as I already pointed out, are directly linked to De Campos's conception of language and textual multilingualism. Apart from this, it contains a group of interlinked quotations from four other languages: English, French, Greek, and Latin. Key terms of the third fragment are the sea, the journey, and the book. The (blank page of the) book is like the surface of the sea, and writing is compared to a trip on the ever-moving ocean of intermingling languages. Plurilingualism is not dealt with explicitly but rendered in the comings and goings,

---

10 Haroldo De Campos, ed., *Ideograma: Lógica, Poesia, Linguagem* (São Paulo: Editora da Universidade de São Paulo, 2000).
11 Haroldo De Campos, *Galáxias* (São Paulo: editora34, 2004) (my translation).

the ups and downs of the ocean. Indirectly, the third fragment is also a reflection on the multilingual writing practice and the status of a plurilingual text and the relationship of the different languages to each other.

"Multitudinous seas": the overlapping and merging of languages and cultures

In this context Alfons Knauth's remarks on a polyglot poetics are particularly revealing. Knauth mentions in his essay *poethik polyglott*, in which he draws a tentative open-ended typology of multilingual texts what he calls the "nautical model."

> The sea is, so to speak, the syntagmatic axis of the Babel paradigm. It separates the languages and unites them at the same time. [...] From a genetic point of view, the sea precedes the mythical construction of the Tower of Babel: It brought about multilingualism and strengthened it. [...] In this way, [...] the internal and external linguistic polyglotism came into being. [...] On one hand, the sea establishes a real contact between the different languages, on the other it embodies a metaphorical analogy for languages [and their relation to each other]: its many-voiced sound is an expression of multilingualism, [...] and its continuous movement an expression of the constant merging or mixing of languages.[12]

Interestingly enough, this – basically linguistic – conception can also be found in Ian Chambers's recently published historical and cultural reflection on the Mediterranean. Chambers translates Knauth's vision of a multilingual sea into a concrete sociohistorical context. The metaphor he makes use of, however, is fundamentally the same. Chambers introduces the notions of diversity and multilateral exchange and reinterprets translational exchanges in an intercultural sense. He stresses both the heterogeneity and unity of the Mediterranean, but this model could ultimately be applied to any form of cross-cultural contact and exchange, highlighting its contradictory nature. By defining the Mediterranean as a closed, circumscribed space, a "complex echo chamber" in which multiple fluxes bounce and rebound, "transforming and transmuting each other,"[13] he interprets the classical vision of unity against its grain. The very metaphor of unity, the sea shaping the coastlines, is here reinterpreted in a plural, polyglot

---

[12] Alphons H. Knauth, "poethik polyglott," *Dichtungsring* 20 (1991), 61 (my translation).
[13] Ian Chambers, *Mediterranean Crossings. The Politics of an Interrupted Modernity* (Durham, NC: Duke University Press, 2008), 48.

sense. Chambers speaks of the "open, creolized complexity"[14] and "the polylinguistic and polycultural composition of a hybrid,"[15] "multiple and mutable Mediterranean."[16] "The seeming solidity of the lands, languages, and lineages that border and extend outward from its shores here become an accessory of its fluid centrality."[17] In this ever-shifting liquid world the foreign is already contained within the familiar, the same way the foreign quotations are in De Campos's text. Chambers speaks of Arab elements to be discovered in the very heart of Christianity, as, for instance, in

> the Arab letters on Christ's cloak in Giotto's Crocifissione. [...] In this doubling and displacement, the very closure sought by cultural monotheism [...] is sundered and dispersed. The image and what it narrates, is no longer possessed by a single mode of telling. History, the Mediterranean, returns, rewriting and recounting the narrative, freeing it, from the fixed moorings of a unilateral meaning, allowing it to drift into their accounts.[18]

It is all about a "floating semantics."[19] In this metaphorical context borders are successfully blurred. Currents mix and mingle on different levels and in manifold ways:

> The tributary histories that flow into the "modern" [...] Mediterranean, also suggest deeper and more dispersive currents. Rather than [...] a logic of barriers to be breached and differences to be bridged [...] overlapping territories and intertwined histories suggest a less rigid, more open comprehension of the making of a multiple Mediterranean.[20]

Multiplicity and liquidity complement each other. "[Borders are porous, particularly so in the liquid materiality of the Mediterranean [...] borders are both transitory and zones of transit. They repeatedly draw our attention to the labor of

---

14 Ian Chambers, *Mediterranean Crossings. The Politics of an Interrupted Modernity* (Durham, NC: Duke University Press, 2008), 55.
15 Ian Chambers, *Mediterranean Crossings. The Politics of an Interrupted Modernity* (Durham, NC: Duke University Press, 2008), 32.
16 Ian Chambers, *Mediterranean Crossings. The Politics of an Interrupted Modernity* (Durham, NC: Duke University Press, 2008), 9.
17 Ian Chambers, *Mediterranean Crossings. The Politics of an Interrupted Modernity* (Durham, NC: Duke University Press, 2008), 2–4.
18 Ian Chambers, *Mediterranean Crossings. The Politics of an Interrupted Modernity* (Durham, NC: Duke University Press, 2008), 131–132.
19 Ian Chambers, *Mediterranean Crossings. The Politics of an Interrupted Modernity* (Durham, NC: Duke University Press, 2008), 79.
20 Ian Chambers, *Mediterranean Crossings. The Politics of an Interrupted Modernity* (Durham, NC: Duke University Press, 2008), 2–5.

translation."²¹ These metaphors of fluidity and liquidity articulate another history and another space. Chambers speaks of the dangers of a solid, solidified sea: "the solidifying of the Mediterranean transform[s] a site of transit into a mounting barrier."²² "The Mediterranean [...] continually 'betrays' all attempts to freeze its composite components into a homogeneous image." This view of "the sea, as the site of multiple mediations and memories [...] delivers us over to a fluid geography that [...] challenges the very being and becoming European and modern." This fluid geography allows us to discover new connections, an "unsuspected cartography" that disrupts "the rigid grids of national geographers."²³ The Mediterranean itself becomes this way a complex metaphor for translation processes and intercultural exchanges:

> The sea itself, [is] not so much [...] a frontier or barrier between the North and the South, or the East and the West, as an intricate site of encounters and currents [animated by] the continual sense of historical transformation and cultural translation which makes it a site of perpetual transit.²⁴

Besides the idea of ever-moving and constantly recombining currents, Chambers introduces another spatial metaphor, very much akin to the metaphor of the constellation, to articulate the mutable transitoriness and complex heterogeneity of the sea: the archipelago. In an archipelago the single cultural elements are bound together in a fragmented network of interlinked points, "an unfamiliar constellation"²⁵ without any rigid inner and outer boundaries or any clear-cut hierarchical orientations. The idea of the archipelago is furthermore connected in the book to the intricate pattern of the arabesque, whose cultural origin is highly significant in a Mediterranean context. This "inconclusive figuration"²⁶ recalls Deleuze's concept of the baroque fold, which brings together that which a linear

---

21 Ian Chambers, *Mediterranean Crossings. The Politics of an Interrupted Modernity* (Durham, NC: Duke University Press, 2008), 5.
22 Ian Chambers, *Mediterranean Crossings. The Politics of an Interrupted Modernity* (Durham, NC: Duke University Press, 2008), 68.
23 Ian Chambers, *Mediterranean Crossings. The Politics of an Interrupted Modernity* (Durham, NC: Duke University Press, 2008), 131.
24 Ian Chambers, *Mediterranean Crossings. The Politics of an Interrupted Modernity* (Durham, NC: Duke University Press, 2008), 32.
25 Ian Chambers, *Mediterranean Crossings. The Politics of an Interrupted Modernity* (Durham, NC: Duke University Press, 2008), 133.
26 Ian Chambers, *Mediterranean Crossings. The Politics of an Interrupted Modernity* (Durham, NC: Duke University Press, 2008), 18.

Eurocentric vision of history would like to hold apart.[27] From this intercultural point of view, De Campos's multilingual fragment assumes a completely new meaning. An aspect that would be worth pursuing is the relationship of the notions of hierarchy, linearity, and border, which both de Campos and Flusser view as a highly problematic theoretical construction.[28]

Multilingualism and intertextuality

Besides thematizing the plurilingual text in the metaphor of the sea and containing five short interconnected passages in four different languages, the third fragment also introduces six foreign authors and one composer, thematically linked to each other and the main subject: Shakespeare, Homer, Ovid, James Joyce, Pierre Boulez, Stéphane Mallarmé, and Ezra Pound. In *Galáxias* multilingualism is always also an eminently intertextual phenomenon. The fragment begins with a quotation from Shakespeare's *Macbeth* (Act 2, Scene 2, 59): "multitudinous seas incarnadine." Macbeth looks at his bloodstained hands and comes to recognize that his guilt can never be washed off, not even by the vast sea. Even Neptune's green immense ocean would end up by being stained by it. "This celebration of the sea-book," writes De Campos, "begins with a verse by Shakespeare, [...] referring to the multitudinous sea that changes from green into red-blood, favorite verse of Ezra Pound and also Borges."[29] The initial image of the tainted surface of the ocean, possibly a metaphor for the multilingual text (a sea of Portuguese words dotted by the stains of other languages floating on its surface and dissolving into it) is taken up later on by the image of the sea as the speckled fur of a panther. *Incarnadine* means "pink" and is used as a verb.

The second Greek quotation also thematizes the many colors of the sea as a metaphor of the multilingual text: "Óinopa pónton cor de vinho" (the color of wine) comes from Homer's *Odyssey* and is also used in Joyce's *Ulysses*. In the first chapter of the book Mulligan describes the sea as "snotgreen." The third short Latin quote, "iris nuntia junonis," can be found in Ovid's *Metamorphoses* (I, 270–271). The full text reads as follows: "Nuntia Junonis varios induta col-

---

[27] Gilles Deleuze, *Fold: Leibniz and the Baroque* (Minneapolis: University of Minnesota Press, 1992).
[28] Rainer Guldin, "Ineinandergreifende graue Zonen. Vilém Flussers Bestimmung der Grenze als Ort der Begegnung," in *Topographien der Grenze. Verortungen einer kulturellen, politischen und ästhetischen Kategorie*. Ed. Christoph Kleinschmidt and Christine Hewel (Würzburg: Königshausen & Neumann, 2011a), 39–48.
[29] Haroldo De Campos, *Galáxias* (São Paulo: editora34, 2004), 119 (my translation).

ores / Concipit Iris aquas" (Iris, the messenger of Juno, clad in robes of many hues, draws water from the ocean). Iris is the iridescent wind, constantly changing its plumage, feeding water to the clouds – another image of fluid, dissolving borders. The fourth quotation, "pli selon pli" (fold by fold), is a piece of classical music for soprano and orchestra by French composer Pierre Boulez, who worked on it from 1957 to 1962, a piece of work in progress very much like De Campos's *Galáxias*. The composition is in five movements, each based on a poem by Stéphane Mallarmé. The title itself is taken from another poem, *Remémoration d'amis belges,* not used in the piece: "Que se dévêt pli selon pli la pierre veuve" (That fold by fold the widowed stone unrobes itself). Mallarmé describes how the mist covering the city of Bruges gradually dissolves. In the same way through the five movements, a portrait of Mallarmé is slowly revealed. This quotation refers also to the many-layered intertextual form of the multilingual text. Mallarmé, on the other hand is a key figure for the aesthetic conception of *Gálaxias*. Flusser refers to Mallarmé's poem *Un coup de dés jamais n'abolira le hazard* in his discussion of the contradictory relationship of intention and chance in De Campos's work.

The last untranslatable Greek word of the fragment, "polúphloisbos," found in Homer's *Iliad* (I.34), onomatopoeically recalls the rolling of the waves and leads the reader back to the beginning of the fragment, the vision of the endlessly moving and transforming ocean. Ezra Pound uses the term to describe the onslaught of the tide onto the shoreline and its subsequent withdrawal.[30]

All quotations are thematically linked to each other and to the main themes of the fragment. De Campos introduces both horizontal and vertical relations between the different passages – Joyce's *Ulysses* refers to the *Odyssey,* Pierre Boulez's piece of music builds on a textual layer by Mallarmé, and Pound is referring to the *Iliad* – echoing thus the syntagmatic and paradigmatic aspects of languages. The passages consistently stress open-endedness and manifold iridescence, characteristics of the sea but also of the multilingual text. How do these quotations from other languages interact with the Portuguese text? They are not just juxtaposed to the main text and do not behave as a foreign body within the dominant language universe but entertain with each other and the Portuguese text a series of complex and flexible relationships that ultimately question any kind of clear-cut linguistic delimitation. In this way, the content is once more integrated into the formal setting. De Campos's description of the sea is at the same time a metaphorical representation of the relationship of the single languages to each

---

[30] Haroldo De Campos, *Metalinguagem* (São Paulo: Vozes, 1976), 29, and *Galáxias* (São Paulo: editora34, 2004), 120.

other. The fine web of intertextual quotations positioned next to each other and within one another mirrors and comments on the fluid relationship of the different languages.

The third fragment, as all others, has neither a clear beginning nor a definitive ending but can be considered as a segment cut out of a flowing, multilayered text-web. To accentuate this impression there are no page numbers, no punctuation, and everything has been written without capital letters. The length of the different verses keeps changing. De Campos uses, above all, enjambements to link one verse with another. In the short introduction to the German translation he describes his writing project, deconstructing the notions of linearity, hierarchy, and border.

> envisage a book. of one hundred pages. or nearly. [...] the first and the last one firm. [...] the others detached and *interchangeable* [...] that is, *without beginning nor ending.* [...] the pages *reversible. replaceable. exchangeable.* the stream of signs. on each page a constant element: the journey or the book. or the travel book. or the book travel. [...] things as they drift past the eye and the ear. in thought. [...] fact and fiction, *without distinction.* that which is gone and that which might have been. that which is. external monologue. without psychology. things. people. visions. contexts. connections. *without originmiddleend. without narration.*[31]

Even if within the fragment itself no clear-cut thematic divisions can be made out, as one thematic strand meshes with the other, a series of interlinked aspects, mixing with each other, are gradually introduced, leading to new linguistic permutations on the phonetical and morphological level. The first image of the speckled sea comes from Shakespeare's *Macbeth,* from a fictional, textual second-hand world. A trip on a boat follows, a journey across a multilingual ocean. The bow of the ship – here De Campos introduces the (problematic) sexual metaphor of the sea as a female body to be plowed by a (male) writer. The blood dripping from Macbeth's hands and the violence it implies might be linked to the process of writing and the pulsating vulva of the sea that shimmers and gleams like a rainbow. De Campos compares the sea to the freckled skin of a panther and its unceasing surging and heaving to the orgasmic up and down of a voluptuously squirming (female?) body. About half way through the fragment a new element is introduced, a comparison with the book, whose countless pages and immeasurable contents echo the multifarious multiplicity of the sea. The fragment ends with a view of the stern of the ship, ripping the ocean apart. In the end, thus, the text circles back to the beginning, to the polymorphic, end-

---

31 Haroldo De Campos, *versuchsbuch galaxien* (Stuttgart: edition rot, 1966) (my translation, emphasis added).

lessly moving surface of the ocean. Thus, De Campos's third fragment is above all a reflection on the unfathomable complexity of a manifold linguistic reality that has neither beginning nor end and that can only be described in a tentative, metaphorical way. The ocean with its horizontal and vertical structure is an apt metaphor both for the workings of a multilingual text and for the inner complexity of single languages. Both juxtaposition and layering, the syntagmatic and the paradigmatic, are described in terms of liquidity.

In his translation, Flusser respected the overall form of the fragment: There is no punctuation, and the whole text is uncapitalized. Unlike in Portuguese, in German this has a very different significance and unquestionably strengthens the visual impact of the text as a flow of words. Flusser left the quotations from other languages in their original form. In a German context, however, these passages assume a very different phonetic and morphologic role. Paradoxically enough, faithfulness to the original leads here to transformation. Flusser changed the length of the single verses drastically, with no apparent reason, doubling the total length of the text and thus altering radically its outer form. The main problem with the Portuguese text with regard to translation is the extremely dense, inextricable web of alliterations, assonances, and internal rhymes. In many instances, Flusser came up with astonishingly imaginative solutions. Most of the time, he had to sacrifice the meaning of the Portuguese original, or at least part of it, to phonetics and morphology. With regard to De Campos's writing strategy based on the threefold variation of phonetics, morphology, and semantics, one could say that apart from single instances the first two levels of the Portuguese original, sounds and letters, have mostly found an adequate German counterpart. Overall meaning has been reproduced in the translation, but many details have been lost or substituted with new ones. Some words or word groups have been omitted, others slightly altered, and sometimes the German words have generated their own fields of variation: Flusser definitely transposed the generative principle of the Portuguese text into his German translation, saving the most innovative aspect of De Campos's multilingual writing. Interestingly enough, many of Flusser's philosophical and essayistic texts also rely heavily on alliteration, assonance, and wordplay.[32] Concrete Poetry and probably also the translation of the two fragments from *Galáxias* must have left an imprint on Flusser's style.

In some instances, Flusser developed implicit metaphorical aspects of the source text: At the beginning of the fragment he describes the bow of the ship

---

32 Rainer Guldin, "Writing Philosophy," in *A filosofia da ficção de Vilém Flusser*. Ed. Gustavo Bernardo Krause (Rio de Janeiro: Annablume, 2011b), 387–406.

ripping the ocean apart in terms of a plow dividing its surface, which has now become a field to be cultivated. In other instances, he has added new imagery, mostly prompted by the generative rule of alliteration and assonance. He calls the ocean a "garstige gargantuasee," literally the "foul gargantuan sea," adding a further, thematically appropriate intertextual connection to the work of another multilingual poet, François Rabelais, who plays a major role in Mikhail Bakhtin's formulation of heteroglossia and dialogicity. Once again, multilingualism, intertextuality, and interculturality meet and merge in a comprehensive constellation. Flusser creates new internal rhymes – "gefälle/welle," "bröckelnden/bröseln" – and discovers homophonies that are possible only in German. He creates neologisms to condense single passages, such as "raubtiergepelzt," literally "predator-furred." However, there are also a few imprecision to be made out. In these instances solutions remaining closer to the original meaning would probably have been better. In the second half of the fragment, furthermore, one can detect a much greater freedom with regard to the original. This tendency grows even stronger toward the end of the text. Flusser's interventions increase drastically. The solutions he finds make sense in the context he has created, but in some cases they lead away from the meaning of the source text. Interestingly enough, this change in translation strategy corresponds to the point where De Campos introduces the new key term "book," that is, they begin at the very juncture where he consciously interferes with the phonetic flow of word associations. Flusser's change of attitude could be a conscious reaction to and implicit criticism of De Campo's intervention in favor of (political?) meaning.

The following significant examples illustrate the extremely fragile and volatile balance of the three interlinked linguistic levels. Flusser translates "mas a escuma mas a espuma mas a espumaescuma do mar" as "aber das schäumen aber das bäumen aber das schäumenbäumen der see." "Bäumen" – from "sich aufbäumen," (to rise up against) – is linked not only homophonically to "schäumen" (to foam, to froth) but also from the point of view of meaning. In other instances, Flusser extended the game of alliteration to whole passages. This way, "no verde vário no aquário equóreo o verde flore" becomes "im gegliederten grün im geglasten gewässer das grüne gegrase." The Portuguese assonances based on "á" ("vário" and "aquário") and "ó" ("equóreo") have been substituted by the use of "ü" and "ä," whereas the alliterative "v" of the Portuguese text has been substituted by the letter "g," used six times instead of three. The last example shows how Flusser's translation toward the end turns more and more into a recreation dictated by the logic of the target language: "mas o mar reverte mas o mar verte" becomes "aber die see versieht aber die see versiert die verse diverse." The last three words have been added. They are a result of the previous alliterative use of the letters "d" and "v" substituting the letters "m" and "v" in the original.

Translation as recreation

Flusser's extremely creative dealings with the Portuguese original do not contradict De Campos's translation theory. This is probably one of the main reasons why he accepted the publication of the fragments. In fact, in an early essay about translation as a form of creation and criticism, *Da tradução como criação e como crítica*,[33] H. de Campos distinguishes three different forms of information. Whereas documentary and semantic information can be easily translated into other codes and different languages, aesthetic information withstands this process because of its very fragility, that is, because of the impossibility of separating form and content, which are inextricably intertwined. Poetry can be codified only in the way it has been transmitted by the author; in other words, aesthetic codification is always identical to its original codification. It is because of this fundamental untranslatability that aesthetic information can be recreated only by working out isomorphic poetic bodies in different languages. In this way the aesthetic information embedded in the two texts will still be distinct, but the two texts will belong to the same isomorphic system. Haroldo de Campos uses a metaphor to describe this process. The translation creates a sort of delicate crystalline twofold structure recalling the very fragility of the aesthetic information itself. The two texts "will be different as far as language is concerned, as isomorphic bodies, however, they will crystallize within the same system."[34] The translation of a poetic text is therefore always recreation, or parallel creation.

This specific conception of the actively creative role of translation processes complies with Flusser's own vision. Flusser did not translate any other poetic texts, apart from the two fragments of De Campos's *Gâlaxias*. In his own practice of self-translation and his general view of the workings of translation itself – not only when applied to essayistic and philosophic texts but also when considered as a universal principle of transformation and transposition between languages, cultures, and forms of discourse – translation operates as a means of discovering

---

[33] Haroldo De Campos, "Da tradução como criação e como crítica," in *Metalinguagem e Outras Metas: Ensaios de Teoria e Crítica Leterária*. Ed. Haroldo De Campos (São Paulo: Editora Perspectiva, 1992), 31–48.
[34] Haroldo De Campos, "Da tradução como criação e como crítica," in *Metalinguagem e Outras Metas: Ensaios de Teoria e Crítica Leterária*. Ed. Haroldo De Campos (São Paulo: Editora Perspectiva, 1992), 34 (my translation).

and deploying hitherto hidden facets of the original, thanks to the very moment of untranslatability.

As the previous considerations have shown, the transatlantic translational route from São Paulo to Stuttgart and back opens up manifold insights into Haroldo de Campos's and Vilém Flusser's work, revealing a series of theoretical, thematic, and stylistic convergences. Moreover, their collaboration sheds an interesting light on the possible relationship of the processes of multilingual writing and translating, the nature of the plurilingual text, and the functioning of intertextual and intercultural interactions in general. The metaphors discussed here – the constellation, the sea, the archipelago, the net, the crystal, the fold – suggest a fundamental conceptual consonance. They form a (meta)constellation of their own, stressing open-endedness, flowing boundaries, and dissolving hierarchies with a strong denial of any form of progressive linearity.

Furthermore, De Campos's and Flusser's (pluri)linguistic model and their dynamic view of translational processes as creative acts could be used to reinterpret intercultural dialogues. From the point of view examined here, cultures are not self-contained unities but constantly shifting, overlapping, and merging entities, without clear-cut borders. Cultures (and languages, for that matter[35]) are not countable. They always already contain signs of other cultures. Contamination and mixing are inevitable: *KulturConfusão*. Finally, intercultural exchanges could be viewed as creative translational acts during which the foreign and the familiar are playfully reinvented.

References

Chambers, Ian. Mediterranean Crossings. The Politics of an Interrupted Modernity (Durham, NC: Duke University Press, 2008).
De Campos, Haroldo. Galáxias (São Paulo: editora34, 2004).
De Campos, Haroldo, ed. Ideograma: Lógica, Poesia, Linguagem (São Paulo: Editora da Universidade de São Paulo, 2000).
De Campos, Haroldo. "Da tradução como criação e como crítica," in Metalinguagem e Outras Metas: Ensaios de Teoria e Crítica Leterária. Ed. Haroldo De Campos (São Paulo: Editora Perspectiva, 1992), 31–48.
De Campos, Haroldo. Metalinguagem (São Paulo: Vozes, 1976).
De Campos, Haroldo. versuchsbuch galaxien (Stuttgart: edition rot, 1966).

---

[35] See Robert Stockhammer, Susan Arndt, and Dirk Naguschewski, "Einleitung. Die Unselbstverständlichkeit der Sprache," in *Exophonie. Anders-Sprachigkeit (in) der Literatur*. Ed. Robert Stockhammer, Susan Arndt, and Dirk Naguschewski (Berlin: Kulturverlag Kadmos, 2007), 15.

Deleuze, Gilles. Fold: Leibniz and the Baroque (Minneapolis: University of Minnesota Press, 1992).
Flusser, Vilém. Bodenlos. Eine philosophische Autobiographie (Düsseldorf und Bensheim: Bollmann Verlag, 1992).
Flusser, Vilém. "Indagações sobre a origem da língua," in O Estado de São Paulo. Suplemento Literário, São Paulo, 29 April 1967.
Flusser, Vilém. Jude sein. Essays, Briefe, Fiktionen (Mannheim: Bollmann Verlag, 1995).
Flusser, Vilém. Zwiegespräche. Interviews 1967–1991 (Göttingen: European Photography, 1996).
Gomringer, Eugen. "die konkrete poesie als übernationale sprache," in zur sache der konkreten poesie I. Ed. Eugen Gomringer (Sankt Gallen: erker, 1988), 51–52.
Gomringer, Eugen. "vom vers zur konstellation. zweck und form einer neuen dichtung," in eugen gomringer worte sind schatten, die konstellationen 1951–1968. Ed. Eugen Gomringer (Reinbeck bei Hamburg: Rowohlt, 1969), 277–288.
Guldin, Rainer. "Translation, Self-Translation, Retranslation: Exploring Vilém Flusser's Multilingual Writing Practice," in Das Spiel mit der Übersetzung. Figuren der Mehrsprachigkeit im Werk Vilém Flussers. Ed. Rainer Guldin (Tübingen: Francke, 2004), 99–118.
Guldin, Rainer. "Ineinandergreifende graue Zonen. Vilém Flussers Bestimmung der Grenze als Ort der Begegnung," in Topographien der Grenze. Verortungen einer kulturellen, politischen und ästhetischen Kategorie. Ed. Christoph Kleinschmidt and Christine Hewel (Würzburg: Königshausen & Neumann, 2011a), 39–48.
Guldin, Rainer. "Writing Philosophy," in A filosofia da ficção de Vilém Flusser. Ed. Gustavo Bernardo Krause (Rio de Janeiro: Annablume, 2011b), 387–406.
Knauth, Alphons H. "poethik polyglott." Dichtungsring 20 (1991): 42–80.
Stockhammer, Robert, Susan Arndt, and Dirk Naguschewski. "Einleitung. Die Unselbstverständlichkeit der Sprache," in Exophonie. Anders-Sprachigkeit (in) der Literatur. Ed. Robert Stockhammer, Susan Arndt, and Dirk Naguschewski (Berlin: Kulturverlag Kadmos, 2007), 7–27.

Contributors

Thomas O. Beebee is Distinguished Professor of Comparative Literature and German at the Pennsylvania State University. His fields of specialization in research and graduate teaching are European literature of the early modern period; criticism and theory; epistolarity; translation studies; and law and literature. His publications include the books *Clarissa on the Continent, The Ideology of Genre, Epistolary Fiction in Europe, Region and Nation in Modern European and American Fiction,* and *Millennial Literatures of the New World, 1492–2002.*

Fernando Clara is Professor Auxiliar com Agregação in German at the Universidade Nova de Lisboa. His book publications include the co-edited *Europe in Black and White* (2010), *Outros Horizontes* (2009), *Mundos de Palavras* (2007), and the co-edited *Portugal-Alemanha-África* (1996).

Marlen Eckl received her PhD in history from the University of Vienna (2009). She has published on Jewish-Brazilian literature, emigration, and exile and is a board member of the Casa Stefan Zweig in Petrópolis, Brazil.

Anke Finger is associate professor of German and media studies and comparative literary and cultural studies at the University of Connecticut. Her research areas include German and comparative modernism, aesthetics, media theory, interculturality, and interart studies. Her publications include two books on the total artwork, Vilém Flusser's *The Freedom of the Migrant: Objections to Nationalism* (2003) and a co-authored introduction to Vilém Flusser, available in Portuguese and German from the University of Minnesota Press (2011), and she cofounded and co-edits (with Rainer Guldin) the online journal *Flusser Studies*.

Wolfgang Fuhrmann teaches film studies at the University of Zurich. He studied drama and film at the Ruhr-Universität Bochum and film and television studies at the University of Amsterdam. In 2003, he received his PhD from the University of Utrecht with a project on colonial cinematography. Between 2005 and 2008 he directed the research group on "Film and Ethnography in Germany 1900–1930," funded by the German Research Foundation. In 2007, he was Deutscher Akademischer Austausch Dienst Assistant Professor at the University of British Columbia. His many publications concentrate on colonial and ethnographic films and early cinema.

Rainer Guldin, a professor at Università della Svizzera Italiana, Switzerland, teaches German language and culture at the Faculty of Communication Sciences of the Università della Svizzera Italiana in Lugano, Switzerland. His numerous publications include monographs on Vilém Flusser's philosophy, the art and aesthetic history of clouds, metaphors of the body, the cultural and political meaning of landscapes, and many articles on Flusser, translation, British literature, and intercultural communication.

Andrew W. Hurley holds a degree in law and a PhD in German studies (University of Melbourne). He is the author of *The Return of Jazz: Joachim-Ernst Berendt and West German Cultural Change* (Berghahn Books, 2009), *Into the Groove: Popular Music and Contemporary German Fiction* (Camden House, forthcoming), and various articles on popular music and cultural history in Germany and elsewhere. He is a senior lecturer in international studies at the University of Technology, Sydney.

Gabi R. Kathöfer is an associate professor of German studies at the University of Denver. She has published a monograph, *Auszug in die Heimat: Zum Alteritäts(t)raum Märchen* (Georg Olms Verlag, 2008), on spaces of alterity in nineteenth-century German fairy tales, and numerous articles on nineteenth- and twentieth-century German culture and literature. Her current research explores politics of identity in German immigrant communities in Brazil and homelessness in German cultural history.

Christopher Larkosh is an associate professor of Portuguese at the University of Massachusetts Dartmouth. His research interests include Brazilian and comparative literature, literary theory, and translation studies. Some of his articles can be found in the journals *Translation Studies, Portuguese Literary & Cultural Studies, Flusser Studies, Annali d'Italianistica, TTR:traduction, terminologie, réduction, TOPIA: Canadian Journal of Cultural Studies, Social Dynamics,* and *The Translator,* as well as a number of edited volumes. He has edited a collection of essays titled *Re-Engendering Translation: Transcultural/Sexual Practice and the Politics of Alterity* (St. Jerome, 2011) and is currently writing a book on Lusophone transnationalisms and diaspora cultures.

Ricarda Musser directs the Media department at the Ibero-American Institute in Berlin and is research advisor for Brazil, Chile, and Portugal. She received her PhD in 2001 with a dissertation on the library system in Portugal; her research interests include travel, eighteenth- and nineteenth-century literature, German migration to Latin America, and German–Brazilian cultural relations.

Horst Nitschack is an associate professor at the Universidad de Chile, where he coordinates the doctoral program at the Centro de Estudios Culturales Latinoamericanos. He has co-edited *Trans*Chile* (2010), *Brazil and the Americas* (2008), and *Hannah Arendt* (2008).

Ute Ritz-Deutch received her doctorate from Binghamton University, State University of New York in 2008. Her dissertation is titled *Alberto Vojtěch Frič, the German Diaspora, and Indian Protection in Southern Brazil, 1900–1920: A Transatlantic Ethno-Historical Case Study.* Her research interests are in ethnohistory, immigration studies, German-Brazilian relations, German diaspora, Atlantic history, colonialism and imperialism, nation building, indigenous rights, and human rights. She currently teaches in the History Department at SUNY Cortland, State University of New York.

Ulrike Schröder is professor of German language and literature at the Universidade Federal de Minas Gerais in Belo Horizonte, Brazil. Her numerous publications include *Liebe als sprachliches Produkt* (2004), *Brasilianische und deutsche Wirklichkeiten* (2003), *Kommunikationstheoretische Fragestellungen in der kognitiven Metaphernforschung* (2012), and articles and book chapters on pragmatics, metaphors, speech styles, and intercultural communication.

Edith Wolfe has a PhD in art history from the University of Texas at Austin (2005), with a specialization in twentieth-century Latin American modernism. She is the recipient of SSRC (Social Science Research Council), IDRF (International Dissertation Research), Fulbright, and AAUW (American Association of University Women) fellowships. Her dissertation is being revised for publication as a monograph titled *Significant Others: Lasar Segall, the Brazilian Avant-Garde and the Cosmopolitics of Modernism (1922–1945)*. She is currently the assistant director of the Stone Center for Latin American Studies at Tulane University and co-curated the exhibition *Re-Aligning Vision: Alternate Currents in Latin American Drawing.*

Index

Abrahams, Roger D.   161
Adorno, Theodor W.   140
Africa   8, 16, 29, 96, 146, 150, 152, 161, 181, 271, 273, 280, 282, 284
Alencar, José de   95, 201, 209
Amado, Jorge.   251
Amaral, Tarsila do   268, 280, 282–285, 290
Amazon   95, 99, 203, 205f., 214
Amazonia   107, 112, 209, 212, 232, 264
America   3, 7, 23, 34, 53f., 62, 74, 85, 87f., 95, 101, 112, 129, 138, 146, 154, 161–163, 166, 173f., 193, 202f., 206, 219, 224, 238, 249, 278f., 288
American Folf Blues Festival   143
ancient Greek culture   73, 95, 111, 112, 280, 311, 312
Andrade, Mário de   9, 15, 84, 95, 101, 113, 123, 201f., 204–206, 208–216, 268, 282, 287
Andrade, Oswald de   9, 12, 95, 201–205, 208f., 213f., 268, 282, 284, 290
Angola   258
anthropology   2, 4, 21, 34, 73, 95, 97, 99, 103, 106, 113f., 174
anthropometric theory   105
anthropophagy   72f., 202–205, 208, 214
appropriation, intercultural   137
Aquarela do Brasil   224f.
Arekuna   101, 205
Arendt, Hannah   264
Argentina   143, 181f., 223, 249, 253
Arnau, Frank   225, 230, 241
Art négre   280
Auslandsorganisationen (AOs)   184
authenticity   2f., 74, 159, 162, 267, 273, 287f.
avant-garde   140, 153, 201f., 208, 267f., 275f., 278, 280, 282, 290, 296f.
Avelar, Idelber   255

Baden Baden   139
Bahia   122, 148–150, 152f., 184
Bakhtin, Mikhail   315

Bandeira, Manuel   204, 210, 213, 268
Barroso, Ary   224
Bayer Leverkusen   130
Bayreuth   128
Becher, Ulrich   223, 225, 232–235, 241f.
Beethoven, Ludwig van   127
Belém   99
Beller, Manfred   48
Belo Horizonte   122, 126
Ben, Jorge   43
Benjamin, Walter   262f.
Bense, Max   301–304
Berendt, Joachim-Ernst   137, 139–143, 145–148, 151f., 154f.
Berger, Paulo   44
Berlin   14, 23, 27–32, 36, 44, 57f., 76–78, 80f., 87, 97–101, 104, 108, 126, 129, 134, 141–145, 147f., 151, 173, 181–183, 190, 192, 204f., 208, 214, 223, 227f., 230, 239, 261, 268, 276, 317
Berlin Jazz Days   137, 140, 142, 146f.
Beyfuss, Edgar   183
Bildungsroman   202, 205f., 213, 215
Binzer, Ina von   80, 84
Bismarck, Otto von   86
Blankett, John   53
Blome, Rainer   144
Blumenau   3, 12, 23–28, 30f., 37f., 77, 79, 181f.
Blumenbach, Johann Friedrich   46
Blut und Boden   243
Bodenlos   236, 240, 303–306
Böhm, Johann Heinrich   56
Border Thinking (Mignolo)   2, 269, 276, 292, 297
Borges, Jorge Luis   248
bossa nova   13, 137–143, 145–149, 152f., 155
Boston   254
Boulez, Pierre   311f.
Braganza   221
Branqueamento   83
Brasília   14, 240f.
Brasilianischer Romanzero   234, 241f.

Brasilidade   224, 284, 286, 288
Brasilien. Bildnis eines tropischen Großreiches   225, 227
Brasilien oder die Suche nach dem neuen Menschen   235f., 240
Brazil   1–3, 7–16, 21–38, 43–45, 47–62, 71–90, 95–101, 104, 108, 110, 119–122, 124–129, 131–134, 137–139, 141–150, 152–155, 163, 174, 180–195, 201f., 206f., 209–213, 219–243, 248, 253, 255, 258, 263–265, 267–269, 277–280, 282–284, 286, 288–291, 293, 295f., 307
Brazil: Land of the Future   223, 226, 236–238
Brazil (Nature and Nation)   43
Brazilian national myth   219, 225
Brazil's discovery   7, 74, 202
Brazilwood Manifesto (Oswald de Andrade)   284
Brill, Marte   225, 228f., 238
Brunn, Gerhard   97
Bündchen, Gisele   12
Buenos Aires   26, 139, 249
Bugre   21f., 24, 26f.
Bugreiro   23
Byrd, Charlie   141

Cameron, Lynne   164f.
Caminha, Pero Vaz de   48, 219
campanha de nacionalização   120, 224
Campos   122, 301–307, 309, 311–317
Canção do exílio   220f., 235
cannibalism   3, 7, 9, 12, 50, 71–74, 80, 88, 90, 203f., 215
Canstatt, Oscar   44
Carlos, Roberto   254
carnival   144, 204, 254, 271f.
Carvalho, Itala Gomes Vaz de   126, 203, 220, 222
Celso, Afonso   221f.
Cendrars, Blaise   240, 280
Certeau, Michel de   44
Chambers, Ian   308–310
Chateaubriand, François-René de   209
Christ, Jesus   51, 75

civilization   3f., 9, 72, 82, 90, 95, 102, 106–110, 112, 203f., 207, 214, 269, 271, 278f., 297
Coelho, Paulo   22, 26, 251
Coffee: The Epic of a Commodity   232
Coimbra   220
colonial fantasies   8, 11, 71, 96f.
colonialism   30, 53, 55, 60, 71, 73, 88, 155, 201, 271, 278
colonization   2, 11, 43, 62, 71, 78, 84, 86, 88, 96, 207, 265
colonization process   2, 11, 44, 62, 71, 78, 86, 96, 207, 265
Columbus, Christopher   73
commericalization   147, 155
Commissão Promotora da Defesa dos Indígenas   35
conceptual metaphor   159f., 164–166, 168, 175
Concrete Poetry   302–305, 314
Congresso Panamericano de Tuberculose   129
cool jazz   146
Cooper, James Fenimore   209
Correa, Djalma   149, 151, 153
Corumbá   108, 110
Cuiabá   100, 108, 110f., 113
Cultural hybridity   2, 179
Cultural Imperialism   194
Cultural Policy, Brazilian   134
Cultural Policy, German   134f.
Curtius, Ernst Robert   60
Czierský, Otto   122, 126

da Cunha, Euclides   112f.
Damm und Fluß (Theweleit)   262
d'Andrade e Silva, José Bonifácio   46
Darwin, Charles   109
Dave Pike Set   149–151, 154f.
de Campos, Haroldo   16, 301f., 304, 306f., 311–313, 316f.
de Moraes, Vinícius   138
Deleuze, Gilles   159, 247, 311
Der Schmelztiegel   228f., 238
Der verchromte Urwald   230, 241
Deutschbrasilianer   11, 12, 13, 21, 23, 25, 27, 30, 32, 36, 38, 186, 189, 192

Deutsche Akademie München 121f., 124, 132
Deutsche Zeitung (São Paulo) 194
Diaspora (Jewish, African) 21, 26, 28, 31, 79, 290
Die Brücke 269f.
Die Weltbühne 242
Dix, Otto 271
Döhl, Reinhard 301
Dohm, Christian Wilhelm 47, 52
Doldinger, Klaus 141, 145, 148f., 153f.
Domingues, Ângela 59
Donaueschingen Musiktage 155
Dresden 53, 268f., 271f., 276
dual state (Germany-Brazil) 247f., 251
Dufresne, David 161
Dylan, Bob 143

Eckart, Anselm Franz Dominik von 47, 52
Edenism 222
Ehrmann, Theophil Friedrich 54, 58
Eldorado 220
emigration 2f., 8, 11f., 71–82, 86–90, 96, 269, 271, 275
émigré writers 225, 227, 229, 237f., 243
empire 21, 27f., 44, 71, 77f., 82, 85–87, 96, 220, 225, 278
Enlightenment/Enlightenment project 124, 216, 275, 291, 296
erotomania 145
Eschwege, Wilhelm Ludwig von 43, 58, 61
Estado Novo 13, 120, 216, 224
Estermann, Alfred Adolph 45
estrangeiro 44, 233
ethnography 11, 96, 98f., 102, 107
Europe 3, 10f., 27, 32, 51f., 57, 59–62, 72f., 75f., 79, 83, 96f., 102, 110, 112, 140, 144, 155, 201, 207, 223, 227, 230, 236–238, 242f., 249, 256, 275, 277–279, 282, 288, 290, 297, 302
European cultural hegemony 249
exile 2, 220, 225, 227f., 230, 235, 238, 241f., 291f., 296
exotic 50, 71, 75f., 79, 97, 107f., 110, 126, 139, 151f., 189, 195, 207, 219, 226f., 234, 270f., 274
exoticism 43, 223, 229, 267, 276

exoticization 127, 137, 152
Expressionism 267–273, 276f., 296
expropriation 139, 207

Farage, Nádia 98f.
Fascism 263
Fassbinder, Rainer Werner 262
favelas 284, 293
Felixmuller, Conrad 271, 277
Ferraz, Geraldo 268, 286f.
Fibel für Deutsche Schulen 131
flora and fauna, Brazilian 219, 227f., 230f.
Flusser, Vilém 16, 225, 235f., 240, 301–306, 311, 314, 317
Folkwang Museum, Dresden 269–271
Forster, Johann Reinhold 53
Foucault, Michel 265
France 4, 16, 48, 59, 61, 97, 125, 228, 279, 282
Franzbach, Martin 44
free jazz 140, 142, 153f.
Freud, Sigmund 80, 204
Frič, Alberto 21, 23, 25f., 28, 32
future potential 15, 236, 238–243

Garden of Eden 219f., 222, 224, 226, 228–230, 234f.
Gatzhammer, Stefan 52
Gaúcho culture (southern Brazil) 253
Gaze, colonial 76, 272
GDR, East Germany 137
Genet, Jean 262
genocide 249
German Brazilian Cultural Film Service (Deutschbrasilianische Kulturfilmdienst [DKD]) 184
German-Brazilians 11, 21, 24, 27–29, 31f., 36, 38, 189, 192
German Latin American Institute 223
Germany 1–4, 8–12, 15f., 23, 27, 29–33, 36–38, 43–45, 48, 51–57, 59–61, 71, 75, 77, 79, 86–89, 96–98, 100, 111, 114, 119–127, 129–135, 137, 140–144, 146, 150, 152f., 159, 162, 174, 179f., 182, 184–186, 189–191, 195, 201, 206, 213, 223, 225, 227f., 239, 247–251, 257, 263f., 267f., 271, 275–277, 286

Getz, Stan 139, 141f., 146
Giessen 98, 100
Gilberto, Astrud 139, 142
Gilberto, João 138
Gilcher, Friedrich 132
Gilroy, Paul 291f.
Gleichschaltung 120
Gluck, Christoph Wilibald 127
Goethe, Johann Wolfgang von 15, 148f., 154, 205f., 213f., 223
Goethe Insititute 121
Goethe-Institut 121f., 137, 140, 142, 147–150, 152–154
Gomes, Carlos 125f., 128
Gomringer, Eugen 301f.
Gonçalves Dias, Antônio 220f.
Görgen, Hermann Mathias 233
Görgen group 233f.
Gorme, Eydie 140
Gran Chaco 100
Great Depression 290
Grönemeyer, Herbert 261
Grupo Baiafro 149–151, 153f.
Gruppe 1919 268, 271, 277
Guarnieri, Mozart Camargo 127
Guattari, Félix 159, 247
Guettard, Jean-Étienne 46

Habsburg 221
Hammerdörfer, Karl 59
Hannover, Infantry Regiments of 55, 60
Hartmann, Günther 58
Hays Code 191
Heimat 76, 181, 186, 189
Heine, Heinrich 132
Hempel, Paul 103, 106
Hermannstädter, Anita 58, 100, 102
Hesse, Hermann 14, 251
Heuberger, Theodor 122, 128, 132
Hieber, R. 123
Higson, Andrew 180f., 189
hip-hop 13, 159–163, 172, 174
Hitler, Adolf 124, 263
Hocks, Paul 45
Hoffmann, Johannes 234
Hoffmann-Harnisch, Wolfgang 225, 227

Hoffmannsegg, Johann Centurius Graf von 58
Homer 73, 311f.
homosexuality (gay, queer, LGBT) 259
Humboldt, Alexander von 57, 75f., 97, 206f., 227
hybridity 4, 95, 109, 112, 151, 155, 179, 288–291
hybridization 3, 6f., 13, 137, 146, 160, 214
Hymes, Dell 174

identity 2f., 8–11, 13, 21, 23, 29, 31, 34, 37f., 60f., 71–74, 77, 79–82, 84, 88–90, 95, 112f., 159, 180, 202, 204, 220, 249, 252f., 256–259, 269, 276f., 279f., 288, 290, 292, 296f.
ideology 87, 120, 124, 140, 152, 154, 186, 189, 215, 235, 243, 249, 254, 260, 262, 278, 289
Ihering, Hermann von 25f., 32–35
Images (Imagology) 10, 43, 48, 60, 80, 90, 106, 114, 123f., 165, 188f., 204, 225, 234, 243, 247, 261f., 278, 282, 286, 289–293
Immigrant/Emigrant/Immigration 3, 8f., 14f., 23, 31, 33f., 71, 77f., 81–86, 88f., 97, 120, 122, 180–182, 184f., 224, 233, 236, 239f., 268, 286, 289, 292–294, 296, 307
immigration 2, 5, 8f., 29, 31, 33, 43, 77–79, 82–85, 88, 134, 180, 182, 267, 280
Imperialism, German 87f.
India 12, 21–26, 28, 31–36, 53, 55, 79, 95f., 101f., 107, 113f., 128, 152, 155, 201, 203, 207–209, 278, 282, 288, 290
Indian Protection Service (Serviço de Proteção aos Indios) 21f., 37
Inquisition 50f., 53
Instituto Histórico e Geográfico do Brasil 61
Instituto Nacional de Música 126
Instituto Teuto-Brasileiro de Alta Cultura 121, 129, 132f.
interculturalities 1, 7, 15, 71f., 89f.
internationalism 145, 223
interracial sexual encounters 145

intertextuality 11, 54, 112, 173, 311, 315
Ipuriná 108

Jacob, Heinrich Eduard 223, 225, 232f., 239
James, William 204
Jameson, Frederic 265
Jannings, Emil 130
Japan 146, 165, 224, 307
Jazz Meets the World 146
Jobim, Antônio Carlos 138, 148
Johnson, Mark 160, 164, 166
Joinville 30, 79, 128
Josetti, Rodolpho 129
Journal of the São Paulo Museum (Revista do Museu Paulista) 101
Joyce, James 311
Jürgensen, Renate 52

Kaingang 21f., 24–26, 33f., 36f.
Kandinsky, Wassily 268
Katz, Richard 225, 230–232, 243
Knauth, Alfons 308
Koch, Robert 130
Koch-Grünberg, Theodor 8, 12, 95, 98f., 103–111, 204f., 214
Kochman, Thomas 161
Koellreutter, Hans-Joachim 148
Koller, Hans 141
Kosche, Christian T. 59
Kövecses, Zoltán 160, 164f., 171
Kraus, Michael 98, 100, 102f., 108
Kreiser, Walter 233, 242
Kriegel, Volker 149–153
Kubitschek, Juscelino 241
KulturConfusão 1f., 11, 15, 195, 257, 317
Kulturfilm (cultural film) 183, 188

La Condamine, C.M. de 48, 55
Lacan, Jacques 265
Lachmund, Charley 126
Lakoff, George 160, 164, 166
Land der Zukunft. Reise in Brasilien 223
Lange, Otto 271
Langsdorff, Georg Heinrich von 51, 59, 220
Langstedt, Friedrich Ludwig 55f.

Latin America 9f., 16, 28, 31, 33, 78, 83–85, 87f., 96, 121, 134, 142, 182, 193, 201, 203, 207f., 235, 255, 282, 284
Lebensraum 243
Leerssen, Joep 48
Leipzig Conservatory of Music 126
Levin, Ira 263
Ley, Charles David 49
Lichtenstein, Heinrich 58
Lima, Jorge de 292, 294
Lindenberg, Johann Bernhard Wilhelm 46
Lindley, Thomas 47, 54, 58
Link, Heinrich Friedrich 58
Lins, Álvaro 211, 216
Lippmann, Horst 137, 142
Lisboa, Henriqueta 211
Lloyd, Jill 269, 271f.
Lombroso, Cesare 105
Loreley 132
Lukács, Georg 209, 213f.
Lüning, C.F. 47
Lutz, Adolpho 130

Machado de Assis, Joaquim Maria 95
Macunaíma 15, 95, 101, 201f., 204–206, 208–216, 282
Malagrida, Gabriel 47
Mallarmé, Stéphane 305, 311f.
Manaus 99, 108, 110
manifesto antropófago 9, 72f., 88, 203
Manuela (German singer) 140
Marc, Franz 268
Maristany, Cristina 126
Martini, Friedrich Heinrich Wilhelm 46
Martins, Amélia de Rezende 122f.
Martius, Carl Friedrich Philipp von 8, 220
Marx, Karl 14, 144
Mata Atlântica 231f.
Mato Grosso 108
May, Karl 97
MC 161, 167–170, 175
Medeiros, Sérgio 102
Mediterranean 308–310
Meidner, Ludwig 271
Mengele, Josef 263
mestizo 108f.
Mignolo, Walter 2, 276

Mignone, Francisco   126
migration   10, 31, 75, 77f., 84, 88f., 180f., 206, 268, 275, 286, 291, 297
military dictatorship, Brazilian (1964-1985)   13f., 163, 203, 253, 255
Minas Gerais   187, 228, 284
Minimal Societies (Noll)   254
modernism, Brazilian   9, 15, 203, 267f., 272, 285, 290, 295–297
monsters (sharks)   264–266
Monteiro Lobato, José Bento Renato   251
Montez, Luiz Barros   55
Müller, Joseph   59
Mulligan, Gerry   138
multilingualism   301, 307f., 311, 315
Münch, Ernst   53
Münchner Medizinische Wochenschrift   129
Murr, Christoph Gottlieb von   52
Música Folklórica Argentina   143

nation state   88
national anthem, Brazilian   112, 221, 235
National Cinema   180–182, 189, 194
national flag, Brazilian   221
national identity, Brazilian   88, 224
National School of Fine Arts, Rio de Janeiro   278
National Socialism   124, 143, 156
National Socialist German Workers' Party (NSDAP)   184
Natural History   58, 228
naturalists   8, 59, 220, 227
nature, Brazilian   7f., 62, 79, 219–221, 225, 231f., 235f.
Nazis   188, 223, 225, 242, 249
Nazism   225, 242, 263
Nebgen, Christoph   52
Neto, Wadi Gebara   143
Niklas, Peter   155
Nimuendajú, Curt Unckel   98
no man's land   239, 240
Nöhden, Georg Heinrich   58
Nohel, Otto Adolf   128
Noigandres group   301, 303
Nolde, Emil   269f.
Noll, João Gilberto   15, 251, 254, 256, 258, 260

North America   10, 75, 88, 97, 138f., 141, 147, 153, 155, 255
Northwest Railroad (Estrada de Ferro Noroeste do Brasil)   25

Oberacker Jr., Karl Heinrich   57
Obermeier, Franz   44, 203
Ohff, Heinz   144
Old Republic (Brazil)   83, 88, 279, 290
Olinda School ((São Paulo)   185
Olympic Games   134
Ossietzky, Carl von   233, 242
Ost-Jude (Eastern Jew)   275
Other, colonial   269, 277
Ovid   311

Pallas, Peter Simon   46
Pantanal   100
Papavero, Nelson   57
Paquetá   231
paradise   15, 43, 56, 219–221, 224, 227–231, 233f., 236, 296
Paraguay River   110
patriotism   221, 267, 269, 289
Paulista Museum (Museu Paulista)   25
Pechstein, Max   269
Peixoto, Afrânio   123
Peoples of Culture   95
Peoples of Nature   58, 95, 97f.
Personal Narrative of Travels to the Equinoctial Regions of America During the Years 1799-1804   228
perversion   147, 259
Petersen, Wolfgang   261
Pfeiffer, Ida   8, 79
Pignatari, Décio   301f.
Pinto, Olivério Mário de Oliveira   58
Pitta, Sebastião da Rocha   54
Pombal, Marquis of (Sebastião José de Carvalho Melo)   51, 53, 57
popular music, Brazilian   137–139, 142, 145, 147, 150
Porque me ufano do meu país   221
Porto Alegre   13, 122, 185f., 219, 249, 253–256, 258
Portugal   45, 47–53, 56, 58–61, 220
Pound, Ezra   307, 311f.

Powell, Baden   143, 145, 147, 154
Prado, Paulo   222
Pragglejaz   164, 166
Pratl, Josef   128
primitive   106, 208f., 249, 267, 270–273, 275f., 278f., 282, 290, 297
Primitivism   267, 269–272, 278
Pro Arte   121, 128, 131, 133
Prochnow, Jürgen   261f.
promising future   222f., 237–239, 241–243
pseudo-civilization   109
psychoanalysis   10
Purim, Flora   151

race   8f., 33f., 62, 78, 83, 85, 109, 112, 126, 145, 223, 279f., 284, 287f., 296f.
racial democracy   14, 145, 237, 295
racialization   10f.
racism   87
rap   13, 159–163, 165–175, 249
Rau, Fritz   137, 142–144
Raynal, Guillaume Thomas François   46, 51, 55
Recife   122
refugees of Nazism   219
Reichsmusikkammer   127
Religion (Church)   9, 47, 51, 73, 163, 175, 289
Rescher, Hubertus J.   3, 45, 76
reterritorialization   13, 160, 175
Retrato do Brasil. Ensaio sobre a tristeza brasileira   222
Rio de Janeiro   21f., 32, 34–36, 44, 47, 55f., 83, 86, 122, 126, 128, 130f., 138, 163, 182, 184, 191–194, 209, 221, 224, 226, 230f., 241, 251, 253, 267, 269, 279, 286f., 294, 314
Rio Hacha   98
Ritter, Karl   124
Robertson, Roland   159
Roda Becher, Dana   242
Roda Roda, Alexander   233, 242
Rolling Stones, The   143
Romero, Sílvio   83, 85f.
Rondon, Cândido Mariano da Silva   33–35
Röntgen, Konrad   130
Roraima   96, 98f., 101f., 204

Rotermund, Wilhelm   131
Ruesenberg, Michael   145
Ruffato, Luiz   250f.

Saba/MPS   140, 145, 147
Sábato, Ernesto   254
Sabino, Fernando   210
Saint-Hilaire, Étienne Geoffroy   58
Saludos Amigos   224
samba   138, 141, 145, 152, 223f., 235, 242, 284
Santa Catarina state, Brazil   12, 22–28, 30f., 35f., 101, 128, 181, 185, 232, 264
Santiago de Chile   129
São Paulo   9, 13, 16, 21f., 24–26, 32–36, 38, 45, 48, 113, 122, 129, 163, 174, 183–185, 187, 189, 191–194, 209, 228, 238, 250, 253, 263, 268, 278f., 284, 289, 303, 317
Schaumburg-Lippe, Friedrich Wilhelm Ernst zu   56
Schendel, Mira   303, 306
Schlager   140–142
Schmidt, Paul Ferdinand   275
Schmidt, Peter   45
Schneider, Ulrich Johannes   44
Schoppe, Amalia   76
Schrank, Franz Paula von   59
Schreiner, Claus   137–139, 142f., 147f., 150f., 153f.
Schüler, Heinrich   223, 227
Schulgrammatik der deutschen Sprache (German School Grammar)   131
Science (European)   61
Secessionist movement   268
Segall, Lasar   15, 267, 269–279, 281, 284, 287–289, 291–295
Seidenraupen   227f., 230, 239
Seixo, Maria Alzira   49
Semana de Arte Moderna (Modern Art Week, São Paulo)   278
sertão   231f.
sexual relationship, lack of (Lacan)   245
Shakespeare, William   213, 311, 313
Shtetl   276
Sieber, Friedrich Wilhelm   57, 59
Sievers, Wilhelm   107f.

Simon, Hugo   225, 227f., 230, 239
Sinzig, Pedro   132
Siusí   106f., 113
Sixteenth International Congress of Americanists   21, 23
Slaves/Slavery   8f., 35, 53f., 60, 78, 82f., 265, 280, 292
Sociedade Brasileira de Tuberculose   130
Society of Jesus (Jesuits)   52, 60
source domain   164, 166, 168, 170
Sousa, Celeste H. M. Ribeiro de   48, 220, 235
South America   8, 10f., 21, 23, 26, 29f., 36, 44, 52, 60, 71, 74–76, 80f., 87–90, 97f., 100, 122, 144, 148f., 154, 180–184, 192f., 223, 232, 238, 242f., 249
Spielberg, Steven   264
Spix, Johann Baptist von   8
Sprengel, Matthias Christian   47, 53f.
Staden, Hans   2f., 7, 11, 72–74, 81, 88, 185
Steen, Gerard   164f.
Steller, Georg Wilhelm   46
Stendhal   208f., 251
Stresemann, Erwin   57
Stuttgart   12, 14, 16, 45, 75, 101, 162, 182f., 187f., 204f., 207f., 213, 223, 227, 301, 303f., 313, 317
Stuttgart School   301
Stutzer, Therese   81
submarines (U-boats)   247, 250, 257f., 263, 266
Südwestfunk (SWF)   139

target domain   164, 166, 168, 170, 172
Taulipang   101, 205
Tavares, Marly   144
terrestrial paradise   219f., 222, 225, 227, 230f., 233, 235
Teuto-Brazilians   9, 84, 119, 186, 190
Theweleit, Klaus   260
Third World   155, 265
Toop, David   161
totalitarianism   15, 247, 262, 264
tourism   97, 144
transcreation   307
translation   10, 16, 34, 44, 47, 49, 51–55, 58, 61, 98, 101f., 104, 121, 123, 129, 141, 179, 205f., 208, 213, 219, 221, 226, 237f., 249f., 254, 256, 258, 260, 263, 267, 301–305, 307f., 310f., 313–316
transnational   6, 14–16, 32, 179, 181, 195, 248f., 259, 261, 302
Transnational Cinema   179
trauma, postdictatorial   236, 255
travel literature   31, 222
travel writing   71f., 75, 80, 96, 288
travelers   45, 49, 56f., 61, 75f., 79, 81, 189, 203, 206, 222, 292
Treece, David   138f., 254–256, 258
Treibhaus Südamerika   232f.
Trocadéro Museum, Paris   280
tropicalismo   149
tropics   97, 201, 203, 206, 236
Tübingen   31, 60, 98, 100, 202, 206, 208, 303
Tuckey, James Hingston   47, 54
twen (magazine)   139–141, 143, 145, 147
Tzoref-Ashkenazi, Chen   55

Uberaba   98
UFA Palácio   193f.
UFA Pornos   191f., 195
ufanismo   221
Ullmann, Hermann   223
Ulrici, H.   129
United States   4f., 11, 16, 33, 57, 97, 139, 146, 216, 224, 232, 242, 251, 254, 306
universalism   154f., 272, 286, 296
Universum Film AG (Ufa)   182
Unterhaltungsmusik   140, 147
Unverricht, Walter   129
Urwaldbarock   234

Vargas, Getúlio   120, 124, 216, 224
Vargas regime   26, 224
Veigl, Franz Xavier   47
verbal dueling   161, 173
Verdi, Giuseppe   128
Verissimo, Luis Fernando   248–250
Verlé, Heinrich   123f.
Vespucci, Amerigo   48, 55, 219
Vianna, Frutuoso   127
Vieira, António   51
Villa-Lobos, Heitor   1

Vilnius   268
virgin forest   228, 230–234
Virtual Sex   247
Vitória   122
von Behring, Emil   130
von den Steinen, Karl   28, 36, 97f., 100, 109
von Schlippenbach, Alexander   154
Vorbrodt, Martin   131
Voswinkel, Stephan   155

Wader, Hannes   143
Wagner, Richard   128
Waldeck, Prince Christian von   51
Walther-Bense, Elisabeth   301
war metaphor   166f., 172–174
Wasserman, Renata   112
Wassermann, Georg   233
Wassermann, Jakob   233
Weber, Max   173
Weber, Oscar   97
Wehrs, Georg Friedrich   46f.
Weimar Republic   191, 223
Weltbühne trial   242
Weltpolitik   86
West Germany   137, 139f., 148f., 153

Wied-Neuwied, Alexander Philipp Maximilian zu   43, 60, 76
Wilhelm Meister   15, 202, 205f., 209, 212f., 215f.
Wilke, Jürgen   45
Wink, Georg   44, 61
Wochenschau (weekly review)   185
Wolf, Peter   52
world literature   204, 251
world music   138, 146, 150, 153–155
World War I   28–30, 207, 222, 268, 271, 276
World War II   26, 162, 182, 193, 241, 249, 251, 258

Xingu   36, 96f., 100, 102f., 108–111
Xokleng   21–25, 27, 36f.
Xuxa   12

Zantop, Susanne   8, 71, 89
Zedler, Johann Heinrich   49f., 53, 56, 60
Zeh, Johann Eberhard   59
Zehder, Hugo   277
Zimmerman, Andrew   113f.
Žižek, Slavoj   247, 259, 265
Zweig, Stefan   62, 223, 225–227, 236–238, 244, 251

www.ingramcontent.com/pod-product-compliance
Lightning Source LLC
Chambersburg PA
CBHW030606230426
43661CB00053B/1862